S0-BSI-874

History of Universities

VOLUME X

1991

History of Universities

VOLUME X

1991

Oxford University Press

1991

History of Universities is published annually as a single volume.

Papers for publication in History of Universities as well as books for review should be sent to the editor, Dr. L. W. B. Brockliss, Magdalen College, Oxford, OX1 4AU, United Kingdom.

A leaflet 'Notes to OUP Authors' is available on request from the editor.

Details of subscription rates and terms are available from Oxford Journals Subscription Department, Walton Street, Oxford OX2 6DP, United Kingdom.

British Library Cataloguing in Publication Data
(data available)
ISBN 0 19 822728–0

Library of Congress Cataloging Publication Data
(data available)

Typeset by Latimer Trend & Company Ltd, Plymouth
Printed in Great Britain by
Biddles Ltd, Guildford and King's Lynn.

Contents

Articles

Conference Reports

Essay Review

Book Reviews

Bibliography

Meeting the Costs of University Education in Northern France, *c.* 1240–*c.* 1340

Jean Dunbabin

Did medieval universities really encourage social mobility? Or did they simply reinforce social privilege, allowing those who could afford to take degrees to monopolize high positions in church and state and justify their possession by reference not only to birth but also to educational advantage? Whatever their view of the situation after about 1350, most historians who have considered it regard the thirteenth and early fourteenth century *studia generalia* as genuinely open to talent, offering a career ladder to those who might otherwise have been denied promotion.[1] This view is not founded on statistics—too little is known about student populations (except those of Oxford and Cambridge) before the late fourteenth century to admit of even crude analysis.[2] It is, rather, an impression based on evidence culled from many different kinds of sources, university and college legislation, particular careers, hints in royal and papal accounts, anecdotes in chronicles, and perhaps most cogently from the relative absence of evidence for participation in university study by members of the high aristocracy whose life stories are known. 'It is clear that the universities of the thirteenth and fourteenth centuries were not aristocratic institutions'[3] is a conclusion reinforced by the apparently striking contrast between them and the late fifteenth-century universities in which those of noble birth were conspicuous.

But the relative absence of great noblemen among the alumni of the early universities does not necessarily imply that the students were drawn overwhelmingly from the non-aristocratic classes. To confine the argument to northern France and to the French students of Paris and Orléans in the thirteenth and early fourteenth centuries, it is worth recalling the very large body of historical literature[4] devoted to demonstrating that knights were clearly accepted within the ranks of the French aristocracy by the early thirteenth century at the latest. Therefore in the early part of our period it would be anachronistic to categorize the sons of knights and lesser lords as belonging to 'the middling ranks' of society. That is not how they would have been perceived by their contemporaries. And while division of inheritance and financial pressures in the late thirteenth and early fourteenth centuries undoubtedly threatened many members of this class with loss of status, a legal career, preceded by a university education, became a popular route to avoiding this fate. In other words, for certain members of the landed classes, the universities acted as a buffer against downward social mobility.

However, the significance of this point depends on the percentage of sons of knights and lesser lords among the student population of Paris and Orléans in the period. In the absence of statistics, there will always be room for argument on the subject. But the *prima facie* case that among French students the percentage was high derives its cogency from the distribution of the population during the period. In 1250, of France's fourteen to fifteen million inhabitants, only around one and a half million lived in towns. And while by 1340 the percentage of towndwellers had substantially increased, they still formed a small minority of all Frenchmen. It is the contention of this paper that, although townsmen were almost certainly disproportionately well represented in the northern French universities, it is implausible that they were in the majority; and that rural dwellers beneath the ranks of the lesser aristocracy could not normally afford a university education. Therefore it is unwise to underestimate the role of the landowning classes as consumers of what the universities provided.

Despite occasional statements to the contrary,[5] it is now generally accepted that French university education was expensive even in the thirteenth century. There were in the first place fees to be found for almost all courses; and although these were not apparently very heavy, they were a powerful disincentive to the impoverished.[6] In addition students had to pay for board and lodgings at rates that inflated fast in university towns where demand was high.[7] And those who wished either to determine as bachelors or to incept as masters faced rapidly increasing bills for the privilege.[8] It was not surprising that the vast majority of students apparently chose not to incept. But even remaining at university long enough to determine was a struggle. Where the relatively rich could easily find themselves in financial embarrassment, those with nothing to fall back on must have found the going tough indeed.

At the university of Paris, the cost of living so occupied men's thoughts that all dues came by the second half of the thirteenth century to be calculated in terms of the *bursa*, the average amount spent by one student in a week (excluding the wages of his servant if he had one). The surviving evidence for *bursae* in royal accounts, college foundation charters, and university legislation, offers a very schematic view of student expenditure, with a large degree of conformity between the sums spent by those studying the same subject, and substantially greater sums recorded for those studying theology than for the arts men. Clearly the figures represent, not so much actual outgoings, as what the university and the nations were willing to accept as an equitable basis for taxation. But unless the university officials were extremely gullible, the artificial element in the compilation of their figures should not seriously impair their value as average indicators of student need. On this evidence it is possible to chart the rising costs of maintenance for a Paris student from the middle of the thirteenth to the middle of the fourteenth centuries. Whereas St. Louis thought a clerk required between 1s. 7½d. p. and 3s. 3d. p. (2s. t. to 4s. t.) a week, by 1333 most of the English–German nation who determined in arts spent 4 s.p., although a few managed on 3 s.p. From the beginning of the fourteenth century most college fellows in arts got rather more.[9]

Figures like this demand some refinement. Whereas those in receipt of royal or collegiate munificence can usually be assumed to be better off than average, the 1333 figures for the English–German nation probably relate to the ordinary students. If one assumes (as William of Saône did in calculating the needs of the theologians in his college[10]) that residence was required for 45 weeks of the year, then most arts students by the end of our period spent 9 1.p. per year, and some got by on 6 1. 7s. 6d. p. Before 1350 there was, however, a provision for much poorer men: those who could only afford 1s. 4d. p. per week (3 1.p. a year) might subdetermine (qualify as bachelors by assisting in the examination of richer patrons who bore the fees for them). But this stipulation presupposes both that subdeterminers were a distinct minority and that they already had patrons to fend for them.[11] In order to obtain some indication of weekly costs for ordinary Paris students in the reign of St. Louis, the figure for 1333 should probably be reduced by rather more than half.[12] It must then have been possible for a poor scholar with a patron to get by, if he could subdetermine, on about 1.1. 10 s. p. for a year; but the average scholar would need at least 3 1.p., probably nearer 4.1.p. And in addition all would have to pay for their classes, their examination dues (if they took them), and books and parchment. These were substantial disbursements. Since the cost of living for students was probably higher than for people in general,[13] it can be assumed that scholars of Orléans could not trim their outgoings much below those of their Paris counterparts. In fact their frequent clashes with the townsfolk may have added considerably to their financial problems. In 1312, for example, they complained that merchants sold food to their servants at much higher rates than they charged other people, that rents were raised excessively, and that landlords removed any standard fittings from student lodgings.[14]

There was, however, one important respect in which the cost of university education fell during our period. Whereas the 1252 statutes of the English–German nation of Paris insisted that all candidates for determination in arts must have reached their twentieth year and have attended lectures on arts for a minimum of four years (five appears to have been the norm) at Paris or some other *studium generale*, well before 1350 the arts faculty was allowing youths of fourteen who had attended lectures in arts for two years to determine.[15] This considerable drop, both in the duration of the course and in the minimum age of the bachelors (whether or not most bachelors were actually as young as this), will have lightened the financial load and made entry to the higher faculties much easier. The same ends were served when the earlier Paris stipulations on teaching for two years after inception in the arts faculty before entering the theology faculty were quietly ignored,[16] and when precise restrictions on entry to the faculty of canon law were relaxed. Although no early statutes survive from Orléans, the scarcity of known Masters of Art among the many law graduates of that university lends weight to Innocent IV's lament that large numbers failed to complete their arts studies before rushing into Roman law;[17] here, too, early attempts at restrictive entry requirements appear to have foundered. Therefore the rising cost of maintenance in a university town will have been offset by the shortened length of the arts course for all students, and by the ease of access to the higher faculties for the more ambitious. As a consequence higher education was probably available to roughly the same economic groups in the middle of the fourteenth century as it had been in the middle of the thirteenth.

The declining age of arts students increased the importance of paternal guidance in career patterns, which must in any case always have been substantial. In an age when elementary schooling in Latin was far from universal, even for children of the aristocracy, decisions had to be taken early. Parents engaging a tutor for their son or sending him at seven or eight to a grammar school in a neighbouring town would automatically begin to think ahead to the question of whether he should go to a university in his teens. The advantage of so doing grew more obvious in the later thirteenth and the early fourteenth centuries, as lucrative careers in ecclesiastical courts beckoned those who had academic training in Roman and canon law. Fathers now calculated that an investment of three or perhaps four years' fees and living costs for some at least of their younger sons would not only free the family inheritance from potential encumbrances but also turn their offspring into positive assets to their lay brothers. Considerations of utility strongly recommended the study of law. And here the emergence of Orléans contributed greatly to easing the financial burden. Although Bologna remained till the last decade of the thirteenth century the ideal place for acquiring legal qualifications (legal studies in Paris being curtailed by the 1219 prohibition on the teaching of Roman law), only wealthy families could normally afford to send their sons so far from home. Orléans, where the law school was established by 1235 and which in the second half of the thirteenth century attained a European reputation under Jacques de Revigny and Pierre de Belleperche, was far more accessible to the upper classes of northern France.[18] And there is every indication that they took advantage of it. If less of a magnet to the international community than Paris, Orléans was more important in the education of Frenchmen.

Early planning to cover the costs of university education was desirable, but not easy in a period of inflation, which may explain the frequency of begging letters from students to their fathers.[19] And circumstances might change, preventing fathers from assisting their sons as far as the sons wished. I imagine many northern scholars faced the predicament described by Pierre de Luzenac to the inquisitor Geoffroi d'Ablis in 1308: his family ran out of money to support both him and his brother at the schools in Toulouse, and since his father had found a job for Pierre, he had to return home at once.[20] His fate was similar to that of the student in a model letter who boasted to his father of his fame in dialectic, and asked to be allowed to go on to theology, for which he would need to buy a Bible. The father replied that, although he was pleased to hear of his son's progress, he could not afford to keep him any longer.[21] It was not, apparently, that those of moderate means underestimated the value of education for their sons; merely that they considered a short exposure as valuable as long residence. And in this they may well have been right, at least initially. At a period when very few students took degrees, in the eyes of potential employers the duration of a man's studies was probably less significant than the fact of his having been at university. But this became less true as the bachelors' grade grew commoner.

As might be expected, paternal generosity was sometimes limited by the jealousy of other sons; Jacques de Revigny, the famous Orléans lawyer, told of a scholar whose father refused to give him anything, 'not even books. His brothers incited the father to this behaviour, saying "our brother is a clerk; that's enough for him; he does not need money." '[22] But worse might befall a scholar whose father's death left him entirely at the mercy of his brothers. A letter in an Orléans formulary vividly illustrates this predicament. In order to continue his studies in civil and canon law at Orléans, a certain clerk had sold his patrimony—presumably to a kinsman. Now, when he was on the point of attracting briefs and only needed a small amount of financial assistance, his rich brother would not help him. He called on the archdeacon of Amiens to persuade the hard-hearted miser of his duty.[23] The mention of a precise recipient argues for this letter being based on a genuine original. Here, then, the student himself had miscalculated the amount he would need to qualify; and his brother was too short-sighted or too pressed by other problems to bail him out. More imaginatively, the famous parody *Evangelium secundum marcem auri et argenti* begins: 'At that time was John studying the arts in Paris without any money. Thus he was bothered and busy over many things, and, raising his eyes to heaven, he said to Jesus, "Lord, does it not concern you that my brother has left me in Paris with no money? Tell him therefore that he should help me." And Jesus responded: "Indeed, money is needed for those studying in Paris." '[24] If Pons of Provence's attractive model letters for Orléans students were based on reality, sisters were less hard-hearted, more willing to protect their siblings from wretchedness;[25] but normally they must have been less capable of rendering effective help.

Important though the nuclear family was in supporting students, its significance was at least equalled by that of rich clerical uncles. Perhaps particularly in the thirteenth century, when the prohibition on clerical concubinage was becoming increasingly effective, those who had attained eminence in the church and enjoyed benefices felt a strong family obligation to assist their emulators of the next generation. Besides, they were more likely than the average father to appreciate the rewards of university education. So Walter de Cantelupe, bishop of Worcester, helped his nephews Thomas and Hugh at the beginning of their scholastic careers, setting an example that Thomas imitated for his own nephew until that youth determined in arts at Paris.[26] St. Louis' clerk Pierre de Lassy, who was killed at the Battle of Mansurah, was discovered to have been educating three nephews and four other relations at schools in Paris and elsewhere; his grateful king took on the burden of their schooling until they acquired benefices.[27] In the late thirteenth century Pierre de Mornay, king's clerk and bishop of Orléans, steered his two nephews Étienne and Philippe into legal careers after they had studied at Orléans.[28] Because the elementary education prerequisite for a university career was obtainable in cathedral cities, uncles who had prebends in cathedral chapters were often given responsibility for their nephews at a relatively early age; the relationship, with its consequent economic dependence, simply continued until the nephew became self-sufficient. The custom relieved a lay family of yet another mouth to feed, while offering celibates a substitute for the domesticity now denied them. It had many advantages. But it usually worked in favour of those who were in any case well off. However, if Salimbene was correct—his malicious tone inspires doubt—in alleging that Ancher Pantaléon was genuinely poor, then the support of his uncle who became Pope Urban IV catapulted him from deprivation into the highest ranks of the church.[29]

While careful family strategies might marginally increase educational opportunity, they could not often open doors to those whose income was well below the required level. Superficially it seems reasonable to suppose that in the middle of the thirteenth century students could only be drawn from families rich enough to provide them with a very minimum of 1 l.p. per annum if they also had a suitable patron, or at least 3 l.p. per annum if they did not; by 1333 the equivalents were 3 l.p. and about 7 l.p. The problem of establishing which families fell into these categories is seriously compounded by the fact that regular wage-earners, though their numbers were increasing during the thirteenth and fourteenth centuries, remained only a small part of the working population in this period. Nevertheless the few indications we have suggest that even the aristocrats among villagers had no hope of raising sufficient cash from their earnings to send their sons to university. Neither the blacksmith who, in the 1240s, earned 5 l.p. per annum plus bread, beer, and eggs, nor the sergeant of the royal forest who earned 4 l. 10s. p. per annum could have given up such a substantial share of their income as would have been needed, even for the cheapest kind of higher education. And their successors throughout the thirteenth century, plagued by stagnant wages and rising prices, would have been in a less good position. Only when wages began to rise as fast as prices in the early fourteenth century did their prospects improve; and by that time the cost of living in Paris and Orléans had soared well beyond their pockets.[30]

Most peasants, however, did not earn regular wages; and most had as their objective the attainment of self-sufficiency, rather than the accumulation of profit. But some small-holders with acreage enough to produce a surplus and also convenient access to an urban market may have profited from the erratically rising grain prices of the thirteenth century and the sky-high prices of the first two decades of the fourteenth—though since these were the result of appalling weather in northern France, particularly in 1315 and 1316, most small-holders will have joined their richer neighbours in watching the destruction of their crops by floods and storms.[31] A tiny minority of fortunate peasants in Picardy (where land prices rose, against the general trend[32]) were rich enough to afford university education for their sons, whether or not they thought it a good investment. Still, the fluctuations which accompanied the overall rise in grain prices in the thirteenth and early fourteenth centuries will always have rendered those students dependent on grain surpluses for their maintenance peculiarly vulnerable to temporary shortages of cash[33]—an irritant affecting the sons of the landed aristocracy as well as those of small-holders. But peasants were usually unable either to buy the land some impoverished nobles offered up for sale, or to take up the new leases on large estates to be intensively cultivated for the expanding urban market. It was a minority of their social superiors, men of knightly rank, who successfully exploited the best opportunities for making land pay in generally unfavourable circumstances.[34]

The argument thus far has suggested that non-aristocratic landowners had a very slim chance of launching their sons into one of the professions for which university education was becoming a requirement. But the premiss that income was crucial to the ability to pay might be questioned. Some parents may have risked their capital. The peasant in Rutebeuf's poem *Li Diz de l'Universitei* who sold (or leased) his *arpent* or two of land in order to send his son to the Paris schools[35] suffered severely thereby, since he lost his own home in the process. Rutebeuf's aim in writing the poem was to castigate students who wasted their time and other peoples' substance in rioting when they should have been studying; his didactic purpose was therefore compatible with exaggerating the extent of parental self-sacrifice. Yet had there been no students from backgrounds as poor as this, the poem's lesson would have been lost on its readers (as indeed it would also have been had they constituted more than a tiny minority). The relation between literature and life is always highly debatable. Yet it would be unfair to discount totally Rutebeuf's testimony. By the thirteenth century the land market was sufficiently developed to permit risk-taking on this scale; but the fate of the peasant was hardly an encouragement to others to emulate him.

It was probably less uncommon to take the risk on one's own behalf. Students who inherited property were free to do what they liked with it; the Paris arts masters revealed in 1284 that some of them fell into this category.[36] Those who could not afford to pay others to work their land will have sold it and lived on their capital. In 1224 in the court of the official of the archdeacon of Paris the clerk Manasses began a suit against his relations, requiring them to provide him with food while he studied. Though the official ordered the family to comply, they appealed against his judgement to the archdeacon. But before the case was heard it was settled out of court. Manasses was to have at once his share of the inheritance, 5 *arpents* of land and 100 sous; in return he promised to claim nothing further from his family, not even his share of future legacies. If one of his brothers predeceased him, he would not inherit unless he had by that time returned to his family the land or its value in money.[37]

Effectively Manasses was equated with a daughter receiving a dowry at her marriage; he was being cast off. It was a harsh arrangement. In accepting it, he took a considerable risk with his future, for if things went wrong, he would have no-one to turn to for help.

This case has interested social historians, because it points to the continued existence of corporate family properties into the thirteenth century. In fact Manasses was relatively lucky; unlike the younger son of a holder in military tenure, he had an established right to his share of the family property, small though that was. Although his 100 *sous* would not have lasted for more than about two years, he was at least able to do what he wanted. Yet the unfavourable terms he obtained proved that his family had an acceptable legal ground for refusing to feed him while he qualified. Many a less determined youth from the same kind of background would have been discouraged by the lack of familial obligation. Furthermore Manasses's brothers' attitude shows that they at least did not regard the university as a substantial career ladder; the lowly position in ecclesiastical administration that could be predicted as his reward for study was too insignificant a step to be of benefit to his relations. He must therefore take his own risks. Theirs was doubtless a realistic view of the situation, given Manasses's lack of social status to reinforce his potential educational achievements.

A peasant who would not risk drawing on his capital might think of taking out a loan, offering his land in pledge. Although there is considerable evidence for money-lending in this period, the sources shed little light on the borrowers; would-be students and their fathers may, for all we know, have been common enough. Yet the prohibitive rates of interest charged—St Louis in 1234 reckoned that a third of all debts to Jews was composed of interest, Philip IV attempted to limit the interest charged at the Champagne fairs to 20 per cent[38]—would soon have bankrupted anyone whose income was too small to cover university costs in the first place. Resorting to loans may have helped through moments of crisis; even the rich Englishman Thomas Cantelupe had to avail himself of a Parisian money-lender's services.[39] But as a long-term solution to poverty it was worse than useless. Thus the economic facts of life told hard against the great majority of northern France's rural dwellers in the education stakes.

For the majority of town-dwellers, circumstances were not very different. The small towns of Champagne, Normandy, Brittany and the Ile de France were still economically dependent on the agriculture of the surrounding area. Though they provided employment for a few artisans and shop-keepers, and during the course of our period were likely to attract the services of at least some notaries, a lawyer or two, and perhaps an academically-trained doctor, they remained essentially centres of exchange rather than production. The chances of any but their richest inhabitants being able to pay university costs were therefore only marginally greater than those of their neighbours in the countryside.

It was, of course, very different for the merchants and bankers of the Champagne fair towns until the end of the thirteenth century, and for the denizens of Paris (150,000 inhabitants in *c.* 1250) and the towns of Flanders and Picardy (taken together 180,000 inhabitants in *c.* 1250)[40] throughout the period. There coin circulated fast, even in 1200; and there production, above all of cloth, made a substantial contribution to the economy. It would be folly to deny that the student bodies of Orléans and Paris drew quite disproportionately on the inhabitants of these towns; even a casual glance at the known masters of arts and theology at Paris—Walter of Bruges, Jacques of Douai, Henry of Ghent—proves their significance. The excellent grammar schools in the Flemish towns[41] prepared boys more than adequately for higher education, and may in part explain what seems to have been the relatively broad social distribution of Flemish students. If the conclusions of the only published study of graduates in an urban community, Christine Renardy's *Les mâitres universitaires dans la diocèse de Liège*, can be applied even approximately to neighbouring Flanders in this period, then there was a high proportion [35%] of bourgeois graduates.[42] The sons of great merchants and of the ruling oligarchs were joined at the universities by those from less privileged backgrounds, the offspring of professional men, of royal or aristocratic servants, perhaps even of successful craftsmen and of shop-keepers. Economically active towns apparently gave rise not only to sufficient wealth to pay for study but also to a competitive atmosphere in which the value of academic qualifications was appreciated. And with growing prosperity the demand for higher education rose. But lest the contribution of the Flemish and Picard towns be exaggerated, we must remember how few and how comparatively small they were, even allowing for almost a century of vigorous growth after 1250 (Ghent, the largest, had a population estimated at around 60,000 by the middle of the fourteenth century[43]). Together they were certainly important contributors to the establishment and expansion of the two north French universities; but their urban élites which were the principal source of students were too numerically restricted even by 1340 to provide a large and regular supply.

Paris with its densely inhabited heartland and its straggling suburbs automatically commands attention as potentially an impressive recruiting ground for students. Because those living at home could cut costs substantially, it is a plausible contention that university education was more widely available to Parisians than to others. And if the less fortunate could see in it a path to relatively secure jobs in the burgeoning royal bureaucracy, then they will have had an added inducement to seek it. Furthermore Paris was home to a substantial group of merchants, bankers, speculators, lawyers, doctors, and members of royal, episcopal, or aristocratic entourages, who could well afford university education for their sons if they chose to invest in it. Yet the insignificance of Parisians among known members of the university, the obscurity of the French nation in university affairs, and the emphasis in the records on 'foreigners', all seem to indicate that the inhabitants of the capital were at best lukewarm about the advantages they might derive from their most famous educational institution.

It is clearly less than satisfactory to argue for the aristocratic contribution to French university life on the grounds that non-aristocrats who both wanted and could afford it were too few and far between to make up the majority of students. But the proposition has the merits of being compatible, both with such other information as we have, and with economic reality. The serious financial problems faced by some members of the lesser aristocracy in the later thirteenth and early fourteenth centuries certainly debarred them from aping their noble superiors, but not from providing tuition fees for their sons. The owner of the 200 l.t. per annum regarded as the bare minimum necessary to support the knightly estate could easily afford to pay his student son's expenses; and if he were temporarily embarrassed, he had only to raise a loan by mortgaging his land. Besides, he was in a better position than most to find a patron for his son, perhaps by turning to one of his social equals whose newly achieved financial prosperity was on the brink of carrying him into the highest ranks of the nobility. And once that son had acquired the necessary education, he could be confident of finding occupation compatible with his birth, either in the ecclesiastical or in the secular bureaucracies. For the lesser aristocracy, university education was an almost risk-free investment.

However, the proponents of the view that universities were open to talent and provided important career ladders will regard the argument thus far pursued as unconvincing. For them the question of cost is minor, because they believe that a sufficiently able scholar would either be supported during his university years by charity or patronage, or could find ways of supporting himself. Their contention does not require them to consider how most students paid for their education; all that is needed is a demonstration that a significant minority of poor but clever men penetrated the system and benefited by it. What constitutes a significant minority is seldom discussed; usually a few case histories are enough to establish the point.[44] And little if any attention is paid to the fact that the plum jobs in church and state continued to go to those who were fitted for them by birth.[45]

Clearly it is impossible to refute this assertion in the terms in which it is usually proposed. Some poor but clever men did manage to get through university and establish themselves in careers that would otherwise have been closed to them. Therefore for them the university proved to be a career ladder. But in order to demonstrate any significant contribution to social mobility it would be necessary to show that, had a particular individual not studied, he would not have gained promotion. In fact France in the pre-Plague period was far from lacking in opportunities for able laymen without Latinate educations, in royal administration, in aristocratic households, in mercantile activities, in money-lending, in local law courts, and in estate management. It cannot be assumed that the lay world was impervious to talent. But because precise evidence concerning lay hierarchies other than royal administration is relatively skimpy, less is known about promotion there than in the church, where graduates were usually rewarded. Nevertheless the regular appearance of new noble families should warn us against underestimating the dynamism of French society in this period.

Most historians who have discussed the matter are in fact less interested in charting social mobility than in demonstrating that education paid. They therefore portray upwardly-mobile students as men propelled by innate ability and hard work. Yet many actually owed as much to a patron as the average layman who ascended the ladder of royal administration.[46] Royal generosity to students has been well recorded: Philip IV lavishly supported his godson Philippe de Villepreux (perhaps a converted Jew) while he was studying, probably at Orléans.[47] Philip VI educated at his own expense Robert le Coq, the younger son of his *bailli* at Orléans, a favour for which Robert was later accused of being ungrateful.[48] Patrons further down the social scale might have more narrowly self-interested motives. The abbot of St. Germain des Près hoped to earn goodwill at Rome by offering to provide pensions for four papal nominees; but the demand that he support one scholar to the tune of 20 l.p. per annum threatened to bankrupt the monastery, and he had to plead to be released from his promise.[49] Similarly good intentions may often have waned in the face of exaggerated demands.

Patronage was not only offered; it was actively sought, especially by mature students with substantial financial needs. By pure luck evidence has survived for Marsilius of Padua's joint-stock plan to finance a theology course. In 1328, two years after the notorious author's flight to the court of Lewis of Bavaria, the archbishop of Arles discovered that Marsilius had raised 20 l. p., a loan of 9 gold florins, and another loan of unknown amount, from Italians resident in Paris, to pay his bills while he studied. This money he had absconded with when he fled from France; and the angry donors were now demanding restitution. As potential benefactors they had been a carefully selected group. Two of them, both medical men, had presumably been Marsilius's colleagues in the period 1319–26 when he was working as a doctor in Paris; a third was described as 'master of the king of France', and the last, a member of the Bardi family, was himself a student and therefore liable to be sympathetic.[50] It is unlikely that their charitable assistance to the spread of theological learning would ever have come to light had they not subsequently heartily repented of it, and tried to prosecute Marsilius's page as an accomplice in his master's crime.

The commonest form of patronage was the provision by a rich student of board and lodging for a poorer one, in return for some form of service. Marsilius of Padua's dependant Francis of Venice informed the archbishop of Arles in 1328 that in laying his master's table and serving him wine he had performed the usual tasks that would be expected of a young Italian scholar. In return Marsilius apparently provided Francis with accommodation, took him for walks, and supervised his spending money.[51] It was an advantageous arrangement, not least for the parents of young boys, who must have been relieved to place their offspring under the tutelage of adults, whether or not they valued the cut in costs. In fact Francis's tasks might have been performed by any noble youth for his lord. But more was expected of others; Ancher Panteléon had to buy the meat for his fellow students.[52] And there were also servants who were expected to do the shopping, cook, and carry books for a whole group of students.[53] But if the burdens could be quite heavy, those who performed them (like fags in the public schools of old) may have seen them as a tedious and irritating initiation ritual on the path to social and intellectual advancement.

Whether the poor servants employed by colleges fell into the same mould may be doubted. When Robert de Sorbon laid down that his fellows should employ *beneficiarii* who would combine studying with seeing to the college's wants, he seems to have envisaged rather older and underprivileged men who would otherwise be denied the opportunity to study theology.[54] As this form of employment spread to other colleges, the absence of clear personal relationships between individual scholars and the servants as a body would tend to disparage the position of the latter. But if becoming a *beneficiarius* did indeed constitute one of the very few ways in which a genuinely poor man might attain a university degree, it is particularly unfortunate that known examples are lacking.

An advantageous variant on the theme open to older and more competent men was to secure a permanent position in the household of a wealthy scholar. S(imon?) de Bockland became secretary to a professor of canon law in Orléans, and in return for his labours was fed and lodged.[55] Richard de Swinfield served Thomas Cantelupe for fourteen years during the time that Thomas was studying in Paris, Orléans, and Oxford. That Richard's duties involved attending his master to lectures may be inferred from his own ultimate acquisition of a theology degree; though Thomas's canonization process does not record it, Richard probably subincepted under Thomas, thereby graduating at the latter's expense.[56] William of Saône's stipulation for his college in 1280 that any scholar who entered the service of a rich man should automatically lose his college allowance suggests that this was a very common ambition among the less well off students.[57] It is, however, probable that by the middle of the fourteenth century, when rich youths took to hiring rooms in colleges, the number of such openings had seriously dwindled.

Service of any sort answered the potential student's major difficulty of how to pay for board and lodging. But there was competition for these jobs, and connections were very important in securing them. In fact, the known cases strongly suggest that patronage within universities usually followed the same rules as it did in the rest of society; the protégé's talent mattered rather less than his family's history of service to the family of his patron. If this is true, then universities, far from creating a new means of clambering up the social ladder, simply offered a new arena in which to demonstrate the traditional one.

However Paris university did give rise to one institution that was distinctly new, and that apparently offered the perfect opening to higher education for a young man of ability but no connections—the college in all its forms. These charitable foundations have been much studied,[58] and can therefore be cursorily discussed here. Colleges offered superior living conditions, stimulating company, and an income, to selected grammar, arts, and theology students. Though foundations were few (nineteen, of which seven apparently failed to survive) in the thirteenth century, they multiplied in the first half of the fourteenth. The stipulation in the statutes of Upsala college that those fellows who could not afford to eat the common meals would be exempted from the obligation to attend[59] demonstrates that some genuinely poor students were the beneficiaries of the system. On the other hand, so were some rich ones. Despite papal encouragement to Christians to relieve the poverty of the scholars at the Sorbonne, its earliest masters included Gerard d'Abbeville, whose extant will demonstrates him to have owned large amounts of moveable and immoveable property (the great opponent of mendicant poverty was a distinctly rich man); and Godfrey of Fontaines, from a noble and influential family of Liège.[60] These were hardly *pauperes* in the normal sense of the word. Other colleges, which by their constitutions gave preference to the founder's kin or put the election of members into the hands of great ecclesiastics, were as likely to relieve the relatively fortunate whose purses were somewhat stretched by long study as to assist the truly indigent.

More important in assessing the effect of collegiate charity is the recent calculation by Frank Pegues that perhaps as few as 6.5 per cent of all Paris students belonged to colleges.[61] If this is so, then the tendency in the early fourteenth century to funnel other charitable donations for poor scholars into the colleges[62] will have made survival outside their walls more difficult for the overwhelming majority of students. The privileges of the few enhanced the hardship of the many. Perhaps the poor scholars of the university of Orléans suffered less than once was thought from its failure to attract colleges.

Still, colleges never totally absorbed charitable payments available to scholars once they had begun their studies. The inhabitants of Paris and Orléans, despite their occasional angry clashes with the students, were aware of the suffering endured by those living far from home, and sometimes attempted to alleviate it. The early fourteenth-century Dominican Pierre de la Palud told in one of his sermons of a Paris physician known to him who gave his services free to the poor, charged moderate sums to those who could afford it, spent very little on himself, and put all his excess earnings into bursaries for poor scholars.[63] If the tale lost nothing in its telling, it was directed to an audience in a position to check the facts. Informal giving of this kind is rarely recorded; but the scale of royal benefactions to scholars[64] was so considerable as to make it likely that others imitated their kings. Rescue by a citizen of Paris or Orléans might always save the temporarily destitute student from having to return home; but it was too unreliable to tempt him from there in the first place.

If Pegues is correct in excluding the overwhelming majority of Paris students from the munificence of the colleges, and if private charity within the university towns was concentrated on 'hard luck' cases, it does not mean that all other students had to pay their own way. Recent research by P. Trio[65] has highlighted the efforts of the inhabitants of Ypres, Ghent, Douai and Tournai in establishing confraternities and flying scholarships to encourage educated youths to go on to Paris to read arts and theology. The scale of liberality in this part of the world was so great that in 1350 the chronicler Gilles le Muisis talked of seventy-three inhabitants from Tournai then studying in Paris.[66] If this figure is accurate, then some at least of these students must have been of relatively humble birth; the flying scholarship could be an instrument of meritocracy. But important as this public finance was, it helped only people from a part of France that was, for other reasons, already favoured in its ability to encourage students; it was not specifically targeted to the poor; and it is not known to have assisted scholars of Orléans. Therefore, while it would be wrong to minimize the effects of colleges and of flying scholarships on the social composition of the student body, it would be equally wrong to think of them as principally devoted to assisting the underprivileged. Only sometimes did they have that effect.

The alternative hypothesis favoured by those who see the universities as career ladders is that it was possible for a relatively poor man to work his way through at least two years of study by finding employment in the vacations and in his spare time. Before examining the evidence for this proposition, there are three points to be made. First, because the average age of students declined sharply in the period with which we are dealing, dependence on parents necessarily increased in the early stages of higher education. With the exception of serving a patron, self-help therefore came to be confined chiefly to those engaged on higher degrees. Secondly, some of the ways in which students had scraped a living in the twelfth century became more difficult as the universities grew institutionalized. When schools were still informal groups of students gathered around one master, when there were no degrees or rules about length of study, and when scholars were mobile, financing education could be a very hand-to-mouth business; Abbot Sampson of Bury St. Edmunds recalled with gratitude the holy water seller who had assisted him while he was studying in Paris;[67] John of Salisbury had contrived to tutor children while pursuing knowledge.[68] But in the course of the thirteenth century, as both masters and students became subject to tighter discipline, the part-time scholar became largely a phenomenon of the past. The academic timetable took up an increasing part of each day, with lectures both in the morning and in the afternoon, making moonlighting harder to arrange. And although the vacation increased in length from the single month stipulated by Pope Gregory IX in 1231, it did not grow beyond about seven or eight weeks in the thirteenth century, and the considerable extension in the fourteenth was short-lived.[69] Thirdly and most importantly, the thirteenth and early fourteenth centuries saw a distinct labour surplus in northern France, driving wages down and making employment difficult to find. It is not therefore surprising that almost all the well-known examples of students supporting themselves by working for employers outside the university[70] come either from the twelfth century or from the post-Plague period.

Unlike modern American universities, Paris and Orléans had no buildings for their students to run nor administrative tasks for them to perform. The only obvious exception to the rule was the provision by the English nation in 1339 of a bursary for one Trinello Vesgotus, in return for his offices as scribe when the nation needed one.[71] Otherwise the masters were quite capable of producing any documents that might be required. And despite Guiard of Laon (chancellor of Paris 1237–38) mentioning some students who had to transcribe texts to live,[72] the increasing production of manuscripts by the end of the thirteenth century offered few opportunities for earning a steady income.[73] This is not to deny that the odd lavish commission might bring a very welcome boost to the finances of a scholar with calligraphical skills; nor that it was a sensible use of time for all students to copy texts for their own use. Books benefited them in the classroom, and could be pawned or pledged in time of financial crisis.[74] They did not, however, substitute for an adequate stipend.

For those in the higher faculties at Paris, teaching in the arts faculty could be a valuable supplement to a small income. And this at least the university did facilitate. But the evidence points to a rapid drain of arts masters away from the city to alternative jobs in the provinces,[75] suggesting that rather few found it an enticing prospect. In Orléans, which maintained a much looser structure than Paris and where the teaching of grammar declined during the thirteenth century, those reading law cannot often have financed themselves by tutoring. However one hypothesis is worth entertaining: that in the rapidly expanding court system of the thirteenth and early fourteenth centuries, even reasonably raw students of law were capable of earning some fees by acting as advocates in straightforward cases. If this were true, then some men of more modest means might have scraped by at Orléans, even without patronage; and Jacques de Revigny's student with the unaccommodating family would have had some means of support. Unfortunately the court records of this period fail to name pleaders or advocates; and without this information there is no way of establishing whether a kind of sandwich course existed informally in the law schools.

It is perhaps perverse to regard the holding of ecclesiastical benefices as in any sense work, since students were of necessity non-resident in their parishes or cathedral churches, and left their cures of souls to the care of others. Nevertheless the extent to which university education could be financed by ecclesiastical benefices is obviously crucial to our image of the student body. If ordinary parish priests could enter the university, then clearly it was accessible to relatively underprivileged people; if only canons normally could, then the entry was quite restricted. Unfortunately the absence of episcopal registers from France in this period makes it surprisingly difficult to establish which was the case. Deductions have to be made from papal mandates, from reported instances, and from occasional references in other literature. Any conclusions can only be extremely tentative.

Throughout this period the popes, anxious to increase the number of learned clerics, both encouraged chapters and bishops to assist scholars by granting them livings, and drew up regulations enabling certain categories of student to derive revenues from their benefices while non-resident for study purposes. Initially at least papal policies seem to have been unpopular with some cathedral and collegiate chapters, despite the suitability of their prebends for financing education (they were usually well-endowed and did not carry cures of souls). In 1232 Gregory IX had to insist on the chapter of Tours allowing one of its canons to obtain his stipend while he was studying theology—presumably at Paris. And although chapters when revising their statutes usually made allowance for study leave, some as late as the mid-thirteenth century continued to express fear of abuse.[76] Then things started to change. Those who were already canons were dispensed to go to university, and canonries were granted to students.[77] But since only men of high social standing could usually obtain these, the chief gainers were aristocratic scholars of law at Orléans. Because demand far outstripped supply, papal efforts were mainly confined to ensuring that doctors of theology from Paris got the appropriate reward—as most did. While a few distinguished masters of arts (Siger of Brabant among them) did become members of chapters, and could then if they wished use the revenues to study theology, most masters were not successful.[78] The bitter complaint of the Paris arts faculty in 1316 led Pope John XXII to introduce the system of university rolls to expedite the acquisition of benefices by graduates, but there is no evidence that this innovation had had a significant effect on the financing of theological studies by about 1340.[79]

From the university rolls that survive it is evident that masters and bachelors regarded themselves as deserving of substantial material reward. They expected to be counted among the higher clergy. On the other hand, the popes also encouraged French parish clergy, like their English counterparts, to study grammar or theology in order to improve the general standard of their ministry. French ecclesiastical records are so much worse than English that proof is lacking; but it might be tempting to assume that the Paris theology faculty fulfilled the same role in educating parish priests as did Oxford and Cambridge. On this assumption a very substantial number of more mature men from simple backgrounds and without previous qualification would have received episcopal dispensations to take up residence in Paris, to attend university sermons, hear theology lectures, and improve their standard of Latinity, without normally intending to take a degree. Their benefices would have financed this important period of study leave.[80] But unsatisfactory though it is to postulate a seminal difference between Paris and the English faculties so closely modelled on it, especially when the evidence is very meagre, the few scraps we have do not suggest that this pattern was common in France.

Unlike their English counterparts, French bishops tended to be suspicious of those parish priests who wanted to study. In 1233 the bishop of Dol complained forcefully to Gregory IX about the clerks of his diocese who were drawing revenues from their benefices on the pretext of studying theology.[81] Though a doctor of theology himself, Eudes Rigaud in 1251 would only permit Adam, priest of Yvercrique, to attend the schools if he pledged his church as a bond for his good behaviour; in other words the archbishop deprived Adam of the revenue of his benefice.[82] And this was the only dispensation for study leave granted in Eudes's entire visitation register. Surviving French synodical legislation makes no mention of such dispensations,[83] and Pope Martin IV's privilege of 1281 to royal clerks studying at Paris to draw revenues from their benefices demonstrated the comparative rarity of such grants, despite papal prescription.[84] Although Boniface VIII's bull *cum ex eo* of 1298 should have altered the situation drastically, there are no obvious signs of a rush to Paris in its wake. Indeed the arts faculty in around 1316 complained bitterly of its declining numbers.[85] And in 1314 Pierre de la Palud affirmed that fewer than one parish priest in twenty had ever heard a course of theology lectures.[86] His secular opponent Jean de Pouilly, who denied most of what Pierre said, could not contradict this. Therefore, inadequate though the evidence is, it is not *prima facie* consistent with an extensive use of parochial revenues to finance university education. Perhaps most parishes were too poor to be able to afford it. It appears therefore that those fortunate enough to obtain canonries remained the chief beneficiaries of papally-inspired generosity, and that Paris turned its face from priests who had not completed the necessary preliminary studies.

Claims for the early universities as career ladders ought to be treated with caution. Certainly there were 'lads o' pairts' in Paris and Orléans in the thirteenth and early fourteenth centuries, but they were much rarer than in nineteenth-century Scotland (and a Scottish historian has recently made inroads even on this sacred class[87]). Furthermore, those who did clamber up several rungs usually achieved their elevation by exactly the same means as their brothers in the lay world, that is by entering the service of their betters. The main problem for the social climber was that advancement within the university was easier in Paris with its colleges and charities than in Orléans, but the law studies of Orléans offered a far more marketable qualification. The lucky few from the upper peasantry or the lesser bourgeoisie who acquired scholarships or patronage and then found a career to suit their talents always constituted a tiny minority. The real gainers by university education were, as might be expected, the younger sons of knights, of the urban governing class, or of merchants. And since many of their counterparts in the lay world achieved striking social advancement,[88] too much significance should not be attributed to their years of study. The medieval university mirrored but did not alter the social values of the world around it. We should not romanticize it.

St Anne's College
Oxford

REFERENCES

1. J. Le Goff, *Les Intellectuels au moyen âge* (Paris, 1957), pp. 139–48; G. Leff, *Paris and Oxford Universities in the Thirteenth and Fourteenth Centuries* (New York, 1968), pp. 9–11; A. B. Cobban, 'Medieval Student Power', *Past and Present* 53 (1971), 61; idem, *The Medieval Universities: Their Development and Organization* (London, 1975), pp. 167–9; A. Murray, *Reason and Society in the Middle Ages* (Oxford, 1978), pp. 218–27.
2. See the wise words of J. Paquet in *Revue belge de philologie et d'histoire* 59 (1981), 409 note 1, on Le Goff's contention that the number of poor students declined rapidly at the end of the middle ages: 'Pareille

affirmation est indémontrable, pour la simple raison que l'on ne dispose d'aucune série de données chiffrées avant la fin du XIVe siècle. Pour la même raison, on ne peut affirmer avec certitude que les universitaires fils de bourgeois étaient proportionellement plus nombreux au XIIIe siècle qu'aux deux siècles suivants et que les universités s'aristocratisent avant 1350.'

3. Cobban, *Medieval Universities*, p. 168.
4. For a summary of work on the rise of the knight see P. Contamine in *La Noblesse au moyen âge* ed. Contamine (Paris, 1976), pp. 21–31; for a more detailed treatment by R. Fossier of the situation in Picardy see ibid., pp. 109–14.
5. J. Le Goff, *Les Intellectuels au moyen âge*, pp. 104–7.
6. G. Post, 'Masters' Salaries and Student Fees in the Medieval Universities', *Speculum* 7 (1932), 181–98. *Chartularium Universitatis Parisiensis* (hereinafter referred to as CUP), eds. H. Denifle and E. Chatelain, I (Paris, 1889), no. 515, p. 609. For comparison with the examination fees in southern French universities, see J. Verger in *The Economic and Material Frame of the Medieval University*. Texts and Studies in the History of Medieval Education ed. A. L. Gabriel, XV (Notre Dame, Indiana, 1977), pp. 20–3.
7. The assumption that lodgings were especially expensive in university towns is reinforced by the university of Paris's 1245 attempt to curb rent rises on rooms hired for teaching purposes, CUP I, no. 136, pp. 177–8.
8. Determiners were expected to pay two-thirds of the rent for their master's school; see CUP I, no. 515, p. 608. For the allegation that examinations could be occasions for extortion see ibid, pp. 610, 616. For the general tendency of examination fees to rise rapidly, see J. Verger, note 6, above.
9. F. Pegues, 'Royal Support of Students in the Thirteenth Century', *Speculum* 31 (1956), 460–2; *Auctarium Chartularii Universitatis Parisiensis* eds. H. Denifle and E. Chatelain, I (Paris, 1894), cols. 13 and 14; for *bursae* at the Collège of Navarre, see H. Rashdall, *The Universities of Europe in the Middle Ages* 3rd ed. by F. M. Powicke and A. B. Emden (3 vols., Oxford, 1936), I. 511. There is sound critical comment on the defects of *bursae* as exact indications of student expenditure in E. Mornet, '*Pauperes scolares*. Essai sur la condition matérielle des étudiants scandinaves dans les universités aux XIV et XVe siècles', *Le Moyen Age* 84 (1978), 67–73.
10. CUP I, no. 423, p. 477. I have chosen to take 45 weeks as the norm for the vacation in calculating *bursae* throughout this paper, because the exact fluctuations cannot be charted, and 45 weeks seems to be around the average. But for more details on this, see note 69.
11. CUP II (Paris, 1891), no. 1185, p. 674.
12. This is based on the assumption that St. Louis's gift of 100 s.t. (4 1.p.) per annum to each of the sons of a royal sergeant (Pegues, 'Royal

Support of Students', p. 461) was a marginally more generous than average provision for an ordinary student. Over 45 weeks, this meant a *bursa* of about 1 s. 9 d. p. per week.

13. See note 7.
14. M. Fournier, *Statuts et Privilèges des Universités françaises depuis leur fondation jusqu'en 1789*, vol. I (Paris, 1890), no. 28, p. 31.
15. CUP I, no. 201, p. 228; CUP II, no. 1185, p. 673. See A. L. Gabriel, *Garlandia. Studies in the History of the Medieval University* (Notre Dame, Indiana, 1969), p. 100. The chancellor's complaint against the arts faculty in 1284 (CUP I, no. 515, p. 616) shows the process of contraction occurring.
16. W. J. Courtenay, 'Teaching Careers at the University of Paris in the Thirteenth and Fourteenth centuries', *Texts and Studies in the History of Medieval Education* ed. A. L. Gabriel, XVIII (Notre Dame, Indiana, 1988), pp. 22–4, on students of theology teaching in the arts faculty.
17. CUP I, no. 235, p. 261.
18. E. Meijers, *Études d'histoire du droit. III. Le droit roman au moyen âge* (Leiden, 1959), pp. 3–148; M. Fournier 'La Nation allemande à l'université d'Orléans', *Revue historique de droit* 1888, p. 392.
19. C. H. Haskins, 'The Life of Medieval Students as Illustrated by Their Letters', *American Historical Review* 3 (1887), 203–29.
20. A. Pales-Gobilliard, *L'Inquisiteur Geoffroy d'Ablis et les cathars du comté de Foix (1308–9)* (Paris, 1984), p. 393.
21. Haskins, 'The Life of Medieval Students . . .', p. 221.
22. Meijers, *Études d'histoire du droit. III*, p. 7.
23. C. H. Haskins, 'Orléans Formularies in a Manuscript at Tarragona', *Speculum* 5 (1930), 417.
24. Translated by S. Ferruolo in *The Origins of the University; The Schools of Paris and Their Critics 1100–1213* (Stanford, 1985), p. 113.
25. Haskins, 'The Life of Medieval Students . . .', pp. 212–3, note 3.
26. *Acta Sanctorum*, October, vol. I (Antwerp, 1765) pp. 544 and 553.
27. Pegues, 'Royal Support of Students . . .', p. 461.
28. F. Pegues, *The Lawyers of the Last Capetians* (Princeton, N.J., 1962), pp. 120–3.
29. *Cronica fratris Salimbene de Adam* ed. O. Holder-Egger, Monumenta Germaniae Historica, Scriptores, 32 (1905), 170, refers to him as 'vilis scolaris'.
30. G. Sivéry, *L'Économie du Royaume de France au siècle de Saint Louis* (Lille, 1984), pp. 135–48.
31. ibid., p. 140, tabulates the fluctuations in grain prices. See also H. Lucas, 'The Great European Famine of 1315, 1316, 1317,' *Speculum* 5 (1930), 343–77.
32. Sivéry, *L'Économie*, pp. 118–25.
33. ibid., p. 140.
34. ibid., pp. 131–3.

35. *Rutebeuf. Poèmes concernant l'Université de Paris* ed. H. H. Lucas (Manchester and Paris, 1953), p. 31.
36. CUP I, no. 515, p. 609. See also Pierre de Belleperche on the problems of scholars inheriting, Meijers, *Etudes d'histoire du droit* III, p. 7.
37. F. Olivier-Martin, *Histoire de la coutume de la prevoté et vicomté de Paris* vol. I (Paris, 1922), p. 147.
38. W. C. Jordan, *The French Monarchy and the Jews. From Philip Augustus to the Last Capetians* (Univ. of Pennsylvania, 1989), p. 133, says that in 1234 the government assumed a third of the face value of any bond to be interest. On Philip IV, see Sivéry, *L'Économie*, p. 238.
39. *Acta Sanctorum*, October, vol. I, p. 552.
40. Sivéry, *L'Économie*, p. 14.
41. H. Pirenne, 'L'Instruction des marchands au Moyen Âge', *Annales d'histoire économique et sociale*, 1 (1929), 13–28; D. L. d'Avray, *The Preaching of the Friars. Sermons Diffused from Paris Before 1300* (Oxford, 1985), pp. 36–8.
42. C. Renardy, *Le Monde des maîtres universitaires du diocèse de Liège 1140–1350. Recherches sur sa composition et ses activités* (Paris, 1979), p. 158.
43. D. Nicholas, *The Metamorphosis of a Medieval City: Ghent in the Age of the Artevalds 1302–1390* (Lincoln, Nebraska, and London, 1987), p. 17.
44. Murray, *Reason and Society*, pp. 226–7; Cobban, *Medieval Universities*, p. 190: 'The product of a fairly humble background, he (the average northern student) was likely to regard the university as one of the few or even the sole means of modest social advancement'.
45. See for example J. R. Strayer, *The Reign of Philip IV* (Princeton, N.J., 1980), pp. 45–6; p. 241.
46. See for example R. Cazelles, *La Société politique et la crise de la royauté sous Philippe de Valois* (Paris, 1958), pp. 336–8.
47. Pegues, *The Lawyers of the Last Capetians*, pp. 124–7.
48. Cazelles, *La Société politique*, pp. 255, 299.
49. CUP I, no. 103, p. 153.
50. S. Baluze, *Miscellanea novo ordine Digesta* II, ed. J. Mansi (Lucca 1758), p. 282.
51. ibid., p. 280.
52. Salimbene, MGH, SS 32, p. 170.
53. Pierre de la Palud in Clermont Ferrand, Bibliothèque Municipale, MS 46, fo. 229r.
54. H. Rashdall, *Universities of Europe* I, 508.
55. C. E. Woodruff, 'Letters to the Prior of Christchurch, Canterbury, from University Students', *Archaeologia Cantiana*, 39 (1927), 28, quoted by J. Paquet in 'Coût des études, pauvreté et labeur; fonctions et métiers d'étudiants au moyen âge', *History of Universities* 2 (1982), 22.
56. *Acta Sanctorum*, October, vol. 1, p. 541.
57. CUP I, no. 499, p. 585.

58. Rashdall, *Universities of Europe* I. 497–539; F. Pegues in *The Economic and Material Frame* ed. A. L. Gabriel, pp. 69–76; Cobban, *Medieval Universities*, pp. 126–32; A. L. Gabriel, 'The College System in the Fourteenth-Century Universities' in F. L. Utley ed., *The Forward Movement of the Fourteenth century* (Ohio, 1961), pp. 79–124.
59. A. L. Gabriel, *Skara House at the Medieval University of Paris* (Notre Dame, Indiana, 1960), p. 26.
60. For Gerard d'Abbeville's will see *Aux origines de la Sorbonne. II. Le cartulaire*, ed. P. Glorieux (Paris, 1965), no. 301, pp. 354–8. For Godfrey of Fontaines see C. Renardy, *Le monde des maîtres universitaires dans la diocèse de Liège. Repertoire biographique (1140–1350)* (Paris, 1981), pp. 257–60.
61. Pegues in *The Economic and Material Frame*, p. 75.
62. When Pope John XXII declared in 1329 his intention of giving a fine wrongly exacted from a bishop to the poor scholars of Paris, he simply handed the money over to two colleges; CUP II, no. 910, p. 343.
63. Clermont Ferrand, Bibliothèque Municipale, MS 46, fo. 25v.
64. Pegues, 'Royal Support of Students', pp. 454–62; and in *The Economic and Material Frame*, p. 72.
65. P. Trio, 'The Financing of University Students in the Middle Ages: A New Orientation', *History of Universities* 4 (1984), 1–24; and 'A Medieval Students' Confraternity at Ypres: The Notre Dame Confraternity of Paris Students', *History of Universities* 5 (1985), 14–53.
66. Trio, 'The Financing . . .', p. 9 and note 77.
67. Jocelin of Brakelond, *Chronicle Concerning the Acts of Abbot Sampson* ed. and tr. H. Butler (London, 1949), pp. 43–4.
68. John of Salisbury, *Metalogicon* ed. C. C. J. Webb (Oxford, 1929), pp. 80–1.
69. See above, note 10; and W. J. Courtenay, *Schools and Scholars in Fourteenth-century England* (Princeton, N.J., 1987), pp. 10–13.
70. Paquet, 'Coût des études, pauvreté et labeur . . .', pp. 15–52.
71. *Auctarium Chartularii Universitatis Parisiensis*, col. 27.
72. Quoted by J. Paquet, 'Coût des études, pauvreté et labeur . . .', p. 22.
73. Despite the marked increase in manuscript production in the later thirteenth century in Paris, and the fact that some manuscripts were written a *pecia* at a time, there is no evidence to suggest that students were often employed in producing those not intended for their own use. For a recent study of book production, see R. H. and M. A. Rouse in *La Production du livre universitaire au moyen âge* eds. L. J. Bataillon, B. G. Guyot, and R. H. Rouse (Paris, 1988), pp. 41–114.
74. G. C. Boyce, *The English-German Nation in the University of Paris During the Middle Ages* (Bruges, 1927), pp. 174–6.
75. Courtenay, 'Teaching Careers at the University of Paris', pp. 23–4.
76. F. Pegues, 'Ecclesiastical Provisions for the Support of Students in the Thirteenth Century', *Church History* 26 (1957), 307–18. See also Innocent IV's letter warning of potential abuses, CUP I, no. 145, pp. 182–3.

77. See e.g. the cases cited by Cazelles, *La Société politique sous Philippe de Valois*, p. 299 note 4.
78. CUP II, no. 728, p. 184.
79. D. E. R. Watt, 'University Clerks and Rolls of Petitions for Benefices', *Speculum* 34 (1959), 214.
80. J. Dunbabin, 'Careers and Vocations', in J. Catto ed. *A History of the University of Oxford. Vol. I. The Early Schools* (Oxford, 1984), pp. 567–8.
81. Pegues, 'Ecclesiatical Provisions . . .', pp. 307–8.
82. *The Register of Eudes of Rouen*, ed. and tr. S. Brown and J. O'Sullivan (New York–London, 1964), p. 491.
83. *Les Statuts synodaux francais du XIIIe siècle* vol. I ed. O. Pontal (Paris, 1971); vol. II ed. O. Pontal (Paris, 1983); vol. III ed. J. Avril (Paris, 1988). Although Robert de Courçon's Ordinances of 1213 (CUP I, no. 19, p. 77) do make allowance for parish priests studying at the university, no later university legislation mentions them.
84. CUP I, no. 507, pp. 591–2.
85. CUP II, no. 728, p. 184.
86. Pierre de la Palud in Toulouse, Bibliothèque Municipale, MS 744, fo. 90v, Quodlibet qu. 4.
87. R. D. Anderson, '"In search of the Lad of Parts"; the Mythical History of Scottish Education', *History Workshop* 19 (1985), 82–104; 'Scottish University Professors, 1800–1939: Profile of an Elite', *Scottish Economic and Social History* 7 (1987), 27–54.
88. C. Renardy, *Les Mâitres universitaires* I. 158–9, has summarized the Flemish and Lotharingian evidence for the assimilation after about 1300 of patricians and knights (who together provided 60% of known Liège graduates). For a treatment of the topic in general, see E. Perroy, 'Social Mobility Among the French *Noblesse* in the Later Middle Ages', *Past and Present* 21 (1962), 25–38; P. Contamine, 'The French Nobility and the War' in K. Fowler (ed.), *The Hundred Years War* (London, 1971), pp. 135–62.

The Collegiate Movement in Italian Universities in the Late Middle Ages

Peter Denley

1. Introduction

In the social and institutional historiography of medieval universities Italy has had the part of Cinderella.[1] The Northern European 'system' has been extensively researched, and is largely the basis for our image of medieval universities; but it is still the case that historians outside Italy tend at most to append to their observations a few comments to the effect that Italy was different, without real understanding of why or how this was so. This is nowhere more clear than in the historiography of the collegiate movement. The assumption that Italy has little to offer here is almost universal.

There are several reasons for this. Partly, of course, it is because success and longevity breed their own historiography. There will be historians of Oxford and Cambridge colleges for as long as those colleges continue to flourish. By contrast, hardly any of the Italian colleges survived into modern times, and those that did were transformed, or have histories of discontinuity. But whereas it is now understood, for example, that the Parisian colleges of the fourteenth and fifteenth centuries were an important feature of the university, and they are being studied to the extent that the documents permit,[2] there has been no comparable revival of interest for Italy. Despite anniversaries—of the Collegio Ghislieri and the Collegio Borromeo in Pavia, and the Collegio di Spagna in Bologna[3]—there has been relatively little serious investigation, virtually no comparative study,[4] and many repetitions, especially by Northern European historians, of the statement that they were unimportant. They are deemed to have been fewer, and smaller, than those in the North, and since they were not teaching institutions they have been considered little more than boarding-houses, and as such not really worthy of study.[5]

The purpose of this investigation is to question those assumptions. It does not seek to deny the limits to the significance of the Italian colleges, just to show that, even if they did not play as great a role as their Northern counterparts, they were none the less significant. Much more research needs to be done on this topic; what follows is by way of being a survey of what has been found to date, not the last word on the subject. First, however, it is necessary to place the Italian colleges in the context of their better-understood Northern counterparts. This is one respect in which the consideration of Italian universities as separate in their evolution has been misleading. The Italian collegiate movement took much from Northern examples, had much in common with them, and adapted many of their features while rejecting some others.

The current view of the role of colleges in the late middle ages might be summarized as follows. In Northern Europe the growth of the collegiate movement provided institutional life for an increasing number of students. By its intensification in the fourteenth century it supplied, as Gabriel put it, the 'bridge' between the thirteenth-century 'age of violence and indiscipline' and the more regulated university world of the fifteenth century.[6] It did so in three ways. The first was financial and social. The endowment of colleges helped to pave the way for the fifteenth-century universities by attacking the problem of the funding of study, alongside the papacy's implementation of a system of assigning benefices to students. The dramatic increase in the number of university foundations in the mid-fourteenth century was accompanied by an equally notable growth in the number of collegiate foundations, which together represented, for Delaruelle, the finding of new solutions to new types of educational need.[7] The second contribution is moral, and concerns discipline: by its pious orientation the collegiate movement brought to the attention of university administrators the notion that the academic body could be disciplined. The Parisian reforms of Cardinal d'Estouteville (1452)[8] and the earlier Oxford and Cambridge legislation compelling students to live in colleges or halls[9] came in the wake of this new interest in discipline. Thirdly, the colleges made a specifically academic contribution; to pre-university teaching (specifically to liberal arts teaching), and to teaching that was supplementary to formal university courses. Indeed, in some cases the colleges ended up largely supplanting university teaching, with the growth of college lectureships, an emphasis on disputations and teaching methods more appropriate to a collegiate environment, and eventually, in England, the tutorial system.[10]

Italian colleges by contrast are seen to have failed in these respects. They were not academic; basically they were 'boarding-houses'. Individual ones may have mattered, but the movement as a whole did not.[11] Cobban offered two reasons for this: the wealthier and more mature character of the Italian student population, which meant that there was less need for financial support or, given the existence of student-universities, for peer support; and the prevalence of student controls, which acted as a deterrent to the founders of colleges, which only grew once student power declined (and here Cobban is thinking, it would appear, of the sixteenth century).[12] In other words, the same factors which gave rise to the student-universities in the first place—the age and status of the predominantly law-student population—are invoked as reasons why there was little incentive for the founding of colleges. Likewise the student-universities allegedly controlled teaching; not surprisingly, therefore, where colleges were founded, they did not develop a teaching function. Collegiate teaching represented a challenge to the centralized functions of a university, which could only be successful where the university had little centralized power—for example Paris by the fourteenth century, and, *par excellence*, Oxford.[13]

The validity of this assessment will be examined in all its aspects. First, however, there is a need for definition, and condemning the Italian colleges for their failure to develop a teaching role raises it immediately. The term 'college' is useful for bringing under one head institutions founded for a range of motives, but usually having in common in the middle ages the caritative aim of providing places for poor scholars. Beyond that, though, colleges could have a wide range of functions, and distinctions must be made. At one extreme, the term can include the graduate colleges of Oxford and Cambridge, richly endowed, independent, and democratically run as institutions of graduate fellows can easily be. These have no real parallels on the continent other than that of the Sorbonne which preceded them and to an extent provided them with a model, and they are not of concern here. Nor, incidentally, shall we be concerned with the Oxford-type halls or Cambridge-type hostels, unendowed establishments for undergraduates, useful as far as the authorities were concerned for discipline, and attractive to undergraduates as accommodation with controlled rents and conditions.

These institutions were not colleges and they were indeed declining by the end of the fifteenth century as the colleges began to take on undergraduates. The nearest parellel on the continent to such halls or hostels was the Parisian-style *pedagogicum*, a hall of residence attached to a college to which members originally went to be taught. Its precursor, the *pedagogicum* discussed by d'Estouteville in his 1452 reforms, grew out of informal or semi-formal arrangements with a teacher, and was often in effect a private school; that is another institution again, and the illustration of the role it played is one of the more durable features of Ariès' otherwise much-criticized book *Centuries of Childhood.*[14] Such private schools certainly existed in Italy, but to our knowledge only at the pre-university level, although the practice among university teachers of taking student-lodgers—and consequently giving them access to their books and expertise—seems to have existed at least in the early days of the University of Bologna, and quite possibly beyond. This study, however, will concentrate on colleges which

1. were essentially for students studying one of the main university subjects, theology, law, medicine or arts[15]
2. were endowed with possessions or some other source of income[16]
3. had some sense of community or of a common way of life embodied in their statutes, or, where there are no extant statutes, some expression of that intention in the documents pertaining to their foundation.

They were not necessarily self-governing (although this was often the case), and they did not necessarily feature a formal teaching role.

That is a good working definition[17] of most colleges outside England, the ones with which comparisons can most usefully be made for present purposes.[18]

The first point that needs stressing is that these colleges were more numerous in Italy than has been realized. In his 1961 survey of European colleges in the middle ages, Gabriel counted sixteen Italian foundations before 1500; one in the thirteenth century, ten in the fourteenth, five in the fifteenth.[19] But we know now of thirty-seven, as well as at least another ten which were at one stage projected,[20] and no doubt there were other attempts at foundation that were lost to posterity. Of course this is hardly dramatic compared to, say, Paris with its forty or so colleges in 1500.[21] Moreover, some of these colleges did not last very long or amount to very much. In some cases only the foundation documents survive; and this study will not dwell for long on foundations such as the Collegio Grassi, established in 1457 in Turin for four students. Most, however, were more significant than that, and of course small-scale foundations are equally common in Northern Europe. In any case, the urge to found colleges in itself is worth examining.[22] Appendix I lists the known and attempted foundations, and Appendix II summarizes their histories in more detail; it must be stressed, again, that the information collected is provisional, and is not intended to be exhaustive.

2. The First Italian Colleges: Bologna and Northern Influences

The first phase of Italian collegiate foundations was essentially Bolognese, but in a sense also very French. It was Franco-Italian links that ensured that that particularly French contribution to university development, the colleges, had an echo in Italy. The first known Italian college was typical of this: Zoen Tencarari, a Bolognese who became Bishop of Avignon, made provision in his will of 1257 for a college at Bologna of eight students, to be chosen from Avignon or the area. He provided an endowment of 24 *lire bolognesi* per annum, together with property, to be administered by the Prior of S. Michele in Bosco. No statutes survive, and as is typical of such early foundations, very little is known about its early history.[23]

We have more information about the second foundation, the Collegio Bresciano, and its founder, Guglielmo Corvi da Brescia, who also had important French connections. Corvi had studied and taught medicine and philosophy at Paris, Padua and Bologna—where he had been a pupil of Taddeo Alderotti—and he had been doctor to two popes, Boniface VIII and Clement V. From about 1290 he had amassed a very impressive number of benefices and lucrative appointments.[24] A good deal of this wealth was bequeathed, by his will of 7 May 1326, to a college of up to fifty students in arts, medicine and canon law. A building was to be bought and adapted specially for the purpose, and the founder also drew up statutes for the new college. Guerrini, the first historian to have investigated the Bresciano, speculated that the college was based on the model of the Sorbonne, which had been founded in the mid-thirteenth century and whose statutes date from 1274, and other historians have repeated this diagnosis in copy-cat fashion;[25] but it is difficult to see how this can be, since the Sorbonne was a college specifically for graduates, with different requirements, and there are no similarities, either in structure or in content, between the two sets of statutes beyond those which one might expect to find in common among any bodies of collegiate statutes.[26] It would be safe only to say that it is quite possible that the example of the many Parisian colleges, among which the Sorbonne had a position of pre-eminence by virtue of both age and influence, influenced Corvi's thinking.[27]

One similarity with French colleges generally is the constitutional arrangement of an outside controlling authority. In the Sorbonne this was a body of governors including the Chancellor, the doctors of theology, and the rector and proctors of the university;[28] in the Bresciano it was a *magister* or *gubernator*, who had jurisdiction over the students' internal presiding officer, known, as in the Sorbonne, as *prior*[29] (in all later Italian colleges he was called *rector*, as indeed was the case in the Bresciano itself by 1388).[30] Another feature which may well derive from French models was that the statutes envisaged a paid teacher *in artibus*—whose lectures, however, not only *collegiati* but all students of the university could attend.[31] Much has been made of this, no doubt because it is not only the first example of a teaching appointment within an Italian college, but also one of the very few made in our period. A more significant feature is the way in which the growth of the college was planned into its foundation. Although eventually fifty places were envisaged, and the building acquired was to cater for this number, only eight places were initially funded (at 15 *lire bolognesi* per annum, or a total endowment of 120 *lire bolognesi*).[32] Brescian students were to have preference in selection, which was in the gift of the Archdeacon of Bologna; but anyone who in the future endowed a place—at 15 *lire bolognesi* per annum—would thereby acquire the perpetual *ius presentandi* for that place. Organic growth was built in, just as in the early Oxford colleges.[33]

It should be mentioned in passing that the international dimension of Italian collegiate foundations is echoed in other attempts of the period. In 1334 a college for Italian students was established in Paris, the Collège des Lombards, as a result of the efforts of four Italians resident in France and the support of the French king. The college had a chequered history in the late middle ages, and was eventually given to a community of Irish priests in 1677. Its main problem was the difficulty in maintaining continuity over a period in which Franco-Italian relations went through so many fluctuations; but the persistence of attempts to keep it going is significant.[34] Another episode which has escaped the attention of university historians altogether is the attempted foundation of a college at Bologna by a follower of Guglielmo da Brescia, the medical doctor Pancio da Controne of Lucca. Pancio spent much of his working life in England, where he became medical adviser to Edward II and Edward III. His will, made in London in June 1338, two years before his death, left possessions to the value of 2,500 *lire bolognesi* for the foundation of a college for twelve students, three each in arts, medicine, canon and civil law. That the college did not materialize may be connected with the financial crisis in England—Pancio was one of Edward III's chief creditors—and the Lucchese had to wait until the seventeenth century until a college for them was established at Bologna.[35]

Most of the other Bolognese colleges of the middle ages were founded in the 1360s, a period of intense university and collegiate development throughout Europe and particularly in France. These foundations all bear the hallmark of experimentation, and inevitably therefore of mixed success. One, the Collegio Fieschi, for Genoese students, first conceived of in 1361, seems to have had only the most shadowy existence before the sixteenth century.[36] Another, the Collegio Reggiano, was not originally intended as a college at all. By his will of 12 October 1362 Guido da Bagnolo, doctor of medicine and counsellor to the Lusignan King Peter I of Jerusalem and Cyprus (and incidentally one of the objects of derision in Petrarch's *De sui ipsius et aliorum ignorantia*) intended to distribute financial help to poor students. In 1371 his executors invested the legacy in land, and in 1384 it was united with the estate of the Reggian Gaspare Tacoli. Whereas in 1393 there is mention of 'scholares de Regio', by 1405 these were listed as 'collegiati et de Collegio regino', and are thus referred to thereafter.[37] It is interesting to note how naturally a group of scholars with an endowment could come to be considered a college; indeed, at this stage the system did not yet favour individual endowment of scholarships.

A more deliberate, though less successful, foundation was that of Urban V. The contribution of this pope to the furtherance of education has only recently come to be appreciated; he was responsible for the nurturing of many French *studia*, and especially for the creation of a number of small preparatory *studia* in Provence, as well as being influential in more than one Italian foundation.[38] His own plans for a college in Bologna—only recently discovered—included places for twenty students of the Papal States, an endowment of 4,000 gold ducats, and the purchase in Avignon of a large collection of books for the foundation library. Urban died before writing the statutes, and it is a pity that we do not, therefore, have his statement of what he intended for the college. The fact that the rector of the college was not a student, and not elected, but an outsider appointed directly by the Pope, suggests that they would have been unusual. Nor did the 4,000 ducats unfortunately materialize, and nothing is heard of the college after his death.[39] It seems that it may have been incorporated in that founded by his successor, Gregory XI, whose foundation of 1370–71 was effectively the largest Bolognese initiative to date. Thirty students were to be incorporated, as well as six chaplains and fifteen servants; a house in the Via Castiglione was bought for the purpose, and in 1372 a library of 193 volumes was added to the foundation. The college was even to have a medical physician charged with visiting sick students. Again, a number of innovations strike the historian. The college was to admit only students of law, fifteen canonists and fifteen civilians—here was a pope setting up a college for civil as well as canon lawyers;[40] twenty were to be poor students from the dioceses of Limoges and Tulle, ten from the Papal States. That these last were to be presented by four doctors, two canonists and two civilians, teaching at Bologna is also unusual; most founders, secular or ecclesiastic, tended to leave these matters to bishops or other ecclesiastics.[41]

The fate of all these foundations was very mixed. The Collegio Avignonese was already in financial difficulty in the early fourteenth century; by 1413 it boasted only one student,[42] and that great despoiler of the Bolognese colleges, John XXIII, confiscated its property.[43] Although it was restored after his deposition, the number of students had in 1420 to be reduced from eight to three to match the meagre resources, and in 1436 it was incorporated in the Gregoriano.[44] The Bresciano, too, never grew to anything like the envisaged capacity, still housing only eight students in 1388, and only six in 1403–4.[45] It too came under pressure from Baldassare Cossa, later John XXIII,[46] and was incorporated in the Gregoriano, in 1437, at the third attempt to do so.[47] The Gregoriano itself was not undented by the vicissitudes of both the town and the university. As early as 1373 it was in crisis because of the absence of its rector; in 1391 it was reported that the college had been closed for three months; in 1411 there were only nine students to participate in the election of a rector.[48] The Gregoriano, too, suffered at the hands of Cossa,[49] and despite the additions of the Avignonese and the Bresciano it did not survive beyond 1452, when the combined revenues of the three colleges passed to the convent of S. Domenico.[50] Even the Reggiano continued only under duress, surviving an attempt at closure by Sixtus IV only by vigorous protestation by the students.[51]

The history of these colleges is not well known to us. One could speculate that they failed for a variety of reasons, not least their size, the difficulties experienced by the University of Bologna at the turn of the fourteenth and fifteenth centuries, and the fact that as attractions to students they never seemed really to catch on. But one college of the 1360s did survive, and indeed more than that; the Collegio di S. Clemente, or Collegio di Spagna, in some ways the most influential Italian foundation of the late middle ages. Its founder and moving spirit, Cardinal Gil Albornoz, was the champion of resurgent papal authority in the Papal States, and the acquisition of Bologna (1360) was the climax of his career. Once in control of Bologna, Albornoz was eager to work for the town and the university; he was influential in obtaining for the university the right to teach theology (1364), and he also, with first Innocent VI and then Urban V supporting him, wished to leave his own personal mark on the university in the form of a college.[52]

Several factors can be seen at work in the creation of the Spanish College. The oldest, hitherto neglected, was the tradition of Spanish interest in the university of Bologna; García García has found references to no fewer than 114 Spanish students at Bologna in the period 1300–30, suggesting that the attempt to found a college rested on very firm ground.[53] The interest and support of Pope Urban was also important, as was the impact of Albornoz's own academic experiences. The statutes of colleges at Paris, Perugia, Montpellier and Toulouse were all influential, and are referred to in his statutes;[54] particularly Toulouse, where Albornoz had studied and Urban had engaged in substantial reform of the Collège de Saint-Martial. But what came out of all this was something also highly original. The statutes of the Collegio di Spagna—we have only the revised version of 1375–77—are certainly the most comprehensive of any Italian college, and must surely be among the most comprehensive of any European college.[55] Sixty detailed statutes run into over a hundred pages in a modern edition. Every area is spelt out in detail; they give us a very clear picture of how the college should run.

The Spanish College was to have thirty students (the founder's twenty-four could be increased within a decade), eight in theology, eighteen in canon law, and four in medicine or arts.[56] All places were reserved for Spanish (i.e. Iberian) students, and non-Spaniards could only be admitted by default (even then, no Bolognese were to be admitted). No member of a religious order was to be admitted.[57] But places were also to be evenly distributed over the Iberian peninsula; not more than one student from one city or diocese, not more than two from one province. The right of presentation was vested in a long list of bishops and other ecclesiastics. Whenever a vacancy arose, letters were to be sent to all those eligible to present for it—even the sums that could be spent on this were laid down. Places were to be kept for ten months, to enable the successful applicant to make travel arrangements, and to ensure efficiency over the long distances involved there were to be overspill facilities outside the college.[58] The statutes laid down how prepared the students had to be; canonists had to have a grounding in grammar, theologians and students of medicine in grammar and logic; any student who was presented and accepted but who on arrival turned out to be ill-prepared could study outside the college for up to two years, after which he might take up his place if his progress had been satisfactory.[59] No student with an income of over fifty florins could be admitted, the exception being the rector, in whom wealth was considered to bring prestige to the college.[60] Scholars might stay for seven years, eight in special cases; if they brought honour to the college by obtaining a lectureship they might remain for a further three years.[61]

The internal organization of the college was sophisticated. The statutes elaborate in detail on the duties of chaplains, servants, cooks, the procurator,[62] and the main officials, the rector and four councillors. These were students, to be elected by all students of the college over the age of eighteen. The rector had to be at least twenty-five years of age, a cleric, and a Spaniard; the councillors—one a student of theology, two of canon law, one of medicine—had to be over twenty years old.[63] The rector was in overall charge of day-today administration and of discipline; he did however come under the Cardinal Protector (Fernando Albornoz, Archbishop of Seville), the final resort in unresolved cases of dispute, and this figure and another relative, Gomez de Albornoz, Vicar-General of Ascoli, were to undertake annual visitations of the college.[64] An ultimate limitation of the power of the rector and councillors was that no reform of the statutes of the college could be enacted by them; only the pope, on the recommendation of the Cardinal Protector, could do that.[65] But apart from that the students had wide powers and responsibility, including the day-to-day management of the estate, visitation of properties, and so on.[66]

The bulk of the statutes is devoted to matters of discipline. Students were obliged to attend mass daily (they had a choice of two services) and confess once a year;[67] they had to attend classes;[68] the use of the library was regulated, and books might not be taken out from it, even by the rector.[69] There were to be no guests (except, with the rector's permission, relatives), no boarding overnight of strangers,[70] and no sleeping out of the college.[71] It was forbidden, on pain of expulsion, to have women in the college (though an exception was made for old ones who might, with permission, come in to look after the sick).[72] Gaming, dancing, and the playing of instruments were forbidden;[73] the kitchen and cellar were out of bounds,[74] students were not to insult their fellows,[75] bear arms,[76] strike a student,[77] or murmur against the rector.[78] The penalty for most of these offences was temporary exclusion.

Berthe Marti, who edited the statutes, called them 'an ingenious compromise between the excessively democratic organization of the University of Bologna at the time and the Cardinal Founder's ideal of discipline, law and order'.[79] It is the latter quality that strikes us most, though the statutes are significant in both respects, for they served as a basic model for the colleges founded in Italy thereafter. None of these colleges had statutes as detailed, and many departed from this model in a variety of ways, but most drafters of statutes consulted them, and in matters of discipline they were widely adopted. Here the Spanish College had by now the advantage of Bologna's place as *doyen* of Italian universities, to be consulted even where there were earlier precedents (for example, the Perugian influence on the Spanish College statutes).[80] But it is not just for its statutes that the Spanish College is significant. For the rest of the period it remained the oldest large surviving foundation in Bologna.

It was undoubtedly the best-endowed.[81] Its resources—cash—were invested, methodically, in property by Fernando Albornoz in the 1370s and managed with great care thereafter,[82] and the college thus began with an incomparable advantage over those foundations which took on the ramshackle estates of some defunct monastery or *ad hoc* purchases of land. It was the first college in Italy to have purpose-built accommodation, and the buildings, which survive today, are Italy's main example of collegiate architecture.[83]

In one sense, though, the contribution of the Spanish College to Italian university history was limited. Its alumni were Spanish. A long tradition of influence on the Spanish intellectual, political, and cultural world began with its foundation,[84] but it played no corresponding role in Bologna, where its virtual independence from the university was only occasionally placed in jeopardy by the fact that theology was taught in the college.[85] Nor indeed did it play such a role in the rest of the Italian university system. Perhaps its independence in this sense contributed to its success, and it was certainly thought of as an ideal establishment, to be copied in whatever ways were possible; but in the competitive world of the establishment of colleges—which is what it soon became—the Spanish College is *sui generis* and plays little direct part.

3. The Spread of the Collegiate Movement in the Late Fourteenth Century

The 1360s saw the first attempts at college foundation known to us from Italian universities outside Bologna, and two of these were successful. Both were influential, and in both cases the personal interconnections speak for themselves. The first is the Collegio Gregoriano, or Collegio di S. Gregoria Magno, also known later as the Sapienza Vecchia, at Perugia. Founded by Cardinal Niccolò Capocci, Bishop of Frascati, in 1360, this college has recently been the subject of intensive archival research.[86] The foundation was part of a three-fold benefaction, as was to become popular; a grammar school and a *misericordia* or hospital were also founded.[87] In the college forty places were envisaged (by 1368 this had already been increased to fifty), to be drawn from all over Europe, again with a detailed list of bishops entitled to present candidates. Capocci's role as educator is important; in many respects he deserves to be considered alongside Albornoz, who was made a cardinal on the same day as Capocci and who died the year before him (1368). He wrote simple but clear statutes for the college (which, as has been seen, were consulted in the drafting of the Statutes of the Collegio di Spagna, and others later on), and his expertise was valued by Urban V who involved him in the setting up of the Urbaniano.[88] The Sapienza Vecchia appears to have had a prosperous history (despite insolvency in 1403). The Perugians, who had given their vigorous support to the whole enterprise from the outset,[89] were so satisfied with it that early in the fifteenth century they encouraged the establishment of a second college.

The other successful foundation of the 1360s, that of the Collegio Tornacense in Padua, is more hidden to view, as is the history of the Paduan colleges generally. Modern historians of Padua have largely ignored the colleges, and the older histories are substantially discordant. In 1363 a Bolognese doctor of law, Pietro Boatieri, obtained permission and tax exemptions from Francesco I da Carrara to use the possessions of Albizo Brancasecchi of Lucca, canon of S. Marie de Tournai, for the foundation of a college for six students of canon law, two each from the dioceses of Ferrara, Treviso and Padua (two further students from the diocese of Tournai were later added). Property was purchased in the Via Pozzo del Campione (from which the college derived its alternative name, Collegio Campioni), and the institution opened its doors in 1366. Statutes were drawn up in that year by the Bishop of Padua, Pileo da Prata, and the Abbot of S. Cipriano di Murano, who had joint oversight of the college. Over the following decades the wealth of the college was significantly increased, and its continuity is attested by a series of published and unpublished documents.[90]

The Tornacense may have figured as part of a larger plan by Francesco I. At about the time of the Tornacense proposal (1363/4) he is reported as having founded a college for twelve students of law—by which may have been meant civil law[91]—while in 1369 the will of a doctor of medicine, Bartolomeo Campo, left funds 'ad sustentationem collegii artistarum et medicorum si contingat illud fieri per magnificum d. Franciscum de Carraria'.[92] If there was such a tripartite plan it never matured; the law college is mentioned once (1371) as having four students, while Campo's bequest appears to have remained a dead letter. It was not a good time for new initiatives. With the outbreak of the Schism the rush of collegiate foundations in Italy, and with it the first, experimental phase of the phenomenon, came to a temporary halt. There were no more foundations until the 1390s. But then there was a flood, all in Padua, one of the few Italian universities to survive the vicissitudes of the period relatively unscathed. The Paduan initiatives of previous decades were now built on; nine fresh foundations were attempted in fourteen years. All but one were modest efforts, chiefly by teachers of the university. For example, in 1394 the heirs of Jacopo di Arquà, a doctor of medicine, opened a college with his estate; in 1398 Niccolò da Rio's will provided the resources which eventually led to the foundation of a college for six or more students in arts and medicine. Others were more modest still, endowing studies rather than aspiring to institutional status. Pietro Garfrano, a Cypriot merchant resident in Venice, left an endowment in 1393 for four Cypriot students, one in theology, one in law, two in medicine/arts, though in the event funds only ran to supporting two; Andrea da Recanati in 1397 left money for four students from Osimo who seem to have acquired a residence if not actually formed themselves into a college.[93]

These and several others—and the Paduan tradition continues right into the mid-fifteenth century—remind us that to look at the whole question of provision for poor scholars takes us into an even less documented area of grants, scholarships, and bequests; and the mass of foundations and bequests at the turn of the century, as well as testifying to the vigour of the Paduan *studio*, may be taken as evidence of the harsh climate which made such provision necessary. The only Paduan foundation of the period to achieve pre-eminence, apart from the Tornacense, was the Collegio Pratense, founded in 1394 by Cardinal Pileo da Prata, designed for twenty students, and endowed with a yearly income of 5,000 ducats, a sum which ensured it prosperity for several decades. Michele Savonarola, who in the 1420s was appointed rector for life of the college, described it in 1446 as a 'Sapienza' (a term increasingly common since first Perugia and then, formally, Siena had adopted it for colleges); the building he described had forty-two student rooms.[94] Again, the importance of international connections is significant. The Tornacense and the Pratense were the only major Paduan foundations; Pileo, who as bishop of Padua had drafted the statutes for the Tornacense in 1366, and had been instrumental in the establishment of theology and the constitutional struggles of the arts faculty at Padua in the 1360s,[95] was a figure of international significance, whose career took him throughout Northern Europe, and particularly to England, where as papal envoy he was involved in the awarding of privileges to the University of Cambridge.[96] Similarly the large number of college foundations at Padua—the largest perhaps after Paris and the English universities—reflects Padua's increasingly international status as a university, a respect in which it arguably outstripped Bologna by the fifteenth century.

4. The Collegiate Movement in the Fifteenth Century

At the same time that various Paduan academics and others were making by no means always successful attempts at charitable endowment, a college of an entirely different kind was in gestation. In 1388, a year after yet another 're-launch' of their precarious, indeed hitherto unsuccessful university, the Consiglio Generale of Siena deliberated

> quod in civitate senarum ordinetur et sit domus sapientie in qua morari possint pauperes . . . sine aliqua expensa tam fienda pro comune.[97]

Twenty-seven years were to elapse before their deliberation could take full effect. The two major enabling factors were, first, an offer by the Bishop of Siena, Francesco Mormille, in 1392 of the buildings and assets of a declining hospital, the Casa della Misericordia, in Siena, and secondly the confirmation of that gift in 1408 by Pope Gregory XII, along with a series of bulls arranging the transfer. Even then, the interruptions and difficulties experienced by almost all Italian universities in those years ensured that the Casa della Misericordia was not cleared, and the doors of the new Casa della Sapienza not opened, until 1415, when the first scholars took up their places.[98]

I have written elsewhere about the University of Siena and its college.[99] The main features of this pioneering experiment will be rehearsed again here because it was so very different from anything seen hitherto in Italy or, to my knowledge, elsewhere. What was revolutionary about the Sienese Sapienza derives (as does what was revolutionary about the university as a whole) from the extreme degree of communal control exercised. The college was from the outset, and for the whole duration of its existence, run entirely by the town authorities. The Bishop of Siena, in making his original offer of the Casa della Misericordia, laid down no conditions, and there was at no stage any question of his being given any say in the running of the college. In its early days the rector was a communal appointee not connected with the university; eventually, after much dissatisfaction with the appointees and possibly some protests from the students, Siena went over to the by now traditional, Spanish College-style, system of a student rector elected by the student members of the college. But that was only achieved by the alteration of his status; his powers were whittled down, a *camarlengo*—who was a town official—being put in to run the administration of the estate and the domestic side, while more and more decisions fell to the *savi dello studio e della Sapienza*, as they were now called, and to higher communal bodies. Even the election of the student rector was tightly controlled by the commune, which took the opportunities of disagreements amongst the scholars to impose their own preferred candidate. Likewise the drafting of statutes, all legislation to do with Sapienza, and all exemptions granted to that legislation, were in the hands of town committees.[100]

A corollary of this control was a blatantly utilitarian approach. This is nowhere more evident than in the matter of the admissions policy, which in the hands of communal officials soon resulted in a complete reversal of the originally stated intention. The 1388 resolution talked of poor scholars, as did the 1392 proposal of the bishop; the Sapienza was to be open only to students from the town or *contado* of Siena. But within six months of its opening in 1415 it was decided to admit only *forenses* in order to attract more of them to the *studium*,[101] and in 1422 it was established that only one student per town (and its *contado*) could be admitted.[102] The rapidity of this volte-face is striking, and raises the possibility that the original plan was formulated in the way that it was in order to obtain ecclesiastical approval. Even more dramatic was the change in social composition which took place once foreigners were admitted. By 1434 the Sapienza was charging an admission fee of forty florins, raised to fifty florins in 1437.[103] The justification for this was given in a document of 1445; 'e perciò che molti sono ricchi e non poveri'.[104] Far from being a deterrent, the admission fee was accompanied by ever-growing pressure on places. The deal offered was now out of the question for truly poor students, but for those who could afford the fee it was none the less attractive; seven years' board and lodging for fifty florins to be paid in advance (later frequently payable in instalments).[105] With this change students too well-off to qualify as 'poor' were presented with the opportunity of a place in a residential college; it was immensely popular. And, as Catoni has shown, the commune used this attraction to the full, reserving control over admissions to the *Concistoro* or priorate itself, and thus placing itself at the helm of a powerful weapon of patronage.[106] It is no exaggeration to say that from the foundation of its Sapienza this much-travailed university never looked back, and never closed its doors again. The success of the college was the success of the *studium* as a whole; it became the 'membro principale dello Studio',[107] and eventually its main venue for lectures, while by 1481 pressure on places had reached the point where the commune began to lay plans for a second college.[108]

It would be too much to say that Siena became an important model for Italian colleges. But its influence on the collegiate system in Italy does seem to me very significant. The immediate and immense popularity of what might be described as a secular college in 'neighbouring' Siena seems certainly to have given an incentive to the Florentines, who in 1429 resolved to accept Niccolò da Uzzano's proposed bequest for a Sapienza; and although nothing came of this plan, when the Florentines did eventually build a Sapienza, in Pisa, at the end of the century, some Sienese characteristics do appear to have been copied (for example the provision of lecture rooms).[109] The effects of Siena's innovation were not confined, though, to 'secular' foundations. The charging of entrance fees was a highly significant development. Although the Sienese Sapienza was not the first to do this—Perugia's oldest college introduced it in 1417 for law students[110]—it was the first to make it a universal requirement, and the eminence of the Sienese university in the mid-fifteenth century, and the international character of the Sapienza's membership, made this development particularly visible. By the end of the fifteenth century the Collegio Pratense at Padua was charging a fee, and both it and the Sienese Sapienza had reached more sophistication in what was available. At the Pratense admission was fifty ducats 'una tantum' for forty years, or eighteen ducats per annum,[111] and here, as in Siena, complaints about commerce in rooms were rife;[112] in Siena, as well as a variety of *pro rata* arrangements, by the late fifteenth century the possibility had appeared of entry for *mezzo tempo*, in recognition of the fact that the type of scholar eligible for this kind of college was more likely to be one who wished to sample the attractions of several universities rather than to study in the same place. And this is typical of the problems of the Sapienza. A secular foundation, run by the commune for paying students, it frequently found the interests of those students, as well as the interests of the institution, to be at odds with the religious, corporate, and collegiate ideals of the Spanish College and other models which its own statutes had imitated. Disputes about internal government and the appointment of rectors, indiscipline amongst the students, jealousies over rooms and resentments over the—to seculars—excessively demanding regulations were endemic and the constant concern of the documents. The utilitarian approach had its advantages but also some drawbacks. There was, for example, little concern over whether the students were actually studying,[113] and Siena's Sapienza was, typically, the only substantial foundation not to possess a library.[114] That it did not have one from its foundation stems of course from the fact that it was not founded by an ecclesiastic or academic benefactor; but it is remarkable that, with the commune devoting so much care and effort to the prosperity of the institution, nobody thought to attempt to put one together.

The Sienese Sapienza had a wider influence in more general terms. By opening up the collegiate system, publicly and spectacularly, to students who were not poor, it helped to give a new lease of life to the movement. More and more joined in the attempt. The fifteenth-century foundations came in clusters, a phenomenon which can be explained partly by interconnections and rivalries and partly by the changing fortunes of the university system in the wake of changing political circumstances. The Florentine initiative of 1429 is contemporaneous with the foundation in Pavia of the Collegio Castiglioni by Cardinal Branda Castiglioni, who two years previously had in fact obtained papal permission to found a college in Rome; a few years later Eugenius IV announced plans for a Roman foundation (1433); meanwhile the Perugians were establishing a second Sapienza.[115] In the 1450s, with the final advent of peace (Peace of Lodi, 1454, and the formation of the Italic League, 1455), again a number of important initiatives can be recorded; the Torrisani in Padua (1454), the Capranica in Rome (1456 onwards), the Grassi in Turin, the Sacco in Pavia. And again the 1480s saw feverish activity to establish new colleges by the Florentines, the Sienese, the Pavians, the Perugians and popes and cardinals in Rome.

By this stage the possession of a college or colleges was the norm rather than the exception for an Italian university. Niccolò da Uzzano's proposal for Florence of 1429 talked of a Sapienza as a 'singolare ornamento mancante', and proposed it 'a similitudine di quelle che sono in tucte l'altre città che hanno studio'.[116] This is of course an exaggeration, but not a great one; only Ferrara, Parma, Naples and Catania did not, to my knowledge, have any colleges at the time, or indeed before 1500, though when the University of Catania was founded in 1444 it was ensured that the Papal Bull of foundation allowed the establishment of 'domos pro uno vel pluribus collegio seu collegiis'.[117] Interesting light on the attitudes to collegiate foundations is cast in an unpublished letter of 1 October 1484 to the commune of Siena from Giovanni Battista Caccialupi da S.Severino, a distinguished lawyer, long-serving teacher and official in Siena and writer on education. Caccialupi writes from Rome, where he has run into his old friend, Angelo Gherardini da Amelia, now Bishop of Suessa. Gherardini confides in him, 'perche fummo compagni in studio ad Perugia', that he has decided to found a new Sapienza there, 'nella quale voleva spendere parecchi migliaia de' ducati'. The pope is happy with the plans, and a prime site, 'in capo della piazza dove già fu la ciptadella', has been obtained. Caccialupi expresses his regret. He wishes he had known about this plan, because he would have persuaded Gherardini to found it in Siena instead, where there is enthusiasm for a new Sapienza, and where a site has also been found. What a pity, exclaims the bishop. If he hadn't already started with Perugia he would gladly have done it in Siena. If the Perugian plan came unstuck he would let Caccialupi know.[118]

As often happens, this document came to light during research on a different topic. Attempts to found colleges may have been wider than we think; in several cases the failures are only known to us accidentally, for they never reached the point of impinging on university or civic records. The same must be true of the largely unexplored practice of endowing places or scholarships. The oldest known example of this is the will of Michele de' Cesis, a Pistoiese doctor of medicine who in 1383 founded two scholarships to enable one student from Pistoia and one from Modena to attend the Universities of Bologna or Padua.[119] Pistoiese administrative records show this endowment to have survived and been used in the fifteenth century. The Bolognese foundation for Brescians, the Paduan one for students from Osimo, or Alberti's unsuccessful attempt to acquire a house in Bologna to provide places for members of his family,[120] suggest that the practice of assisting students from a specific locality or family was not uncommon. Other examples are known from Pistoia, Lucca, and from Sicily.[121] It is better documented by the sixteenth century, when for example Giulio Turini, of the small Tuscan town of Pescia, funded several scholarships for Pescians at the University of Pisa,[122] and when in 1512 Bartolommeo Bolis, a Paduan cleric, funded six places at the Sapienza in Siena, thus reopening it, at least theoretically, to poor students.[123] This appears to be the first instance in which additional places in an existing college were founded by a new benefactor, something perhaps optimistically envisaged by the founder of the Bresciano at Bologna almost two centuries previously. It reminds us, though, that the foundation of colleges and the provision of scholarships are basically two sides of the same coin, the financing of higher education; our understanding of the collegiate system will be incomplete until more is known about the other aspects of charitable provision.[124]

5. The Late Medieval Italian Colleges Compared

How far is it possible to categorize and to group this plethora of foundations? To what extent can they be described collectively? The remainder of this article will attempt to establish common features and to highlight some disparities. Much more could be said; the comparative study of statutes alone merits another article. What follows is a necessarily provisional sketch.

The colleges vary considerably in the profession or status of their founders. Categorization, both of colleges and of their founders, of course has an element of arbitrariness about it. However, if we include those colleges (e.g. the Reggiano at Bologna) which may have originated as non-residential endowments, of the thirty-seven whose foundation can be considered to have taken place successfully (however short-lived they may have been), twelve were founded by ecclesiastics not involved in university teaching; two by popes, six by cardinals, two by bishops, one by an apostolic protonotary, and one by a canon.[125] Nineteen originated through academics, usually in their own university; eleven were founded by doctors of medicine, seven by lawyers, and one by the widow of a lawyer with his estate. Five were founded by lay persons or authorities; two by civic authorities, and three by individuals. (One college, Padua's Casa di Dio, is of unknown origin.) It should be said immediately that this last group is the least significant. The Sienese Sapienza is unique as a successful secular foundation; the Florentine Sapienza had the misfortune to open on the eve of the Italian wars, while the Fieschi (founded by a Count), the short-lived initiative of Francesco I Carrara, and the Cypriot endowment established at Padua by a merchant made a negligible impact.

As Bruno Pagnin has pointed out, the two main categories of founder, ecclesiastical and academic, really give rise to two different types of college.[126] The most striking difference is of scale; inevitably the foundations of academics were much more modest in their aspirations, and not surprisingly much less sure of success. It would be fair to guess, though, that they also represented a natural, and possibly more 'grass-roots', response to perceived and immediate needs. In this respect it is interesting that there were more foundations for students of medicine/arts than of law; this is in contrast to the proportion of teachers and students in the Italian universities, where law predominated over medicine/arts almost everywhere. It may perhaps be explained by the greater need for subvention among these students than among those of law, or at least by a greater desire to provide for them than for those who were destined for a more lucrative profession.[127] At Padua and to a lesser extent Pavia, where the majority of these colleges are to be found, their number may have compensated for their small dimensions to add a significant route to university study; but their chronic precariousness ultimately seems to have ensured that few of them survived into the modern period.

Apart from the Sienese Casa della Sapienza, all the largest and most important colleges in the fifteenth century—the Spanish College at Bologna, the Pratense at Padua, the Castiglioni at Pavia, the Capranica at Rome, the two Sapienze of Perugia—were founded by ecclesiastics, and all but one of these by cardinals. An examination of these founders reveals two features. All of them had experience of more than one university, either through attendance or, in later life, through administrative responsibility of some sort. Moreover, many of them had contacts, possibly influence, with each other. It has already been noted how many of the fourteenth-century founders of colleges had wide experience on which they could draw. Cardinal Pileo da Prata is perhaps the best example; his experience of universities extended as far as Cambridge, and he was involved with several Italian colleges, drafting the statutes for the Paduan Tornacense in 1366, intervening to reform the Gregoriano at Perugia in 1392,[128] as well as attempting a foundation at Bologna (1383) before his success with the Pratense at Padua in 1394.[129] In the fifteenth century such range is not uncommon. Cardinal Branda Castiglioni, founder of the Collegio Castiglioni at Pavia, had studied and taught at Pavia and in 1389 had been involved in negotiations with Pope Boniface IX for a bull to legitimize its *studium generale*; but he had also attempted a college foundation in Rome two years before the successful foundation at Pavia, had been involved in papal educational policy in Hungary, and was in contact, particularly through his participation at Councils, with Aeneas Silvius and other figures of influence in educational matters (such as Cardinals Albergati, the reformer of the Bolognese colleges, and Cesarini, later reformer of the Castiglioni).[130] Cardinal Domenico Capranica had studied at Padua and Bologna, and had experience of Siena, Florence and Perugia, where he was involved in the administration of the Sapienza Vecchia, before founding a college in Rome.[131] Angelo Gherardini, who unsuccessfully attempted to found a third Perugian college in 1484, also knew several Italian universities; he had studied at Bologna and Florence, taught in Siena, and visited Pavia before settling in Perugia where he was in turn rector of both Sapienze. He had also been in the service of Cardinal Capranica.[132] It is perhaps worth noting that his interlocutor and former fellow-student in the anecdote quoted above, Giovanni Battista Caccialupi, had had a long and distinguished career as teacher of law in Siena, during which he had written an influential treatise on legal education.[133] Other cardinals actively concerned in college foundation included Francesco Todeschini-Piccolomini, later briefly Pope Pius III, who was involved, alongside Caccialupi, in the Sienese attempt to establish a second Sapienza in the 1480s, who was named as one of the two executors of Cardinal Stefano Nardini in the will which established the Collegio Nardini in Rome.[134]

Education was clearly an important area of involvement among senior churchmen. Paolo Cortesi's instructions in his treatise on cardinals (1510) that founding a college was a worthy object of a cardinal's beneficence seem already to be being observed.[135] One can of course only speculate as to the nature and importance of the connections between these figures. It may be significant, for example, that Cardinal d'Estouteville, the reformer of the university of Paris (1452), lived in Rome from his appointment in 1439 until his death in 1483, and was certainly aware of what was happening at the *studium urbis*;[136] but no specific evidence of connection with Italian reformers can be established. A final case, the career of Cardinal Niccolò Forteguerri, is offered as an excellent illustration of the ecclesiastical interconnections of the Italian academic world. A distant relative of Aeneas Silvius (to whom, once he became Pope Pius II, Forteguerri owed advancement), he went from Pistoia to study at Bologna with one of the scholarships endowed by Michele de' Cesis in the fourteenth century. He soon followed his mentor, the Pistoiese law teacher Filippo Lazzari, from Bologna to Siena, where he took his degree and taught. In 1472 he is found as one of the executors of Leon Battista Alberti, with the task of setting up a small college at Bologna for members of the Alberti family. Forteguerri's own contribution was a highly original one; twelve scholarships for Pistoiese students at Bologna, and, to prepare them for university, a Sapienza at Pistoia itself, which, while not a university or even university-level institution, was closely modelled on contemporary university colleges.[137]

The two types of college foundation may have differed clearly in scale and prospects, but apart from this they had a great deal in common, which justifies taking them together. Inasmuch as one can deduce anything from standard formulaic explanations in wills, the motives of these founders are highly conventional and similar (I am of course excepting the civic foundations). They are in the first instance altruistic; they endow facilities for poor scholars who otherwise would not have access to higher education, in a community whose life-style and regulations would give them the maximum opportunity for the pursuit of their studies. In return, the founder would be commemorated by a mass or prayers on the anniversary of his death, and more generally by being remembered as the founder of a college which would probably bear his name. There is little point in speculating about the extent to which the foundation would improve his reputation within his lifetime (in cases where the endowment took immediate effect), although the information that three years after the foundation of the Collegio Grassi in Turin (1457) its founder, the jurist Giovanni Grassi, was the only teacher in the university to have his lecture room rebuilt might point us in that direction.[138] But one other bonus, of significance to lay and ecclesiastic founder alike, was the right known in Northern Europe as the right of Founder's Kin, the right for relatives of the founder to places in the college.[139] An early instance in Italy, quite possibly modelled on English examples, is the will of Pancio da Controne (1338) which intended a college in Bologna exclusively for his relatives;[140] the proposed Bolognese foundation of Leon Battista Alberti (1472) is another instance, though he did stipulate that any surplus places could be filled by non-relatives.[141] The custom of privileging Founder's Kin in the treatment they were to be given in the college (as opposed to preference in the obtention of places) does not appear to have been copied.

Provision for founder's kin is frequently stipulated, and it is the main exception to the general rule that college places were available only to students from outside the town.[142] Niccolò da Uzzano, for example, stipulated that no Florentine citizen or descendant of a Florentine citizen might enter his proposed college, except members of his family, who had first to prove that they were *bona fide* students.[143] The provisions for founder's kin were not necessarily sufficient to forestall opposition to a foundation from the benefactor's family—at Pavia, Raimondo Marliani's heir contested his will, 'retinens contra omne jus ne dictum Collegium fieret'[144]—but it might go some way towards placating them, and, in the case of the small-scale provisions made by academic founders, more than that. Indeed, the right of members of the founder's family, or of other designated families, to present candidates for admission could get out of hand; the 'protectors' of the Pratense at Padua had to attempt to impose a check on the practice in the fifteenth century.[145]

Founders usually had firm notions of the regions from which they wanted their students to come. Many of the small colleges were founded for a largely local clientele; this is particularly true of the Paduan colleges, whose founders were mainly from the north-eastern region of Italy anyway. Some, however, paid respect to the traditions of the earlier period in catering for ultramontanes, the Ancarano (Bologna) and the Marliani (Pavia) being examples.[146] Catone Sacco in fact founded his college expressly for ultramontanes.[147] At the grander end of the spectrum, Cardinal Albornoz, as has been seen, made very detailed provisions for the presentation of candidates for the Collegio di Spagna from all over the Iberian peninsula, and Cardinal Capocci, founder of the Sapienza Vecchia in Perugia, extended this across Europe. The question naturally arose whether all those entitled to present would remember to do so. The Brescians had to be reminded, in the early fifteenth century, that there was a college in Bologna for them,[148] while in the early fifteenth century the Avignonese, originally intended for students from Avignon, admitted students from elsewhere, including a Milanese student.[149] Most provisions therefore had fall-back arrangements. The Marliani statutes even mentioned the possibility of negligence of the ultramontanes at presenting candidates; this late measure (1487?) may well have been drawing on the experience of other colleges.[150] The admission of native students—for example Bolognese citizens as fall-backs at the Bresciano (1403)[151]—was therefore not unknown.[152] Colleges with less elaborate regulations had it easier. The administrators of admissions to the Sienese Sapienza could and did vary their choices of student according to expedient, although they soon discovered that it was in their interests, and in the interests of the students in the college, to keep a rough balance between regional and national groups.[153]

Founders also usually stipulated the subjects that the students should be studying. Again, there is a great variety; smaller colleges were more often single-subject institutions for the study of the discipline of their founder—law at the Ancarano,[154] canon law at the Tornacense,[155] arts/medicine at the Ridium.[156] (The only college intended exclusively for students of theology was the Torrisani.)[157] The larger colleges tended to welcome the whole spread of subjects but carefully stipulated proportions. The Bresciano, aiming at fifty students but anticipating a minimum of eight, had to have at least two canonists, two students of medicine, and four artists;[158] the Spanish College, as has been seen, within a decade of its foundation provided for eight theologians, eighteen canonists, and four students of medicine. If this last figure seems low, the statutes, in providing for a reserve position, show that if anything it was feared that it would be too high, since few wanted to come from Spain to Bologna to study medicine.[159] There is a revealing discrepancy in the attitudes of the colleges to the two branches of law. The traditional wariness of mixing theology and civil law—the main reason why civil law was not officially taught at Paris, and why theology was so late in coming to the Italian universities—was very much present in the fourteenth century. Of the forty students envisaged by Niccolò Capocci in his provisions for the Sapienza Vecchia at Perugia, six were to be theologians, four to six civilians, and the rest canonists; the low number of civilians was justified by the now often quoted statement 'quod advocationis officium maxime in partibus Italie dapnationis est anime'.[160] And the Spanish College took that further, and followed the example of the Bresciano in not having civilians at all. What is not so often quoted, though, is the fact that as early as 1369 the revised Perugian Sapienza Vecchia statutes, providing now for fifty students, fixed the proportion at thirty students in canon law or theology and twenty civilians.[161] And this was followed by the Gregoriano, in which thirty places were to be evenly divided between canonists and civilians.[162] Later colleges have less compunction. The Sienese, in deciding in 1422 that twenty-five out of the thirty students in their Sapienza were to be lawyers, made no distinctions, declaring simply

> la [*sic*] facultà di ragione canonica e di ragione civile sono quelle, che fanno venire in grande degnità e stato quelli che seguitano, e più honore riportano a le città che niuna facultà che l'uomo studi.[163]

The length of stay permitted in the colleges varied, though not greatly (until the Sienese began to offer places for *mezzo tempo*). Around six or seven years was the norm—five years for students of medicine and of canon law in the Bresciano,[164] and for non-theological students in the Marliani.[165] The shortest period was four years (for arts/medicine in the Zanetini),[166] exceptionally, the 'scholares Auximani' were entitled to ten years.[167] In the Pratense the period of residence was reduced in the 1460s from seven to six years because funds were scarce and only eight out of twenty places could be filled.[168] One condition about which the statutes are unanimous is that students might not outstay their term. Only in special cases was the term extended—to ten years in the Capranica,[169] and in the Collegio di Spagna, as has been seen, by a year at a time, up to a maximum of ten, for those who held office or brought distinction to the college by winning a lectureship. Minimum and maximum ages, too, are usually stipulated, and it will not surprise historians of universities to discover considerable range here; in the Gregoriano at Bologna students had to be over twenty before entering and under thirty before leaving,[170] while in the Capranica the extremes were fixed at fifteen and thirty-five.[171] This leads one to the conclusion that the level of preparedness required before admission—something very difficult to assess even where the statutes make mention of it—must in practice have varied considerably. Students had to leave before their time was up if they graduated (though at Siena one of the conditions of entry into the college was that they undertook to take a degree at the end of their period of residence),[172] and they also had to leave prematurely—in those colleges where poverty was still a prerequisite—if they acquired an income exceeding a stated figure (20 *lire bolognesi* in the Bresciano,[173] 50 florins in the Collegio di Spagna, in the fourteenth century;[174] 25 florins in the Capranica in the mid-fifteenth).[175] But of course it was also by no means unknown for students to leave earlier for other reasons—in the fee-paying Sienese Sapienza because they had had enough of that university and wanted to move on, or in any of the colleges because they had contravened the code of discipline.

Another area in which there is a variety within an overall pattern is the constitutional framework of the colleges. All of them were put under the overall control of an outside personage or body, which acted as a visitor and court of appeal and had to be consulted on matters of reform or serious disciplinary cases. In a few colleges this involved the university. At Bologna the Ancarano was placed under the jurisdiction of the (student-)university of lawyers, with the bishop and the *anziani* of Bologna as 'fall-backs'.[176] The Pratense came under the prior of the College of Lawyers (though the bishops of Padua were closely involved too),[177] and the Spinelli under the prior of the artists and the doyen of the Spinelli family,[178] while the Ridium was placed under the joint control of senior members of the College of Artists, the founder's family, and Paduan guilds.[179] In Siena the Sapienza came under the direct control of the *savi dello studio*, now known as *savi dello studio e della Sapienza*, and behind them of the town's main governing committees.[180] Almost all the other colleges were under ecclesiastical supervision, whether founded by ecclesiastics or not.

Under that tier came the chief executive official of the college, the rector. Most colleges adopted the model of the Collegio di Spagna here, of a student rector, elected by the students, and assisted by four *consiliarii*, also elected. (An early but short-lived exception was the Urbaniano.)[181] In the Spanish College the rector had to be a cleric over the age of twenty-five, and held office for two years,[182] in most fifteenth-century colleges this was reduced to one year, with perhaps the provision—as in the Capranica—that he could serve for a second year if elected unanimously.[183] The Marliani statutes declared that he had to be a citramontane in order that he should be more versed in the demands of the job; no other statutes made such a stipulation.[184] The student-rectorship, an echo of the student-rectorship of the university, was an important feature, and attempts to have it otherwise, or to deny the students the right to elect their rector, were fiercely contested. The provisions at the Ancarano, where from the outset the student-rector and *consiliarii* of the university of lawyers could nominate the rector of the college if the students were unable to reach a decision, led to a long and unhappy history of conflict over this post.[185] On the other hand, at the Sapienza Vecchia of Perugia, mismanagement by the rector resulted first in communal restriction of his powers and then, after episodes of student violence, in the removal of the students' right to elect him.[186] Moreover, the founders and supervising authorities were wary about giving control of finances and estates to students; so the rector and *consiliarii* were usually assisted by a procurator (Spanish College),[187] *negotiorum gestor* (Castiglioni)[188] or *camarlengo* (Siena),[189] often an official from outside the college, allegedly in order that they need not get too distracted from their studies.[190] This system of two key officials became widespread. The Sienese Sapienza, again unusual by virtue of the circumstances of its foundation, opened with a single official, a rector, appointed by the commune; within two decades Sienese citizens were being appointed. By the second half of the fifteenth century the students had gained the right to appoint one of their numbers as rector, but increasingly power was vested in a new official, the *carmarlengo*, and later in a *governatore*, who answered directly to the communal authorities.[191]

It is difficult to generalize about the tenor of life and the problems faced by these colleges in the fifteenth century. None the less it is clear that, despite the very different types of foundation, the notion of what a college ought to consist of and how it ought to be run was widely agreed. In matters of discipline the Spanish College statutes continued to be taken as the norm. Though they were often simplified, the spirit of them was ever-present. However much college statutes differed, they mostly addressed the same set of issues, in varying degrees of detail. The government of the college, the powers and duties of the rector, discipline at table and in rooms, basic rules of conduct, regulations about access to the library, all feature with great consistency. Many of the statutes lay down the quantity and quality of food and drink to be distributed. The extent of provision might vary considerably; many of the small foundations give each student a pension in addition to board and lodging,[192] while as has been seen some of the larger (and more successful) colleges were charging substantial entrance fees.

These statutes merit fuller investigation. As sources for collegiate life, however, they suffer from the limitations of all initial legislation in that they reflect the intentions of the founders much better than they can illustrate the history of the colleges in practice. Many subsequent reforms are clearly responses to crises or inadequacies in the original legislation. It is these sources which tell us, for example, of the conflicts over the role of the rector at the Ancarano,[193] the abuses of allocation of places of the Pratense,[194] and the chronic shortage of funds which led many colleges to reduce their intake at various stages. The richest picture, however, must come from other administrative and anecdotal documents. So far, only the Sapienza of Siena has provided the historian with a full, day-to-day account of all aspects of college life.[195] The wealth of Sienese sources is directly related to the degree of communal control over the Sapienza, and is unlikely to be repeated elsewhere, though substantial records have also been found for Perugia. It can only be hoped that further evidence is uncovered, particularly for the two universities where smaller colleges proliferated, Padua and Pavia.

6. Conclusions

The fourteenth century saw the introduction in Italy of an institution that had become popular in Northern Europe, and particularly in Paris and, in different forms, in Oxford. The influence came particularly from Paris, and affected Bologna above all, spreading from there. By the late fourteenth century the movement was temporarily faltering (as indeed was the Italian university system as a whole), except in Padua where a host of small foundations was attempted at the end of the century. In the fifteenth century the movement spread across the system, becoming competitive and integral to university development in some places.

Conclusions are hardly possible in a broad and necessarily incomplete survey of this kind. But some trends and features are worth noting, even if one cannot generalize from one or two examples across the entire system. I would suggest that the Italian colleges contributed to the university scene particularly in the following respects:

1. The colleges' role in stimulating the development of the university system as a whole. The energies that went into nurturing an Italian *studio* through the vicissitudes of competition and the instability of the period received a considerable boost by the fashion for colleges, and much effort was spent on acquiring them. The stability of the Sienese *studio* in the fifteenth century owed much to the Sapienza; to an extent the same could be said of Perugia. The rhetoric of administrators of existing colleges supports this claim, as might be expected. More telling, perhaps, is the phrase used by Leon Battista Alberti in correspondence about his proposed bequest; he wished to found one of those 'chollegi e sapienzie che sono il mantenimento degli Studii'.[196]

It may at first seem surprising that I see the colleges as playing a positive role in the university. The proportion of university students in a college was always small,[197] and colleges have traditionally been seen as weakening or fragmenting university power.[198] In fact the areas in which conflicts might be expected tended to be kept in abeyance. The notion that the colleges threatened the universities by reason of their independence was kept in check, because the Spanish College students were members of the student-universities, and other colleges followed that example.[199] It is true that in Perugia the students of the Sapienza Vecchia were at the end of the fourteenth century given exemption from the jurisdiction of the rector of the university—a weak figure there in any case[200]—but other colleges took long in following suit; in Siena it was only in the mid-sixteenth century that the *sapientini* pressed for and obtained some sort of independent status.[201] This worked partly because in the Collegio di Spagna, as later for example in the Castiglioni, college students were debarred from the rectorate or vicerectorate of the university.[202] Other potential causes of conflict were soon defused; Urban V's demand that the students of his new college should be exempt from the costs of taking a degree met with frosty opposition.[203]

What suffered, of course, in this relationship was the capacity of the colleges to become centres for teaching. Except in the Bresciano, the only subject officially permitted was theology, in which lectures were held in the Collegio di Spagna in the fourteenth century and in the Pratense[204] and the Castiglioni in the fifteenth.[205] As theology fell outside the ambit of the student-universities and the main colleges of doctors, this was not a problem; its teaching was already fragmented across the *studia* of the religious orders, and one more chair was not likely to be controversial. Indeed, it was accepted that lectures in theology were valuable to students of all subjects in a college, as part of their moral training, just as it was acceptable for a solitary chair in theology to appear on the law university lecture-list at Bologna for the benefit of the canonists. But there was absolutely no formal teaching of other subjects. The use of college rooms for lectures (Siena, Florence), preliminary grammar coaching, disputations, 'practice teaching', *repetitiones* can all be found occasionally, but no more than that. Yet it would be wrong to see this in such a negative light. There were no complaints that the colleges were not providing tutorial teaching or separate lectures. Colleges in Italy were simply not conceived of as having that role; it remained with the *studium*.[206]

The colleges also helped the growth of the universities in another way; they contributed the first university buildings. Only the Spanish College, the Pratense and the Sapienza in Pisa had purpose-built accommodation, and Michael Kiene, who has surveyed Italian collegiate architecture, detected no obvious stylistic homogeneity either among those or among other plans which did not come to fruition. But the achievement is none the less real, and, together with the many projects of conversion of existing buildings to colleges, is a preliminary to the much more extensive construction of university buildings in the sixteenth century.[207]

2. The social role of the colleges. Most of the foundations aspired to provide places for poor students. The extent to which they achieved this must be debatable. Apart from the limited numerical significance of the colleges, the fact that some of them soon went over to charging fees is significant; even if the fee was low enough to constitute an attraction and an enabling factor for the less wealthy, it clearly put such places beyond the reach of the really poor. Detailed work is possible on the records of Siena, Perugia and the Spanish College at Bologna, where we have at least the names of students who entered the colleges.[208] Elsewhere the situation is less hopeful. But much work remains to be done here before any conclusions can be reached; it will need to be integrated with study of the social composition of the universities themselves, and the investigation will need to work both outwards from the institutions and inwards from the communities whose members attended them.

Insofar as a trend towards college places for wealthier students can be established, it clearly foreshadows developments that are well documented for the sixteenth and seventeenth century, in Italy as well as elsewhere.[209] Claudia Toniolo Fascione's work on enrolment statistics for the Sapienza at Pisa in that period provides perhaps the best-documented illustration of a college that had become geared overwhelmingly to the needs of the bourgeoisie.[210] The institutional consequences also find an echo in the north. The reluctance of aristocratic or at any rate well-off students, whether in the Sapienza of Siena or the Pratense at Padua, to accept disciplinary restrictions originally designed for quasi-religious communities of poor students, has many northern parallels already in the fifteenth century, particularly in disputes over residence requirements, the obligation to eat at a common table, and the exclusion of women.[211]

We are on firmer ground in assessing the geographical aspects of college membership. The extant admissions lists show that the colleges increasingly provided incentives for mobility between universities. They were particularly attractive to ultramontanes. Large numbers of Iberian and German students came to study in Italy, and many came in the hope of finding a collegiate place. Bologna, Padua and Siena were especially famed in Germany, Bologna and Siena were the particular targets of Iberian student migration. That this traffic was (apart from the ill-fated Collège des Lombards at Paris) one-way is no accident; and colleges, a northern import into the Italian system, may have helped attract northerners southwards in offering a comparatively familiar brand of institutional security, and moreover doing so at a time when the nations of the student-universities were largely in eclipse.[212] In this respect the Italian colleges are a good illustration of the artificiality of the crude division that is normally made between northern and southern models of university.

3. The role of the colleges in perpetuating ecclesiastical influence on the Italian universities. The image of Italian universities as secular places of study, in contrast to the Northern European universities, is incomplete and crude. The endowment, legislation, and administration of colleges was a way of contributing to and influencing the student world and the teachers' world; indirect, but significant.[213] And this in turn is one of the many ways in which the Italian universities demonstrate continuity; ecclesiastical influence and state control, far from appearing suddenly with the Counter-Reformation, go back to the fourteenth and fifteenth centuries which largely shaped the universities of the early modern period.

Department of History
Queen Mary and Westfield College
University of London
Hampstead Campus
Kidderpore Avenue
London NW3 7ST

REFERENCES

1. A view often expressed by the founder of this journal, the late Charles Schmitt. I would like here to record my debt to Dr Schmitt, from whose early encouragement I greatly benefited. Earlier versions of this paper were read to the Seminar on Late Medieval Italian History at the Institute of Historical Research, University of London, and a seminar on Italian Renaissance History at the University of Oxford. I am indebted to the participants of both seminars for their comments and suggestions. Laurence Brockliss, Giuliano Catoni, Marie Denley, John Fletcher, Michael Kiene, Kate Lowe, and Giovanni Minnucci made useful points and directed me to material I might otherwise have missed. I should like also to record my debt to the staff of the Archivio di Stato di Siena, the Biblioteca Marciana, Venice, and the Biblioteca Apostolica Vaticana for assistance with microfilms, to Dott. Patrizia Angelucci Mezzetti and Padre Ugolino Nicolini for their warm and enthusiastic help in tracing two Perugian *tesi di laurea*, and particularly to Dott. Luciana Rea of the Archivio Antico della Università, Padua, for her indefatigable labours on my behalf during and after my brief visit there.
2. See esp. the work of A. L. Gabriel; e.g. *Student Life in Ave Maria College, Medieval Paris*. Publications in Medieval Studies, University of Notre Dame, 14 (Notre Dame, Indiana, 1955); *Skara House at the Medieval University of Paris*. Texts and Studies in the History of Mediaeval Education, 9 (Notre Dame, Indiana, 1960); 'Preparatory Teaching in the Parisian Colleges during the Fourteenth Century', *Revue de l'Université d'Ottawa*, 21 (1951), 449–83, repr. in his *Garlan-*

dia. Studies in the History of the Medieval University (Notre Dame, Indiana, 1969), pp. 97–124.

3. E.g. E. Verdera y Tuells (ed.), *El Cardenal Albornoz y el Colegio de España*, 6 vols. (Bologna, 1972–79: Studia Albornotiana, vols. 11–13, 35–7); *I Quattro Secoli del Collegio Borromeo di Pavia. Studi di Storia e d'Arte Pubblicati nel IV Centenario della Fondazione 1561–1961* (Milan, 1961); M. Bendiscioli *et al.*, *Il Collegio Universitario Ghislieri di Pavia*, 2 vols. (Milan, 1966–70).
4. A partial exception is B. Pagnin, 'Collegi universitari medievali' in *I Quattro Secoli*, pp. 229–42, which examined the colleges of Bologna, Padua, and Pavia in the context of the European collegiate movement; see also J. M. Fletcher, 'The Spanish College—Some Observations on its Foundations and Early Statutes', in Verdera y Tuells (ed.), *El Cardenal Albornoz*, ii. 73–91, and A. L. Visintin, 'Due Collegi universitari del tardo Medioevo', in *Il Collegio Universitario Ghislieri*, ii. 299–311 (comparing the Collegio di Spagna, Bologna and the Collegium Sapientiae, Freiburg im Breisgau, but incorporating other comparisons as well).
5. E.g. A. B. Cobban, 'The Role of Colleges in the Medieval Universities of Northern Europe, with Special Reference to England and France', *Bulletin of the John Rylands University Library of Manchester*, 71 (1989), 49–70 (pp. 64–5).
6. A. L. Gabriel, 'The College System in the Fourteenth-Century Universities', in F. L. Utley (ed.), *The Forward Movement of the Fourteenth Century* (Columbus, Ohio, 1961) pp. 79–124; repr. as extract (Baltimore, 1962), esp. pp. 28–9.
7. E. Delaruelle, 'La politique universitaire des papes d'Avignon—spécialement d'Urbain V—et la fondation du Collège Espagnol de Bologne', in Verdera y Tuells (ed.), *El Cardenal Albornoz*, ii. 7–39 (p. 9).
8. P. Ariès, *Centuries of Childhood* (tr. London, 1962: 1986 edn.), pp. 151, 158, 159, 169; J. Verger, 'Les Universités françaises au XVe siècle: crise et tentative de réforme', *Cahiers d'Histoire*, 21 (1976), 43–66 (pp. 64–5).
9. A. B. Cobban, *The Medieval English Universities: Oxford and Cambridge to* c.*1500* (Aldershot, 1988), p. 148.
10. Cobban, 'The Role of Colleges', esp. 53–9.
11. Cobban, 'The Role of Colleges', pp. 64–5, 70.
12. Cobban, 'The Role of Colleges', pp. 65–6. A third factor implicit in Cobban's argument is that in universities where there were no salaried lectureships, there was a danger that the university would lose its teachers; colleges became a vehicle for providing and guaranteeing teaching. Italy, to the forefront of the movement towards salaried lectureships (Cobban, 'Elective Salaried Lectureships in the Universities of Southern Europe in the Pre-Reformation Era', *Bulletin of the John Rylands University Library of Manchester*, 67 (1984–85, 662–87),

had less need for such collegiate provision. Cobban, 'The Role of Colleges', p. 68.

13. This argument presupposes acceptance of the traditional view of Bologna as model for Italy and home of student power (Cobban, 'Medieval Student Power', *Past and Present*, 53 (1971), 28–66; idem, *The Medieval Universities: their Development and Organization* (London, 1975, chs III and VII), a view which is questionable (P. Denley, 'Northern and Southern Models of the Medieval University', in C. O'Boyle and R. French (eds.), *The Origins of the Universities: Learned Disciplines in Revolution*, forthcoming).
14. Esp. ch. 7.
15. I avoid the terms 'undergraduate' and 'postgraduate' here because they are less meaningful in the Italian context; although the arts course was considered ancillary and preliminary to medicine, a qualification in arts was not a prerequisite for the study of medicine, and still less so for law. This is another aspect of Italian university history that is little understood. Denley, 'Northern and Southern Models'.
16. Cobban, 'The Role of Colleges', p. 50: 'The common factor underlying college differentiation was the act of endowment made for educational purposes. It is this endowed state of the college which distinguishes it decisively from the rented hall or hostel or hospice'.
17. J. M. Fletcher, 'The History of Academic Colleges: Problems and Prospects', in D. Maffei and H. de Ridder-Symoens (eds.), *I collegi universitari in Europa tra il XIV e il XVIII secolo.* Atti del Convegno di Studi della Commissione internazionale per la storia delle Università, Siena-Bologna, 16–19 maggio 1988. Orbis Academicus IV (Milan, 1991), pp. 13–22, proposes a typology of colleges which I have borne in mind in what has been said above. I am grateful to Dr Fletcher for a preview of his article and for permission to cite it.
18. It should be emphasized that these student colleges should not be confused with the 'Colleges of Doctors' that are also present in the Italian university system; these were guilds of doctors which awarded degrees, provided pools of expertise for the town, and protected the interests of their members, but have no physical or residential aspect. Cf. Denley, 'Northern and Southern Models'.
19. Gabriel, 'The College System', pp. 32–4.
20. There are obvious difficulties of categorization where evidence is scanty, but the overall figure is an accurate indication of what has come to light so far.
21. They are listed in L. Thorndike, *University Records and Life in the Middle Ages* (New York, 1971), Appendix II, pp. 433–48, with map facing p. 448.
22. On foundations and motives, A. L. Gabriel, 'Motivation of the Founders of Medieval Colleges', in P. Wilpert (ed.), *Beiträge zum Berufsbewußtsein des mittelalterlichen Menschen.* Miscellanea Mediaevalia III (Berlin, 1964), pp. 61–72, repr. in Gabriel, *Garlandia*, pp. 211–

23; on the mechanics of drawing up foundation statutes see also V. G. Davis, 'English Collegiate Statutes in the Later Middle Ages' (forthcoming). I am grateful to Dr Davis for sight of this piece and permission to quote it.

23. Rashdall doubted whether the endowment actually provided for residence as opposed to pensions, though this was clearly the case by the fifteenth century (H. Rashdall, *The Universities of Europe in the Middle Ages*, eds. F. M. Powicke and A. B. Emden, 3 vols. (Oxford, 1936 edn.), i. 198). For general references on the Avignonese, and the colleges described in what follows, see Appendix II below.
24. On Guglielmo, P. Guerrini, 'Guglielmo da Brescia e il Collegio Bresciano in Bologna', *Studi e memorie per la storia dell'Università di Bologna*, VII (1922), 55–116, esp. pp. 60–8; N. Siraisi, *Taddeo Alderotti and his Pupils. Two Generations of Italian Medical Learning* (Princeton, N.J., 1981), esp. pp. 49–54.
25. Siraisi, p. 70; G. P. Brizzi, 'I collegi per borsisti e lo Studio bolognese. Caratteri ed evoluzione di un'istituzione educativo-assistenziale fra XIII e XVIII secolo', *Studi e Memorie per la Storia dell'Università di Bologna*, n.s. IV (1984), 9–48 (p. 15); A. Pérez Martín, 'El Colegio Vives', in Verdera y Tuells, (ed.), *El cardenal Albornoz*, vi. 118–25, and A. Sorbelli, *Storia dell'Università di Bologna*, i (Bologna, 1944), p. 119.
26. The 1274 Sorbonne statutes are in H. Denifle (ed.), *Chartularium Universitatis Parisiensis*, I (Paris, 1899), 505–14.
27. Of course some statutes make explicit reference to those of the Sorbonne as their model, even if they then go on to differ in matters of detail. However where references are not explicit, and where the textual tradition is not unambiguously clear, it is best to observe the principle that 'the similarity between medieval college statutes makes it difficult to trace the influence of one set of statutes upon another—one must be hesitant to claim that one statute is a source for another'. D. Sanderlin, *The Medieval Statutes of the College of Autun at the University of Paris*. Texts and Studies in the History of Mediaeval Education, 13 (Notre Dame, Indiana, 1971), 20.
28. Rashdall, *The Universities of Europe*, i. 508.
29. Statute 28, Guerrini, p. 108.
30. C. Piana, *Nuovi documenti sull' Università di Bologna e sul Collegio di Spagna* (Bologna, 1976), p. 170, n. 3. The older term survives, however; in 1404 the five remaining scholars elected one among their number to be their *prior*; ibid., p. 609.
31. Guerrini, pp. 95–6.
32. About 7½ Florentine florins each, or a total of 60 florins. P. Spufford, *Handbook of Medieval Exchange* (London, 1986), p. 73.
33. Guerrini, pp. 93, 109.
34. The Collège des Lombards is now the subject of a monograph by R. Manno Tolu, *Scolari italiani nello Studio di Parigi. Il 'Collège des Lombards' dal XIV al XVI secolo ed i suoi ospiti pistoiesi*. Quaderni

della Rassegna degli Archivi di Stato, 57 (Rome, 1989). Cf. also eadem, 'La "Domus pauperum scolarium Italorum" a Parigi nel 1334', *Archivio Storico Italiano* 146 (1988), 49–56. Its chequered history is not unlike that of a similar German attempt, studied by A. L. Gabriel, 'The House of Poor German Students at the Mediaeval University of Paris', in F. Prinz, F.-J. Schmale and F. Seibt (eds.), *Geschichte in der Gesellschaft. Festschrift für Karl Bosl zum 65. Geburtstag* (Stuttgart, 1974), pp. 50–78. The Collège des Lombards was the only college for Italians to be founded outside Italy in this period; for the next attempt, K. J. P. Lowe, 'Cardinal Francesco Soderini's Proposal for an Italian College at Paris in 1524', *History of Universities* IV (1984), 167–78.

35. A. Mancini, 'Emigrati italiani del Trecento', *Annali della Regia Scuola Superiore Normale di Pisa* ser. ii, vol. i (1932), 335–46 (the will is published on pp. 343–6). On Pancio, C. H. Talbot and E. A. Hammond, *The Medical Practitioners in Medieval England: a Biographical Register* (London, 1965), pp. 234–7; and N. Siraisi, *Taddeo Alderotti*, pp. xix, 17–18, 50, on his links with Guglielmo. I am grateful to Dr Paul Brand for drawing my attention to Pancio's will.
36. Pérez Martín, 'El Colegio Vives', pp. 124–5; Piana, *Nuovi documenti*, pp. 62–3.
37. Piana, *Nuovi documenti*, pp. 170–1, 366–7, 430, 581–2; C. Piana, *Nuove ricerche su le Università di Bologna e di Parma* (Quaracchi, 1966) pp. 433–61.
38. Delaruelle, loc cit.
39. Piana, *Nuovi documenti*, pp. 153–62; Brizzi, pp. 15–16.
40. See below, pp. 53–4.
41. Piana, *Nuovi documenti*, pp. 162–9; Pérez Martín, 'El Colegio Vives', pp. 122–3. The documents are published in *Chartularium Studii Bononiensis*, II (Bologna, 1913), 243–346.
42. Piana, *Nuove ricerche*, p. 405. It has to be said that this was at a particularly bad moment in Bologna's history, indeed in the history of the Italian universities generally.
43. Piana, *Nuove ricerche*, pp. 410–11.
44. *Chartularium Studii Bononsiensis*, IV (Bologna, 1919), 89–91.
45. Piana, *Nuovi documenti*, pp. 170, 416, 612.
46. Guerrini, p. 76.
47. *Chartularium*, IV, pp. 92–4.
48. Piana, *Nuovi documenti*, pp. 166–9.
49. Piana, *Nuove ricerche*, p. 386.
50. Pérez Martín, 'El Colegio Vives', pp. 122–3.
51. Ibid., pp. 120–2.
52. The fullest introduction to Albornoz and the college is now B. M. Marti, *The Spanish College at Bologna in the Fourteenth Century* (Philadelphia, Pa., 1966), which includes an edition and translation of the 1375–77 statutes.
53. A. García García, 'Escolares ibéricos en Bolonia, 1300–1330', in

Estudios sobre los orígenes de las universidades españolas. Homenaje de la Universidad de Valladolid a la Universidad de Bolonia en su IX Centenario (Universidad de Valladolid, 1988), pp. 113–34.

54. E.g. Statute 4 (Marti, p. 146). This passage also refers to statutes of a college in the Spanish town of Osma (with which Albornoz was connected), which has not been explained by historians.
55. The considered view of Fletcher, 'The Spanish College', pp. 79–80.
56. Statute 2 (Marti, pp. 128–32). *Pace* Fletcher, 'The Spanish College', p. 78, these were not graduate students; the Italian system did not even require a degree in arts for study in a higher subject, see note 15 above.
57. Statute 2 (Marti, pp. 130–1).
58. Statutes 3 and 4 (Marti, pp. 132–48).
59. Statute 5 (Marti, pp. 150–2).
60. Statute 6 (Marti, pp. 152–6).
61. Statute 7 (Marti, pp. 156–62).
62. Statutes 9–14 (Marti, pp. 168–204).
63. Statute 21 (Marti, pp. 238–48).
64. Statutes 39 (Marti, pp. 314–24) and 59 (pp. 314–16).
65. Statutes 18 (Marti, pp. 226–8). On the external authority over the college, A. Pérez Martín, *Proles Aegidiana. Los colegiales desde 1368 a 1977*, 4 vols. (Bologna, 1979), i. 74–8.
66. Statutes 13 (Marti, pp. 194–200) and 37 (pp. 306–8).
67. Statutes 11 (Marti, pp. 176–82) and 28 (pp. 272–4), and p. 32.
68. Statute 30 (Marti, pp. 276–8).
69. Statutes 24 (Marti, p. 256) and 32 (pp. 282–6).
70. Statute 23 (Marti, pp. 252–4).
71. Statute 34 (Marti, pp. 294–8).
72. Statute 29 (Marti, pp. 274–6).
73. Statutes 50–51 (Marti, pp. 334–6).
74. Statute 52 (Marti, pp. 336–8).
75. Statutes 40–41 (Marti, pp. 324–6).
76. Statute 43 (Marti, pp. 328–30).
77. Statutes 45–46 (Marti, pp. 330–2).
78. Statute 49 (Marti, p. 334).
79. Marti, p. 10.
80. Denley, 'Northern and Southern Models', cit. note 13 above.
81. A point emphasized by Fletcher, 'The Spanish College', pp. 80–1.
82. Cf. J. Ríus Cornado, 'Las propiedades urbanas del Colegio de España en Bolonia (1459–1490)', in Verdera y Tuells (ed.), *El cardenal Albornoz*, v. 307–48. The surviving estate records of the college were extensive enough to yield a substantial monograph: P. Iradiel, *Progreso agrario, desesquilibrio social y agricoltura de transición (La propiedad del Colegio de España en Bolonia, siglos XIV y XV)* (Bologna, 1978: Studia Albornotiana, 34).
83. M. Kiene, 'L'architettura del Collegio di Spagna di Bologna: organizzazzione dello spazio e influssi sull'edilizia universitaria europea', *Il*

Carrobbio, IX (1983), 234–42; idem, 'Die Bautätigkeit in den italienischen Universitäten von der Mitte des Trecento bis zur Mitte des Quattrocento', *Mitteilungen des Kunsthistorischen Institutes in Florenz*, XXX:3 (1986), 433–92 (esp. pp. 455–76).

84. Cf. the analysis of Pérez Martín, *Proles Aegidiana*, i. 90–104, which however shows the real period of influence to be after 1500. See also J. Sánchez Herrero, 'Los colegiales sevillanos del Colegio Español de San Clemente de Bolonia (1368–1600)', in *Estudios sobre los orígenes de las Universidades españolas*, pp. 135–204.
85. A point made in E. Armstrong's charming 'The Spanish College in the University of Bologna', in his *Italian Studies* (London, 1934), pp. 273–94 (pp. 277–8). Fletcher, 'The Spanish College', pp. 83–5, stresses the integrality of Albornoz's encouragement of theology teaching with the foundation of the college, and the link between the college and theology teaching for seculars in particular (pp. 83–6).
86. By Mirella Sebastiani ('Il collegio universitario di San Gregorio in Perugia detto la Sapienza Vecchia', unpublished *tesi di laurea*, Università degli Studi di Perugia, Facoltà di Lettere e Filosofia, Anno Accademico 1966–67), who showed that the foundation date was 1360 not 1362 (pp. 27–8 esp.).
87. The foundations were not, however, linked in the English fashion with places at the college reserved for pupils from the school. The triple foundation foreshadows the recommendations of Paolo Cortesi at the beginning of the sixteenth century on the caritative activity of cardinals (below, p. 50).
88. Piana, *Nuovi documenti*, p. 155.
89. Sebastiani, esp. pp. 7, 65, and her Appendice I, pp. 32–8, 59–67, etc.
90. For bibliography see Appendix II below.
91. The term *legge* is often used in contrast to canon law.
92. A. Gloria, *Monumenti della Università di Padova (1318–1405)* (Padua, 1888), ii. 76.
93. See Appendix II below for full references to these and other Paduan foundations.
94. M. Savonarola, *Libellus de magnificis ornamentis regie civitatis Padue*, ed. A. Segarizzi, *Rerum Italicarum Scriptores*, n. ed., XXIV, xv (Città di Castello, 1902), pp. 55–6. Cf. G. Fabris, 'Il Collegio Pratense', in *L'arte che rivive nella rivoluzione fascista nell ripristino del Collegio Pratense riscatto a sede della legione 'Patavina' M.V.S.N.* Supplemento de *Il Milite*, VI (1929), repr. in his *Scritti di arte e storia padovana*, intr. L. Lazzarini (Cittadella, 1977), pp. 151–71 (pp. 157–8), and M. Kiene, 'Die Bautätigkeit der italienischen Universitäten', pp. 477–9.
95. P. Stacul, *Il Cardinale Pileo da Prata*. Miscellanea della Società Romana di Storia Patria, 19 (Rome, 1957), 15–16, 23–4, 291–2; G. Fabris, 'Pileo da Prata', in *L'arte che rivive*, and in his *Scritti di arte e storia*, pp. 125–49.

96. P. N. R. Zutschi, 'Some Inedited Papal Documents Relating to the University of Cambridge in the Fourteenth Century', *Archivum Historiae Pontificiae*, 26 (1988), 393–409, esp. pp. 396–9, 401–3, 406. I am grateful to Dr Zutschi for drawing my attention to this aspect of Pileo's career.
97. Archivio di Stato di Siena (hereafter ASS), *Consiglio Generale*, 196, c. 67v, 23 June 1388.
98. For these developments, G. Catoni, 'Genesi e ordinamento della Sapienza di Siena', *Studi Senesi*, LXXXV (1973), 155–98.
99. P. Denley, 'The University of Siena, 1357–1557', unpublished D.Phil. thesis, Oxford, 1981; revised version *Commune and* studium *in Late Medieval and Early Renaissance Siena*, in Saggi e Documenti per la Storia dell'Università di Siena, 2 (Milan, 1991, forthcoming).
100. Denley, *Commune and* studium, Part IV.
101. ASS, *Consiglio Generale*, 207, c. 95r, 12 August 1415.
102. ASS, *Casa della Misericordia*, 1, cc. 53v–54v, 14 December 1422; L. Zdekauer, *Lo Studio di Siena nel Rinascimento* (Milan, 1894, repr. Bologna, 1977), pp. 161–2, 96–7.
103. ASS, *Casa della Misericordia*, 1 c. 56v, and *Concistoro*, 413, c. 13v, 17 November 1434; *Casa della Misericordia*, 1, c. 85r, and *Statuti*, 47, c. 212v, 29 May 1437.
104. ASS, *Casa della Misericordia*, 1, c. 57v, 18 March 1445.
105. Compare this with the estimate of L. Martines, *The Social World of the Florentine Humanists 1390–1460* (London, 1963), p. 117, that in this period 'the yearly expenses of a young man enrolled in a university away from home averaged about 20.0 florins', while 'servants were paid from 9.00 to 20.0 florins yearly'. Unskilled and skilled labourers in Florence could expect wages significantly better than that (although of course board and accommodation would not be included): R. Goldthwaite, *The Building of Renaissance Florence* (Johns Hopkins, Baltimore, 1980), Appendix 3, esp. pp. 436–8.
106. G. Catoni, 'Il comune di Siena e l'amministrazione della Sapienza nel sec. XV', in *Università e Società nei secoli XII–XVI*. Centro Italiano di Studi di Storia e d'Arte, Pistoia, Nono Convegno Internazionale, Pistoia, 20–25 settembre 1979 (Pistoia, 1982), pp. 121–9.
107. ASS, *Consiglio Generale*, 219, c. 117r, 25 February 1437; the phrase, and others like it, become standard.
108. See below, Appendix II.
109. On the relationship between Sienese and Florentine attempts at college creation, P. Denley, 'Academic Rivalry and Interchange: the Universities of Siena and Florence', in P. Denley and C. Elam (eds.), *Florence and Italy. Renaissance Studies in Honour of Nicolai Rubinstein* (London, 1988), pp. 193–208 (pp. 201–3). It should be noted that, although much of the emphasis in the documents of the period—and by subsequent historians—is on the lecture rooms that were to be provided (thus providing a focus for the university) the Florentine Sapienza was to be a residential collegiate foundation as well.

110. Sebastiani, 'Il collegio universitario di San Gregorio', p. 76, and her Appendice II, pp. 284–5. The charge was forty or fifty florins. Perugia's second college, the 'Sapienza Nuova', had followed suit by 1443 with a fee of forty florins for all, raised in 1445 to fifty florins; Giuliana Nardeschi, 'Le costituzioni della "Sapienza Nuova" dell' Anno 1443', unpublished *tesi di laurea*, Università degli Studi di Perugia, Facoltà di Magistero, Anno Accademico 1971–72, pp. 71–2, 102.
111. Statutes of Bishop Jacopo Zeno (between 1460 and 1481), rubric 7; in *Fondazione Collegio universitario Pratense, Padova* (Padua, 1960), n. p.
112. Fabris, 'Il Collegio Pratense', pp. 158, 160.
113. Contrast for example the Tornacense statutes, rubric 14 (Biblioteca Marciana, Venice, ms. Lat. XIV.288 (=4635), c. 4r).
114. Here I must differ from G. Minnucci, 'Documenti per la storia dello Studio senese (secoli XIV–XVI)', in G. Minnucci and L. Košuta, *Lo Studio di Siena nei secoli XIV–XVI.* Orbis Academicus; Saggi e Documenti di Storia delle Università, III: Saggi e Documenti per la Storia dell'Università di Siena, 1 (Milan, 1989), pp. 13–314, about the significance of an inventory which he publishes (pp. 102–9) as 'probabilmente della Sapienza'. In all the extensive documentation of the daily life of the Sapienza in the period there is not a single mention of a library.
115. For information on these and subsequent colleges, see below, Appendix II.
116. A. Gherardi, *Statuti della Università e lo Studio Fiorentino* (Florence, 1881), pp. 211–12.
117. R. Sabbadini and M. Catalano-Tirrito (eds.), *Storia documentata dell'Università di Catania, I. L'Università di Catania nel secolo XV* (Catania, 1898, repr. Bologna, 1975), p. 65 (18 April 1444). The Commune of Catania, like many other Sicilian towns, had previously given scholarships to citizens wishing to study in Northern Italian universities; ibid., pp. 8–12.
118. ASS, *Concistoro*, 2056, no. 53 (1 Oct. 1484). For the only published information on this project, P. Pellini, *Dell'historia di Perugia* (Bologna, 1664), pt. 2, p. 818.
119. On the Cesis scholarships, see most recently Manno Tolu, *Scolari italiani nello Studio di Parigi*, p. 61.
120. See below, Appendix II, under Bologna.
121. Cf. P. Denley, 'Governments and Schools in Late Medieval Italy', in *City and Countryside in Late Medieval and Renaissance Italy: Essays Presented to Philip Jones*, eds. T. Dean and C. Wickham (Hambledon, 1990), pp. 93–108 (p. 106).
122. J. C. Brown, *In the Shadow of Florence. Provincial Society in Renaissance Pescia* (Oxford, 1982), p. 178.
123. P. Piccolomini, 'Bartolomeo Bolis da Padova e la sua fondazione per lo Studio di Siena', *Archivio storico italiano*, ser. V, 36 (1905), pp. 144–52.

124. On the attitudes of teachers who made such bequests, alongside the donation of books, etc., as part of what was considered the obligation to transmit one's learning, J. Agrimi and C. Crisciani, *Edocere medicos. Medicina scolastica nei secoli XIII–XV* (Naples, 1988), pp. 124–5.
125. See below, Appendix I for a conspectus of foundations, and Appendix II for more details of the founders.
126. Pagnin, 'Collegi universitari medievali', pp. 241–2.
127. Siraisi, *Taddeo Alderotti*, p. 54, claims of the Bresciano—the first Italian college to be founded by an academic—that 'it is . . . probably true that Guglielmo's statutes contain an implied criticism of the attitudes and priorities of the lawyers and physicians of Bologna and of what Guglielmo perceived as an excessively vocational emphasis in the *studium*'.
128. Sebastiani, 'Collegio universitario di San Gregorio', p. 67, and her Appendice, I, pp. 70–1.
129. See above, pp. 42–3.
130. See esp. A. L. V. Visintin, 'Il più significativo precedente del Collegio Ghislieri: il Collegio Universitario Castiglioni (1429–1803)', in *Il Collegio Universitario Ghislieri di Pavia*, I (Milan, 1966), 51–89 (pp. 52–4); and F. Zambelloni, 'Il Collegio Castiglioni, prima istituzione collegiale pavese', in *Il Collegio Ghislieri: 1567–1967* (Milan, 1967), pp. 211–16 (esp. pp. 212–14).
131. See esp. M. Morpurgo-Castelnuovo, 'Il cardinale Domenico Capranica', *Archivio storico della Società Romana di Storia Patria*, LII (1929), 1–142 (pp. 87–8).
132. See esp. B. Geraldini, 'La vita di Angelo Geraldini scritta da Antonio Geraldini', *Bullettino della Società Umbra di Storia Patria*, II (1896), 41–58, 473–532 (pp. 56, 58, 473–9).
133. Johannes Baptista Caccialupus, *De modo studendi et vita doctorum tractatus* (Venetiis, 1472). Bibliography on Caccialupi is in Minnucci, 'Documenti per la storia dello Studio senese', p. 270.
134. C. Marcora, 'Stefano Nardini Arcivescovo di Milano', *Memorie Storiche della diocesi di Milano*, III (1956), 257–488 (esp. pp. 352). On this figure see A. A. Strnad, 'Francesco Todeschini-Piccolomini, Politik und Mäzenatentum im Quattrocento', *Römische Historische Mitteilungen*, 8–9 (1964–66), 104–425; on his involvement with the Sienese Sapienza, Denley, *Commune and* studium, Part IV.
135. Paolo Cortesi, *De Cardinalatu libri tres* (Casa Cortese, 1510), f. ciii. For further examples of cardinals' activity in this respect, Lowe, 'Cardinal Francesco Soderini's Proposal', pp. 167–78.
136. P. Partner, *The Pope's Men. The Papal Civil Service in the Renaissance* (Oxford, 1990), pp. 121, 189.
137. The literature on Forteguerri is diffuse. See most recently L. Gai, 'Niccolò Forteguerri nei suoi rapporti con l'ambiente culturale pistoiese nel Quattrocento', *Studi Storici Pistoiesi*, 1 (1976), 57–72; S.

Ciampi, *Memorie di Niccolò Forteguerri istitutore del Liceo e del Collegio Forteguerri di Pistoia nel secolo XV* (Pisa, 1813); Q. Santoli, 'La biblioteca forteguerriana di Pistoia', *Accademie e biblioteche d'Italia*, VII (1929), 65–82; idem, *La biblioteca forteguerriana di Pistoia* (Pistoia, 1932); A. Zanelli, *Del pubblico insegnamento in Pistoia dal XIV al XVI secolo* (Rome, 1900); Manno Tolu, *Scolari Italiani*, p. 70; Strnad, 'Francesco Todeschini-Piccolomini', p. 175.

138. E. Bellone, *Il primo secolo di vita della Università di Torino (sec. XV–XVI). Ricerche ed ipotesi sulla cultura nel Piemonte Quattrocentesco* (Turin, 1986), p. 79.
139. Cobban, 'The Role of Colleges', pp. 63–4; J. M. Fletcher and C. A. Upton, 'The Cost of Undergraduate Study at Oxford in the Fifteenth Century: the Evidence of the Merton College "Founder's Kin"', *History of Education*, 14 (1985), 1–20 (pp. 4 seq.); G. D. Squibb, *Founders' Kin. Privilege and Pedigree* (Oxford, 1972), esp. pp. 5–10, 14, 34–5.
140. Above, p. 35, and Appendix II.
141. See Appendix II.
142. The other notable exception is the Capranica, where eighteen places were reserved for students of Roman birth. Morpurgo-Castelnuovo, pp. 92–3.
143. Gherardi, *Statuti*, pp. 235–6.
144. Z. Volta, 'Del collegio universitario Marliani in Pavia', *Archivio Storico Lombardo*, ser. II, 9/19 (1892), 590–628 (p. 605).
145. Fabris, 'Il Collegio Pratense', p. 156.
146. On the Ancarano, Brizzi, pp. 59–60; on the Marliani, Volta, 'Del collegio universitario Marliani', esp. p. 609.
147. Z. Volta, 'Catone Sacco e il collegio di sua fondazione in Pavia', *Archivio Storico Lombardo*, ser. II, 8/18 (1891), 562–600 (esp. pp. 581, 591).
148. Guerrini, p. 77 (1431). Cf. Manno Tolu, *Scolari italiani*, p. 75, on a similar problem in Pistoia in remembering the existence of places in the Collège des Lombards at Paris.
149. Piana, *Nuovi documenti*, pp. 170, 414–15, 508, 663, 726 and 731; idem, *Nuove ricerche*, pp. 407–10, 412, 414–17.
150. Volta, 'Del Collegio Universitario Marliani', p. 609.
151. Piana, *Nuovi documenti*, p. 416.
152. On the other hand Marti's assertion that the Gregoriano at Bologna 'liberally provides for the support of three scholars from Bologna' (*Spanish College*, p. 147 n. 15) seems to me to rest on a misunderstanding of a papal privilege of 1373, which granted the *anziani* of Bologna the perpetual right to present three candidates to the college 'secundum formam Statutorum dicti Collegii' (i.e. not Bolognese students). *Chartularium Studii Bononiensis*, ii. 313–14.
153. Denley, *Commune and* studium, Part IV.
154. Brizzi, pp. 59–60.

155. Statute 8, Archivio Antico della Università, Padua (hereafter AAUP), 602, n.c.
156. Gloria, i. 104. For a list of subjects specified, see below, Appendix I.
157. J. Facciolati, *Fasti Gymnasii Patavini* (Padua, 1757), ii. 85. By the seventeenth century it was taking students of law and medicine as well. The Nardini in Rome is often described as a theological college but in fact it accepted students in canon law and, provided they were intending to proceed to theology, arts. Marcora, p. 350.
158. Guerrini, pp. 108–9.
159. Statute 4 (Marti, pp. 142–4).
160. A. Rossi, 'Documenti per la Storia dell'Università di Perugia', *Giornale di Erudizione Artistica*, VI (1877), 53.
161. G. Ermini, *Storia dell'Università di Perugia*, 2 vols. (Florence, 1971 edn.), i. 397.
162. *Chartularium Studii Bononiensis*, ii. 291.
163. Zdekauer, *Lo Studio di Siena nel rinascimento*, p. 162.
164. Guerrini, p. 110.
165. Volta, 'Del Collegio Universitario Marliani', p. 616.
166. Gloria, ii. 256 (30 August 1391).
167. F. M. Colle, *Storia scientifico-letteraria dello studio di Padova*, 4 vols. (Padua, 1824–25), i. 114; AAUP, 731, c 271r.
168. Fabris, 'Il Collegio Pratense', p. 158.
169. Morpurgo-Castelnuovo, p. 94.
170. *Chartularium Studii Bononiensis*, ii. 291.
171. Morpurgo-Castelnuovo, p. 94.
172. ASS, *Casa della Misericordia*, 1, c. 103v (4 April 1476).
173. Statute 7 (Guerrini, pp. 95, 109). This was the equivalent of about 10 Florentine florins (see above, n. 32).
174. Statute 6 (Marti, pp. 152–6).
175. Morpurgo-Castelnuovo, p. 94.
176. Malagola, *Statuti*, p. 200; Brizzi, p. 60.
177. Fabris, 'Il Collegio Pratense', pp. 152, 155–60. The bishops soon took over from the jurist prior.
178. AAUP, 731, cc. 20r, 254r–255r.
179. The guilds had the right of presentation, subject to confirmation by the others. Colle, p. 114. Guilds also played a prominent part in Nicollò da Uzzano's proposed Florentine Sapienza (Gherardi, esp. 237–8).
180. Denley, *Commune and* studium, Parts II and IV.
181. See p. 36 above.
182. Above, p. 38.
183. Morpurgo-Castelnuovo, p. 97.
184. Volta, 'Il Collegio universitario Marliani', p. 618.
185. Malagola, *Statuti*, p. 200 n. 1; Piana, *Nuove ricerche*, esp. pp. 427–9; Brizzi, p. 60.
186. Sebastiani, pp. 74–5 (1417), 94–5 (1467).
187. Statute 12 (Marti, pp. 182–94).

188. Visintin, 'Il più significativo precedente', p. 59.
189. Denley, *Commune and* studium, Part IV.
190. Visintin, loc. cit., n. 188 above.
191. Denley, *Commune and* studium, Part IV.
192. For example at Padua the scholars of the Zanetini were provided with thirty lire per annum; those of the Descalzi twenty-five (Gloria, ii. 256, 373); the Grassi in Turin offered 'duodecim florenos parvi ponderis Sabaudie' (T. Vallauri, *Storia delle Università degli Studi del Piemonte* (Turin, 1845–46), pp. 321).
193. Above, p. 56.
194. Fabris, 'Il Collegio Pratense', pp. 158–60.
195. Denley, *Commune and* studium, Part IV.
196. G. Mancini, 'Il testamento di L. B. Alberti', *Archivio Storico Italiano*, LXXII (1914), II, 20–52 (p. 20).
197. If the average size of student population can be estimated at 200–400 (with slightly larger figures for Padua and Bologna and significantly larger ones for Padua), then the college population might comprise at most a quarter to a third of the total; in many *studii* it would be substantially less.
198. Cobban, 'The Role of Colleges', pp. 65–6, and n. 12 above.
199. Marti, p. 23.
200. Ermini, I, p. 397.
201. Denley, *Commune and* studium, Part IV.
201. On the Collegio di Spagna, Statute 30 (Marti, p. 278); cf. A. L. Visintin, 'Due collegi universitaria del tardo Medioevo', in *Il Collegio Universitario Ghislieri di Pavia*, II (Milan, 1970), 299–311 (pp. 306–7): on the Castiglioni, Visintin, 'Il più significativo precedente', p. 58.
203. Brizzi, pp. 15–16, n. 13.
204. Fabris, 'Il Collegio Pratense', p. 158.
205. Visintin, 'Il più significativo precedente', p. 63.
206. The judgement of Brizzi, p. 18, that the colleges failed to develop because they were unable to develop a teaching role may stand if contrasted directly with Oxford and Cambridge colleges, but in other respects is an unduly pessimistic assessment.
207. M. Kiene, 'L'architettura del Collegio di Spagna'; idem, 'Die Bautätigkeit in den italienischen Universitäten'; idem, 'Die Palazzo della Sapienza—zur italienischen Universitätsarchitektur des 15. und 16. Jahrhunderts', *Römisches Jahrbuch für Kunstgeschichte*, 23/24 (1988), pp. 221–71.
208. Pérez Martín, *Proles Aegidianae* (Spanish College); for Perugia, Sebastiani, Appendice II, and late fifteenth-century archival series (advice from Padre Nicolini); for Siena, Zdekauer, pp. 180–91, for a late fifteenth-century list, and Denley, *Commune and* studium, part IV, for analysis and references to the abundant archival material.
209. Cf. Kagan, commenting on the sixteenth and seventeenth centuries: '... the establishment of scholarship colleges at a number of univer-

sities did provide new educational opportunities for a limited number of impoverished youths. But did such scholarships go to the poor in the sense of those at the bottom of the scale? Studies are few but it appears that many of the places in these colleges went to nobles who could not otherwise afford university study. In other words, despite . . . the general increase in enrolments, this phenomenon probably did not depend on any widening of [the] university's social base'. R. L. Kagan, 'Universities in Italy, 1500–1700', in D. Julia and J. Revel (eds.), *Les Universités européennes du XVIe au XVIIIe siècle: histoire sociale des populations étudiantes* (Paris, 1986), pp. 153–86 (p. 163).

210. M. Claudia Toniolo Fascione, 'Il Collegio della Sapienza di Pisa nella Toscana del Seicento: provienza culturale, sociale e geografica delle richieste di ammissione', in Maffei and Ridder-Symoens (eds.), *I collegi universitari in Europa*, pp. 33–45.

211. I owe information on such examples to John Fletcher, who has written on several aspects of this trend; e.g. J. M. Fletcher and C. A. Upton, '"Monastic Enclave" or "Open Society"? A Consideration of the Role of Women in the Life of an Oxford College Community in the Early Tudor Period', *History of Education*, 16:1 (1987), 1–9, and in a forthcoming article on the college university.

212. The only exception being the German nations at Bologna and Padua. In the sixteenth century nations experienced a revival at Italian universities. Denley, 'Northern and Southern Models'.

213. Cf. Cobban's observation that in France and England 'the colleges were barometers of the ecclesiastical penetration of the universities' ('The Role of Colleges', p. 66).

Appendix I

Chronological Table of Italian College Foundations founded before 1500[1]

Date[2]	Town	College	Founder[3]	Places[4]	Subject[5]
1256	Bologna	Avignonese	Zoen Tencarari, bishop of Avignon	8	
1326	Bologna	Bresciano	Guglielmo Corvi da Brescia (dr. of medicine)	8–50	arts/med/can
1338x	Bologna		Pancio da Controne da Lucca (dr. of medicine)	12	arts/med/law
1360	Perugia	Gregoriano/Sap.Vecchia	Cardinal Niccolò Capocci	40/50	law
1361..	Bologna	Fieschi	Count Pepiniano Fieschi		
1362	Bologna	Reggiano	Guido da Bagnolo (dr. of medicine)	9	
1363	Padua	Tornacense/Campioni	Albizo Brancasecchi da Lucca (canon of Tournai)	6/8	can
1363/4	Padua		Francesco I Carrara	12	law
1364	Bologna	S.Clemente/di Spagna	Cardinal Gil Albornoz	24/30	theol/can/med/arts
1364	Bologna	Urbaniano	Pope Urban V	20	can[6]
1369..	Padua	Campi	Bartolomeo Campo (dr. of medicine)	3–4	arts/med
1370	Bologna	Gregoriano	Pope Gregory XI	30	law
1383x	Bologna		Cardinal Pileo da Prata	25	can
1385	Padua	S.Caterina/Arquà	Jacopo di Arquà (dr. of medicine)	10	arts/med
1388–1415	Siena	Casa della Sapienza	Commune of Siena	30/40	law/arts/med
1391..	Padua	Zanetini	Giacomo Zanetini (dr. of medicine)	8	arts/med
1393	Padua	Cypriot students	Pietro Garfrano (merchant)	4	all

Chronological Table of Italian College Foundations founded before 1500[1]

Date[2]	Town	College	Founder[3]	Places[4]	Subject[5]
1394–99	Padua	Pratense/del Santo	Cardinal Pileo da Prata	10	can
1397	Padua	'scholares Auximani'	Andrea da Recanati (dr. of medicine)	4	arts/med
1398–1405	Padua	da Rio/Ridium	Niccolò da Rio (dr. of medicine)	6	arts/med
1400..	Padua	Descalzi	Ottonello Descalzi (dr. of law)	4	law
1405..	Padua	Casa di Dio			
1412..	Padua	Curtosi	Lodovico de' Curtosi (dr. of law)	8	law
1414–	Bologna	Ancarano	Pietro d'Ancarano (dr. of law)	8	law
1425–	Perugia	Gerolimiano/Sap.Nuova	Benedetto di Alberto Guidalotti, bishop of Recanati	40	law
1427x	Rome		Cardinal Branda Castiglioni		all
1429	Pavia	Castiglioni	Cardinal Branda Castiglioni	24	all
1429x	Florence	Sapienza	Niccolò da Uzzano (banker)	40–50	no restrictions
1433x	Rome		Pope Eugenius IV		
1439	Padua	Spinelli	Belforte Spinelli (dr. of law)	4	arts
1446	Padua	Engleschi	Francesco degli Engleschi (dr. of medicine)	4	arts/med
1454	Padua	Torrisani/Trevisano	Taddeo de Adelmari da Treviso	8	theol
1456–	Rome	Capranica	Cardinal Domenico Capranica	31	theol/arts/can
1457	Turin	Grassi	Giovanni Grassi (dr. of canon law)	4	law/theol
1458	Pavia	Sacco	Catone Sacco (dr. of law)	12	law/theol
1472x	Bologna		Leon Battista Alberti	2	
1472–87	Pavia	Ferrari da Grado	Gian Matteo Ferrari da Grado (dr. of medicine)	3	med/theol/can
1475	Pavia	Marliani	Raimondo Marliani (dr. of law)	12	all
1480–84	Rome	Nardini	Cardinal Stefano Nardini	20	theol/can/arts[7]

[illegible]	[illegible]		[illegible] of Suessa		
1487–93..	Pisa	Sapienza	Commune of Florence		law
1489..	Pavia	Griffi	Ambrogio Griffi, apostolic protonotary	8	arts/med/law
1489–x	Pavia		Bregonzo Botta (Sforza official)		
1499	Pavia	Bossi	Polissena Bossi, widow of Matteo Bossi (dr. of law)	4	arts
?..	Pavia	Dataro	Lazzaro Dataro (dr. of medicine)		

1. For ease of reference, the universities functioning in Italy in the fifteenth century are listed below.

University	**Date(s) of foundation**
Bologna	C12
Padua	1222
Naples	1224, C15
Siena	1240s, 1357
Rome (*Studium Urbis*)	1303
Perugia	1308
Pisa	1343 (1472, Florence-Pisa)
Florence	1349
Pavia	1361
Ferrara	1391
Parma	(C14, C15)
Turin	1405
Catania	1444

2. '..' denotes a college of which no evidence survives for this period beyond the act of foundation: 'x' denotes a college which failed to reach even that stage. The distinction can sometimes be arbitrary, and should be regarded as provisional.
3. Where more than one person was involved in successive stages of foundation, the name of the first or principal founder is given.
4. Number of places envisaged at the moment of foundation. Where a second number is given after a slash, this indicates a change made soon after foundation.
5. 'Can' indicates canon law, 'law' indicates both canon and civil law.
6. The first students admitted were all canonists, though the books acquired included civil law codes. No further evidence available.
7. Only artists preparing to go on to study theology were admitted.

Appendix II

Profiles of Italian College Foundations to 1500

The summary of successful and attempted college foundations is intended as a 'checklist' and provisional guide. The bibliography is intended to give summary indications of the best means of access to the sources, not to be exhaustive.

BOLOGNA

A number of surveys provide a fuller guide to the literature than is possible here. Most recent is G. P. Brizzi, 'I collegi per borsisti e lo Studio bolognese. Caratteri ed evoluzione di un'istituzione educativo-assistenziale fra XIII e XVIII secolo', *Studi e Memorie per la Storia dell'Università di Bologna*, n.s. IV (1984), 9–48, with appendices pp. 49–172. Brief summaries in A. Pérez Martín, 'El Colegio Vives', in *El cardenal Albornoz y el Colegio de España*, ed. E. Verdera y Tuells, VI (Bologna, 1979: Studia Albornotiana, 37), 118–25, and A. Sorbelli, *Storia dell'Università di Bologna*, I (Bologna, 1944), 224–8. The fullest survey is C. Piana, *Nuove ricerche su le Università di Bologna e di Parma* (Quaracchi, 1966), pp. 337–41.

Collegio Avignonese

Founded in 1257 by Zoen Tencarari, Bishop of Avignon, for eight students from Avignon and the surrounding area. After chronic financial difficulties its remaining assets were transferred to the Collegio Gregoriano in 1436.

Sources: No statutes survive. For documents and references, Brizzi, p. 11; Piana, *Nuove ricerche*, pp. 405–18; idem, *Nuovi documenti sull'Università di Bologna e sul Collegio di Spagna* (Bologna, 1976), i. 169–70.

Collegio Bresciano

Founded in 1326 by Guglielmo Corvi da Brescia, doctor of medicine at Bologna and archdeacon, originally for eight scholars, to be increased to fifty, in arts, medicine and canon law. It was united to the Collegio Gregoriano in 1437.

Sources: P. Guerrini, 'Guglielmo da Brescia e il Collegio Bresciano in Bologna', *Studi e memorie per la storia dell'Università di Bologna*, VII (1922), 55–116, published the foundation documents including the college's statutes (1326, with additions of 1341; pp. 107–14). See also Piana, *Nuovi documenti*, pp. 170, 416, 609–10, 612; and Brizzi, pp. 14–15 for further references.

The will of the doctor of medicine Pancio da Controne of Lucca (June 1338) envisaged a college at Bologna for twelve students of his family, three each in grammar or arts, medicine, canon, and civil law. The college failed to materialize. A. Mancini, 'Emigrati italiani del Trecento', *Annali della Regia Scuola Superiore Normale di Pisa*, ser. ii, I (1932), 335–46 (the will is pp. 343–6), and see p. 35 above. Despite this publication the initiative has escaped the attention of Bolognese historians.

Collegio Fieschi

The history of this college, for Genoese students, can be followed from its re-foundation in 1508; it has only recently been appreciated that its origins lay in the will of Count Pepiniano Fieschi in 1361 (with codicil of 1364). That this was not entirely a dead letter is suggested by a solitary document of 1427 relating to the 'Collegii dominorum de Flisco in Bononia rector'. (Piana, *Nuovi documenti*, pp. 62–3).

Sources: Piana, loc. cit.; Pérez Martín, 'El Colegio Vives', pp. 124–5.

Collegio Reggiano

In 1362 Guido da Bagnolo, doctor of medicine, made provision for the distribution of funds for poor students from Reggio. In 1384 the estate of Gaspare Tacoli, also of Reggio, was added to this, and eventually the 'scholares de Regio' are referred to as 'collegiati et de Collegio regino' (1405). Piana, whose study of this is the most detailed to date, has reservations about classifying this as a college in the same sense as the other Bolognese foundations; there is no evidence as to its site, and some evidence that its scholars lived dispersed; in other words, it may have been a mechanism for distributing funds rather than an actual institution.

Sources: Piana, *Nuovi documenti*, pp. 170–1, 366–7, 430, 581–2; idem, *Nuove ricerche*, pp. 433–61.

Collegio di Spagna

Founded in 1364 by Cardinal Gil Albornoz, for twenty-four Iberian students (soon raised to thirty); see text for fuller history.

Sources: A substantial literature is available for this well-documented college. See esp. B. M. Marti, *The Spanish College at Bologna in the Fourteenth Century* (Philadelphia, Pa., 1966), with an edition and parallel translation of the statutes of 1375–77; Piana, *Nuovi documenti*, esp. pp. 62–153; idem, *Nuove ricerche*, pp. 338–85; and the many collected essays in E. Verdera y Tuells (ed.), *El Cardenal Albornoz y el Colegio de España*, 6 vols. (Bologna, 1972–79: Studia Albornotiana, vols. 11–13, 35–37). The students of the college have been studied by A. Pérez Martín, *Proles Aegidiana. Los colegiales desde 1368 a 1977*, 4 vols. (Bologna, 1979); vol. 1 for the fourteenth and fifteenth centuries and for a comprehensive introduction.

Collegio Urbaniano

Founded in 1364 by Pope Urban V, and probably incorporated into the Gregoriano at an early stage, the Urbaniano was rediscovered by Piana. Provision was made for twenty students, though by 1370 it was already down to fourteen.

Sources: Piana, *Nuovi documenti*, pp. 153–62; Brizzi, pp. 15–16.

Collegio Gregoriano

Along with the Collegio di Spagna, the major Bolognese foundation, instituted by Pope Gregory XI in 1370–1, with provision for thirty students and substantial endowment. The Gregoriano survived for eighty years; in 1451 Nicholas V gave its revenues (by then including those of the Avignonese and the Bresciano) to the Dominicans, and in 1452 it was suppressed (an attempt to revive it in 1452 appears to have been unsuccessful).

Sources: Piana, *Nuovi documenti*, pp. 162–9; idem, *Nuove ricerche*, pp. 385–405; Pérez Martín, 'El Colegio Vives', pp. 122–3; G. Zaoli, 'Lo Studio Bolognese e Papa Martino V', *Studi e Memorie per la Storia dell'Università di Bologna*, 3 (1912), 107–88, esp. pp. 122–34, and edn. of 1372 statutes pp. 163–88; *Chartularium Studii Bononiensis*, II (Bologna, 1913), 243–346 (1372 statutes pp. 289–313, collating two mss.), and IV (Bologna, 1919), 89–97.

In 1383 Cardinal **Pileo da Prata** set aside sums for the foundation of a college for 25 canonists in Bologna, which was still his intention in 1399, by which time his successful foundation, the Collegio Pratense at Padua, was already in operation. The bequest had to be overridden in 1407 by the Venetian authorities to allow the funds to be transferred to the Pratense. Fabris, 'Il Collegio Pratense' (see under Pratense), pp. 151–2, 155.

Collegio Ancarano

The will of the jurist Pietro d'Ancarano (12 October 1414) provided that, in the event of his sons not producing heirs, his estate should be used to found a college for eight law students 'paupers et dociles'. This eventually took place, and the college was in operation by 1442. The statutes were drawn up in 1464 (but have not survived). The college was active until its suppression in 1781.

Sources: Despite its longevity, no history of the college has been written. On what is known of its history to 1500, Brizzi, pp. 19 and 59–67 (with description of later archival holdings); Piana, *Nuove ricerche*, pp. 418–33; *Novi documenti*, pp. 171, 892–5.

A. V. Antonovics, 'The Library of Cardinal Domenico Capranica', in C. H. Clough (ed.), *Cultural Aspects of the Italian Renaissance. Essays in Honour of Paul Oskar Kristeller* (Manchester, 1976), pp. 141–59 (p. 148), claims that a college was founded at Bologna by Cardinal Niccolo Albergati. Albergati was charged by Pope Martin V to reform the Bolognese colleges (G. Zaoli, 'Lo Studio bolognese e papa Martino V (1416–20), *Studi e memorie per la storia dell'Università di Bologna*, 3 (1912), 107–88 (pp. 129–31)), but I know of no evidence that he attempted a foundation himself.

Similarly, the list of Bolognese university colleges should not include the **Collegio dei 10 chierici** or **Collegio Grassi**, listed by Pérez Martín ('El Colegio Vives', p. 124, as the college of 12 clerics), who garbles the story of its foundation. The will of Leon Battista Alberti (1472) left 1,000 ducats for the purchase of a house to enable two members of the Alberti family to study at Bologna. With the re-foundation of the University of Florence–Pisa the following year, and the prohibition of study elsewhere for Florentine citizens, the original intention became unrealizable. Alberti's will provided that if no students from the Alberti family presented themselves other poor students at Bologna could benefit, and so Alberti's Bolognese executor, Antonio Grassi, set in motion the foundation, making the necessary purchases (1473–74), taking over the patronage of the college, and drafting its statutes. Once his fellow executor, Niccolò Forteguerri, had died he changed his mind, and by 1478 had obtained a derogation of the will from Sixtus IV which made this sum over to a foundation for ten boys in service at the cathedral. (The political changes of the 1470s, and particularly the rift between Florence and the Papacy, must have facilitated this.) No more is known of the foundation's history. L. Ferrari, 'Il testamento di Leon Battista Alberti e la data della sua morte', in *Nozze Soldati-Manis, Firenze, il III agosto MCMXII* (Città di Castello, 1913), pp. 33–52; G.

Mancini, 'Il testamento di L.B.Alberti', *Archivio Storico Italiano*, LXXII (1914), II, pp. 20–52 (esp. pp. 23, 30–5); on the manuscript containing documents regarding its foundation and its statutes, *Catalogo della raccolta di statuti, consuetudini, leggi, decreti, ordini e privilegi dei comuni, delle associazioni e degli enti locali italiani, dal medioevo all fine del secolo XVII*, I (Rome, 1943), 211–12.

FLORENCE/PISA

In 1429 the banker **Niccolò da Uzzano** proposed the foundation of a college for forty or fifty students. One of the main reasons given was the fear of lack of discipline among students. Detailed plans and provisions were made, and building work begun, but the project languished and was never completed. The documents are published in A. Gherardi, *Statuti della Università e lo Studio Fiorentino* (Florence, 1881), pp. 210–15, 230–9; E. Spagnesi, *Utiliter edoceri. Atti inediti degli Ufficiali dello Studio fiorentino (1391–96)* (Milan, 1979), pp. 69 seq.; P. Denley, 'Academic Rivalry and Interchange: the Universities of Siena and Florence', in *Florence and Italy. Renaissance Studies in Honour of Nicolai Rubinstein*, eds. P. Denley and C. Elam (London, 1988), pp. 193–208 (pp. 202–3).

The revival of the *studio*, and its transfer to Pisa in 1473, eventually (1487) led to a fresh proposal for a college of law students. Construction began almost immediately but was halted at the death of Lorenzo de' Medici in 1492, and little was heard of it in the period to 1503. The Sapienza that eventually played such a key role in the sixteenth and seventeenth centuries was however developed out of this project. A. F. Verde, *Lo Studio fiorentino 1473–1503*, 4 vols. (Florence, 1973–85), iv. 655, 718–19, 793–4, 798, 807–10, 866, 902, 923–4, 1022, 1071–2, 1080; cf. Denley, loc cit.

PADUA

Despite intense scholarly interest in the University of Padua in the late middle ages, the many small colleges founded there have barely been studied; even the two most successful ones, the Pratense and the Tornacense, have been neglected despite the existence of archival material. The standard histories list the foundations with varying degrees of accuracy: esp. A. Gloria, *Monumenti della Università di Padova (1318–1405)* (Padua, 1888), I, 103–5; F. M. Colle, *Storia scientifico-letteraria dello studio di Padova*, 4 vols. (Padua, 1824–25), i. 107–14; J. Facciolati, *Fasti Gymnasii Patavini* (Padua, 1757), i. 18–19, 24–9; ii. 4, 82–5; A. Riccoboni, *De*

Gymnasio Patavino commentariorum libri sex (Padua, 1598), pp. 10–11; more recent summaries in L. Montobbio, *Splendore e utopia nella Padova dei Carraresi* (Padua, 1989), pp. 265–71. The Archivio Antico della Università, Padua (hereafter AAUP), has several volumes of documents relating to these colleges which none of these historians appear to have used (vols. 601–3, 607, 731).

Collegio Tornacense/Collegio Campioni

In 1363 Pietro Boatieri, a Bolognese lawyer, obtained permission from Francesco I da Carrara to use the possessions of Albizo Brancasecchi of Lucca, canon of S. Marie de Tournai, for the foundation of a college for six canonists. The statutes were drawn up and the college opened in 1366; its history appears to have been continuous throughout the period.

Sources: Montobbio, pp. 265–8; Gloria, p. 103; Colle, pp. 108–11, garbling the story of the foundation; Facciolati, i. 18–19. The 1366 statutes are in AAUP 602 (later copy); the 1429 statutes are in the Biblioteca Marciana, Venice, ms. Lat. XIV.288 (=4635), cc. 2r–27v. Further documents (later copies) in AAUP 602, n.c., 607 pp. 5–25, and 731 cc. 286r–316r, 323r–27r.

In 1363/4 **Francesco I Carrara** founded a college for twelve students of (civil?) law. Apart from a document of 1371 no more is heard of it. Montobbio, p. 265; Gloria, i. 103; ii. 86.

Collegio Campi

In 1369 Bartolomeo Campo, doctor of medicine, bequeathed possessions and revenues towards the college for students of arts and medicine proposed by Francesco Carrara, or, if that did not materialize, to provide for three or four scholars (who were also to be allowed to use his library). No further evidence about this attempted foundation has come to light. Colle thought that this and Francesco's own law college were merged into the Tornacense, but adduces no evidence.

Sources: Montobbio, p. 269; Gloria, i. 103; ii. 76.

Collegio di S. Caterina/Collegio Arquà/de Arquado

In 1385 Jacopo di Arquà, a doctor of medicine, left money to a variety of beneficiaries and expressed the hope that some sort of charitable foundation might ensue. In 1394 his heirs opened a college for medical students with the revenues from the estate (valued at 5,500 ducats), which apparently sufficed for ten scholars. The college survived into the early modern period, though little of its subsequent history is known.

Sources: P. Sambin, 'Il testamento del professore di medicina Giacomo da Arquà (Buda, 9 settembre 1385)', *Quaderni per la Storia dell'Università di Padova* 7 (1974), 73–7; Montobbio, pp. 269–70; Gloria, i. 104; ii. 289; Colle, p. 111 (on subsequent history as well); AAUP 602, n.c.; 607, pp. 41–4; 731, c. 20v; contemporary description in M. Savonarola, *Libellus de magnificis ornamentis regie civitatis Padue*, ed. A. Segarizzi, *Rerum Italicarum Scriptores*, n. ed., XXIV, xv (Città di Castello, 1902), 41.

Another famous doctor of arts and medicine, **Giacomo Zanetini**, stipulated in his will of 1391 that his house should be turned into a college for eight Padual or Trevisan students of arts and medicine; they were to receive 30 lire per annum as well as food, but once they had taken their degree and were launched in their careers they were obliged to give towards the dowries of poor girls. Again, the outcome of the project is unknown. Montobbio, p. 270; Gloria, i. 103; ii. 256.

Pietro Garfrano, a Cypriot merchant resident in Venice, left an endowment in 1393 for four Cypriot students, one in theology, one in law, two in medicine/arts, though in the event funds only ran to supporting two. Colle, pp. 112–13; AAUP, 731, cc. 65r–66v (copies of his will).

Collegio Pratense (also known at various stages as Collegio del Santo/dei Santi Girolamo e Prosdocimo di Padova/del Cardinale/dei Furlani)

The original foundation (1394) by Cardinal Pileo da Prata intended the college to be for ten poor students of canon law. In 1399 the number was raised to twenty, but two decades elapsed before we can be sure that it was operational. The first statutes were drawn up around 1430 by the Bishop of Padua, Paolo Donato. Thereafter its history is well-documented, with a number of revisions of its statutes. It was in continuous existence until 1945.

Sources: Brief history in G. Fabris 'Il Collegio Pratense', in *L'arte che rivive nella rivoluzione fascista nel ripristino del Collegio Pratense riscatto a sede della legione 'Patavina' M.V.S.N.* Supplemento de *Il Milite*, VI (1929), repr. in his *Scritti di arte e storia padovana*, intr. L. Lazzarini (Cittadella, 1977), pp. 151–71; publication of all the documents, including various redactions of the statutes, in the collection of essays and documents *Fondazione Collegio universitario Pratense, Padova* (Padua, 1960); contemporary description in Savolarola, *Libellus*, pp. 55–6; see also the standard Paduan sources (above).

Scholares Auximani

Andrea da Recanati, a medical doctor practising in Venice, in 1397 left money for four students in medicine or arts from Osimo, the town in the Marches that had subsidized his studies at Padua. Eventually these students, known as the 'scholares Auximani', seem to have acquired a residence if not actually formed themselves into a college. Colle, p. 114; AAUP 731, cc. 271r–75r (copies of his will).

Collegio da Rio/Ridium

In his will of 1398 Niccolò da Rio, another doctor of medicine, provided that, should his brother and heir Daniele, a doctor of law, die without sons, his estate should be used to found a college for six or more students in arts and medicine. Daniele's will (1405) repeated this, and the college eventually came into being, surviving into the nineteenth century.

Sources: Montobbio, pp. 270–1; Gloria, i. 104; ii. 330–1, 434; Colle, p. 114.

In 1400 the jurist **Ottonello Descalzi** left resources for the support of four poor law students to the tune of 25 lire each; the students were to be chosen by the rector of the Citramontanes, the prior of the college of doctors of law and the vicar of the bishop. Montobbio, p. 269; Gloria, i. 105; ii. 373.

Casa di Dio. A solitary document of 1405 mentions a 'collegii scolarium Domus Dei'. The *contrada* Casa di Dio was known for its law schoolrooms, but no more can be constructed out of this mysterious reference. Montobbio, p. 269; Gloria, i. 105; ii. 436.

A college for eight law students was envisaged by **Lodovico de' Curtosi**'s will of 1412, again virtually the only document to survive. Facciolati, ii. 4; AAUP, 731, c. 88r–v.

Collegio Spinelli

Belforte Spinelli, a law teacher at Padua, founded a college in 1439 for four arts students, two from Padua, one from Treviso and one *forestiero*.

Sources: AAUP, 731, cc. 254r–55r, 257r–58r; Riccoboni, p. 11.

Collegio Engleschi/di Pontecorvo

Plans for this college date from 1446, when the Florentine doctor of arts and medicine Francesco degli Engleschi left funds for a college for four poor students in arts and medicine. Ten years later another doctor of medicine, Stefano Dottori, whom Engleschi had appointed his executor in matters regarding the college, in turn made the college his heir.

Sources: AAUP, 731, cc. 108r–119r; Facciolati, ii. 82–3; on the role of Dottori, T. Pesenti Marangon, *Professori e promotori di medicina nello studio di Padova dal 1405 al 1509. Repertorio bio-bibliografico* (Padua, 1984), pp. 115–16.

Collegio Torrisani/Trevisano

In 1454 Taddeo de Adelmari of Treviso, another doctor of arts and medicine, made provision for eight students of theology. This is the only college of this period founded for theology students alone.

Sources: AAUP, 731, cc. 219r–25r; Facciolati, ii. 84–5.

PAVIA

B. Pagnin, 'Collegi universitari medievali' in *I Quattro Secoli del Collegio Borromeo di Pavia. Studi di Storia e d'Arte Pubblicati nel IV Centenario della Fondazione 1561–1961* (Milan, 1961) pp. 229–42 (esp. pp. 239–41), gives a useful survey; older ones are G. Vidari, *Frammenti cronistorici dell'Agro Ticinese*, 4 vols. (Pavia, 1891), iii. 61–117 (which abounds with inaccuracies), and *Memorie e documenti per la Storia dell'Università di Pavia*, II (1878), 65–76.

Collegio Castiglioni

Founded in 1429 by Cardinal Branda Castiglioni, the first Pavian college was intended to house 24 students in all subjects. In 1440 a chair of theology was established in the college.

Sources: A. L. Visintin, 'Il più significativo precedente del Collegio Ghislieri: il Collegio Universitario Castiglioni (1429–1803)', in *Il Collegio Universitario Ghislieri di Pavia*, I (Milan, 1966), 51–89; F. Zambelloni, 'Il Collegio Castiglioni, prima istituzione collegiale pavese', in *Il Collegio Ghislieri: 1567–1967* (Milan, 1967), pp. 211–16; R. Maiocchi, *Codice Diplomatico dell'Università di Pavia* (Pavia, 1905–15) II. 1, esp. pp. 251–61 (incl. summary of 1429 statutes), 319–20, 360–86 (incl. 1437 reforms), 391–2, 397–8, 404–6, 409–10; II.2, pp. 414–22, 428–30, 443–4, 446, 458–60, 463–6; *Memorie e documenti*, pp. 65–70; M. G. Albertini Ottolenghi, 'Il Collegio Castiglioni', in A. Peroni, M. G. Albertini Ottolenghi, D. Vicini and L. Giordano, *Pavia. Architetture dell'Età Sforzesca* (Turin, 1978), pp. 153–66.

Collegio Sacco

The eminent jurist Catone Sacco established a college for twelve students of law or theology in 1458; it is known to have been operational by 1482, but closed by 1525.

Sources: Z. Volta, 'Catone Sacco e il collegio di sua fondazione in Pavia', *Archivio Storico Lombardo*, ser. II, 8/18 (1891), pp. 562–600 (statutes published pp. 590–5).

Collegio Marliani

In 1475 the jurist Raimondo Marliani founded a college for twelve students in any subject, four of whom were to be ultramontanes. His will was contested by his heirs in 1481. Little is known about the college's fate.

Sources: Z. Volta, 'Del collegio universitario Marliani in Pavia', *Archivio Storico Lombardo*, ser. II, 9/19 (1892), pp. 590–628 (statutes published pp. 608–28).

Collegio Ferrari da Grado

The foundation of the doctor of medicine Gian Matteo Ferrari da Grado (1472) instituted a college for three members of his family studying medicine, theology or canon law. His books were left to the college. It was opened by 1487. In 1521 the bequest was transformed into scholarships.

Sources: B. Pagnin, 'Collegi universitari medievali', in *I Quattro Secoli del Collegio Borromeo di Pavia. Studi di Storia e d'Arte Pubblicati nel IV Centenario della Fondazione 1561–1961* (Milan, 1961), pp. 229–42 (p. 240); *Memorie e documenti*, p. 74.

Collegio Griffi

By his will of 4 Sept. 1489 Ambrogio Griffi, apostolic protonotary and a former student of medicine at Pavia, founded a college for eight students in arts, medicine or law, three from Varese, three from Milan and two from Lodi. Statutes were approved by Ludovico il Moro and Pope Alexander VI in 1496. The college was subsumed into the Castiglioni in 1770.

Sources: Pagnin, loc. cit.; *Memorie e documenti*, pp. 71–2 (excerpt of his will on p. 72).

Collegio Bossi

Apparently founded in 1499 by Polissena Bossi, widow of Matteo Bossi, a law teacher at the university of Pavia, this college had four places for arts students who were members of his numerous family.

Sources: Pagnin, loc. cit.; *Memorie e documenti*, p. 75.

At the end of the fifteenth century a senior functionary of the Sforza, **Bregonza Botta**, provided for a college in a series of wills (19 October 1489, 22 July 1496, and 24 October 1503). There is no trace of a college having been founded, to the extent that this attempt has escaped the literature on the university. E. Motta, 'Morti a Milano dal 1452 al 1552', *Archivio storico lombardo*, XVIII (1891), 241–86 (p. 285); *Dizionario biografico degli italiani*, 13, p. 364.

Of the **Collegio Dataro** all that is known is that it was founded by Lazzaro Dataro, a doctor of medicine. It appears to have closed temporarily in 1496, but reappears in documents of 1532. P. Vaccari, *Storia dell'Università di Pavia* (Pavia, 1957 edn.), p. 111; *Memorie e documenti*, p. 75; C. Magenta, *I Visconti e gli Sforza nel Castello di Pavia*, I (Milan, 1883), p. 579, n. 2.

PERUGIA

Collegio Gregoriano/Sapienza Vecchia

Founded by Cardinal Niccolò Capocci in 1360 (Mirella Sebastiani has shown this, not 1362, to be the date), the Sapienza Vecchia flourished for the rest of the middle ages, encouraging the Perugians to start a second college early in the fifteenth century. The statutes preceded those of the Collegio di Spagna and influenced them.

Sources: M. Sebastiani, 'Il collegio universitario di San Gregorio in Perugia detto la Sapienza Vecchia', unpublished *tesi di laurea*, Università degli Studi di Perugia, Facoltà di Lettere e Filosofia, Anno Accademico 1966–67; U. Nicolini, 'La "Domus Sancti Gregorii" o "Sapienza Vecchia" di Perugia. Il periodo delle origini', in D. Maffei and H. de Ridder-Symoens (eds.), *I collegi universitari in Europa tra il XIV e il XVIII secolo*. Atti del Convegno di Studi della Commissione internazionale per la storia delle Università, Siena-Bologna, 16–19 maggio 1988. Orbis Academicus, IV (Milan, 1991), pp. 47–52; idem, 'S. Giovanni da Capestrano studente e guidice a Perugia (1411–1414)', *Archivum Franciscanum Historicum*, LIII (1960), 39–77 (pp. 44–9); G. Ermini, *Storia dell'Università di Perugia*, 2 vols. (Florence, 1971 edn.), i. 394–8; Capocci's will in A. Ciaconius and A. Oldoino, *Vitae et res gestae Pontificum Romanorum et S.R.E. Cardinalium* (Rome, 1677), ii. 511–16; statutes in A. Rossi, 'Documenti per la Storia dell'Università di

Perugia', *Giornale di Erudizione Artistica*, VI (1877), 52–9, more recently and with later additions in Sebastiani, Appendice III, pp. 206–353.

Collegio Gerolimiano/Sapienza Nuova

Attempts to found a second Perugian college from 1425 at the instigation of Benedetto di Alberto Guidalotti, Bishop of Recanati. After much negotiation with the papacy, it opened in 1443 with forty scholars.

Sources: Ermini, i. 398–405; Giuliana Nardeschi, 'Le costituzioni della "Sapienza Nuova" dell'Anno 1443', unpublished *tesi di laurea*, Università degli Studi di Perugia, Facoltà di Magistero, Anno Accademico 1971–72.

1484 an attempt was made by Angelo Gherardini da Amelia, bishop of Suessa, to found a third college. Detailed arrangements were made and permissions granted, but the project does not seem to have yielded results. Ermini, i. 400, n. 164; P. Pellini, *Dell'historia di Perugia* (Bologna, 1664), pt. 2, p. 818; Archivio di Stato di Siena, *Concistoro*, 2056, n. 53 (1 Oct. 1484) (see above, p. 47).

ROME

Summary of Roman colleges in D. S. Chambers, 'Studium Urbis and the *Gabella Studii*, in C. H. Clough (ed.), *Cultural Aspects of the Italian Renaissance* (Manchester, 1976), pp. 68–110 (pp. 83–4).

In 1427 **Cardinal Branda Castiglioni** was authorized to set up a college and draft statutes. The project appears to have been abandoned when Castiglioni switched his attentions to Pavia, where two years later he founded the Collegio Castiglioni. R. Valentini, 'Gli istituti romani di alta cultura e la presunta crisi dello "Studium Urbis" (1370–1420)', *Archivio storico della Società romana di storia patria*, LIX (1936), 179–243 (pp. 212–15, 235–7).

Eugenius IV announced his intention to establish a college in 1433; nothing came of this (Chambers, p. 83).

Collegio Capranica

In 1456 Cardinal Domenico Capranica began the process of establishing a college which would occupy his palace after his death (1458). He drew up extremely detailed statutes, and left the college his extensive library. A feature of the college was its closeness to the university which was involved in its administration.

Sources: Summary in *Dictionnaire d'histoire et de géographie ecclésiastique*, 11, cols. 941–3; fuller discussion in M. Morpurgo-Castelnuovo, 'Il cardinale Domenico Capranica', *Archivio storico della Società romana di storia patria*, LII (1929), 1–142, esp. pp. 85–116, 137–42 (documents); statutes in Biblioteca Vaticana, MS Barb. Lat. 1625, pp. 1–82 (I have been unable to consult the 1705 edition cited in *Dictionnaire ... ecclésiastique*).

Collegio Nardini

In 1480 Cardinal Stefano Nardini, like Capranica, set aside part of his palace for a future college. This was established by his will of 1484, and by 1489 it had already been reformed. The college was for poor students of theology or canon law (students had daily to attend a lecture in each subject), though arts students who intended to progress to one of these subjects were also admitted. Nardini stipulated that the Collegio Capranica's statutes were to be adopted. The twenty places were, however, soon reduced to six, and the college was suppressed in the eighteenth century.

Sources: G. Zippel, 'Il palazzo del Governo Vecchio', *Capitolium*, VI.2 (1930), 366–8, 376; C. Marcora, 'Stefano Nardini Arcivescovo di Milano', *Memorie Storiche della diocesi di Milano*, III (1956), 257–488 (esp. pp. 325–7, and the will, published on pp. 349–52).

SIENA

Casa della Sapienza

The Sienese college was first proposed in 1388, and was created out of a declining hospital, the Casa della Misericordia, and its estates. It finally opened its doors to students in 1415. It was unique among the Italian colleges in being founded and exclusively controlled by the state, and was the second, after the Gregoriano at Perugia, to charge an admission fee. Competition for places was fierce, and this was used by the authorities for diplomatic purposes. The Sapienza became the main focus for the university, and the wealth of surviving records pertaining to it is unparalleled in Italy.

Sources: G. Catoni, 'Genesi e ordinamento della Sapienza di Siena', *Studi Senesi*, LXXXV (1973), 155–98 (publishing the foundation statutes, pp. 177–82); idem, 'Il comune di Siena e l'amministrazione della Sapienza nel sec. XV', in *Università e Società nei secoli XII–XVI*. Centro Italiano di Studi di Storia e d'Arte, Pistoia, Nono Convegno Internazionale, Pistoia, 20–25 settembre 1979 (Pistoia, 1982), pp. 121–9; P. Denley, 'The University of Siena, 1357–1557', unpublished D.Phil. thesis, Oxford, 1981; revised version *Commune and* studium *in Late Medieval and Early Renaissance Siena*. Saggi e Documenti per la Storia dell'Università di Siena, 2 (Milan, 1991, forthcoming).

In the 1480s and 1490s attempts were made to found a second Sapienza; land, permissions and funds were obtained and Siena's two most eminent architects, Giuliano da Sangallo and Francesco di Giorgio Martini, drew up plans for the building. The project was thwarted by the pan-Italian crisis of the 1490s. L. Zdekauer, *Lo Studio di Siena nel Rinascimento* (Milan, 1894, repr. Bologna, 1977), pp. 79–81; P. Denley, 'Academic Rivalry and Interchange: the Universities of Siena and Florence', in P. Denley and C. Elam (eds.), *Florence and Italy. Renaissance Studies in Honour of Nicolai Rubinstein.* (London, 1988), pp. 193–208 (pp. 202–3).

TURIN

Collegio Grassi

In 1457 Giovanni Grassi, a law teacher, founded a college or 'Sapienza' for four poor students.

Sources: E. Bellone, *Il primo secolo di vita della Università di Torino (sec. XV–XVI). Ricerche ed ipotesi sulla cultura nel Piemonte Quattrocentesco* (Turin, 1986), pp. 78–81; T. Vallauri, *Storia delle Università degli Studi del Piemonte* (Turin, 1845–46), pp. 318–25 prints the document of foundation.

In 1482 **Sixtus IV** planned a college for 24 students, but this does not appear to have materialized. Bellone, pp. 83, 85.

The Medieval Students of the University of Salamanca*

Antonio García y García

1. Introduction

The University of Salamanca has had a chequered history. The difficult early stage in the thirteenth and fourteenth centuries (1218/1219–1380) gave way to a period of consolidation, beginning at the end of the fourteenth century and running until the end of the Middle Ages (1381–1500). This was followed by the golden age of the University in the sixteenth century when its numbers and reputation were at a height. The University later experienced gradual but irregular decline until the first half of the twentieth century, when it again grew in importance. These vicissitudes notwithstanding, it was the foremost of the Spanish universities until the end of the ancien régime. This article only discusses the University during the late middle ages, from its foundation until the latter part of the reign of the Catholic King and Queen, Ferdinand and Isabella.

The University, established in the winter of 1218–19, found its first patron and author of its first statutes (1254) in King Alphonso X (1252–84). The protection of the Crown was also evident during the reigns of John II of Castile (1406–54) and of the Catholic King and Queen (1474–1516). Amongst Popes noted for their protection of Salamanca were Benedict XIII and Martin V. The former in 1381 as cardinal legate gave the University a set of statutes, which have not survived, but which formed the basis for others which he gave as Pope in 1411. Martin V was author of the statutes of 1422, which remained in effect until the early modern period was well advanced. The local Salamancan church contributed to the University in several ways. Besides helping to provide buildings and personnel, it endowed the University with a third of the tithes of the diocese of Salamanca, which were applied towards the payment of the teaching staff. In addition to the above, the late medieval University had other benefactors of lesser importance whose assistance is recorded in University documents.[1]

On the basis of the available documentation, I shall attempt to determine the geographical background of the students who came to Salamanca in the late middle ages and whether their extraction was from the nobility, the bourgeoisie, or the poorer classes. I shall also discuss briefly the sources of funding for university studies as well as the distribution of the students amongst the various faculties.

No general work on the University of Salamanca in the late medieval period which uses modern historical methods exists. A first attempt to provide such a study is to be found in the two chapters on this subject in the first volume of the new *Historia de la Universidad de Salamanca*.[2] The reader is referred to these two chapters for a detailed account of the historical background to the present article, as well as for information about the rather scant existing bibliography on the medieval period of the University of Salamanca.

In an attempt to organize the available information, I shall distinguish between the difficult early period of the University of Salamanca from its foundation in the winter of 1218–19 to 1380, and the period of consolidation, from 1380 to 1500. The dates are approximate.

2. The Difficult Early Period: from the Foundation to 1380

The source material for the history of the University of Salamanca in the late middle ages provides no direct information on the students of the thirteenth century nor those of the first forty years of the fourteenth; thus we are unable today to determine their total numbers, social origin, sources of financing, or any other details other than those which may be inferred from the existing information from the end of the first half of the fourteenth century, assumptions which would be unreliable. In the author's opinion, all that can be assumed retrospectively is that nearly all the scholars were clerics, for the most part canon lawyers, and to a much lesser extent students of civil law, and that secular clergy financed their studies principally by means of ecclesiastical benefices, while members of the regular clergy were provided for by the order to which they belonged.

Such official and private books as may have existed for the fourteenth century in which were recorded the names of scholars of the University of Salamanca have now been lost. This unfortunate gap can only be overcome, albeit very inadequately, using the documents contained in the *Bulario* and *Cartulario* of the University. For the period 1343–80 there are fifty-one references to students in about fifty documents, corresponding in all to thirty-five scholars. However some of these were studying in more than one faculty; hence the presence of fifty-one entries in Table I (see Appendix below). These documents provide information about the students' diocese of origin, to what category of the clergy they belonged, whether they were bachelors or students who had not yet obtained this degree, the faculty in which they studied (although this information is frequently omitted) and the benefices for which they were applying (where this is the case). It is evident that nearly all were clerics bound for the Church. Admittedly, according to contemporary canon law, applicants for ecclesiastical benefices need only to have been tonsured and were not necessarily destined for a career in the clergy. But in this case it must be stressed that students who appear for the first time in a document as clerics continue to appear as such in later *acta*, even in those sometimes written several years afterwards. In fact there are only two laymen to whom reference is made at all in these documents. One was the physician to the King of Navarre, Angel de Costefort, who graduated from Salamanca in 1362, having been financed by a donation from his King, Carlos III, amounting to 73 *libras*, 19 *sueldos* and 11 *dineros carlines*.[3] The other was not a student but a doctor of both canon and civil law called Juan Alfonso, who asked that he and his wife might choose a confessor *in articulo mortis*. Obviously, the fact that all but two of the thirty-five scholars discussed here were bound for the Church does not give much indication about the number of lay students who may have attended Salamanca contemporaneously.

It has been affirmed that in respect to thirteenth and fourteenth century Bologna,[4] most of the scholars were clerics and that amongst these the predominant group held canonries. At Salamanca the proportion of clerics was probably greater than at Bologna. Of the thirty-five members of the University discussed here, eighteen were canons, thirteen are described simply as clerics, one was a priest, and one a deacon. One thing seems clear from this documentation: those who were not canons wished to be so, and those who were often aspired to another or other subsequent canonries. Interestingly in this period, there was no monk or member of the regular clergy who asked for or received an ecclesiastical benefice, which was not the case in the following period. The only student who was a member of the regular clergy in these registers was the Navarran Franciscan Pedro de Isaba, who in 1355 received 12 *libras* from the Infante Luis of Navarre, brother of King Carlos II the Bad, to attend the 'schools of Salamanca'.[5]

To interpret correctly this information, it is necessary to point out that in most cases the sources reveal that the students were studying at the University at the moment the document was written. In some cases, however, the students seem to have studied prior to this date so that it is likely that some became canons after leaving the University. In the case of several students, the relevant document does not say that they had studied at Salamanca at all, simply that the University of Salamanca requests ecclesiastical benefices for them. It can only be assumed they were or had been students of Salamanca. There are also two cases in which enrolment at Salamanca was based only on the fact that those involved were important personages who had established foundations for students at Salamanca.

Finally, it must be asked what can be known about the average total attendance at Salamanca in this period 1343–80 for which there is only specific information about thirty-five students. Again, there is no direct evidence of the total number of students. But a register of 1378 does exist[6] in which the person in charge of the school of the *Decretals* states that in them 'at least 200 scholars' could be seated, which allows us legitimately to suppose that there was another hall of the same capacity for the schools of the *Decretum* (The *Decretals* of Gregory IX and the *Decretum* of Gratian were the chief texts read in the faculty of canon law.) Table I (although obviously biased towards clerics) suggests that canonists far outnumbered civilians. Supposing that the latter did not exceed one hundred, it would seem that in 1378, the number of canon- and civil-law students was about 500. Table I also suggests that the number of scholars who studied in the other faculties (theology, arts and medicine) was much lower too. In all, the scholars must have numbered about 1,000 at most. Such a relatively small total number of students *c.* 1378 allows us to suppose that the number must have been much smaller in the thirteenth century, about which, as mentioned above, we have no sources at all.

In the period 1347–80, it should be said, total attendance may have fluctuated wildly. At different times during this century Castile was subject to plague, drought, and bad harvests. To what extent these factors have affected attendance, however, cannot be ascertained.

In the documentation no mention at all is made of the social origin of the students identified. We can only presume they were mainly from the bourgeoisie, as was the general tendency of the time, and as can be observed in the following period at Salamanca for which the documentation reveals the existence of a mere handful of poor students and nobles, implying that the rest were drawn from the middle classes. Certainly there can have been few poor students at the University at the time. One way of assisting such students was through the provision of free accommodation in hostels and university colleges. These institutions appeared late at Salamanca compared with their date of introduction in the universities of France and England. In Salamanca in this period only a few of these institutions were created, such as the hostels for sixteen scholars of canon and civil law, whose establishment in Salamanca was undertaken in 1364 by a canon of Burgos, Alfonso Pérez.[7] Pérez was a great collector of ecclesiastical benefices, some of which even gave rise to litigation over their rightful ownership. As compensation he was required to establish the aforementioned hostel, although we do not know if it ever opened its doors.

3. Period of Consolidation of the University of Salamanca, 1381–1500

The University of Salamanca grew in importance from the 1380s, principally due to the protection given by Benedict XIII, especially after his dispute with the University of Paris. In addition to the two sets of statutes he gave to the University of Salamanca mentioned above, Pope Luna also granted the University's request in 1403 that 318 of its members be given ecclesiastical benefices (Table VI). In addition, he was responsible for the organization and consolidation of the theology faculty, which had hitherto been operating in the

Dominican and Franciscan convents of Salamanca, and only in the University itself on an impermanent basis. While we are uncertain of the date that the theology faculty was first established, Benedict XIII's reorganization dates from 1395–96. To achieve this, he took maximum advantage of the material and intellectual resources of the two great mendicant orders, the Franciscans and the Dominicans. He created five chairs, three in the University and two in the Dominican and Franciscan convents of St Steven and St Francis, whose standards were recognized to be high. At the same time the cathedral chapter was affiliated to the theology faculty on the same terms as the mendicant orders. These measures produced a larger influx of students wishing to study theology at Salamanca, and throughout the fifteenth century teachers emerged, not only of local but worldwide importance, such as Juan de Segovia, Juan Alfonso de Mella, Alonso de Madrigal and others.

The other faculties also improved in quality and expanded in numbers of students, but they did not attain the standard of the two law and theology faculties.

The special protection of Juan II of Castile and above all the Catholic King and Queen was also very influential in consolidating and strengthening the University after 1380.

This is the context in which to view the comments made below on the students of the University of Salamanca during this second period of consolidation which precedes the University Salamanca's golden age in the sixteenth century.

A few years after the outbreak of the papal schism the University of Salamanca sent a *rotulus* to the Avignon Pope, Clement VII, soliciting ecclesiastical benefices and, exceptionally, spiritual graces or dispensations for the University's professors and especially its students. The *rotulus* was accepted by the Pope on 29–31 October 1381. This was the first known occasion on which a Pope granted a large number of ecclesiastical benefices (to several hundred fortunate people) at the request of the University of Salamanca (see Table II). There were doubtless two reasons for this concession: Salamanca and the kingdom of Castile were already of considerable importance in the academic world and in contemporary Christian politics; in addition, the Avignon Pope needed the support of the universities, which easily could transfer their obedience from Avignon to Rome, or back again if they did not receive special treatment when this was demanded.

Scholars on the *rotulus* came from nearly every diocese of the two kingdoms of Castile and Portugal. But no student came from Navarre. This had not been the case among the groups of scholars identified from the period 1343 to 1380 which, as mentioned above, include a layman and a Franciscan from the kingdom of Navarre, if admittedly both were maintained by the royal family of the kingdom.

Apart from the diocesan clerics, a Benedictine from the Monastery of Samos (diocese of Lugo) appears in the 1381 *rotulus*, who asked to be appointed a prior in Santiago or Braga. The faculty in which he studied is not supplied.[8] Conversely, there is a cleric from the diocese of León who aspired to a benefice whose collation was in the hands of the monks of the monastery of Sahagún.[9]

Of the students on the 1381 *rotulus*, several were bachelors and of these, some were recruited as teachers. Admittedly, to obtain a bachelor's degree a period of teaching was obligatory for experience in 'reading' or 'teaching' formed part of the *curriculum studiorum*. In these cases, however, it would appear that the bachelors occupied paid teaching positions, which was, in principle, against the statutes, since such teachers were required to be licentiates or doctors. Presumably, the shortage of qualified teachers led to this lowering of the statutory requirements. On this *rotulus* benefices were also requested for eight doctors or masters: for a Franciscan doctor of theology, four doctors in canon law, one in civil law and two in music.[10] Music, at this point, did not constitute a faculty, but was rather a unique discipline taught in the *schola cantus*.[11] However, no scholar appears in the *rotulus* who claimed to be studying music. On the other hand, one of the music masters was definitely at the same time a scholar of canon law.[12] But studying in two faculties or teaching in one and studying simultaneously in another was a relatively common occurrence in Salamanca.[13]

This *rotulus* contains little indication of the social background of the scholars. Social class is only denoted in the case of noblemen, of whom eleven are mentioned, amongst others, Gonzalo Gómez de Aguiar, son of Prince Fernando, in turn son of the King of Castile, Enrique II.[14] On the other hand, another student is said to have been the son of the beadle of the University,[15] who presumably was not a nobleman, but who none the less was an influential person in the university corporation.[16]

Although there is no specific evidence to support this, it can be supposed that the remaining students were drawn from the bourgeoisie. In other *rotuli* of this kind there is specific mention of poorer students, their poverty stated as being the reason for requiring the benefice solicited. In the 1381 *rotulus*, however, no one claims poverty as an excuse.

Thirty-three students appear in a second *rotulus* of 13 October 1392. In it are listed benefices or graces sought for scholars belonging to ten dioceses all within the kingdom of Castile. In addition to the bachelors and simple students, only one doctor (of law) appears in this *rotulus*. His presence has not been recorded in Table III. One of the students held the position of university *consiliarius* that year.[17]

More interesting than the *rotulus* of 13 October 1392 for purposes of this discussion is the *rotulus* of 9 August 1393, by means of which the same Avignon Pope Clement VII granted benefices to 113 Salamancan scholars from twenty-three dioceses of the kingdom of Castile as well as to a monk from the monastery of Santo Domingo de Silos (diocese of Burgos) who studied canon law (see Table IV). Seventeen were bachelors of canon law and eight of civil law; eleven were students of civil law, one of arts, and one of theology; in the case of thirty-four their faculty is unknown.

Examination of the evidence also shows that just as most of the students were studying law, so most of the professors soliciting benefices were lawyers. Benefices were solicited for three doctors in civil law, three in canon law, one licentiate *in utroque iure* who was also a bachelor of arts, two licentiates in canon law, and one licentiate in canon law who was also a student in civil law. It seems odd that no teacher of theology appears; this is undoubtedly due to the fact that these teachers usually were members of mendicant orders, who rarely solicited ecclesiastical benefices. We do not know if the teachers in medicine of this date were laymen and hence excluded from soliciting for benefices. Indeed, we do not even know if the faculty had a significant number of students in this period, albeit far fewer than the number of students in the law faculties and the theology faculty.

A student who 'per septennium in Studio Salamantino scholas grammaticales tanquam bachalarius rexit'[18] is also mentioned, as is another who had similarly taught for seven years in the grammar schools. In this second case there is no indication of the supplicant's current teaching position or any other activity.[19]

As regards the information on social extraction, the *rotulus* lists the son of the nobleman, Arnaldo Bonal (doctor of decrees),[20] a son of a military man,[21] and the son of Antonio Sánchez, doctor of canon law and *auditor* of the King of Castile.[22]

A fourth *rotulus* exists dated 16–17 October 1403 presented to the pope by the Bishop of Niza and soliciting benefices for thirty-three members of the University of Salamanca (see Table V). It does not appear to have been granted, perhaps because Benedict XIII was about to accept another *rotulus* of 318 scholars only a few days later. In addition to the students from the twelve dioceses of the kingdom of Castile this list contains the name of a Frenchman from the diocese of Oloron, who was a student of canon law. Distributed according to faculty, this *rotulus* contains the names of two BAs, three bachelors of canon law, and two in civil law, plus two students in arts, twenty-three in canon law, and one in civil law.

The second largest surviving *rotulus* of all is that granted by Benedict XIII on 19–23 October 1403 (see Table VI). In it appear the names of 318 scholars, plus the names of those who appear as teachers (one doctor of civil law, another of canon law, and a licentiate of civil law). Another teacher, a Toledan cleric, is also mentioned, who was responsible for the 'cathedra cantus' and was studying canon law.[23]

These 318 students were drawn from twenty-seven dioceses of the kingdom of Castile and from three French dioceses (two from Mende and one from Oloron). From the kingdom of Aragon, there were only two scholars from the diocese of Saragossa. Significantly, no Portuguese is recorded, undoubtedly because the Portuguese kingdom had refused obedience to Pope Luna. There also appear three members of the Third Order of Saint Francis and a canon regular from the collegiate church of San Isidro de León.

Amongst these scholars, two are listed as belonging to the nobility[24] and one as a military man.[25]

By faculty, in descending order of numerical importance, there were 102 whose faculty is unknown, twenty-three bachelors and ninety-eight students in canon law, ten bachelors and twenty students in civil law, fifty-seven students in arts, seven in theology, and a single BA. There was also a bachelor in *utroque iure*[26] and a bachelor in both canon law and arts.[27] One of these students was *consiliarius* of the University[28] and another its syndic.[29]

During this period three university colleges were founded: one of the five *colegios mayores* (the *Colegio de San Bartolomé*) and two of 'minor' ones (the *Colegio Viejo de Oviedo*, known vulgarly as 'Bread and Coal', and the college of the Archbishop of Toledo, Alfonso Carrillo). It must be emphasized that the terms *colegio mayor* and *colegio minor* refer to a later period. There was no difference in legal structure between the two types of college, only a difference of importance. Eventually, there were six *colegios mayores* in the Spanish university system, of which four belonged to the University of Salamanca. The *Colegio de San Bartolomé* was the only one founded in the middle ages.

These three colleges were founded for poor scholars, as is indicated by the very title of the first statutes of the *Colegio de Oviedo: Ordinatio Collegii pauperum scholarium civitatis Salmantinae*. This college was founded by Gutierre de Toledo in 1381, who drew up some preliminary statutes to enable it to open, the title of which is transcribed above. The definitive statutes date from 1386 and were amended in the seventeenth century. In the founder's *Ordinatio*, it was set out that the college was established for six poor scholars to study canon law, to be chosen from the candidates from the diocese of Oviedo. Should there be an insufficient number of these, then candidates from the dioceses of Toledo and Palencia could be elected instead.[30]

The minor Salamancan college founded in 1479 by Archbishop Alfonso Carrillo de Acuña offered twelve places for students from the Archbishopric of Toledo or from other dioceses if there was an insufficient number of candidates. The scholars were required to study either in the faculties of theology or canon law.[31]

The first statutes of the *Colegio de San Bartolomé* were drafted in 1414–16. They were adapted from the statutes of the *Colegio de San Clemente de los Españoles* established at the University of Bologna. San Bartolomé's founder was Diego de Anaya y Maldonado, then Bishop of Cuenca, hence the name also given to the college, *Colegio de Cuenca*. The founder later became Bishop of Salamanca and subsequently Archbishop of Seville. The college was intended to provide places for fifteen poor scholars drawn only from the kingdom of Castile, of which five were to study theology and ten canon law. The statutes of 1414–16 were drafted definitively in 1435, amended in 1437, then amended further on other occasions.[32]

Undoubtedly, the preference given to students of canon law in filling the places in these colleges only reinforced the numerical dominance of the faculty of canon law, which almost certainly existed from the university's inception. It is also one of the reasons why attendance in the faculty continued to increase during the sixteenth century while in other countries the number of canonists fell in relation to the numbers studying civil law or other subjects of greater interest.

4. Conclusion

The papal *rotuli* of requests or collective petitions for ecclesiastical benefices for poor students are an important source for medieval university history, despite their limitations, especially in the period of the Avignon popes, who tried to attract supporters thereby. The chief country to benefit from this rich manna was France. Castilians benefited in their hundreds from papal munificence during the Great Schism, but Frenchmen were rewarded in their thousands. In 1378 French universities presented Pope Clement VII with a total figure of 4,788 requests for benefices for students. In 1403, they sought 4,478 benefices from Pope Benedict XIII.[33] The largest *rotulus* of graces for Salamanca benefited only slightly more than 300 students; over the epoch of the Great Schism only 825 Salamancan students are known to have sought papal aid.

Obviously, the *rotuli* of requests say relatively little about the total student population at the date of their presentation. Not all students had the qualifications that permitted them to be included in the list of petitioners. Fortunately for Salamanca we have another apparently insignificant but actually quite important source from which to determine the total number of students in 1378, as we have already seen. Working from information about the capacity of the lecture hall for students of canon law following a course on the *Decretals*, we have estimated that at this date there were some 1,000 students at Salamanca. This figure, high for a Castilian or any other Iberian university in the period, was modest compared with many contemporary Italian, French, and English universities.[34] Clearly, too, the collegiate provision at Salamanca was meagre compared with the great universities of northern Europe. In both respects, moreover, the University of

Salamanca at the turn of the fifteenth century was in no way comparable with its successor in the reign of Philip II. At its zenith in the late sixteenth century Salamanca enrolled 5,000, not 1,000, students per annum and boasted fifty colleges, not three.[35]

Facultad de Derecho Canónico
Apartado 541
Universidad Pontificia de Salamanca
37000 Salamanca
Spain

REFERENCES

*Translated from Spanish by Kathy Ross Landazabal.

1. V. Beltrán de Heredia, *Bulario de la Universidad de Salamanca* vol. I (Salamanca, 1966): hereinafter cited as BUS; idem, *Cartulario de la Universidad de Salamanca* vol. I (Salamanca, 1970): hereinafter CUS.
2. Various authors, *Historia de la Universidad de Salamanca* (3 vols., Salamanca, 1989–90), i. 13–34 'Los difíciles inicios (Siglos XIII–XV)' and 35–48 'Consolidaciones del s. XV': hereinafter HUS.
3. CUS, i. 639, no. 59.
4. S. Stelling-Michaud, *L'Université de Bologna et la pénétration des droits romain et canonique en Suisse aux XIIIe et XIVe siècles* (Geneva, 1955), pp. 130–1.
5. CUS, i. 637, no. 56.
6. CUS, i. 646–7, no. 71.
7. BUS, i. 393–4, no. 109, and BUS, i. 396–7, no. 113.
8. BUS, i. 439, no. 70. A similar case is found in BUS, i. 442, no. 147.
9. BUS, i. 451, no. 327.
10. BUS, i. 434–5, nos. 4–8.
11. BUS, i. 441 and 443, nos. 132 and 161. Cf. BUS, i. 568, no. 33.
12. BUS, i. 443, no. 161.
13. BUS, i. 442–3, nos. 148, 161, 166, etc.
14. BUS, i. 441, no. 117.
15. BUS, i. 443, no. 159.
16. See the chapters cited in HUS, note 2 above.
17. BUS, i. 491, no. 7. For this office see the chs. cited in HUS, note 2 above.
18. BUS, i. 504, no. 104.
19. BUS, i. 504, no. 98.
20. BUS, i. 501, no. 45.
21. BUS, i. 501, no. 46.
22. BUS, i. 501, no. 47.

23. BUS, i. 568, no. 33.
24. BUS, i. 567, no. 11; BUS, i. 580, no. 279.
25. BUS, i. 573, no. 121.
26. BUS, i. 567, no. 5.
27. Ibid., no. 14.
28. Ibid., no. 9.
29. Ibid., no. 10.
30. L. Sala Balust, *Constituciones, estatutos y ceremonias de los antiguos colegios seculares de la Universidad de Salamanca* vol. I (Madrid, 1962), pp. 73–7.
31. Ibid., pp. 95–104.
32. Ibid., vol. 3 (Madrid, 1964), pp. 7–194.
33. J. Verger, *Les Universités au moyen âge* (Paris, 1973), pp. 124–5.
34. See esp. T. H. Aston, 'Oxford's Medieval Alumni', *Past and Present* 74 (1977), 6–10; G. D. Duncan and T. A. R. Evans, 'The Medieval Alumni of the University of Cambridge', *Past and Present* 86 (1980), 35, 74–5.
35. L. E. Rodríguez San Pedro Bezares, *La Universidad Salmantina del Barroco. Periodo 1598–1625* 3 vols. (Salamanca, 1986).

Appendix

The following tables contain the most important information about the six lists of students analysed above. They are followed by a final table which summarizes the content of its six predecessors. The abbreviations used are: A = Faculty of Arts; C = Faculty of Canon Law; L = Faculty of Civil Law; T = Faculty of Theology; M = Faculty of Medicine; ? = faculty unknown.

I. Students of the University of Salamanca from 1343 to 1380

Diocese	*Bachelors*						*Students*						*Total*
	A	C	L	T	M	?	A	C	L	T	M	?	
Astorga	1	1	1										3
Burgos		4						1				1	6
Coimbra				1									1
Cuenca								1				4	5
León		1											1
Lugo							1						1
Mondoñedo												4	4
Osma							1						1
Oviedo												1	1
Palencia												1	1
Pamplona					1								1
Salamanca			1					4				1	6
Santiago								1					1
Seville		1											1
Toledo		1										5	6
Tuy							1					1	2
Religious				2									2
Unknown		4	4										8
Total	1	12	6	3	1		3	7				18	51

II. *Rotulus* of Clement VII for the University of Salamanca, 29–31 May 1381

Diocese	*Bachelors*						*Students*						*Total*
	A	C	L	T	M	?	A	C	L	T	M	?	
Astorga		1						2	1				4
Avila							4	5		2		5	16
Badajoz												1	1
Braga							1					1	2
Burgos	1	3					6	14				8	32
Calahorra							4	21		1			26
Ciudad Rodrigo								2	1			2	5
Coimbra		1							1				2
Córdoba							4	6				8	18
Cuenca								5	1			3	9
Evora							1	1	1				3
Jaén		1						1					2
León		1					10	7	4			3	25
Lisbon									1				1
Lugo		1					1	2				2	6
Mondoñedo								3					3
Orense							1	2					3
Osma							2	2				2	6
Oviedo								1	3				4
Palencia		1					9	13	2			7	32
Plasencia												2	2
Porto												1	1
Salamanca	1	1	1				11	11	3			5	33

II. *Rotulus* of Clement VII for the University of Salamanca, 29–31 May 1381

Diocese	*Bachelors*						*Students*						*Total*
	A	C	L	T	M	?	A	C	L	T	M	?	
Santiago		2					5	11				1	19
Segovia							1	2				1	4
Seville							4	1				3	8
Sigüenza							3	1					4
Tarazona		1											1
Toledo							6	13				3	22
Tuy								2					2
Zamora							6	14				1	21
Religious												1	1
Origin Unknown		1					3	3	1			2	10
Total	2	14	1				82	145	19	3		62	328

III. *Rotulus* of Clement VII for the University of Salamanca, 12 October 1392

Diocese	*Bachelors*						*Students*						*Total*
	A	C	L	T	M	?	A	C	L	T	M	?	
Avila		3						2	2			1	8
Burgos			1					1				1	3
Lugo								1					1
Osma		1											1
Oviedo			1					1				1	3
Palencia			1					1	1				3
Santiago								2				2	4
Segovia		1							2			3	6
Toledo		1	1									1	3
Zamora								1					1
Total		6	4					9	5			9	33

IV. *Rotulus* of Clement VII for the University of Salamanca, 9 August 1393

Diocese	*Bachelors*						*Students*						*Total*
	A	C	L	T	M	?	A	C	L	T	M	?	
Avila		1						2	1			4	8
Burgos								4				3	7
Cádiz								2					2
Calahorra								1				1	2
Córdoba								3					3
Coria												1	1
Cuenca			3					4	1				8
Jaén		1								1			2
León	1	2						3				1	7
Lugo												1	1
Majorca												1	1
Mondoñedo		1											1
Osma		3						1					4
Palencia			2					5				2	9
Plasencia			1						1			1	3
Salamanca	1							4	3			7	15
Santiago								1				4	5
Segovia								4					4
Seville								1	1				2
Sigüenza							1	1.				1	3
Toledo		8	2						3			4	17
Tuy												1	1
Zamora		1						3	1				5
Religious												1	1
Origin Unknown												1	1

V. *Rotulus* for the Benefit of the University of Salamanca, addressed to Benedict XIII, 16–17 October 1403

Diocese	*Bachelors*						*Students*						*Total*
	A	C	L	T	M	?	A	C	L	T	M	?	
Avila			1				1	1					3
Badajoz	1							1					2
Burgos	1							2					3
Córdoba									1				1
León								5					5
Orense		1											1
Oloron								1					1
Osma		1						1					2
Palencia		1						1					2
Plasencia								1					1
Salamanca			1				1	5					7
Seville								3					3
Sigüenza								2					2
Total	2	3	2				2	23	1				33

VI. *Rotulus* of Benedict XIII for the University of Salamanca, 19–23 October 1403

Diocese	*Bachelors*						*Students*						*Total*
	A	C	L	T	M	?	A	C	L	T	M	?	
Astorga		1					1	1				8	11
Avila		1	3				10	7	4	1		4	30
Badajoz							1	1					2
Burgos	1	2					4	8	2	2		8	27
Calahorra							4	6				2	12
Cartagena								1					1
Ciudad Rodrigo							1	1	1				3
Córdoba		1					1						2
Coria							2					3	5
Cuenca								6	1			3	10
Jaén								1					1
León			3				6	9	1	1		6	26
Lugo							2						2

Oloron					1				1
Orense		1		1	3			3	8
Osma		1						2	3
Oviedo		2		3	9		1	1	16
Palencia		2		3	8			4	17
Plasencia					1				1
Salamanca		2	3	8	11	2	1	25	52
Santiago		2			7			8	17
Segovia		1			1			5	7
Seville		3		1		6		8	18
Sigüenza		1			4			3	8
Toledo		2	1	5	1	1		4	14
Tuy					2			2	4
Zamora				2	3	1		2	8
Saragossa				1	1				2
Religious					3		1		4
Origin Unknown					1	1			2
Total	1	23	10	57	98	20	7	102	318

VII. Summary

Diocese	*Bachelors*						*Students*						*Total*
	A	C	L	T	M	?	A	C	L	T	M	?	
Astorga	1	3	1				1	3	1			8	18
Avila		5	4				15	17	7	3		14	65
Badajoz	1						1	2				1	5
Braga							1					1	2
Burgos	3	9	1				10	30	2	2		21	78
Cádiz								2					2
Calahorra							8	28		1		3	40
Cartagena								1					1
Ciudad Rodrigo							1	3	2			2	8
Coimbra		1		1					1				3
Córdoba		1					5	9	1			8	24
Coria							2					4	6
Cuenca			3					10	2			7	22
Evora							1	1	1				3
Jaén		2						2		1			5
León	1	4	3				16	24	5	1		10	64
Lisboa									1				1
Lugo		1					4	3				3	11

Mondoñedo		1				1	4			4	10
Oloron							2				2
Orense		2				2	5			3	12
Osma		6				3	4			4	17
Oviedo		2	1			3	11	3	1	3	24
Palencia		4	3			12	28	3		14	64
Pamplona					1						1
Plasencia			1				2	1		3	7
Porto										1	1
Salamanca	2	3	6			20	35	8	1	38	113
Santiago		4				5	22			15	46
Segovia		2				1	7	2		9	21
Sevilla		4				5	5	7		11	32
Sigüenza		1				4	8			4	17
Tarazona		1									1
Toledo		12	4			11	14	4		17	62
Tuy						1	4			4	9
Zamora		1				8	21	2		3	35
Zaragoza						1	1				2
Religiosos				2			3		1	2	8
Origin unknown		5	4			3	4	2		3	21
Total	8	75	31	3	1	145	315	55	11	222	866

The University of Prague, Czech Latin Schools, and Social Mobility 1570–1620

Jiří Pešek

The last decades of the sixteenth century and the early ones of the seventeenth century are usually treated as an inglorious period in the history of Prague University. It is often argued—mainly on the basis of nineteenth century historiography—that the instruction provided paid little attention to the practical needs of early-modern society and to contemporary progress in the natural sciences. The University, it is claimed, played no part in the generation of novel ideas and concepts and its curriculum and organization remained wedded to a medieval tradition. The list of charges could go on. But it is advisable to raise the question whether these charges are justified or whether they are anachronistic in light of the historical role of the University in the decades before the outbreak of the Thirty Years War. Most of these charges might also be levelled against other universities and academies in neighbouring countries of the time, whose structures resembled those of Bohemia and where the role of institutions of higher education was similar. We should rather consider the performance of the University and the municipal Latin schools with which it was closely associated from the position of what people at the time expected of higher education. The present paper concentrates on one aspect of the social history of the University during this period: the career opportunities for the University's graduates who came from relatively humble backgrounds.

Until the 1960s we had only a superficial knowledge of the social composition and career orientation of graduates from the Protestant University of Prague in the last third of the sixteenth and the beginning of the seventeenth centuries.[1] This knowledge was based on generalizations from individual cases and small local samples. The loss of the old University register of matriculands and graduates, the lack of supplementary sources, and above all the apodictic status of the opinions of nineteenth century historians (especially those expressed in the monumental works of Zikmund Winter on the character and quality of Prague University before the Battle of the White Mountain and on the fate of its students), all resulted in an underestimation of the significance of the *studium* around 1600 for Czech society, especially for the bourgeoisie.[2] Studies by F. Šmahel and M. Truc in the 1960s on the numbers and origin of Prague students represented the first breakthrough in an understanding of the history of the University.[3] But it was only in the 1980s that substantial progress was achieved. In keeping with the pan-European trend of quantitative history and prosopography, F. Šmahel and other scholars subjected the then available sources to global socio-historical analysis.[4] At the same time, more importantly, a remarkable collection of primary source material on the history and composition of the Prague academic community was published.

In this context, it is necessary to mention in the first place the completion of the series *Enchiridion renatae poesis Latinae in Bohemia et Moravia cultae*. This contains the biography of all Czech authors of occasional poetry before 1620.[5] It has been possible to show that three-quarters of Prague graduates of the period under review wrote verses in Latin, evidence that the *Enchiridion* is a prosopographic source of extraordinary value.[6] Shortly afterwards the reconstructed register of graduates was published for the period 1586–1620 as a continuation of the extant dean's book, the source of our knowledge of graduations before 1585. In addition, the reference book of the University rector, covering the period of the 1560s to the 1580s and containing the names of the Latin school students who turned up for formal matriculation in the University register was made available.[7] As a result, for the second half of the sixteenth and the early seventeenth centuries, it is now possible at least partially to chart the regional origin of the University's students, to describe in some detail its social role, and to indicate what career opportunities were open to its graduates.

Prague University in the period under review was a state institution in which were intermingled the humanism of Melancthon, a native Reformation tradition, the German Reformation, and later on Calvinist ideas. With respect to the curriculum Prague University remained in the grip of traditional Aristotelian ideas but these were given a Melancthonian gloss and further transformed in the 1590s under the impact of Ramism. Especially during the term in office of the rector Martin Bacháček (a mathematician, astronomer, and friend of Johann Kepler), the content of the University's teaching was partly modernized. Also an incomplete University reform undertaken between 1609 and 1611 endeavoured to reconstitute the four faculties of the *studium*. Since the fifteenth century practically only the faculty of arts had been in operation at Prague, but as a result of the reform some courses were organized under its umbrella which usually belonged to the programme of the higher faculties.[8]

It is necessary to agree with those authors who maintain that the Prague University of Arts offered little instruction of practical use.[9] But were the arts faculties of other European universities or autonomous academies of neighbouring countries orientated in a more practical direction? This was certainly not the case of urban Latin schools and the university arts faculties of other central European countries.[10] On the contrary, the reformers and authors of the school regulations concentrated their attentions mainly on establishing a system of religion and civic education which would serve the needs of the élite in Church and state. The curriculum was necessarily constructed within a framework of Christian humanism (either Protestant or Catholic). Moreover, if impractical, this training was certainly marketable for those from middle-class backgrounds who formed the backbone of the institutions' clientele. Burgesses of central European towns and boroughs demanded value for money and they would not have allowed their sons to acquire a humanist education for nothing. Study was an important investment. Many students on completing their arts education were destined to educate other students. Also, sooner or later they were likely to become clerks to or members of corporations, town communities or provincial assemblies, or to take up a religious career. A graduate had many sought-after skills: a cultural veneer, a practical knowledge of languages, dexterity in formulations, experience in working with texts and handbooks, and a basic knowledge of mathematics. A life of independence and relative poverty at university had also given him moral backbone. Even Latin verse composition or practical musicianship could be marketed as could academic titles.

The Protestant University of Prague in the decades before the Thirty Years War was primarily the school of the Bohemian bourgeoisie. In the period under review 90 per cent of BAs were from Bohemia, 4 per cent from Slovakia (especially from the region near the Bohemian border), and 6 per cent from Silesia (from the region of Polish Silesia and the German towns). Noble students were very rare. Admittedly, students coming from the countryside accounted for 10 per cent of the total over the period and their proportion increased over time (4 per cent 1551–75; 8.2 per cent 1576–99; 11.3 per cent 1601–20). None the less, if an assessment can be made on the available sources, then *all* the University's graduates initially sought an urban career and those who settled in the countryside were limited to those who became priests or exceptionally clerks to great landowners. Most students from the countryside established themselves in towns once they had completed their studies.[11]

In the period under examination almost 1,200 bachelors graduated from the Protestant University, making it an academic institution of small to medium size.[12] Few foreigners visited the country on the international *peregrinatio academica*. It is unlikely that the University produced an excessive number of educated men for the country's needs. As in Franconia the dense network of towns enjoying self-government and boasting inflated bureaucracies was able to absorb huge numbers of graduates.[13] The highly developed parish systems offered another career opportunity. Central Europe did not experience the problems of 'alienated intellectuals' as England in the early seventeenth century supposedly did. At that time between 400 and 500 students graduated from Oxford and Cambridge every year while in Prague only thirty-three young men yearly achieved the BA degree during the years 1601–1620.[14]

The first usually tentative step into practical life for the majority of graduates was to take the post of rector or teacher in one of the urban Latin schools in Bohemia or Moravia which belonged to the network controlled by the rector of the University of Prague.[15] This network may be fairly accurately established on the basis of the preserved official letters of the rectors Martin Bacháček, Jan Bystricky, and Jan Campan, which are contained in the rectors' handbooks of the period 1598–1612.[16] The originally quite meagre network of schools under the University's administration, built up in the very heart of Bohemian Utraquism, gained considerable importance thanks to the dedication of the rector Bacháček just at the turn of the seventeenth century.[17] The University's influence grew stronger practically in the whole of the Czech-speaking region of Bohemia. It extended right up to the Czech-German language dividing line and occasionally beyond it. The Catholic region of Pilzen and a part of southern Bohemia did not belong to the sphere of influence of the University. But few students came to the *studium* from these areas. At the beginning of the seventeenth century the school network became denser and the University's contacts with the schools became even more regular. The influence of the University's rector was extended not only to the schools of the Czech free royal towns, but also to a series of vassal towns, boroughs, and during the last years under review even villages. After 1600 the Rector used to appoint the teaching staff at 114 Latin schools and to verify the quality of their work and their moral decency. Most of the schools in German towns (usually Lutheran) and the schools of Catholic towns were independent. Following the imperial charter of the Emperor Rudolf II in 1609 by which Prague University was put under the jurisdiction of the Bohemian Estates, a decree was issued confirming the sovereignty of the *studium* over all the schools of the kingdom of Bohemia. Thus Prague University achieved the position, at least formally, of being the overseer of the Czech education system.

The University obtained and strengthened its influence over the town schools mainly as the producer and organizer of the 'market' of schoolmasters. During the periods of positive co-operation between the University and the Utraquists and, after 1609, the Reformed Consistory (the highest Protestant body in the country), the rector, who was a member of the Consistory, was helped by the power of the Church. Generally the rector exercised his authority through the aid of personal contacts in town councils, among the clergy, and with the authorities in vassal towns. The University lacked any direct executive authority.

The Czech Protestant educational system, though linked to the University, was established in the second half of the sixteenth century as an open and dynamic system, which in the conditions of the time could not be entirely institutionalized. It required a certain amount of organizational ability to keep it fully operational given the changing balance of religious and political forces. Town councils required schoolmasters and elementary teachers who had a command of the Czech language and were Protestants with guaranteed qualifications. There was a permanent requirement for teachers since the teaching staff of urban Latin schools (which in most cases taught both Czech and Latin) had a rapid turn-over. Teachers continually departed to engage in permanent careers in either the religious or secular field. In the Czech-speaking part of the country, the University of Prague was virtually the unique supplier of Protestant, university-educated teachers. Only schools belonging to the Union of Czech Brethren (the Czech Calvinist Church) were independently staffed but they were few in number in Bohemia. An agreement with the University was the easiest way for towns to acquire teaching staff, especially as the graduates were keen and regularly inspected by the University's rector.

Teaching at all Latin schools was administered by the school administrator (rector) who in the period around 1600 had at least one but in most cases more subordinate teachers.[18] So far it is impossible to draw up a complete list of these teachers and even research done on a regional basis will not be able to supply comprehensive information. But it can be estimated on the basis of the main University sources, from an analysis of the *Enchiridion renatae poesis*, and from available secondary material, that town schools in Bohemia around 1600 required some 300 teachers who had had at least a rudimentary university education.

Towns in western and northern Bohemia (which were Lutheran and German speaking) recruited most of their teachers from Saxon universities, especially Leipzig and Wittenberg, and offered long-term contracts to their employees. Towns in the rest of the country, which were fed by Prague University, preferred a system of 'rotation' which took into account the turn-over of young teachers and their changing qualifications. The system developed probably around the mid-sixteenth century as a result of the limited opportunities of academic *peregrinatio* open to Czech-speaking bourgeois. The main factor was the long distance between central European universities and academic schools and the costs involved in long study trips. Academic grades enjoyed a high prestige in towns thus increasing the interest in acquiring them, but in most cases the burgesses lacked the money to pay for long-term stays in Prague, while the University could not offer many scholarships. Only a handful of boys from noble families could afford a real *peregrinatio academica*.[19] The system of short-term teaching contracts solved the problem. Students after spending a short period at the University were accustomed to take up a post at a school outside Prague where they continued to study at the same time for the BA examination.

Once this was passed, they might continue in the post or switch their position several times in subsequent years. Promotion depended on their qualifications and ability. From schools in small towns they would proceed to those in important educational centres where they would prepare themselves to take their MA. This was to a certain extent a continuation of the restricted educational *peregrinatio* they would already have experienced in their younger days (from local to regional school and then to the University).[20] Through moving from post to post the teachers gained life experience and the contacts necessary for a permanent job.

The University controlled the teachers through this rotation system. In cases where the teachers' rights were not respected, this system also allowed pressure to be brought to bear on the town councils. The University might refuse to appoint a new school administrator to replace the one who had been recalled or left the school. In fact, teachers were members of the University throughout their period of service in the classroom, and theoretically they were supposed to be only under the jurisdiction of the University rector. Furthermore, the rotation system had a unifying impact on the method and quality of teaching throughout the entire territory under the University's supervision. It also guaranteed to the teachers a certain degree of justice in career promotion, vis-à-vis the distribution of more or less lucrative posts (if due weight must always be given to the system of favours and personal contacts with local authorities). The rotation system ensured that the town council or the priest could not make the schoolteacher their subordinate and make him more dependent upon them than upon the University, which guaranteed considerable independence for the teachers. A negative feature of this system consisted in an unavoidable discontinuity in the classroom due to the frequent changes of personnel (in some cases six monthly). But this shortcoming was to a great extent obviated by the unified method of teaching and by the fact that frequent changes involved either only the administrator or subordinate teaching staff.

It goes without saying that considerable effort was required from the University rector to keep the system going. He had to organize and keep a register of everything but, in the first place, he had to ensure a regular and quite large supply of new teachers from among the University's students and graduates. Clearly, new BAs, some thirty in number each year, did not have much difficulty in placing their feet on the first rung of the career ladder. Approximately one-tenth of Prague graduates embarked immediately on a secular or religious career outside the classroom, while the rest served as schoolteachers for a shorter or longer time.[21]

It has been a commonplace to paint the schoolteachers as poor bachelors who depended on public welfare and crumbs from the priest's table. They are seen as destitute beggars, going from one school to another in search of slightly better conditions, able to escape finally from the misery of the classroom only through a humiliating marriage with a wealthy widow. This picture results from a complex of various influences: the distortions of the Romantic era, the poverty experienced by teachers in elementary schools and by supply-teachers of grammar-schools towards the end of the nineteenth century, and the information in medieval and early-modern books in which the poor student-teachers of a town school represented a traditional character. In the period under review a town school was in fact a prestigious guild institution. It served the purpose of the municipality and was integrated into it. The relationship between the school on the one hand and the vicarage on the other, as well as with the religious life of the town community generally, was close and materially rewarding.

The situation of the Latin school teachers in the region under the administration of the University of Prague was unstable but not because of the low social prestige of the teachers, especially the school administrators, or their poverty. It is true that the teachers of small country schools in particular complained of material difficulties in their letters to the rector. But it should not be forgotten that they were young and that the intelligentsia tends to exaggerate its social significance and its problems of status. The main reason why the teaching profession lost its attraction over time was the instability and insecurity of the rotation system. In addition, mature members of the profession felt uneasy about celibacy which applied to all members of the University community until 1609. The general situation of the Latin school administrators did not differ from that of other officials paid by the town community. Their financial income was, if not equal at least comparable (of course taking into account considerable local differences resulting from the size of the school, the funds the town council had at its disposal, and the status the school had acquired in the town thanks to the activities of the preceding administrators). Towards the end of the sixteenth century, the mean income of a school administrator in towns where the payment was also in the form of kind and *carols* (donations by students and others) was approximately 20 to 24 *sixties Meissen groschen*, while in towns where the administrator was totally paid in cash his yearly income was between 40 and 60 *sixties*. But rich towns with important schools paid even more—substantially the same as towns of neighbouring countries. The amount depended on the character of the school, the number of paying pupils, etc. There were cases where the administrators of some rich schools went as far as to refuse the offer to join the University's teaching staff. In the town of Kutná Hora, for instance, the administrator's position was so prestigious that he had hopes of joining the town administration.

The town schools of Czech-speaking Bohemia played a crucial role in providing bourgeois students with the means to finish their studies and gain the necessary qualifications for a professional career outside the classroom. This is suggested, if not confirmed, by the fact that the student and graduate teachers who are known to us through the rectoral records nearly always disappear from view two or three years after they are first referred to. Teaching was definitely a transitory occupation. Those that continued to teach for any length of time were peculiarly rootless characters, such as Nicolaus Spissius of Kutná Hora, son of a town alderman and bookkeeper to the town's royal mint.[22] In 1607 Spissius gained his BA. By 1608 he was serving as a school administrator of the Prague school of St Clement, but by Christmas of the same year he had started working as a tutor to a noble family. Thereafter every year he changed teaching jobs, becoming an MA in 1614. He is last mentioned in the records in 1621 at which date he was administrator to the Tyn school in Prague.

The transitory nature of the teaching profession is also suggested by research in the archives of the city of Prague, where it has been impossible to discover the inventory or testament of a Latin school teacher or administrator who died at a great age.[23] Above all, however, the significant role that teaching played in the career formation of bourgois students can be demonstrated by studying the career orientation of student-teachers recorded in the *Enchiridion renatae poesis*. About 600 of the entries for the period under review concern *literati* who were teachers for a part of their career and about whom enough biographical information survives to permit a meaningful analysis. Ninety of the sample never seem to have graduated, while 190 took their MA degree as well. On average every teacher in the sample was employed at 2.2 schools and only twenty of the *literati* (3.3 per cent) held posts at more than five establishments. These figures, however, should be treated with caution, since it is impossible to produce a complete list of the staff at any school in the late sixteenth and early seventeenth centuries, even the staff of famous establishments. Thus, using a variety of sources it is still only possible to uncover the names of 70 per cent of the administrators and 4 per cent of the subordinate teaching staff at the renowned school of St Henry in Prague New Town in the period 1571–1620.[24] In consequence there is no way of knowing precisely how many years the *literati* in the sample actually spent in the classroom.

The results of the career analysis are given in Tables I–III. The first table shows the initial career choice of former student teachers immediately after leaving teaching. The second table records the most prestigious position obtained in subsequent years, and the third maps career shifts. The data in the *Enchiridion* has been inevitably simplified but an attempt has been made through the relatively detailed system of classification to provide as accurate an account as possible of career orientation.

Table I shows clearly that the largest group of teachers deserted the intelligentsia for a life initially in trade or manufacturing. This was so even in the case of many MAs (40 per cent). Normally entry

Table I. Initial Career of Former Teachers of Latin Schools (the figures are percentages)

Employment	*MA*	*BA*	*Non-grad.*	*Av.*
univ. prof.	17.9	0.0	0.0	5.6
priest	14.2	18.6	23.3	17.9
town clerk	14.7	13.0	10.0	13.1
private clerk, notary, member of other lib. profession	4.2	4.6	4.4	4.5
town councillor	2.1	0.0	0.0	0.7
tradesman, artisan, rentier	40.1	53.6	53.4	49.2
deceased	4.2	9.0	7.8	7.3
emigrant	2.6	1.2	1.1	1.7
Total 100% =	190	323	90	603

to a trade or craft was the result of marriage to a widow. Socially this was perfectly acceptable and it provided the student teacher with a position in society from which he could hope one day to become involved in town government. Entry to the ranks of the bourgeoisie might also be by purchase or inheritance.

Fifteen per cent of MAs became town clerks, while a further 4 per cent became clerks in private practice or entered the legal profession. Two per cent of MAs almost immediately joined the town council. Similar positions were also attained in relatively large numbers by bachelors or non-graduates. The growing bureaucratic town apparatus of town courts and offices needed a bevy of clerks fluent in Czech and Latin, who were capable of working with legal documents, and who had the skill to defend the town's interests at local and national level.

A sizeable group of MAs left schoolteaching to become professors at the University. Despite the fact that the situation of Prague professors was not outstanding it was a stable job, opening the door to both a life of intellectual stimulation and to the best jobs in the offices and town councils of the most important towns, especially Prague. However, even the position of professor at the University was an impermanent one, merely a stepping-stone to a career as a town politician, or more desirable still a post in the supreme body of the Utraquist Church (the Consistory *sub utraque*). This had personal ties with the University for most of the period under review, and its headquarters was in the University itself, in the Emperor Charles' College.

Quite a considerable proportion of Latin schoolteachers went directly into the ranks of the Protestant Church. From among teachers who held an MA, 14 per cent were ordained, while among teachers without an academic grade more than 23 per cent became clergymen.

Finally, mention must be made of two smaller groups. 7.3 per cent of schoolteachers died while at the chalk face, so never progressed to another career. BAs were particularly prominent among this group. Another smaller, but equally unfortunate, contingent comprised teachers who emigrated after the defeat of the Bohemian revolt in 1620. Teachers accounted for about a tenth of all emigrants after the Battle of the White Mountain.

Table II shows the most elevated position reached by former teachers. It is interesting to note that the proportion of MAs who

Table II. The Apex of the Career of Former Teachers of Latin Schools (the figures are percentages)

Employment	*MA*	*BA*	*Non-grad.*	*Av.*
univ. prof.	7.9	0.0	0.0	2.6
priest	16.3	20.4	26.6	20.1
town clerk	14.7	9.3	6.7	10.6
private clerk, notary, member of other lib. profession	5.8	5.9	11.1	6.6
town councillor	16.3	16.7	16.7	16.6
premier councillor	9.0	9.9	7.8	9.3
imperial delegate	1.6	1.6	3.3	1.8
tradesman, artisan, rentier	21.6	26.0	18.9	23.5
deceased or emigrant	6.8	10.2	8.9	9.0
Total 100% =	190	323	90	603

found jobs as town officers did not change. It remained at the level of 14.7 per cent. However, the table hides shifts that did occur within the group as a whole. Some MAs who first became resident in towns through marriage or the purchase of property later availed themselves of an opportunity to make proper use of their qualifications by gaining a clerkship. Others were promoted over time from their position as junior clerks (the town halls of royal towns had quite a numerous office staff) to that of head clerk (*protonotarius* or chancellor). Yet others—former town clerks—quit their office and joined the ranks of the aldermen. In most towns the position of the leading elected official—the burgomaster or head alderman—rotated, but the first burgomaster to take office after council elections always had the highest prestige. For this reason this group of municipal dignitaries has been specifically isolated in Table II, where it can be seen that almost 10 per cent of MAs reached the highest point on the civic ladder. For similar reasons the office of imperial magistrate has also been isolated as a special category. The latter was the imperial representative on the town council directly appointed by the emperor, an office created after the defeat of the Estates in 1547. However, the office quickly lost its repressive character and in the period under review it was customary to bestow the dignity on one of the most outstanding, most esteemed, or wealthiest members of the town council. This honour 'de facto' might also be characterized as the ultimate accolade of a successful career.

At the peak of their career, a smaller proportion of BAs and non-graduates were likely to be town clerks than at the outset. In this respect the performance of both groups differed from that of MAs. On the other hand, all three groups eventually participated in urban self-government in roughly equal proportions. Non-graduates, in contrast, were relatively highly represented at the peak of their career in the group composing private clerks and other professional people. Inevitably, no BAs and non-graduates ever became professors. Their bent was frequently towards the Church. One fifth of BAs reached the pinnacle of their career as priests and 27 per cent of non-graduates. It is interesting to note that in all groups some individuals became priests after only a brief exposure to civic life. Presumably the continuity between the life of a schoolmaster and that of a priest, plus the guarantees of a post in the Church, played a part in their decision to quit quickly the burgess community. Maybe, too, some of our sample found themselves unqualified to compete in commerce and manufacturing.

This increase in the number of former teachers entering the liberal professions was matched by a fall in the proportion at the height of their career-cycle gaining a living as merchants and artisans or living on income from rented urban or suburban property. The proportion among this group formed by MAs and BAs was halved. Among non-graduates the proportion fell to one third. Moreover, the figures are maxima for the survey has not isolated as a special category those who held minor municipal and parish offices, or positions in literary societies, etc.

The extent to which the former teachers eventually penetrated the liberal professions is emphasized in Table III. Twenty-eight per cent of the sample became aldermen in time, 2.5 per cent ended up as professors or other dignitaries of Prague University, more than 17 per cent peaked as clerks, notaries, or members of other private professions, while 20 per cent became priests. In fact, two-thirds of the people covered by the survey were successful in intellectual and socially-prestigious professions. Indeed, about one-third of the sample made its way into the highest echelons of the burgess community. Further social promotion, it must be stressed, was virtually impossible. I am aware that the sources available may influence the outcome of the analysis since there is always more

Table III. Overall Career Pattern of Former Teachers of Latin Schools (the figures are percentages)

Employment	*Starting-point*	*Apex*
univ. prof.	5.6	2.6
priest	17.9	20.1
town clerk	13.1	10.6
private clerk, notary, member of other lib. profession	4.5	6.6
town councillor	0.7	27.7
tradesman, artisan, rentier	49.2	23.5
deceased or emigrant	9.0	9.0
Total 100% =	603	603

information on the career of those who were successful than those who fell into oblivion. Nevertheless, I believe that the survey is sufficiently extensive and representative to allow us to state on the basis of its outcome that middle-class fathers who made some investment in the studies of their sons around 1600 had good reason to do so. Many of the young men who spent the best years of their lives studying 'useless' sciences and teaching in sometimes bad conditions eventually enjoyed careers which they could not have achieved without education.

Moreover, many of these teachers carved out a successful career for themselves in the leading towns of the country. Limiting our sample only to those who were made urban freemen and leaving aside university teachers, clergymen who had no control over where they lived, and of course those who died or went abroad, we find the following: 54 per cent of individuals in the sample of 413 came from royal towns, 74 per cent settled in one, and only 12 per cent returned to their native towns, most of them again royal.

But not only the town's status was important; also its location and its economic and local political significance. Map II indicates that wealthy towns in the regions around the rivers Elbe and Ohře and in the region between the lower Vltava, Ohře, and Elbe generated interest. With the exception of the town of Domažlice the teachers were not tempted to go and live either in the important towns of south-western Bohemia or in the towns located in central Bohemia

Map I.
The birthplaces of former teachers of Latin schools, who settled in the towns Žatec, Domažlice, Hradec Králové

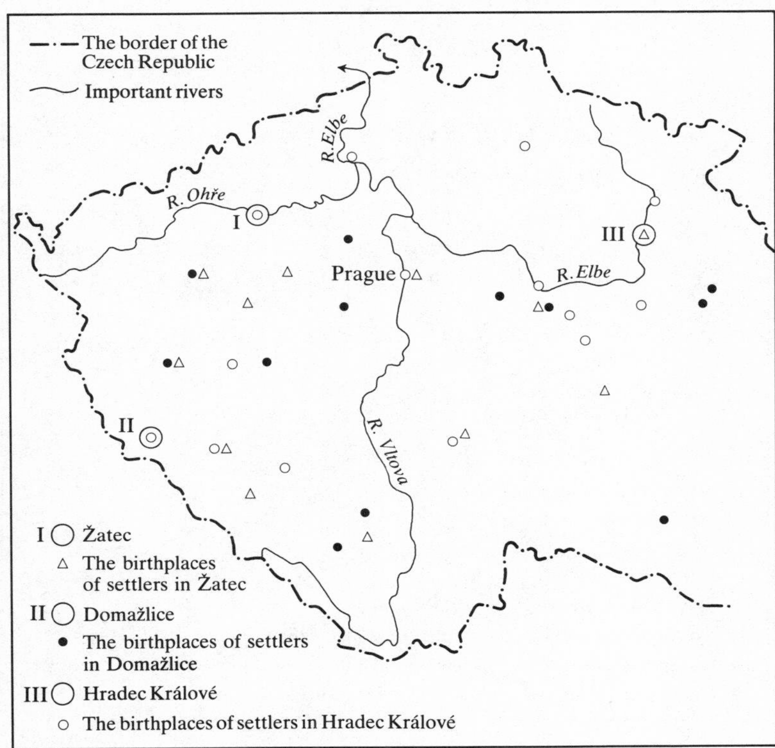

Map II.
The pattern of migration of former teachers of Latin schools

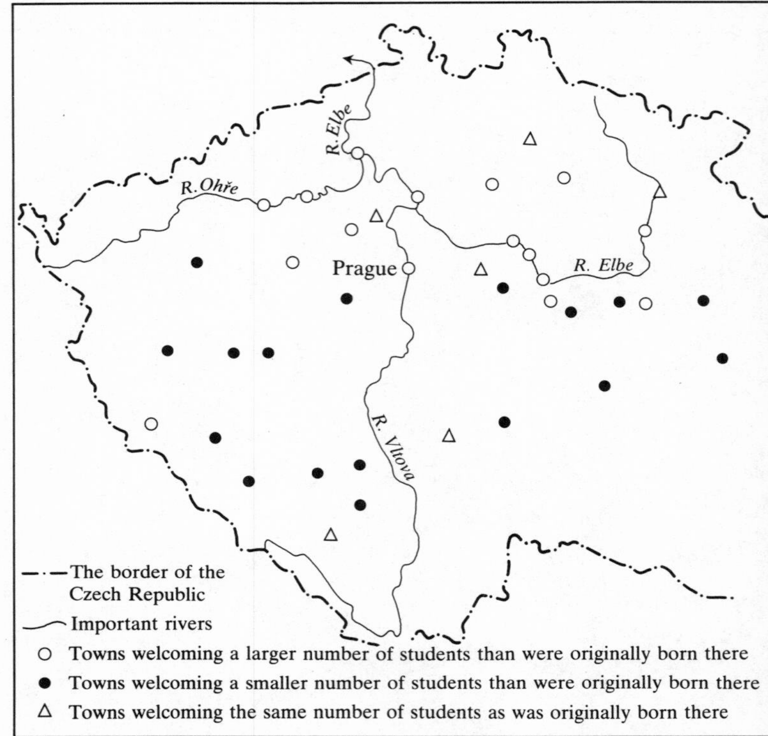

between Plzen and Prague or in the towns of eastern Bohemia south of the river Elbe.

The key royal towns with economic, cultural, local, and political importance, that is those where tens of teachers tried to settle, were the birthplace of relatively, and in some cases absolutely, smaller numbers of *literati* than unimportant vassal towns. Prague, a big city with 60,000 inhabitants, seventeen Latin schools, and the University preparatory school (i.e. the classes of the University whose pupils were too young to be incorporated) is represented in the sample by only forty teachers. Small country towns, on the other hand, which had no more than several thousand inhabitants or even smaller vassal towns are represented by ten or more: Čáslav 17; Klatovy 14; Vodňany 19; Beroun 12; the vassal town of Strakonice 12; to name but a few. Similarly, important royal towns, like Hradec Králové, Mělnik, Litoměřice, Louny, and Slaný, to which the young intelligentsia were particularly attracted, have only between four and eight representatives.

This phenomenon, it must be stressed, is also visible in the pattern of graduations from the University of Prague. Over the period the proportion of graduates from the capital and other important towns clearly decreased.[25] So far we have no satisfactory explanation for this collapse. However, the case of the imperial city of Nuremberg may be instructive. There it seems at this date academic education was not a sufficient guarantee for promotion to the ranks of the urban élite.[26] Arguably, then, in the important towns of the kingdom of Bohemia many offices carried such distinction that they were allocated according to family wealth, guild contacts, etc., rather than academic qualifications *tout court*. This situation probably made burgesses outside the élite look for other ways of family promotion. On the other hand, it can be supposed that the situation did not deter the burgesses of smaller towns from sending their sons to schools in important centres or the capital to foster contacts. Academic education opened up prospects for younger sons from small towns which would not have been otherwise available. Even relatively humble offices in Prague and other important towns would have carried more prestige than the posts open to them at home. Map I shows the widespread geographical origin of teachers who made a career in three medium-sized Bohemian towns. An academic education and a period of service in a Latin school became the means of significant social mobility for gifted young men with limited opportunities: the second sons of well-established families and young men from outside the élite or from smaller and vassal towns. In this way the University and the Latin schools became a mechanism for supplying new blood to the élites of the royal towns. It was a dynamic system which probably worked well until the outbreak of the Thirty Years War. The collapse of the Bohemian rebellion had a dramatic effect on the composition of the urban élites. Over 16 per cent of the *literati* in the sample fled the country, 22 per cent of those who held an MA. For those willing to convert a huge number of vacant posts suddenly beckoned.

Archiv hl. města Prahy
Husova 20
CS 110 00 Praha 1
Czechoslovakia

REFERENCES

1. From 1562 there was an independent Jesuit college in the city of Prague eventually given a quasi-university status.
2. Z. Winter, *Děje vysokých škol pražskych od secessí cizích národu po dobu bitvy bělohorské 1409–1622/ A History of the Academies of Prague from the Secession of the Foreign Nations to the time of the Battle of the White Mountain* (Prague, 1897); Z. Winter, *O životě na vysokých školách pražkých knihy dvoje. Kulturní obraz XV. a XVI, století/ Two Books about the Life of the Academies of Prague. A Cultural Picture of the Fifteenth and Sixteenth Centuries* (Prague, 1899).
3. F. Šmahel and M. Truc, 'Studie k dějinám University Karlovy v letech 1433–1622/ Studies on the History of the Charles University 1433–1622', *Acta Universitatis Carolinae—Historia Universitatis Carolinae Pragensis* IV: 2 (1963), 3–59; F. Kavka a kol, *Stručné dějiny University Karlovy/ A Short History of the Charles University* (Prague, 1964), pp. 77–121.
4. F. Šmahel, 'L'Université de Prague de 1433 à 1622: recrutement géographique, carrières et mobilité sociale des étudiants gradués' in D. Julia, J. Revel, and R. Chartier (eds.), *Les Universités europées du XVIe au XVIIIe siècle. Histoire sociale des populations étudiantes* vol. I (Paris, 1986), pp. 65–88. J. Pešek, 'Manuál rektora Curia-Dvorského: kniha záhadná/ Register of the Rector Curius-Dvorský: an Enigmatical Book', *Acta Universitatis Carolinae—Historia Universitatis Carolinae Pragensis* XXVI: 1 (1986), 97–108.

5. J. Hejnic and J. Martínek, *Enchiridion renatae poesis Latinae in Bohemia et Moravia cultae* (Prague, 1966–82).
6. P. Svoboný, 'Sociální a regionální struktura literárně činných absolventů pražské univerzity v letech 1500–1620/ The Social and Regional Background of Graduates of the University of Prague 1500–1620 Active in the Field of Letters', *Acta Universitatis Carolinae—Historia Universtatis Carolinae Pragensis* XXVI: 1 (1986), 11.
7. K. Beránek, *Baccalaurei et magistri in facultate philosophica Universitatis Carolinae Pragensis ab anno 1586 usque ad annum 1620 determinati* (Prague, 1988); K. Beránek, *Manuale rectoris nomina eorum continens, qui in albo Universitatis Carolinae Pragensis nunc perdito ab anno 1560 usque ad annum 1582 inscripti sunt* (Prague, 1981).
8. J. Petráň, *Nástin dějin filozofické fakulty Univerzity Karlovy/ Outline of the History of the Philosophical Faculty of the Charles University* (Prague, 1984), pp. 49–51.
9. Šmahel, 'L'Université de Prague', p. 67.
10. Cf. e.g. R. Endres, 'Nürmberger Bildungswesen zur Zeit der Reformation', *Mitteilungen d. Vereins f. Geschichte d. Stadt Nürmberg* 71 (1984), 112–15; R. Endres, 'Die Bedeutung des lateinischen und deutschen Schulwesens für die Entwicklung der fränkischen Reichstädte des Spätmittelalters under der frühen Neuzeit' in L. Kriss-Rettenbeck and M. Liedtke (eds.), *Schulgeschichte im Zusammenhang der Kulturentwicklung, Schriften zum Bayerischen Schulmuseum Ichenhausen* vol. I (Bad Heilbrunn, 1983), pp. 144–65; R. Bastiaanse, H. Bots, and M. Evers, *Tot meesten nut ende dienst van de jeught. Een onderzoek naar zeventien Gelderse Latijnse scholen ca. 1580–1815* (De Walburg Pers, 1985), pp. 32–8.
11. Šmahel, 'L'Université de Prague', pp. 74, 76, table 5.
12. Šmahel and Truc, 'Studie k dějinám University Karlovy', p. 47; Beránek, *Baccalaurei et magistri*, p. 16.
13. R. Endres, 'Die deutschen Führungsschichten um 1600' in H. H. Hofmann and G. Franz (eds.), *Deutsche Führungsschichten in der Neuzeit* vol. 12 (Boppard am Rhein, 1980), p. 99.
14. M. H. Curtis, 'The Alienated Intellectuals of Early Stuart England', *Past and Present* 23 (1962), 32; L. Stone, 'The Educational Revolution in England 1560–1640', *Past and Present* 28 (1964), 47–57.
15. Z. Winter, *Život a učení na partikulárních školách v Čechách v století XV. a XVI./ Life and Teaching in the Latin Schools of Bohemia in the Fifteenth and Sixteenth Centuries* (Prague, 1901), pp. 144–200.
16. Archives of the Charles University, MSS B 18, A 13b.
17. J. Pešek, 'M. Martin Bacháček z Nauměřic, rektor univerzity pražské/ Magister Martin Bacháček from Nauměřice, Rector of the University of Prague', *Acta Universitatis Carolinae—Historia Universitatis Carolinae Pragensis* XIX: 1 (1979), 73–94.
18. Winter, *Život a učení*, p. 157.

19. J. Pešek and D. Saman, 'Les Etudiants de Bohéme dans les universités et les académies d'Europe centrale et occidentale entre 1596 et 1620' in Julia, Revel, and Chartier, pp. 89–111; J. Pešek and M. Svatoš, 'Die sozialen Folgen der akademischen Peregrination in den Böhmischen Ländern in der zweiten Hälfte des 16. Jahrhunderts', *Zeszyty naukowe Uniwersytetu Jagiellonskiego DCCCLXX. Prace historyczne* 88 (1989), 51–4.
20. F. Palacký, 'Obyvatelstvo českých měst a školni vzděláni v 16. a na začátku 17. století/ Inhabitants of Czech towns and School Education in the Sixteenth and the Beginning of the Seventeenth Centuries', *Československý časopis historický* XVIII (1970), 355. Palacký's research indicates that three-quarters of town-school pupils in the towns of north-western Bohemia attended, besides the school in their birthplace, between two and four other municipal schools.
21. Šmahel, 'l'Université de Prague', p. 79, table 8.
22. *Enchiridion* V. 150–2.
23. I have consulted Archives of the City of Prague, MSS 1173–5, 1208–14, 1217, 2209, and 2210.
24. Prague at this date comprised a unit of five independent royal as well as tributary towns: Old Town, New Town, Little Town, Hradčany, and Vyšehrad.
25. See Jiří Pešek, 'Nad rekonstruovanou matrikou graduovaných pražské university let 1586–1620/ On the Reconstructed Register of the Graduates of the University of Prague', *Studia Comeniana et Historica* 42: XX (1990), 85. 1433–1622 11 per cent of BAs came from Prague; in the period 1586–1620 only 7.5 per cent. In the same period only twelve MAs came from Prague and twelve from the second city of Bohemia, Kutná Hora, but six came from Vodňany and four from Čáslav and Německý Brod (all small towns).
26. R. Endres, 'Sozial-und Bildungsstruckturen fränkischer Reichsstädte im Spätmittelalter und in der frühen Neuzeit' in H. Brunner (ed.), *Literatur in der Stadt* (Göttingen, 1982), p. 64.

An Academic Counter-Revolution: Newman and Tractarian Oxford's Idea of a University

P. B. Nockles

University reform in the age of liberal revolution took a variety of forms. Historians have tended to focus on only one model of university reform in Britain, that propagated by liberal and radical reformers. However this model, which in the context of the undisputed Anglican hegemony of the two English universities in the early nineteenth century had distinctly secularizing, if not anticlerical overtones, was by no means the only one. This paper concentrates upon a very different, counter-revolutionary scheme put forward by a party in the Church of England no less dissatisfied with the status quo in the University of Oxford than their liberal counterparts. The leaders of this active party expounded, in a rich vein of pamphlet and periodical literature, an alternative educational ideal to that put forward by liberals. It was an ideal shaped by and related to the Oxford context in which it was born, but which at the same time was to provide the ultimate inspiration for one of the classic treatises on the purposes of universities in the English-speaking world, John Henry Newman's *The Idea of a University*.

1. The University Context

Recent scholarship has done something to modify the Gibbonian caricature of intellectual and moral decay as well as torpor and indolence relentlessly propagated by radical and nonconformist critics of late-Georgian Oxford.[1] The internal process of reform from within symbolized by the new examination statutes of 1800 and 1807, represented a genuine tightening up in academic standards and discipline. However, as Colin Matthew has observed in a penetrating analysis of the subject in this journal, the reforms of the 1800s actually reinforced the religious and establishmentarian emphasis of the university.[2] Indeed, it was partly because the basis of those reforms had been conservative and designed to render the Anglican confessional nature of Oxford more of a living reality that the university was subjected to utilitarian critique by the *Edinburgh Review* in 1808–9. The ground of the attack lay in the fact that Oxford was religiously closed as well as apparently educationally 'useless' and non-'professional' in orientation compared to the Scottish and continental universities. As is well known, Oxford's response was spearheaded by a fellow (and subsequently Provost) of Oriel, Edward Copleston.

Copleston's defence of Oxford's classical and collegiate system of education has been well explored by Peter Slee,[3] and requires no further elucidation here. Essentially, Copleston defended the value of a classical education in cultural terms and as an invaluable source of mental training. He did not respond directly to the implicitly theological animus inherent in the repudiation of the principle of Anglican hegemony and a confessional university made by John Playfair and other writers in the *Edinburgh Review*. None the less, it is important not to overlook the religious dimension of this debate, as too many cultural historians of the university have tended to do.[4] Copleston may have left it largely to others to focus on theological implications, but at the root of the Coplestonian ideal of a 'liberal', non-professional education was the notion of Oxford's distinctive 'academic ethos'.[5] The vital element of this ethos was religion and—in particular—the explicit Anglican confessionalism which the Scottish reviewers consciously strove to discredit. As Colin Matthew points out, the reaction to the secularizing trend of the French Revolution had produced a response in favour of Anglican confessionalism at Oxford from the 1790s onwards; a reaction that was in stark contrast to the case of German universities where equally conservative forces had secularized in order to survive.[6] To discuss ideas of university education and reform in this period without a keen sense of awareness of the contemporary religious understanding and function of that education and reform is to ignore a crucial aspect of the controversy and the discourse in which it was conducted.

The successful Parliamentary challenge to the hitherto Anglican confessional nature of English society between 1828–32 inevitably posed a threat to an academic institution bound up with what

Jonathan Clark has characterized as the church-state of England's 'ancien regime'.[7] If the University of Oxford in the early decades of the nineteenth century had appeared in its corporate capacity to stray too far into the realm of national politics, as witnessed by the innumerable petitions drawn up against Catholic Emancipation in the period, this was precisely because the concerns of politics and religion were by definition inseparable for what was, after all, an endowed ecclesiastical institution whose primary aim was not simply to educate and instruct, but to uphold and inculcate Church of England principles. However, with the repeal of the Test Acts, Catholic Emancipation and the Reform Act, a dam burst and the ancient universities, Oxford especially, were exposed to potentially hostile secular influences as never before. The new secularizing challenge took the form of a campaign to admit religious dissenters to the university. Dr Matthew has identified four general categories of response at Oxford to the constitutional revolution of 1828–9[8] and the subsequent attempt to overturn the university's exclusively Anglican character. First, there was a traditionalist resistance to change offered by what the present author describes elsewhere as 'old High Churchmen' or 'the Orthodox'[9] as well as by many Evangelicals. Secondly, there was a 'prudential liberal-conservatism' characteristic of many of that group of divines who held intellectual sway in the Oxford of the 1810s and 1820s and centred on Oriel College, the so-called 'Noetics'. This position was represented by the more conservative of the 'Noetics' such as Edward Hawkins, successor as Provost of Oriel to Copleston who can be himself identified with this standpoint. In practice, it conceded limited internal change but without admitting the broader principle of a non-denominational university. Thirdly, there was an 'assertive reformism' prepared to countenance reform imposed from without, and associated with figures on the more radical wing of the 'Noetics' such as Baden Powell[10] and Thomas Arnold, headmaster of Rugby (R. D. Hampden was probably closer to this category than that of the 'liberal-conservatives'). And, fourthly, distinct from the other categories, there was a counter-revolutionary group represented by what is called the 'Oxford Movement' and its adherents, the so-called 'Tractarians'. It is the unique contribution to the whole nineteenth-century debate involving the status and role of universities and university education which the Tractarians provided, with which this paper is concerned.

What was this 'Oxford Movement', and why is it important for an understanding of the history of Oxford University in the 1830s and 1840s? What had the Oxford Movement, an avowedly theological phenomena, to do with a university and university education?

In essence, the Oxford Movement embodied the initial rallying together in the early 1830s of a band of young Oxford MAs and tutors bound by common ties of friendship and academic partnership. Leadership was provided by John Henry Newman, John Keble, Richard Hurrell Froude, and later, E. B. Pusey, from whose involvement the movement was to attract the nickname 'Puseyism'. The Oxford Movement represented not merely a defence but an attempted restoration of the High Church or 'catholic' tradition in the Church of England as expressed in ecclesiology and sacramental teaching, in direct response to a perceived liberal and Erastian challenge to the Church's rights and independence. Its genesis was dated by Newman to Keble's sermon on 'National Apostasy', delivered at the Oxford Assizes on 14 July 1833. The sermon embodied a protest against the Whig government's supposed parliamentary interference in matters spiritual by the suppression of ten Anglican bishoprics in Ireland. The context of the movement's origin was thus political, but a religious issue lay at its heart. As a religious and theological movement, what became known as 'Tractarianism'[11] was not static, but rather underwent a process of marked evolution over time.[12] Yet, in spite of the shades of theological difference which emerged even within the movement, an intellectual coherence and identity was provided by its philosophical as well as moral and spiritual dimension. It was the philosophical and intellectual character of Tractarianism which ensured that its contribution to the debate over university education would prove to be enormous. For it was a central Tractarian tenet that theology and the claims of dogma could not be compartmentalized, but on the contrary should permeate all branches of knowledge.

As an episode in the cultural, intellectual, and religious history of the nineteenth century, the Oxford Movement has never lacked historians. The theological controversies engendered by the movement, such as the debate over Tract 90, and its leading personalities, notably Newman, are familiar. To a great if often unconscious extent our historical understanding of the Oxford Movement has been coloured by the personal drama of the peculiar religious odyssey of Newman himself, the more especially as it so movingly unfolds in Newman's masterpiece of spiritual autobiography, the *Apologia pro vita sua.* Yet many of the events that form part of Newman's earlier religious history not only represent important chapters in the history of Oxford University over two decades, but are also chapters in the history of ideas about universities and university education. For while Newman's later contribution to this subject, his *Idea of a University* published in the 1850s, has been widely studied, there has been little recognition—with the exception of Dwight Culler's study—of the extent to which the *Idea*, formulated as it was in an Irish context, was the mature fruit of the experiences and theorizing of his Oxford, Tractarian years.[13]

The character of the Oxford Movement bore the imprint of the university environment in which it was forged. There is a case to be made for dating the real genesis of what the one-time 'Noetic' Blanco White called the 'mental revolution'[14] in Oxford represented by Tractarianism in the 1830s to the university's formal repudiation of Sir Robert Peel as its Member of Parliament in 1829 after the latter's volte-face on Catholic Emancipation.[15] It is highly significant that the young Newman, with all the zeal of a convert to the High Church cause, viewed a contest that at one level seemed trivial in almost apocalyptic terms as a 'glorious victory' for 'the independence of the Church and of Oxford' in equal measure. Moreover, for Newman, it was a victory over the multifarious dark forces of 'liberalism', 'march of mind' utilitarianism, Whiggery, radicalism and Dissent. Newman and his incipient followers were already identifying Oxford as a symbol of resistance to these forces; for them the real issue at stake in the Peel election was the preservation of Oxford's moral integrity as the soul of Church and nation. Oxford had 'never turned with the tide of fortune', Newman insisted; it was better to be 'bigotted than time-serving'.[16] Thus, while the occasion of the contest might have seemed from the viewpoint of the older 'Noetics' to have been but a minor episode of internal university politics, both Newman and Blanco White from opposite perspectives sensed that deeper forces were stirring. From now on the need to defend the independence of Oxford as much as that of the Church provided the motivating force in the emergence of the new movement.

Oxford was the 'genius loci' and source of inspiration for Tractarianism. The most famous and immediate product of the movement, a series of publications known as the 'Tracts of the Times' from which the very epithet 'Tractarian' was first derived, may have been addressed to churchmen at large, but soon became notorious as the 'Oxford Tracts'. Of course, this did not mean that the university in its formal, ruling capacity through the Heads of Houses endorsed or was responsible for the movement. On the contrary, for many years the Heads strove to dissociate the university's good name from Tractarian proceedings. In so far as the Tractarians did represent the university, it was the university of 'juniors', the MAs and younger fellows as represented in Convocation. At the same time, Tractarian supremacy at this level also depended on its ability to articulate and orchestrate the feelings of the so-called 'external university' of non-resident MAs which was to play such a crucial part in the debates and votes of Convocation in the 1830s and 1840s. When, as in 1845, it ceased to do this, the days of Tractarian ascendancy were over.[17]

Moreover, the emergence of the Oxford Movement was facilitated by the withdrawal of some of its future leaders from the more immediate concerns of active university life. Newman's resignation as a tutor at Oriel in 1830 after a dispute with the Provost, Edward Hawkins, released him to operate on the broader stage of theological controversy,[18] though the university pulpit remained a vital medium for Newman's spiritual influence on undergraduates and MAs.[19] Furthermore, the lecture room and tutorial office continued in other Tractarian hands to be a major source of the movement's impact on university life. Charles Lloyd, as Regius Professor of Divinity in the mid-1820s, had already demonstrated their potential for raising the theological tone within the university, and several of the future Tractarian leaders testified to the importance of his lectures.[20] As Frederick Oakeley, one-time Tractarian tutor at Balliol and later convert to Roman Catholicism, put it many years later,

> 'The University of Oxford is both a centre which draws to itself all that is powerful in this country, and a source from which those elements return to their several spheres of influence with an immense accession of strength, whether for good or evil. Moreover, Oxford possesses, so far as a Protestant University can possess it, a most valuable apparatus of oral teaching. Its lecture-rooms in the several colleges furnish, to those who preside in them, abundant means of moulding the ductile mind of young in one or another form'.[21]

It was not long before the Whig and anti-Tractarian Warden of New

College, Philip Shuttleworth, was complaining that 'the young men brought up at the feet of the Tractists are now beginning to occupy in great numbers the tutorships of the several colleges, and I fear will in consequence be enabled to do a vast deal of mischief'.[22]

The imprint of the university on the movement was most keenly felt through what can be called its 'ethos' and the spell exerted by historic Oxford over the Tractarian imagination. This spell has been linked to the associationist ideas and aesthetic theories emanating from Scottish Enlightenment thinkers; it was also a product of the influence of Romanticism, imbued with ecclesiastical overtones.[23] An interesting example of the veneration and historical idealism which the presence of Oxford could invoke in contemporary undergraduates is provided by the young Guernsey scholar of Pembroke College, Peter Le Page Renouf, in a letter home to his mother in 1841. Renouf described how he and his friends felt 'it an honour and a privilege to be living here in the dwellings of the good and great of former generations. Oxford is to us a second mother, for it we would willingly spend and be spent, and our eyes are continually turned towards its towers and its groves as the very hills of our earthly Zion'. In contrast, Renouf described the disdain he felt for one of his contemporaries, one Marrett, who did not share these feelings. Marrett, Renouf lamented 'never will be a thorough Oxonian. He has come up imbued with deeply engrained prejudices which time itself can never wear away . . . Marrett has not one spark of poetry or imagination about him'. This prevented him not only from appreciating the architecture of the place in an aesthetic sense, but worst of all, 'the college chapels and other relics of ancient piety he considers as the trumpery productions of a foolish and fatal superstition'.[24]

Newman's own vivid imagination and Romantic sensibility rendered him particularly susceptible to Oxford's spell. The almost apocalyptic mood of resistance to change which he embraced in 1829 was fuelled by potent images of historic Oxford as a 'place set apart' to 'witness to the nation'. Newman recalled that as he walked along the 'old road' from Oxford to visit his mother and sister at Horsepath in that fateful autumn of 1829, 'King Charles and his Bishop [Laud] seemed to rise before him'.[25] This Tractarian identification with an image of historic Oxford also helped instil an urgent sense of special vocation to be best fulfilled simply by remaining 'at their posts' in the university. It could encourage a disdain for 'outsiders' or intruders. As early as 1829, in discussing the invasion of journalists into Oxford to report on the Peel election, Newman was provoked into remarking on, 'their littleness ... amid the buildings of old Oxford, yet wishing to strut with all the bad taste and banausic of republicanism—they understood us about as much as they would Sophocles or Pindar'.[26] It was an attitude evident even in Newman's measured view of his friend and ally in the early years of the movement, William Palmer. Palmer was a graduate of Trinity College, Dublin, and in 1828 incorporated at Oxford. However, for all Newman's recognition of his friend's massive learning, it was still held as a point against him that 'he never had really grown into an Oxford man'.[27]

This disdain was apparent in the somewhat superior attitude which Oxford Tractarians adopted towards the sister university, Cambridge, though the feeling was often reciprocated. Certainly, it is a moot point of conjecture as to whether if Newman had gone to Cambridge, he would ever have emerged as a leader of a religious movement of the character of that which he led at Oxford. Cambridge had a very different theological temper and tradition, intellectual character and ethos. In Oxford Tractarian eyes, Cambridge, by admitting Dissenters without taking degrees, gave rein to boldness, self-will and lack of reverence. As George Moberly, a Fellow and Tutor of Balliol put it in 1834,

> 'how different is their religious system from ours. In our colleges a Roman Catholic, or Socinian, would feel their doctrines denied more or less directly every day of their lives. In the regular course of our religious reading, every form of Dissent would in turn be exposed and refuted. We have instituted, and we wish to perfect, a higher system of religious education than is there possible'.[28]

In short, from an Oxford Tractarian viewpoint Cambridge already had fatally compromised with the forces of latitudinarianism. She was in no position to take a vanguard position in the necessary academic counter-revolution to the forces of liberalism and secularity that Newman was convinced Oxford alone could lead. As Newman put it, 'let Cambridge wish us well, and cheer us to our work. We have at present the post of danger and honour; it may be hers another day!'[29]

For their part, various Cambridge figures were no less disdainful of the state of Oxford. Conscious of its curricular bias towards mathematics and the sciences, Cambridge academics felt that the spirit of their university was more rational, if more prosaic.[30] 'Our teachers preached common sense, and common sense said, stick to your triposes, grind at your mill, and don't set the universe in order till you have taken your bachelor's degree', Leslie Stephen later observed. In response to the common Oxford reproach that Cambridge could not appreciate Newman, Stephen retorted, 'we held that our common sense enabled us to appreciate him only too thoroughly by the dry light of reason and to resist the illusions of romantic sentiment. That indeed was the merit of Cambridge in the eyes of those who were responsible for my education . . . we shrank from all vagaries, whether of the high church or low church'.[31]

Yet it would be quite wrong to overlook the real extent to which warm intellectual debate and enquiry and rational argument played a part in the rise of Tractarianism at Oxford. For in a sense 'Noeticism' was the 'provocative of the subsequent movement'. An acute observer looking back noted in 1852,

> 'it is our object, to appeal to anyone who was acquainted with the inner life of the Oxford religious world twenty and five-and-twenty years ago, whether two very opposite, and now very prominent, parties in the English Church [Tractarian and liberal], are not the development of private discussions and every-day conversations within the walls of Oriel common-room'.[32]

Tractarianism probably could not so easily have taken root at Oxford without the free-ranging intellectual atmosphere of the 1820s in which ideas were readily interchanged and influences, such as those of Whately and Hawkins in their different way over the young Newman, brought to bear.[33] The Tractarians owed more than they later acknowledged to the academic reforms associated with John Eveleigh and Edward Copleston at Oriel, and with Dr Parsons at Balliol and Cyril Jackson at Christ Church. In particular, the Oriel emphasis on the value of intellectual debate and mental activity for its own sake as something more important than a narrowly technical commitment to 'the drudgery of the Schools' also left its mark. It was such priorities that would propel future Tractarians on to the path of desiring to 'set the universe in order'. However, while it was true that it was precisely the same mental activity within Oriel common-room that made some into 'Noetics' and others eventually into Tractarians, it was to be the peculiar character of Oxford's mental training that helped play a part in fostering the appeal of Tractarian ideas. Bishop Butler's moral philosophy, rooted in Aristotelianism, was held in higher esteem than at Cambridge, and permeated Oxford's system of education. It left an indelible mark on Gladstone as well as Newman, Froude and Keble. Many years later, Oakeley pointed out the tendency of Oxford's prevailing Aristotelianism to make men's minds more receptive to Tractarianism:

> 'the Aristotelian ethics, with the Christian philosophy of Bishop Butler as their commentary and supplement, entered into the academical education of all the more cultivated minds of Oxford, and contributed, in a pre-eminent degree, to form their character and regulate their tone ... No one can read Mr. Froude's "Remains", for instance without seeing, that with him, and with those whom he corresponded, the ethical system of Oxford had exercised no small influence in the formation of mental habits ... constantly he used to appeal to this great moral teacher of antiquity ("Old Stole", as he used playfully to call him), against the shallow principles of the day. Thus, then, it was that the philosophical studies of Oxford tended to form certain great minds on a semi-Catholic type'.[34]

One of the insights which the Tractarians drew from Aristotle's teaching was that mere 'head-knowledge' alone was not enough, that 'heart-knowledge' was essential. It is true that sometimes Tractarian theology, infused as it was with poetic and Romantic sensibility, assumed a Platonic temper; Newman attentively studied the Alexandrian Platonists, and his thinking was deeply influenced by them. None the less, the epistemology of Tractarian thought was primarily Aristotelian. Newman and other Tractarians might have been 'born' Platonists, as David Newsome has observed, but they became Aristotelians through their Oxford education.[35]

Given that the rise of the Oxford Movement was partly the product of a spirit of intense intellectual enquiry, it seems something of a paradox that contemporary liberal critics and many later historians should argue that the movement stifled such enquiry and speculation. From the liberal perspective, Tractarianism in the context of the history of Oxford University, has been widely regarded as at best an irrelevance or distraction, at worst, an alien and disruptive force. Thus, for Mark Pattison, a disillusioned and embittered one-time acolyte of Newman who came to embrace an overtly secular viewpoint, the movement in retrospect represented a fatal and damaging diversion from 'the true business of the place'.[36] The point was most forcefully made by one contemporary liberal critic, who wrote of what he called 'Oxford theology' that,

> 'it never could have been produced in a place where scientific thought or historical criticism had flourished. Had Oxford minds understood the laws of evidence, or had they been imbued with the principles of mathematical proof, Newman and his disciples would have laboured in the fire. Had even logic flourished as a science, Puseyism must have been strangled at birth'.[37]

Such charges were misplaced given the influence of Whatleyean logic over ductile future Tractarian minds, and also given Newman's own avowed interest in mathematics and mathematical principles. Yet, whatever the fairness of such a critique, what for many appeared to be the later theological aberrations of Tractarianism did help to reinforce some of the *Edinburgh Review*'s criticism of Oxford's system of education. Demands for curriculum reform voiced by John Playfair in the 1800s and restated by Sir William Hamilton in the *Edinburgh Review* in 1831, seemed to take on a more urgent relevance and meaning. Thus, the more radical university reformers of the late-1830s and 1840s used the perceived need to defend Protestantism in the face of Tractarianism as a conclusive argument in favour of broadening Oxford's curriculum so as to include more practical subjects.

2. The Tractarian Educational Ideal

The essentially Pattisonian viewpoint often echoed by modern intellectual historians is so dependent on narrowly secular presuppositions as to the meaning and role of a university as to do less than justice to the positive, reforming aspect of Tractarian educational ideals, framed as they were in religious terms. This viewpoint fails to engage with a conception of a university that gave ultimate priority to the achievement of religious and moral excellence and preservation of dogmatic truth rather than the pursuit of intellectual attainment alone. Liberal and secular critics of the Oxford Movement often argue that it possessed no definite corporative view of the university, its role in society or even the church: as if the university context were almost accidental, the Tractarians sometimes are portrayed as cynically making use of a privileged position to further theological ends irrelevant to the real needs or ends of a university. Yet the Oxford Movement from its origin did possess a clear and definite version and ideal of the university and its relation to church and nation. It was not that the Coplestonian ideal of university education was jettisoned, but as we shall see, that it was given a much deeper and more explicitly theological colouring and framework. As such, in Dean Church's words, the University of Oxford became 'the fulcrum from which the Tractarians hoped to move the church'.[38] Cathedrals, as another 'catholic vestige' of the economy of the ancient English church, would fulfil a similar role, and the High Church campaign for reform of both institutions often dovetailed. The battles which the Tractarians orchestrated in the mid-1830s against the admission of Dissenters, in defence of subscription to the Thirty-nine Articles at matriculation and in protest over the appointment of Hampden as Regius Professor of Divinity, represented much more than merely defensive operations in favour of the status quo in the manner of the old-fashioned Tory High Churchmen. The latter, along with many Evangelicals, may have rallied to the standard erected by Tractarian zealots at this time to form a 'triple alliance' against the spectre of Whig-inspired, external liberal reform. However, for the Tractarians such contests were occasions for the testing of new theories as well as restatements of old ones. They were motivated by a vision and ideal of a university. It was only when the implications of this vision, which amounted to a veritable counter-revolution, along with the attendant theological developments of Tractarianism, became apparent to the Tractarians' erstwhile allies that the 'triple alliance' broke down and its two other constituent elements emerged as opponents of the Movement.

It was in 1834–5, with the debate over subscription and the proposed admission of Dissenters, that the two essentially contrasting visions of the university surfaced within Oxford for the first time. Previously the university had always presented a united front against external foes.[39] This intellectual divergence was a consequence of the political breach within Oxford made in 1829. Of course, the use of the labels 'liberal' and 'Tractarian' to characterize distinct and opposed ideas about the university can be accepted as valid in only a very qualified sense. As with all such labels, there is an element of 'short-hand'. Colin Matthew is right to insist that many of those in favour of moderate internal reform in 1835, the so-called 'prudential liberal-conservatives' who included 'Noetics' such as Hawkins, never questioned the essentially religious character of the University and certainly did not favour the principle of religious pluralism being accepted at Oxford. Tractarians such as Henry Wilberforce were less than fair in lumping advocates of very limited change such as Hawkins together with radical, secular reformers, as assailants of the 'foundations of the faith' in Oxford.[40] Further confusion in the use of terms is caused by the way in which Newman and other Tractarians could use 'liberal' sometimes in a non-pejorative sense as in 'liberal education'. Pietro Corsi, in his study of Baden Powell, goes so far as to question the use of the term 'liberal' at all for this period as entirely anachronistic.[41] Certainly, for the pre-Tractarian era, where Corsi convincingly has shown that there was a far greater degree of intellectual and even theological consensus between the 'Noetics' (the apparent 'liberals' of the day) and High Churchmen than has usually been assumed,[42] he has a valid point. However, as Corsi argues, one should not underestimate the degree and depth of the intellectual as well as political breach in this consensus after 1829; a breach which by 1834–5 had led to stark polarization within the university. In this new, more troubled era of sharpened theological identity, the older Coplestonian certainties were deemed to be no longer enough as the main bulwark of Oxford's defence against external foes. Within Oxford it was no longer the basis of unity that it had once been. For the Tractarians, 'liberalism'—now defined with secular overtones in a pejorative sense—became a clearly defined threat to all that Oxford still represented in their eyes. At the same time, such a 'liberalism' became associated, however unfairly, with an association of ideas which 'Noetics' in the 1820s would have indignantly repudiated.

The polarization that took place within Oxford from the 1830s onwards may have not been a rift in the sense of the Scottish Disruption of 1843, but it was in all but name a 'great disruption'. Yet the polarization was not, as it is often presented, a one-sided process. In short, it was not simply the result of the Oxford Movement pushing matters to new extremes or, as it were, moving the theological 'goal-posts'. For there was also a shift in theological direction away from the earlier consensus apparent in some of the 'Noetics' and as Corsi convincingly shows, divergences of opinion would emerge even from within the Noetic circle.[43] In pre-Tractarian Oxford few would have denied or seen any incongruity in the epithet of 'Orthodox' or even 'moderate High Church' being applied to such leading 'Noetics' as Copleston, Hawkins and Kebles' Oriel friend, John Davison. In 1814, Copleston had even been happy to describe himself as a High Churchman.[44] Moreover, it was perhaps only in Oxford's peculiar context, that Hawkins's own High Church credentials might have been deemed suspect, though some continued to regard him as a 'moderate High Churchman'.[45] It may have been that it was only for future Tractarians that the Peel election was a cathartic experience, but after 1829, old High Churchmen as well as incipient Tractarians were convinced that some of the 'Noetics', notably Hampden and Baden Powell who had hitherto as Corsi demonstrates, been allied to the High Church camp,[46] were embracing a more self-consciously 'liberal' theological identity. This movement in one direction coincided with an ever more sharply anti-liberal consciousness among Oxford High Churchmen. However, it was Whately who was for a time deemed to be the most dangerous symbol of this perceived trend within 'Noeticism', so that the breach between Newman and his old mentor, Whately, would prove especially bitter. For according to Henry Wilberforce writing many years later, after 1829 there was widely attributed to the influence of Whately, 'a whole new turn to what had formerly been called the Oriel School, a turn towards rationalism'. It is Wilberforce's use of the word 'new' that deserves due emphasis here.[47]

The Tractarian alarm in the mid-1830s at even the very modest proposals of conservative 'Noetics' such as Hawkins was based on the perception that they, albeit unwittingly, seemed to aid the underlying strategy of those whom Matthew labels the 'assertive reformers'.[48] For the Tractarians, the pamphlets not only of Baden Powell but also Hampden in favour of opening up the university seemed designed to 'liberalize' in the sense of 'secularize' Oxford. Moreover, behind such proposals there did undoubtedly increasingly lie certain intellectual and moral presuppositions which struck at the root of the Tractarian idea of the university.

The essence of the liberal position on university reform was made clear by Hampden when he maintained that 'after all, the University is not the Church. It is only accidentally a society of church members, and considered as a literary society, it has surely no right to rest on authority, as the foundation of its lessons in any department of knowledge'.[49] Of course, this begged the key question: was not a university something more than a mere 'literary society'? Matthew, citing this highly significant passage has recognized, it was precisely because the Tractarians held that the university must remain a microcosm of the church that limitations on opinion became appropriate in a way that they could not be if a university was merely 'a society for the diffusion of literary and scientific knowledge', founded, in Lord Melbourne's words, 'for the support of literature and science'.[50] Given this liberal definition of a university and the secular liberal assumption that the universities were only civil institutions 'intended to promote general learning' it was easy for this type of reformer to diagnose a state of declension and corruption.[51] Thus Lord Holland maintained that Oxford had 'deviated from the original institution and has ceased to be either a national or general school for the arts, sciences and philosophy'.[52] Against this, the great bulk of Oxford churchmen would have admitted that the universities were only national institutions 'in so far as they were connected with the National church', but 'in no other point of view were they to be regarded as national institutions, for it could not be pretended even that they were supported by the nation'.[53] Even for conservative 'Noetics' and moderate reformers such as Hawkins, it was axiomatic that the universities were chartered private corporations, which had 'a right to expect that their charters shall not be interfered with, unless they can be shown to have been transgressed'.[54] However, because a minority of more advanced liberal reformers within Oxford such as Baden Powell and Edward Bayley, a university proctor, began to echo the more secularist demands of the university's parliamentary critics such as Lord Radnor pressing for reform from without, the belief grew that such Oxford liberals represented a dangerous 'fifth column'. The apparent collusion of this group with secular Whigs such as Lord Holland and the Melbourne administration gave a sinister political twist to the liberal threat to Oxford in Tractarian eyes.[55] Espousing a utilitarian concept of university education, liberal reformers came to support the admission of Dissenters into Oxford. Baden Powell supported this proposal on the specific ground of his belief, 'that scientific education may be adequately conveyed without blending it with any religious instruction'.[56] Hampden did not go this far but, while broadly supporting a continued supremacy of 'Church of England principles' at Oxford,[57] warmly advocated the admission of Dissenters on specifically religious grounds.[58] On the other hand Blanco White turned the argument the other way, warning Dissenters not even to seek admission to Oxford since that university was incapable of ever living up to the liberal ideal: 'much may be done in the way of internal improvements but I do not conceive it possible to make Oxford an establishment for the promotion of learning in general, as some people wish', he told Hawkins.[59]

In stark contrast, the Tractarians regarded the university 'in the light of a corporate minister of religion'. It was the solemn duty of all her members 'to regard her as the sacred ark wherein the truth has been preserved ... not as sceptical disputants, who would investigate for themselves a new road to the shrine of truth; but as humble and teachable disciples, labouring to ascertain what has been the church's faith and practice'.[60] For this reason, the university ordinance of 1581 which first prescribed the test of subscription to the Articles of matriculation, was invested with peculiar significance as a symbol of church as well as academic authority. It is notorious that Newman especially, as Tract 90 exemplified, was no great friend to the actual theological content of the Articles themselves. As early as 1835 he privately expressed the wish that the Creeds might be substituted for them. What mattered was that subscription to the Articles on matriculation impressed 'upon the minds of young men the teachable and subdued temper expected of them. They are not to reason, but to obey; and this quite independently of the degree of accuracy, the wisdom etc. of the Articles themselves'.[61] Thus, to tamper with this system of subscription was to strike at the keystone of the Tractarian understanding of the 'catholic' character of university education. It was for this reason that the Tractarians such as Henry Wilberforce so bitterly criticized even the modest compromise proposals of Hawkins in favour of a substitute for subscription in 1835. If the act of subscription was the matter of indifference which even liberal-conservatives like Hawkins seemed prepared to concede, then of course it could and should be abandoned in favour of a substitute. However, it was because for the Tractarians subscription exemplified a sacrosanct 'catholic principle' that it had to be preserved at all costs. The arguments of moderates such as Hawkins and Edward Denison that such a substitute might actually prove more exclusive and effective as a confessional test were deemed to be irrelevant, because ultimately for the Tractarians this was not the final and paramount concern.

The Tractarians did not oppose university reform in itself, but took issue with the ideological premises of the measures advocated in parliament and among a minority of advanced liberals within the university from 1835 onwards. As Benjamin Harrison, in response to renewed strictures from the *Edinburgh Review*, put it, 'if our universities are to be regarded properly societies for the diffusion of knowledge, we should have thought that it would have been better to style them societies "for the diffusion of useful knowledge" '.[62] The Tractarians defined education in quite different terms from that of secular liberal reformers. The Tractarian, Henry Woodgate succinctly summed up the difference—'they think Education consists in knowledge; we do not'.[63] A neo-Tractarian, William Sewell, Fellow of Exeter College and White's Professor of Moral Philosophy, was still more uncompromising in refutation of the utilitarian, liberal ideal of education. Sewell insisted that,

> 'we . . . do not consider the communication of knowledge as the chief design of our post, or the grand end of education . . . We are . . . entrusted with the care of the young . . . and our consideration is to form and fashion and bring them to that model of human nature, which in our conscience we think is perfection.
> This model . . . we do not find, and therefore we will not place in the intellect of man. And this is the first grand point in which we differ, wholly and irreconcilably differ, from the maxims of the present day'.[64]

The theory behind Oxford's tutorial system appeared to support this Tractarian view of university education. The conviction that religion came first, 'head-knowledge' second, permeated Newman's stand against Provost Hawkins over Oriel tuition between 1828 and 1830. In Newman's view, the role of a tutor should involve far more than imparting knowledge, possessing a moral, spiritual and pastoral dimension. As he reiterated many years later,

> 'when I was a Public Tutor of my college at Oxford, I maintained, even fiercely, that my employment was distinctly pastoral. I considered that, by the Statutes of the University, a Tutor's profession was of a religious nature. I never would allow that, in teaching the classics, I was absolved from carrying on, by means of them, in the minds of my pupils, an ethical training; I considered a College Tutor to have the care of souls'.[65]

This pastoral concept of the tutorial office could be regarded as inherent in the system of education evolved at Oxford over many centuries. Newman was right to claim countenance from the Laudian statutes in particular, for his view that a tutor 'was not a mere academical Policeman, or Constable, but a moral and religious guardian of the youths committed to him'.[66] Moreover, the Tractarians had good grounds for fearing that this view of the tutorial office was in danger of being lost sight of. That it had come to represent by no means the norm on the eve of the Movement is clear from the rapid growth of private tutors or 'crammers' whose role was the purely technical one of getting their pupils through the Schools. However, this in itself was essentially a short-term response to the marked academic improvements that had been instituted within Oxford since 1800, as the demands of the new examinations placed a strain on the old system.

The intellectual ferment of the 1820s with its concomitant college rivalries for honours and prizes represented a welcome advance over the apparent sloth and lethargy of the preceding century. However, the Tractarians were concerned to prevent the university from degenerating into an education factory on the lines of what Oxford men most despised, 'some Prussian or French academy'. William Sewell in the Tory *Quarterly Review* in 1840 well expressed this viewpoint when he roundly asserted that 'colleges were not mere educating machines; and this is a fact to be stated the more openly, and the more carefully borne in mind, as the narrow utilitarianism of the day has frequently availed to contract the view taken, even in Oxford itself, of their privileges and duties'.[67]

Newman and the Tractarians in general did not carry this reaction against the absolute supremacy of intellectual attainment so far as to make them ever lose sympathy with the basic Coplestonian ideal of a 'liberal education'—the notion 'that the purpose of the curriculum was simply to provide abstract training or mental discipline'. Newman emphasized the independence of mind and antipathy to 'low utilitarianism' of pre-Tractarian defenders and reformers of Oxford's educational system such as Copleston.[68] The Oriel tradition that Copleston had won an outright victory in 1810 in his controversy with the *Edinburgh Review* remained very strong, and Tractarians could appreciate that the genesis of the Oxford Movement itself owed much to the enormous boost to Oxford's self-confidence provided by Copleston's brilliant defence.[69] So strong was the impression that Copleston's defence made on Newman, that as a Roman Catholic in the 1850s he strove relentlessly to persuade an Irish Catholic audience that the true doctrine of the nature of a university lay in that protestant source. None the less, other Tractarians were by no means as unreserved in praise of Copleston's achievement as Newman generally was.

Although the Tractarians owed much to the climate of intellectual stimulus which the Oriel 'Noetics' helped foster, they increasingly came to fault the latter for a certain over-intellectualism and the neglect of the moral and religious dimensions of university education. Even Copleston, though much less unsympathetic to the Oxford Movement than is often assumed, did not escape later Tractarian criticism in this respect. He was criticized for having done too little to effect a moral reformation to match the undoubted intellectual reformation which he inspired within the Oxford of the 1810s and 1820s. As a later Tractarian writer complained, Copleston 'had left a certain high moral tone out of his system at the first start of life, and was never able, and even became physically incapacitated, to nerve up his resolution to be the advocate of that severity of manners and disinterested self-devotion which graced the teaching of his successors in academic life'.[70] Clearly, when viewed against the burning sense of religious mission along with a cultivation of familiarity that seemed to infuse the teaching methods of the next generation of Tractarian tutors, Copleston's somewhat lordly urbane style appears to belong to a different world. Yet Copleston's later private admission that the Oxford Movement itself had actually strengthened his own sense of the importance of 'church principles' is highly significant.[71]

To restore the moral and spiritual dimension of Oxford university education to more of a living reality was as much a central aim of the movement qua the university, as the propagation of high sacramental teaching and the call to 'apostolicity' was its aim qua the Church as a whole. Significantly, when Dean Church defined the Oxford Movement it was primarily as a moral and religious crusade to restore the University in accordance with the spirit of its founders.[72] Far from this necessarily entailing a blind opposition to all curriculum reform, it helped predispose the Tractarians in favour of renovation and renewal. It led to a serious questioning of some acccepted priorities and maxims in university education. That the movement actually favoured a potentially radical reorientation of Oxford's educational system was recognized perceptively by the then young Oxford liberal, A. P. Stanley, in a surprisingly sympathetic article in the *Edinburgh Review* in 1843. Stanley well delineated the philosophical basis of the Tractarian blueprint for reform, when he wrote,

'when first the theological "movement" began . . . there was excited at the same time in both universities, but especially in Oxford, a strong feeling of dissatisfaction with the existing studies and occupations of the place. It was the common language of all those who deemed that the frame and temper of society needed an extensive renovation, that this renovation must begin with the young. The presumptuous turn of mind, the reliance on intellectual ability, supposed to result from instruction addressing itself to the intellect alone, were to be corrected by a strong diversion in favour of a more subjective course of study. The study was to be the formation of moral character by habit, not the imparting of what is commonly called learning . . . Catholic theology, and Moral Philosophy in accordance with Catholic doctrine, were to be the main foundations of the improved education of these newer days; science and literature were not, indeed, to be neglected, but to be cultivated as in subordination only to these great "architectonic" sciences . . .'[73]

Clearly, it was envisaged that a renewed moral dimension and different order of priorities needed to be infused into the otherwise worthy Coplestonian educational model.

3. The Tractarians and University Reform

As long as proposals for university reform could be deemed as likely to further the philosophical priorities described above, then Tractarians could support them enthusiastically. Only if reform proposals appeared likely to subvert the ideal that they favoured would Tractarian resistance become implacable. Their concern for the highest academic standards was genuine. Thus Pusey was later anxious to make clear that the Tractarian orchestration of Convocation's opposition to the Heads' attempt to revise the statutes in 1839 stemmed from a genuine apprehension 'that the Hebdomadal Board would, together with what was really obsolete, bring down good Statutes to a lower standard, rather than wait until our standard should rise to the Statutes'.[74]

It was the same concern for standards that led Newman, unlike many of the old-guard High Churchmen, actually to welcome the publication in 1840 of the original statutes of Magdalen College by the Deputy High Steward of the University, G. R. M. Ward.[75] Ward was a radical university reformer and ideologically poles apart from the Tractarians, but Newman had been a contemporary of his at Trinity and had remained on friendly terms. Ward's was one of many similar publications of Oxford college statutes in English translation, in response to urgings from the University's Chancellor, the Duke of Wellington, that colleges would be better able to fend off the threat of external interference if the obsolete provisions in their statutes were revised.[76] The Tractarians recognized much better than some of Oxford's conservative die-hards that a judicious review of college statutes was necessary. They were quite as genuinely alarmed as any radical reformer at the revelation of abuses and widespread non-observance of statutes that Ward's publication revealed.[77]

To 'liberal' university reformers, the negative Tractarian attitude to some proposals for curriculum extension could easily appear tantamount to anti-intellectual obscurantism and myopia. Newman's own antipathy to such proposals was made clear in a letter to his friend, Charles Anderson, in 1836, when he wrote,

> 'As to Modern Languages, I do not think we ought to condescend to teach them, more than drawing or fencing. Much more may be said for Modern History, but serious difficulties present themselves here . . .—the introduction of modern politics. The present school of philosophers are disgusted with our teaching religion on a positive basis—would they be better pleased if we taught Toryism as well? and it is quite certain that, if we taught the history of the last three centuries, we should interpret it in our own way'.[78]

Yet it is possible to read more into these deliberately provocative comments in a private letter than is warranted. Modern languages had not been envisaged as necessary ingredients for the Coplestonian model of university education as mental training. It was because Newman still doubted whether they deserved to be included in the ambit of a 'liberal education' since their study appeared to involve or encourage a mere technical proficiency, rather than on any more sinister doctrinal grounds, that he opposed their introduction. There is no evidence to support the contention that Newman's attitude was determined by a serious desire to discourage students from reading dangerous continental works.[79] With the study of modern history there was less objection on the score of the 'mental training' criteria, but Newman's fears in this case as to the possible anti-dogmatic uses to which study of the subject might be put, were not as fanciful or absurd as might be supposed in the context of the period. Tractarian misgivings as to the suitability of modern history as an academic discipline were widely shared. Many felt that it could not be 'dispassionately considered' for, as J. A. Froude pointed out, it had become a political weapon, fuelling political and religious dispute.[80] There was contention enough in Tractarian Oxford without the addition of another potential source of dispute. As Slee shows, the process of overcoming such difficulties in Oxford would be slow and halting.

The Tractarians were still more sceptical about the academic value and legitimacy of another, increasingly fashionable subject, the study of political economy. Copleston had admittedly interested himself in this subject, but the extent to which liberal 'Noetics' such as Whately and Nassau Senior had identified themselves with its promotion as a university discipline[81] fuelled Tractarian fears as to the likely anti-dogmatic implications and 'evil frame of mind' which study of the subject was likely to engender among impressionable youth. However, rather than ignore the subject, the Tractarians were prepared to give it consideration so long as it could be taught and studied in strict subordination to the claims of Revelation. Thus they strove hard to influence the way in which the subject was taught, investing its study with more reference to principles of moral philosophy, and testing the maxims of Jeremy Bentham by recourse to Aristotle and Butler. For this reason, the Tractarians pushed their own candidates, first Woodgate, then F. D. Maurice, for the vacant professorship in 1837.[82] When Woodgate protested his ignorance of the subject, his Tractarian supporters pleaded that this was actually a recommendation in their eyes! As Hawkins informed Whately, 'it is thought that to make the Professorship do the least harm we should elect the man who knows the least of the subject'.[83] The idiosyncratic terms in which the neo-Tractarian Roundell Palmer espoused Maurice's candidature in itself represents a revealing expression of Tractarian educational priorities for the university;—

'He [Maurice] is a man who has always taken his philosophical premises as much from the spiritual world revealed to us in the Bible as from the sensible world by which our bodies are surrounded. He would (as I understood) if elected, endeavour to try the popular principles of political economy, by the test of principles higher and more certain than themselves; and particularly to recall the attention of his hearer to that interference of moral considerations which will in practice be sure to effect if not materially disturb those results, which modern economists have generally reasoned out by mere arithmetical calculation. All this seems to me to be very much wanted in the present state of the science; and Oxford is just the place from which it ought to come'.[84]

In the end, Tractarian hopes in Maurice were to be disappointed.[85] However, the very fact that even political economy could be deemed worth bringing within the orbit of the movement's ambitions of 'catholicising' the university shows that for the Tractarians no potential academic discipline could be regarded as immune from the application of their own philosophical principles.

Another characteristic charge against the movement from the liberal and secular perspective has been that it was per se anti-science. The Tractarian attitude to both the natural and physical sciences has been portrayed as a blind, narrow-minded antipathy based on a fear that the dogmatic edifice which the movement extolled might be thereby damaged in any way.[86] It is true that the mental climate of Tractarian Oxford, with the dominance of theological disputes, does not appear to have been conducive to the growth of scientific studies within the University. There was a marked fall in attendance at the lectures of such scientific luminaries as Professor Buckland. As G. L'E. Turner showed in an article in an earlier number of this journal, and as Nicholas Rupke has also demonstrated, there was a steady fall in numbers of undergraduates attending geology, chemistry, and mineralogy lectures in this period.[87] Geology, with its theological implications, remained more popular, but here too Turner traces a dramatic fall in lecture attendance after 1840. Moreover, the situation at Oxford at this period presented a sharp contrast with that of Cambridge where something of a 'scientific network', encompassing not only scientists alone but historians, theologians and other dons, flourished. Scholars such as Adam Sedgwick and William Whewell were at the forefront of this network.[88] Nevertheless it is facile entirely to blame the apparent decline of interest in science at Oxford on the Tractarians. Lecture attendance is but one, not altogether reliable index, of the level of interest. Moreover, it is easy enough to link even this fall in attendance to other academic factors. J. B. Morell and others have conclusively shown that the decline in numbers was largely the product of earlier curriculum reform at Oxford, and in any case, the beginnings of the decline well predated the rise of the Oxford Movement. Turner also suggests that the fall which can be dated from the later 1820s, was the positive reflection of the increasing strictness introduced into the examination statutes which in turn fostered a growing number of private coaches.[89] It was partly the increased demands that this placed on the time of undergraduates that explains the fall in attendance at lectures on subjects not examined in the Schools.

Moreover, at the personal level, it does appear that many future Tractarians when they had been undergraduates or young MAs in the 1820s had been assiduous in attendance at scientific lectures. For instance, Thomas Mozley, albeit an often unreliable witness, later recalled how he and Robert Wilberforce had been eager in their enthusiasm for Buckland's lectures.[90] Furthermore, there were those in the Tractarian entourage themselves closely involved in scientific pursuits. For instance, Newman's friend, Manuel Johnson, the last person whom he saw and bade farewell when he left Oxford for the last time in February 1846, held the prestigious post of Radcliffe Observer, and was always affectionately referred to by Newman as 'Observer Johnson'. The genial Johnson left an abiding impression on Oxford contemporaries. Mozley in his eccentric *Reminiscences* devotes a whole chapter to vivid description of his astronomical labours, about which he clearly had first-hand knowledge.[91]

On the philosophical level, the Tractarians readily accorded scientific endeavour the status of what has been called a 'norm of truth'.[92] As ever, what mattered were the principles on which scientific study were based. As the moral philosopher Sewell put it, 'the sciences which relate to matter ought to be studied upon Christian principles and methods, just as much as the sciences which relate to mind'.[93] As with their intellectual precursors in the eighteenth century, the so-called 'Hutchinsonians',[94] the Tractarians insisted that the Scriptures, duly studied and applied, were the appropriate guide to every species of scientific truth. Like the High Church Hutchinsonians, Tractarians stressed the limitations of physical science, and argued that its claims must be subject to the supremacy of theology. Given the almost constant fluctuations in the prevailing scientific orthodoxy, they felt that a certain scepticism about its claims was only healthy and realistic. As Newman told Pusey in response to the latter's expression of such scepticism following Buckland's own repudiation of some of his earlier theories,

> 'I quite feel what you say about Buckland's "Reliquae". It has made me distrust every theory of geology since; and I have used your words "why take the trouble to square Scripture with facts and theories, which will be all changed tomorrow, and be obliged to begin again?" '.[95]

It was, then, a question of priorities. As Pusey put it, 'all things must speak of God, refer to God, or they are atheistic' and just as 'history, without God, is a chaos without design, or end, or aim', just as 'political economy, without God, would be a selfish teaching about the acquisition of wealth', so 'physics, without God, would be but a dull enquiry into certain meaningless phenomena'.[96] In contrast to the liberal Anglicanism of the Noetic school, this outlook was reflected in a conscious depreciation of natural science and natural theology. Pusey stressed that if nature was not interpreted by the Bible, then the Bible would be brought down to the standard of nature.[97] Natural science was relatively unimportant because 'with matter it began, with matter it will end; it will never trespass into the province of the mind'. For this reason, moral philosophy would always be superior to physical science.[98] As Sewell put it, the former 'brings us into contact with spirit instead of matter—with human beings, and more than human beings, instead of ideal quantities and mechanical laws'.[99]

Nevertheless the Tractarian attitude to actual scientific discovery was both positive and detached. It had little or nothing in common with the truly negative denunciations of geological speculations from Evangelical, so-called 'Scriptural Geologists'. The meeting of the British Association for the Advancement of Science, held in Oxford in 1832, focused university attitudes to the claims of modern science. The geological section of the Association was prominent, and the geological speculations of scientists like Buckland and Charles Daubeny attracted much attention. Rather than the Tractarians, it was the Evangelicals and some die-hard Protestant High Churchmen, given to a literal interpretation of Genesis, who led the assault and in doing so made the mistake of trying to attack the men of science on their own ground. This line of attack was best represented by the Protestant High Churchman, Frederick Nolan's 1833 Bampton Lectures, *The Analogy of Religion and Science*. The points which Nolan made about the underplaying of Revelation in favour of secondary causes operating in the material world, with which Tractarians wholly agreed, were overshadowed by his reliance on discredited geological arguments. This only served to enable the advocates of the claims of science to brand their opponents as fundamentally opposed to all scientific inquiry.[100] The Tractarians did not fall into that trap. The best illustration of the Tractarian attitude to science is John William Bowden's 1839 review in the *British Critic* of the reports of the British Association; a review which won Newman's enthusiastic approval.[101] Bowden dissociated the Tractarian position from that of Evangelicals who denounced recent scientific discoveries because of their supposed inconsistency with a literal interpretation of the Bible. The Tractarians regarded the Church rather than the Bible alone as the chief instrument of Revelation, and did not wish to be confused with those who took such a negative position. Bowden insisted that the progress and prospects of physical science should be watched with an attentive, but not unfriendly eye. He made clear that,

> 'it is not our wish to take part with those who, startled by the tone in which some of its recent discoveries have been promulgated, have subjected it and them, as though essentially opposed to truth revealed, to a general denunciation'.[102]

Science presented man with a view which was necessarily partial and temporal, a view which since it had to do with 'the minor and subordinate system of things visible and tangible', might well appear irreconcilable with his glimpses of 'the higher system of things spiritual and revealed'. The believer had to accept mystery and the limitations of human knowledge. He would have to wait for the ultimate resolution of apparent incongruities. Science could never be a threat to revealed truth as long as it accepted the boundaries and limitations of its spheres of influence and application. In this way, their high doctrine of the Church and the role of mysticism enabled Tractarians to take an essentially detached view. As Bowden put it,

> 'We would watch then the progress of physical science, not from any apprehension of the direct and legitimate results of its career; not as though it were a branch of inquiry to be pursued by its votaries with a timid or apprehensive spirit, as though they might discover too much, might carry their researches too far, and were ever on the verge of abysses in which the faith and peace of the Christian world might be irrevocably engulfed; we

would watch it, because we feel that this pursuit, while, like all others open to man, it has its own attendant moral dangers, is now, from its position and predominance in the world, exposed to those dangers in a highly exaggerated degree'.[103]

It was not science as such, but the new breed of 'gentlemen of science' represented by the activities of the British Association, and the new and radical definition of the meaning and realm of science that they propagated, which the Tractarians repudiated.[104] It is in this context that instances of Tractarian denigration of scientific pursuits as an 'unworthy employment', as cited by Corsi, need to be placed. New claims to absolute intellectual authority, without regard to the claims of Revelation, were propounded by the savants of the British Association. Active officers of the Association openly boasted that it was identified with no dogmatic system. In Oxford, Baden Powell, as Savilian Professor, began to insist that the claims of physical science should be judged quite independently of Revelation.[105] For the Tractarians, the British Association inevitably became a symbol of a prevalent rationalizing and liberalizing spirit, and a representative of 'that anti-Christian pseudo-philanthropy which characterises the fashionable infidelity of our generation'.[106] Moreover, its avowed latitudinarianism or indifferentism was compounded by Whig and Dissenting as well as Cambridge connections—reinforcing the Tractarian view that coming to Oxford, the British Association represented a violation of the purposes of the university and an unwanted intrusion of an alien spirit.[107] The avowed links of the 'gentlemen of science' not only with both ultra-liberal Anglicans and prominent Dissenters, caused the Tractarians (with the growing campaign to force the universities to admit Dissenters in mind) to fear that the scientists represented forces which would secularize Oxford and supplant historic Christianity by a new religion of science and the philosophers who were its hierophants. The British Association was a menace because,

'one of the fundamental principles of their self-formed fraternity was the neglect or oblivion, for certain purposes, of those great landmarks, with reference to which the Universities, like all other ancient religious institutions, were founded, and which it was one of the ends of their foundation perpetually to maintain'.[108]

For Tractarians, science could have a place in university study, but a university properly understood should no more be a mere scientific academy on the recently evolved German model as it could be an academy for the general Arts and literature. Pusey came closest to summing up the Tractarian idea of a university in his evidence to the Hebdomadal Board's reply to the royal commission in 1852:

'The problem and special work of an University, is not how to advance science, not how to make discoveries, not to form new schools of mental philosophy, nor invent new modes of analysis; not to produce works in Medicine, Jurisprudence, or even Theology; but to form minds religiously, morally intellectually, which shall discharge aright whatever duties God, in His Providence, shall appoint to them'.[109]

Tractarian dissatisfaction with the condition of the Church of England, and their advocacy of what Newman called 'a second Reformation', in practice encouraged both intellectual speculation on theological matters and generated reform proposals and positive ideas for curricular extension and the organization of teaching within the university to further that end. For instance, the Tractarians from the start of the movement, pressed for the wider study of church history and liturgy within the university—High Church involvement in the foundation of Durham University and the determination that such subjects should be given paramount attention there, reflected a profound feeling of dissatisfaction with the older universities on this point. As early as 1834, Benjamin Harrison urged that professors of church polity be created at Oxford and Cambridge.[110] In 1837, conscious of the need to improve clerical training at Oxford, the Tractarians supported a private offer to fund a liturgical chair. It was the Heads who rejected the offer.[111]

It was not theological studies alone that the Tractarians sought to promote. Newman favoured an examination for the MA degree, and sought to encourage Mathematics, on the conventional Coplestonian ground that it offered a valuable exercise in mental training. Moreover, the Tractarians did not oppose plans, first mooted in 1839, to revive the decayed professorial system within the university. A fully working professorial system of teaching was closely associated with the German universities, and enjoyed the advocacy of advanced liberals such as Bonamy Price. On the face of it, this was unlikely to appeal to the Tractarians. In practice, however, the neglect of many of the formal duties previously attached to the professoriate placed heavier burdens of teaching upon the college tutors. The revival of the professoriate might better promote the Tractarian ideal of the tutor as pastor, and Newman supported it on these grounds.[112] As William Sewell put it in 1840,

'the result of a change would be so far from that which is found in Germany, that it would at once enable tutors to unite with the instruction of the juniors their own legitimate duties as guides, and friends, and spiritual pastors. It would be an additional bulwark against all that is to be dreaded in foreign systems; because it would make the tutorial system an effective check upon it, instead of an unconscious or unwilling accessory to it'.[113]

In 1839 the proposal was lost in Convocation, but in 1840, the Russell government raised the matter again alongside a proposal to reorganize the Christ Church chapter. A canonry was offered for the Margaret Professor, along with two more for proposed new chairs of ecclesiastical history and biblical criticism. Opposing the admission of Dissenters in the 1830s, Oxford's conservative defenders had stressed the importance of the university's religious training; by 1840 both the Tractarians and protestant High Churchmen were admitting the inadequacy of that training, urging acceptance of the new chairs on the specific ground that the course of studies at the University for the clergy 'are of a character too general and vague to have any sufficient bearing on the future usefulness of the christian Minister'. Protracted negotiations between Dean Gaisford and Archbishop Howley eventually bore fruit in the foundation of the regius chair of ecclesiastical history and pastoral theology, part of whose duties covered those set out for the ill-fated liturgical chair in 1837.[114] The scheme was passed in high hopes. Charles Perry's plea for greater professional and vocational training for the clergy in Oxford—where, in contrast to the preparation of the presbyterian clergy at Scottish universities, evidence of study in theology as a distinct branch of study was not required of ordinands for the Church of England—could not but arouse Tractarian support. Yet the Tractarians came to oppose a new statute to introduce an examination in theology proposed by the Heads in 1842, foreseeing a danger in relegating divinity to the level of just another academic discipline. It would encourage what Newman once described as the 'evil frame of mind' whereby 'the learner is supposed to be external to the system' so that 'the student is supposed to look upon the system from without, and to have to choose it by an act of reason before he submits to it'.[115] Academic politics added another dimension to their opposition, for the Tractarians feared that, by giving the Regius professor of divinity powers to oversee the proposed theology examination, the Heads were placing in the hands of the Tractarians' theological enemy, R. D. Hampden,[116] the power to withhold degrees on an apparently arbitrary assessment of a candidate's anti-Tractarian theological soundness.[117]

4. The Tractarians and Reform of the Colleges

The Tractarians made use of the occasion of Ward's publication of the Magdalen college statutes to call, not for the abrogation of any statutes but for their full observance and restoration of the spirit of 'our Founders'. Neither Copleston nor Davison,[118] still less the robust protestant high church Tories of the Oxford of the 1820s, had much sympathy with the monastic ideal, and Tractarian advocates of reform noted and lamented the 'wordliness' and anti-ascetic temper of even the best in the Oxford of the recent past. In 1838 Newman offered an uncompromising statement of his vision of an Oxford restored on medieval lines, counselling members of the university,

'never to forget that their present life is but a continuation of the life of past ages, that they are, after all, only in a new form and with new names, the Benedictines and Augustinians of a former day. The monastic element, a most important ingredient in the social character of the Church, lingers among them, when the nation at large has absorbed it in the frivolous or evil tempers and opinions of an advanced period of civilisation'.[119]

Moreover, the defence of the monastic ideal and the values of medieval Oxford engendered a conscious repudiation of the complacent, self-satisfied tone of the older protestant High Church Tory champions of the University who while defending existing abuses, inveighed against those supposedly committed by their pre-Reformation forebears. With such Tory churchmen in mind, Newman complained that

'while Oxford never shows so well as when resisting innovation, and rallying round some ancient principle which is emperilled, it never shows so weakly as when, professing such a course, it yet censures or separates from those who centuries ago did the same . . . Hence the common practice . . . of men's purchasing for themselves a licence for what the world calls intolerance and bigotry, by declaiming against the like allied failings in their forefathers, or of hiding, as far as may be, their own modicum of so-called formality and superstition, by denouncing those who had a little more of both than themselves'.[120]

Robert Hope-Scott made a similar point in a review of a translation of the fifteenth-century statutes of Magdalen College, published in 1840. He parodied what might have been the plan of such an article as if composed by a typical Oxford churchman of half a century or more before:

'We should say something about the "curious picture of manners" which these statutes unfold . . . We should then draw attention to the importance of such "evidences" and "monuments" in tracing the origin of customs and the meaning of words. After that we should soundly abuse the schoolmen for dunces, and laugh at the "superstitions of those days". The founder we might call "pious and munificent", hinting all the time that he was far beyond his age; nay, we might go so far as to assert that he was a Protestant, and perhaps succeed in proving him no Catholic. After this we should proceed to James the Second and Dr. Hough, when we should speak at large of Popery, Despotism, and the Bill of Rights. And then, having bestowed no small praise upon the "polite genius" and the "rational religion" of our own times, we might conclude with a hope that Magdalen College might long continue to promote "virtue and good breeding", "letters and civility", in this great and free nation'.

Hope-Scott concluded that 'such a strain would ill satisfy us now', because of the altered circumstances of the time. For the Tractarians, identification with 'the spirit of our Founders' was far more than mere Romantic escapism, or sentimentalism. To them, history was not an old almanac, providing 'curious' records of antiquarianism, but living and able to be rekindled still, the pre-Reformation college statutes offering a counter-revolutionary model of university reform.[121]

In Oriel College, Newman advocated a return to the spirit of the fourteenth-century founder, Adam de Brome, with the Head and the Fellows living together as a brotherhood, sharing a common table, all devoted to a life of study, and using their learning in the service of God. Newman wished to restore 'that portion of the ancient college which had faded away, namely the idea of a resident body of Fellows engaged not in teaching but in advanced theological study'.[122] Comparing the statutes with current practice he found 'only two things which are not in substance . . . observed; the Provost living with the Fellows, and the Fellows residing. This excepts of course the great deviation common to all the Catholic Foundations; the cessation, i.e. of Prayer for the Founders'.[123]

Prayers for the dead being one of the doctrines upheld by the primitive church which the Tractarians wished restored, Keble lamented the cessation of prayers for college founders, regarding it 'as a most lamentable concession to Ultra Protestant fears and jealousies; nor do I think we shall ever be quite right till it is repaired'.[124] Newman himself made a special point of praying for Oriel's founders and benefactors. The other deviations from the founder's intentions proved more difficult to remedy.

The original ideal of holy poverty as a condition for holding a fellowship had been lost sight of from both de Brome's Oriel and Waynfleete's Magdalen. Writing in 1840, William Sewell considered

'The present danger of our universities is in nothing so much as that they neglect the claims of poverty. There is always too much temptation in such institutions to raise a purely intellectual standard, instead of that admirable threefold one which our ancestors maintained, in making good character, good capacity, and poverty, equally requisite for election to fellowships, etc'.[125]

Newman attempted to introduce such criteria into the election of fellows at Oriel, to leaven the college with a body of like-minded men about him. A further problem was that, contrary to the intention of college founders, fellows rarely resided. To rectify these deviations, and further his medieval cenobitic ideal, Newman strove to make sure that Fellows were not lured off to secure livings or to get married, and that they remained in residence, living frugally. The pursuit of learning was to be the object of their lives. They were not necessarily to engage in tuition, but to assist all members of the college in their own line of study. What Newman wanted to rekindle above all, and make the lynch-pin of the restored system, was a common feeling of spiritual and scholarly brotherhood among all members of the society, regardless of academic status.[126]

The authority of the Oriel Provost, Edward Hawkins, and the privileged status enjoyed by wealthy students as Gentlemen-Commoners represented insuperable obstacles to the realization of Newman's dream. Irreconcilable differences between Newman and

Hawkins over the latter, rather than over the role of the tutor as such, underlay the controversy of 1828–30, when Hawkins removed Newman from his teaching position within the college.

Had Keble been elected Provost of Oriel in 1828, Newman's plan night have been realized. Hurrell Froude had urged Keble's claims: he 'would bring in with him quite a new world, that donnishness and humbug would be no more in the College, nor the pride of talent, nor an ignoble secular ambition'[127]—all things which Copleston, for all his virtues and role in raising Oriel to a state of academic greatness, was later to be accused by some Tractarians of fostering. At the time, Newman was unmoved by this, and he eagerly backed Hawkins as 'the more practical man' and one who already had a reputation as a stern disciplinarian. Moreover, as yet, Hawkins was supposed to be in tune with a growing feeling among college tutors and fellows 'that the Heads of Houses usurped', or at least 'injuriously engrossed power in University matters, and that those who did the work, the resident Fellows, not those who had no work to do, should have the power'. However, once Hawkins became Provost, he

> 'did not shrink from declaring that all was as it ought to be, that after all the Masters were a real and effective power in the resident body, that the Proctors efficiently represented them in the Hebdomadal Board, and that no reform was called for. This is what was said in Oriel by his friends as well as by others. They accused him also in their talk with each other, of assuming state and pomp, and of separating himself from his own Fellows, . . . and moreover, of courting the society and countenance of men or rank and name, whether in the world, or in the state, or the Church. They smiled, when instead of speaking of the Provost's "lodgings", he talked about "my house" '.[128]

Newman's concept of the college as a spiritual brotherhood was frustrated by such 'donnishness', and Hawkins's championship of the traditional privileges of the Gentlemen-Commoners sealed the fate of its implementation. The Tractarian ascetic ideal exhibited an antipathy to what Hurrell Froude called 'the gentlemen heresy' among the clergy. As Sheldon Rothblatt has shown, Newman's concept of a 'gentleman' was ambivalent; for Newman realized that the gentleman was more a product of intellectual culture than of Christianity. As the supposed training ground for the Anglican clergy, the Tractarians felt strongly that the real place to set about refashioning the concept, emphasizing the moral and spiritual over secular, social values, was at the source—within the universities. One of the criticisms some Tractarians came to make against Copleston was that he cultivated men of fashion, and had made 'the gentlemanly character too primary and single a consideration'.[129] Hawkins, his successor, also disappointed those who had supported him for the Provostship in 1828 in the hope that he would institute radical internal changes that would reinfuse something of the original intentions of Adam de Brome. In fact, Hawkins was convinced that the Tractarians had misconstrued the intentions of the college founders. He insisted that college fellowships had not, as the Tractarian reformers seemed to imply, been intended by the founders for monastic clergy not for 'merely learned academic' clergy, but for 'a learned clergy qualified to teach the people by their life and doctrine'.[130] In fact this was a traditionalist Anglican position, directed against radical secular reformers like H. H. Vaughan who demanded that fellowships should be applied to the needs of secular learning. Hawkins used it now against the Tractarians, whom he felt were making a false appeal to a spurious medieval ideal. For their part the Tractarians remained convinced that Hawkins's prosaic, legalistic mind quite failed to understand the underlying 'medieval spirit' which they read into the original statutes, and that his essentially patronizing 'high and dry' attitude to Oxford's collegiate founders was akin precisely to that of an earlier generation which Hope-Scott had so remorselessly satirized in the *British Critic*.[131]

The ascetic and 'monastic' ideals of Oxford's early college founders found expression in the special provision that was made for poor scholars. Tractarians maintained that in founding their colleges men such as William of Wykeham and William Waynfleete had aimed at educating poor scholars for the service of the church. For the Tractarians, an apparently excessive regard to the claims of birth and rank, exemplified in the status and special privileges accorded to gentlemen-commoners, had done more than anything to pervert a practical application of the ideals of the medieval founders over the preceding century and a half. It was deemed to have led to a slavery to outward forms while in practice, proving subversive of true discipline. Thus Tractarians wished to strip away what they called, 'the monstrous idol of university etiquette, which in days of gross corruption and general laxity set itself up "as God in the house of God", prescribing a rigid form of outward deference to rank and station, in lieu of that real heartfelt deference to superior worth which could no longer be depended upon for the preservation of university order, when station and dignity had become less a sign of worth than worthlessness'.

The aristocratic and socially stratified world of Cyril Jackson's Christ Church was quite as foreign to the fulfilment of this Tractarian university ideal as were any 'Germanised' blue-prints of the liberal reformers. Both were deemed to neglect the role, value and dignity of the poor scholar. Tractarians complained that 'modern delicacy' had obliterated 'from our universities the entire class of poor and deserving scholars, the very classes for which the colleges at least were founded'.[132] By means of infusing them with such a class, colleges could be rejuvenated in a more plain, ascetic, 'medieval' direction.

Newman's hopes of reforming Oriel on 'monastic' lines were not helped by the fact that the class of poor scholars there had entirely disappeared. At Magdalen, on the other hand, with the continued existence of scholarships, called 'demys', conditions seemed more favourable for such reform. Demyships had originally been intended for the support of poor boys, but their historical idealism blinded Tractarians to the fact that, whatever the founder's intention, these emoluments had not been regularly enjoyed by poor scholars since the seventeenth century at least. However, Hope-Scott had no doubts as to the intentions of Magdalen's founders. He held up the statutes of that college as the ideal model of a body of poor scholars, Fellows and President, all living under a common discipline and on equal terms, united in a common life of prayer, charity, self-denial and theological study, and claimed Magdalen was where such a model could most easily be recreated.[133] He saw in Magdalen the possibility of imitating St Maur, the great French Benedictine monastery which had in the seventeenth and eighteenth centuries flourished as a centre of theological scholarship and deep learning combined with ascetic piety.[134]

Hope-Scott's proposals for Magdalen stood little more chance of realization than Newman's for Oriel. Only at Merton was full advantage taken of the demand for voluntary statute reform in the later-1830s to effect something of a conservative 'counter-revolution' in a college on Tractarian lines. As a fellow of Merton, Hope-Scott managed to get some of his positive ideas into practice, when a committee of Merton fellows was set up by college to implement a reform of its statutes in 1839. As an historian of the college has observed:

'Their first inquiry was into the motives of the founder and the original purposes of benefactions. They did not conceive of the College and its revenues as a bare tablet on which to impress the sign-tokens of their own originality and super-eminent wisdom ... They reported simply that the College was founded mainly for poor students to study theology, though a few, for the good of the Church, might study civil and canon law. The College determined as simply that in future all Fellows save five should observe their founder's intention, and the five might study any branch of jurisprudence'.[135]

In 1846, a further move in an anti-secular direction was taken in direct opposition to the whole trend of liberal reform proposals for the university, with the issuing of new orders that all fellowships in future, save six, should be clerical, or awarded to those intending to take holy orders. However, even here the spirit of counter-reformation was short-lived. Hope's vacation of his fellowship in 1847 heralded a turning of the tide. From then on, it ran strongly the other way. As the college historian put it, 'the appeal to antiquity, which as it stirred Oriel in questions of religion swayed Merton in questions of the reform of study' was discredited. When in 1853 the college finally decided that henceforth only a bare majority should study theology, the Tractarian dream was destroyed.[136] The future lay with the liberal reformers, and such rearguard actions as those at Magdalen and Merton would even become the object of satire.[137]

Although the Tractarian educational ideal was able to make but little headway in the colleges in terms of actual reorganization, it did find classic expression in at least three private schemes carried out by leaders of the movement. Firstly, in 1836, Pusey, increasingly a recluse from what he considered the luxury and self-indulgent life-style of canons of Christ Church, threw his house and income there open to young graduate students, on condition that they studied theology or subjects connected with it.[138] It was in this setting that younger followers of the movement collaborated with him in embarking on the project of the 'Library of the Fathers'. In 1837, Newman took a house in St Aldate's, with the object of 'occupying it with a sufficient number of men without Fellowships, but who wish to stay up regularly in the University'. It was to be 'a reading and collating establishment', carrying on the spade-work for the 'Library of the Fathers' in an atmosphere of prayer, piety and frugality.[139] However, the fullest attempt to recreate something of the spirit of 'monastic' learning suggested by the example of St Maur, which the Tractarians in vain tried to kindle at Oxford, came with the setting up of the community under Newman's informal direction in the cottages at Littlemore, a village three miles south-east of Oxford but part of the parish of St Mary the Virgin where Newman was vicar. Newman's plan owed much to the inspiration provided by Hope-Scott's article. He attempted to realize in 'a complete type or specimen' the very institution which he and his followers had been considering since the earliest days of the movement. The model was medieval in source, and a kind of conscious protest against what Newman increasingly regarded as the almost institutionalized secularity of modern Oxford colleges.[140] Yet, in so far as all these projects entailed something of a conscious retreat, a search for a refuge from the University as such, they represented tokens of defeat of Tractarian hopes of 'catholic' reform of collegiate life within Oxford.

5. The Failure of the Ideal

Newman's followers continued to grapple with the realization of the movement's vision for the university, but most schemes proposed reflected an ever deeper 'opting out' of the attempt to rejuvenate the mainstream of college and university life from within, and became increasingly piecemeal and 'sectarian' in character. The foundation of theological colleges itself reflected the growing sense that the university could no longer fulfil the theological needs of the new generation of ordinands,[141] a reflection of the ever higher standards expected of the clerical office which, in turn, was partly a by-product of the movement. Tractarian proposals for university reform had aimed at making Oxford meet those higher demands and standards. Their defeat helped foster the process of fragmentation and piecemeal improvisation. Pusey, Acland, and Gladstone, despairing of Oxford, even began to contend that cathedrals should become more devoted to the specific ends of clerical education hitherto monopolized by the universities.[142] Elements of the Tractarian educational programme thus continued to be pressed on unsympathetic university authorities, but the original unity of purpose and conception was gone. For instance, in 1848, the earlier demand for better provision for poor scholars as part of a programme of university extension was revived by the Tractarian, Charles Marriott.[143] However, by then, the impossibility of carrying out sweeping internal reforms of the colleges had led to the demand for separate, independent institutions, if need be away from Oxford. The plan for a hall for a hundred or so of such 'deserving scholars' and ordinands to be set up at Worcester college in 1845 envisaged an institution that was in effect separated from, albeit adjacent to, that college.[144] There was no real attempt at integration. Here was the germ of the idea of a separate Tractarian college that found expression in the foundation of Keble. That foundation, in so far as it represented the need for 'separation' and 'refuge' from an increasingly 'secular' Oxford, rather than the original idea of a 'catholic' leavening of all the colleges from within, reflected the ultimate symbol of the failure of the movement's idea of a university.

Given the moral and religious ascendancy which the Tractarians had acquired within the university by the late 1830s, their failure to win university acceptance of more of their educational ideas and have them carried out into practice, might seem a matter of surprise. In many ways, the climate seemed right. The demand for a moral reformation at Oxford—tighter discipline, greater frugality, better vocational training for the clergy—was widespread, and far from confined to followers of the movement. Some of the keenest opposition to the overtly secularizing reform proposals of the more advanced liberals, such as H. H. Vaughan, came from 'prudential liberal-conservatives' such as Copleston and Hawkins. Copleston opposed Vaughan's plan to increase the number of law and medical (and hence, non-clerical) fellowships as 'manifestly at variance with the letter and also the spirit of the original statutes'.[145] Even the emphasis on the pastoral role of the tutor was not an aim unique to the Tractarians. Many Evangelicals and the more religious and earnest among the younger liberal party associated with thc followers of Dr Arnold took a no less high-minded view of the tutorial office. Although, perhaps, they might have represented a minority in the 1830s, by the mid-1840s tutors resembling Churton in *The Collegian's Guide* were more common. Such tutors, according to that manual of undergraduate conduct, were 'men who talked less to their pupils about mere classical and scientific knowledge than about the tone and temper of their minds', who 'regarded lectures and honours as means, and not the only means, to a far more noble end, that end being to send forth to the world, in the whole armour of human learning, and heavenly light, champions of the Church of Christ'.[146] Whatever previous standards had been, it is clear that, by the early-1840s, the Tractarians had no monopoly of moral and religious earnestness in the university. Even Tractarian supporters had to admit that Arnold had done almost as much if not more than Newman to leaven the university with a higher moral and religious tone than in previous generations. As George Moberly, a tutor at Balliol in the 1830s, conceded, 'it soon began to be matter of observation in the University, that Arnold's pupils brought quite a different character with them to Oxford than that which we knew elsewhere—his pupils were thoughtful, manly-minded, conscious of duty and obligation, when they first came to College; we regretted, that they often were imbued with principles which we disapproved, but we cordially acknowledged the immense improvement in their characters in respect of morality and personal piety'.[147] At the same time, protestant high churchmen, conservative evangelicals, and even some of the morally earnest Arnoldian liberals such as A. C. Tait and A. P. Stanley could accept the broad religious principle inculcated by the Tractarians of the paramouncy of the claims of religion in any educational system. What neither of these parties could accept, and what was to make the Oxford Movement's plan for university reform really distinctive and unique, was the nature of the religious principles on which Tractarian schemes for university reform were grounded. Once the Oxford Movement came to be seen as a threat to traditional protestant orthodoxy, and the external radical threat to the university receded, the anti-liberal 'triple alliance' of the 1830s quickly unravelled.

Paradoxically the very earnestness and moral and religious energy of most churchmen and academics of all parties made it more difficult for the Tractarians to achieve their ends than it might have been in the lethargic Oxford of a half-century or more previously. The movement, of course, was a force for earnestness, but earnestness of a particular sort, that did not commend itself to the no less earnest liberals of the Arnoldian school. It stressed self-denial, repose, introspection, quiet study—in its 'Oxford stage' it was often accused of being 'unpractical', out of touch with the modern world and reality. Certainly, it was not in tune with the dynamic, bustling, practical, and 'professional' spirit so characteristic of the early Victorian era, with its demand for utility, efficiency, productivity and high priority given to the creation of wealth. It did not, like the age, set a high value on the 'active' virtues.[148] Even the 'prudential liberal-conservative' category among campaigners for university and educational reform, moral and religious as they were, in so far as they came to stress professionalization and specialization, reflected something of that alien spirit within Oxford—their fascination with the study of political economy being no coincidence in this respect. One contemporary perceptively recognized the collision of two equally earnestly held university ideals when he wrote that,

'The new enthusiasm of reform had to encounter the new reactionary idealizing of the past. The middle classes and the middle ages—things most diverse—came into authority together. There seems nothing in common between men who regarded the colleges as "relics" of a "mischievous medievalism inconsistent with the healthy temper and wider views of modern European life", and conservatives who declared, "It is a blessed thing for the country that there should be some one place fenced around with chapels and with cloisters, where some few men may live and die removed from all this giddiness and din, to preserve even the name of truth and the memory of the past" '.[149]

Had it simply been a matter of Tractarian earnestness engaging old-fashioned Tory Oxford lethargy, there would have been little in the way of a contest or conflict of ideas. It was the challenge of Arnoldian liberalism that made such a conflict inevitable and bitter. Significantly, Newman could candidly admit that had there been an appropriate mental revolution at that time, then the conditions pertaining in the Oxford of the mid-eighteenth century would have rendered the university much more susceptible to being remoulded on the model of St Maur than it was in the more earnest and industrious 1830s. Tractarians might deplore the laxity of the earlier age, but they could not but lament the passing of a more tranquil, contemplative Oxford, while sighing over the lost opportunities of which the University of that period of 'port and prejudice' was guilty in their eyes. As Newman explained,

'Oxford was a place of leisurely thought, of multifarious but undigested erudition, of wayward irregular exertion, of enthusiastic college feeling, of repose relieved by the graceful or splendid sallies of wit. It was a place equally favourable for genius and for abuses. No examinations or class-lists directed the mind either of tutor or pupil to definite objects or and necessary preparations, or raised their eyes from the walls of their college to the University schools, and from the schools to the busy walks of life. Oxford was their home, their resting-place, and had both the advantages and disadvantages of a home; it was a very dear place, but a very idle one. It was not a place of passage, or of lodging for a year or two, or a means to an end, so frequently as it now is. Such a state of things, had its capabilities had been fully understood, might have been productive of most beneficial results; the fault was, not that inducements for exertion were not supplied from without, but that there were no active principles stirring within'.[150]

Thus the Tractarians recognized only too well that the intellectual and even religious ferment of the Oxford of their day had been achieved at a price. A man like the venerable President of Magdalen, Martin Routh, living cloistered in his lodgings for over half a century, buried in his books, seemed the symbol of a bygone age that, for all its sloth and apathy and lack of imaginative historical sense or reverence for the past, was in some senses actually closer to their much cherished 'medieval' Oxford than their own. Above all, they lamented that the Oxford of their day was much less shielded from, and immune to 'harmful' London influences than that of the previous century. The 'renaissance' of the Oxford of the 1810s and 1820s is rightly claimed by Newsome to have been the harbinger of the theological and spiritual 'reformation' of the Oxford of the 1830s. However, it is perhaps doubtful after all whether that intellectual renaissance was, in the long run, conducive to the realization of the Tractarian idea of the university. The spectre of secularization, later associated with the ideal propagated by advanced reformers such as Benjamin Jowett and Goldwin Smith, was already on the horizon. The Tractarian counter-revolution had probably come too late to succeed.

6. Conclusion

Newman's and Tractarian Oxford's idea of a university can be said to have been a refinement and development of Copleston's; 'liberal' in a cultural sense as opposed to merely utilitarian or 'professional' in its educational priorities, but imbued with a far profounder theological and moral dimension. Newman was always explicit in his conviction that it was Oxford's unique collegiate structure that allowed university teaching to transcend the mere dissemination of knowledge and to become an actual agent of moral regeneration. Yet the intellectual dimension, while albeit subjected to moral influence, was by no means neglected. The jibes of a Pattison or a Jowett as to the un- if not anti-intellectual bias of the movement were but an index of their own intellectual prejudices, a reflection of a modern 'scientific' scorn for the nature of the laborious 'ancient' learning beloved by the Tractarians. Pattison himself in the 1850s had been willing to regard the Oxford Movement as having represented no less than the Protestant Reformation a measured step towards enlightenment and moral progress.[151] W. C. Lake, a Balliol friend of Tait and W. G. Ward, clung to this view. In his old age in the 1890s, Lake raised a protest against 'the fashion with some writers ... to speak slightingly of the days of the "Tractarian revival" intellectually'.[152] It still remains something of a fashion to regard the painstaking patristic labours of Tractarians such as Pusey as something of a turning of the back on genuine academic scholarship.[153] This is less than fair, for while the 'forty-eight volumes of the "Library of the Fathers" excite nobody's curiosity now, yet Pusey would have seen them as the great monument of the Movement'.[154]

Newman's vision of a university, which was to find final and full expression in his famous Dublin lectures in the 1850s, was doomed to fail in the Oxford of the 1840s on account especially of the theological direction which the movement came to take. In the last resort, it was the process of disintegration engendered by the divergence of Tractarianism from traditional Anglican orthodoxy that rendered continued Tractarian attempts at fostering educational reform doomed to failure. In short, what finally put paid to the realization of Newman's vision was the divisive impact of Tractarian theology on Oxford, which has been described aptly by Sheridan Gilley as 'nothing less than the destruction from within of the old Protestant high church ideology of unreformed Oxford'.[155]

The disillusioning experience of increasingly bitter theological disputes with the Heads of Houses led the Tractarians to turn their backs on the 'official' university, abandoning their original design of transforming Oxford as a whole by 'leavening the lump'. Had the Tractarians remained more faithful to their own original spirit of 1829–33, they would and could have fought much harder than they did against the academic revolution of 1852–4 which involved the first major breach in Oxford's clerical *ancien régime*. Had the rump of the movement been more prepared to sink old differences with the Heads, reuniting the anti-liberal orthodox body of the university, then the secular liberal challenge, so successfully beaten off in the mid-1830s, might have been held at bay for longer. However, as a direct result of Tractarian inspired theological controversy in the 1840s, the conservative forces within Oxford found themselves weakened and divided at a critical time.

For a time it did look as if the 'catholic' party as well as that of the younger Oxford liberals might equally benefit from the waning of the supremacy of the largely protestant High Church Heads in the university. Although subsequently played down by Tractarian partisans such as Pusey's biographer Liddon, elements of common ground between what seemed to be the two 'movement' parties within Oxford opened up the possibility of a so-called 'liberal catholic' party.[156] Certainly, the younger Oxford liberals such as A. P. Stanley and Professor Donkin played a far more active role in actually defending the Tractarians from the assault of the conservative Heads in 1845 than Newman or most other Tractarians would later care to admit.[157] The former showed themselves to be far more tolerant of Tractarian vagaries than the older, more conservative 'Noetics' proved to be. Moreover, some Tractarians did welcome the potential realignment. Dean Church, who more than most first-generation Tractarians fitted the 'liberal-catholic' label, paid tribute to the high moral ethos of the new Oxford liberalism as being much more 'religious' and 'imaginative' than the older Oxford 'Noeticism' with its dry, Hanoverian mistrust of mysticism.[158] Yet, in terms of future university politics, 'liberal-catholicism' was to prove to be less the natural or only viable option for remaining followers of the movement than sometimes has been supposed. In the longer term, liberals gained ever more ground at the expense of 'catholics'. By utterly abandoning the Heads and old Oxford to its fate, the rump of the movement after 1845 only played into more secular liberal hands and eclipsed their own remaining hopes of major influence within the university.

It is true that Pusey made peace with the old guard Heads in the last hours of Oxford's old regime, proving to be 'their best champion'.[159] However, Pusey was the exception among Tractarians in this particular respect. By far the strongest resistance to secular liberal reform came from the old conservative anti-Tractarian forces within Oxford, encompassing not only protestant High Churchmen and conservative Evangelicals, but even 'prudential liberal-conservative' reformers such as Hawkins himself. In comparison, the rump of the movement appeared to accept the overthrow of the old order and its attendant secularization with remarkable equanimity, even appearing to contemplate the abolition of Subscription so long as their own doctrinal position could be maintained as a 'separate tradition'. Thus, when a High Church revival did come about in Oxford in the 1860s, it was by then too late to salvage much of the 'church interest' at the old political level. By that date, according to E. A. Knox who then first went up, the state of Oxford 'was exactly that which Newman had foreshadowed in his last word as an Anglican to Anglicans ... the anti-clerical spirit had gained the upper hand'.[160] It was a state borne out by Isaac Williams, who wrote in sadness to Newman on a visit to Oxford in 1863, 'the whole ethos of the place seemed outwardly changed ... in the discipline of Alma Mater the pastoral and parental spirit seemed changed for the intellectual, so that some old friends said it is no longer Alma Mater but dura Novena'.[161]

The abandonment of the concept of 'Anglican defence' represented the crucial volte-face of the Oxford Movement in the 1840s. Thereafter, no more than secular liberal reformers, did Tractarians regard it as any part of the role of the University of Oxford to fight to defend what they now came to regard as an old, discredited, and disintegrating academic order. It seems that the experience of being at the receiving end of theological censure from academic authorities prompted the dramatic change of tack, causing the Tractarians in effect to jettison their previous academic vision for theological party ends. It is striking to see how ecclesiastical authority as wielded by the university authorities, which had been welcomed in the mid-1830s as a wholesome revival of sacred discipline when applied against the movement's liberal opponents, was suddenly denounced as an illiberal and tyrannical exercise of arbitrary power when applied against themselves in the 1840s.[162] By 1843, the Tractarians had been driven into accepting that the cause of the Church should be separated from that of the 'official University'. In the manner that secular liberals had argued in the 1830s, Henry Woodgate was provoked into arguing 'that the university is only a lay corporation, and therefore has no authority, properly so called, in ecclesiastical matters'.[163] In particular, at the time of the suspension of Pusey from preaching in the university by the Heads, the Tractarian attempt to appeal beyond the jurisdiction of the university to the civil and criminal courts, squared very uneasily with the logic of the whole Tractarian campaign on behalf of the independence of Oxford which had been commenced in 1829. Even a younger generation of High Churchmen who can by no means be exclusively identified as 'Tractarians' came to question the official university's traditional function as theological censor. As Agatha Ramm has perceptively observed with regard to Gladstone's attitude to the clash between Heads and Tractarians in the 1840s, the university had always been regarded as 'a symbol, if any institution was, of the identity of the English church with the English state. Yet Gladstone supported no one of the actions it took to assert its single religious opinion'.[164]

In the 1830s the Tractarians had continued to espouse the cause of a confessional university in a state that was already ceasing to be confessional in its nature. The theological crisis at Oxford from 1841–45 was to reveal the implicit logic of the altered relation between church and state. It infused an urgency into the need finally to reappraise the position of the University of Oxford as a symbol of a church-state identity that no longer accorded with reality. This reappraisal paved the way for the final breach between Church and University; the 'umbilical cord' would be severed. In this way, the crisis of the 1840s in the University engendered by Tractarianism proved a true parent of the university reforms of the 1850s.[165]

Yet, in the last resort, for all the later liberal euphoria about the intellectual improvements for Oxford prompted by these reforms, this Tractarian-induced breach between Church and university would have some less happy side-effects. As was later observed, compared to the Oxford of 1900, the Oxford of 1840 had 'thought and felt and combated for what it thought and the noise of its combatants spread through much of the world'. In short, Oxford simply ceased to be treated as the oracle she once was.[166] Such earlier theological turmoil may not have been conducive to peace and stability, but some at least felt that with the closing of that era, both Oxford and the nation became a duller and less stimulating place. Moreover, one serious apparent legacy of the breach would be a so-called 'crisis of learning' in the Church of England that was to be much lamented later in the century.[167] The Tractarian vision of a university, a vision that saw academic culture being fully integral with revealed religion at every point, was in ruins. The academic counter-revolution inspired by the Tractarians to make that theoretical integration more of a living reality had been fatally checked in the 'odium theologicum' of the 1840s. With the far-reaching university reform of 1854, the Tractarian ideal was to be given its last rites.

The John Rylands University Library of Manchester
Manchester M13 9PP

REFERENCES

1. See L. S. Sutherland and L. G. Mitchell (eds), *History of the University of Oxford* v (Oxford 1986).
2. H. C. G. Matthew, 'Noetics, Tractarians, and the Reform of the University of Oxford in the Nineteenth Century', *History of Universities* ix (1990), 196. Cf. E. G. W. Bill, *Education at Christ Church, Oxford, 1660–1800* (Oxford 1988), ch. 1.
3. P. Slee, 'The Oxford idea of a liberal education, 1800–1850: the invention of tradition and the manufacture of practice', *History of Universities* vii (1988); for the chronology of the debate see A. I. Tillyard, *A history of university reform* (Cambridge 1913), chs ii and iii.
4. See, for instance, S. Rothblatt, *Tradition and Change in English Liberal Education: an essay in history and culture* (London 1976), ch. x. See also, S. Rothblatt, 'The student sub-culture and the examination system in early nineteenth century Oxbridge', in L. Stone (ed.), *The University in Society* (2 vols, Princeton 1974).
5. Slee, 63.
6. Matthew, 197. Cf. W. R. Ward, *Victorian Oxford* (London 1965), 13.
7. See J. C. D. Clark, *English society, 1688–1832: ideology, social structure and political practice during the ancien regime* (Cambridge 1985), 408–20.
8. Matthew, 197.
9. P. B. Nockles, 'Church Parties in the pre-Tractarian Church of England, 1750–1833: the "Orthodox"—some problems of definition and identity', in J. Walsh, C. Haydon and S. Taylor (eds), *From Toleration to Tractarianism: the Church of England,* c. *1689–*c.*1833* (forthcoming).
10. Baden Powell (1796–1860), was Savilian Professor of Geometry from 1827 onwards. For a superb study of his thought, see, P. Corsi, *Science and Religion: Baden Powell and the Anglican debate, 1800–1860* (Cambridge 1988).
11. The first use of the epithet 'Tractarian' appears to have been by the then Master of the Temple, Christopher Benson, in a series of discourses preached at the Temple Church in 1839: C. Benson, *Discourses upon Tradition and Episcopacy* (London 1839), 101. Cf. *British Critic* xxvi (Oct. 1839), 508. Many years later, Newman

confirmed that Benson had indeed been the first to use the term. On seeing the fact mentioned by Sir John Coleridge in his biography of John Keble, Newman remarked, 'Yes—Mr. Benson gave the name "Tractarian" to us in his Sermon. I thought no one recollected this but myself': J. H. Newman to Sir J. T. Coleridge 7 Feb. 1869, C. S. Dessain & T. Gornall (eds), *Letters and Diaries of John Henry Newman* xxxi (1977), 87.

12. See P. B. Nockles, 'Continuity and change in Anglican high churchmanship in Britain, 1792–1850' (Oxford D.Phil. 1982).
13. A. D. Culler, *The imperial intellect: a study of Newman's educational ideal* (New Haven and London 1955). For a recent appreciation of this, see J. M. Roberts, ' "The Idea of a University" revisted', I. Ker and A. G. Hill (eds), *Newman after a Hundred Years* (London 1990), 193–222.
14. J. H. Thom (ed.), *The Life of Joseph Blanco White* (3 vols, London 1845) iii, 131. The accuracy of White's statement in Newman's eyes is evinced by the latter's lengthy citation of it in his own *Apologia*. See, J. H. Newman, *Apologia pro vita sua* (London 1864), 118–19.
15. For a full account of the election, see N. Gash, 'Peel and the Oxford election of 1829', *Oxoniensia* iv (1939), 162–73; H. Tristram, 'Catholic Emancipation, Mr Peel, and the University of Oxford', *Cornhill Magazine* lxvi (April, 1929), 410.
16. J. H. Newman to Mrs Newman, 1 Mar. 1829, A. Mozley (ed.), *Letters and correspondence of John Henry Newman during his life in the English church* (London 1891) i, 202. Cf. J. H. Newman, *Apologia*, 72–3. Newman's attitude was fully in tune with that of the bulk of MAs, for whom the real issue was whether or not the University was to be 'infected by the liberality of the age, and is willing to sacrifice experience to expedience'. *The substance of two speeches delivered in Concovation on Thursday February 26th, 1829* (Oxford 1829), 5.
17. This theme will be explored more fully by the present author in, P. B. Nockles, 'The Great Disruption: the University and the Oxford Movement', M. G. Brock and M. C. Curthoys (eds), *History of the University of Oxford*, vi. (forthcoming).
18. Newman would even later claim that had he not then given up tuition at Oriel, there would have been no Oxford Movement. See J. H. Rigg, *Oxford High Anglicanism* (London 1899), 53.
19. C. J. Shairp, *John Keble* (London 1866), 17; A. I. Dasent, *John Thadeus Delane, Editor of "The Times". His life and correspondence* (2 vols, London 1908) i, 20; W. Lockhart, *Cardinal Newman: Reminiscences of fifty years since* (London 1891), 5–6; C. E. Mallett, *A history of the University of Oxford* (3 vols, London 1927) iii, 241–3. Significantly, the University Vice-Chancellor, Ashurst Gilbert could privately complain to the Chancellor, the Duke of Wellington, 'that Mr Newman has availed himself of the opportunity for making his parish pulpit much more an organ for propagating his views among those who are educating for the church, than the plain instruction of

an ordinary congregation'. A. T. Gilbert to Wellington, 26 Dec. 1839, Wellington MSS Southampton University Archives 2/250/65.

20. F. Oakeley, *Historical Notes on the Tractarian Movement* (London 1865), 12–14. Cf. J. H. Philpot, *The seceders, 1829–1869* (London 1930), 15. Cf. [Baden Powell], 'Jowett and the Broad Church', *Westminster Review* xvi (July 1859), 44; W. J. Baker, *Beyond Port and Prejudice: Charles Lloyd of Oxford* (Orono, Maine 1981), 214–15.
21. F. Oakeley, 180. This point was also borne out by a hostile observer, who commented, 'young and plastic minds coming to Oxford with a trembling veneration for the place and its association . . . formed materials admirably suited, and ready for the purposes of the "conspirators". To hundreds thus coming every year to Oxford, the Fellow or the tutor of his college, a canon of Christ Church, and the occupant of a professorial chair, would be objects of a degree of fear and of reverence, their notice a condescension and their lessons the utterances of infallibility'. *Oxford Protestant Magazine* i (October, 1847), 384.
22. P. Shuttleworth, 19 June 1841 (copy) Bodleian Library, Oxford MS. Eng. Hist. c. 1033, f. 230. However, a contemporary American observer insisted that it was the MAs rather than undergraduates who were the most susceptible to Tractarian influence: C. A. Bristed, *Five Years in an English University* (London 1873), 82. By 1845, it was actually estimated that among the resident members of Convocation in Oxford made up of MAs, those prepared to support the Tractarians could command a majority of nearly four to one. J. Bateman, *Tractarianism as described in Prophecy. A word to the wise on the Oxford Crisis* (Oxford 1845), 43.
23. See S. Gilley, 'John Keble and the Victorian churching of Romanticism', in J. R. Watson (ed.), *An Infinite Complexity: essays in Romanticism* (Edinburgh 1983), 226–39.
24. P. Le Page Renouf to Mrs J. Le Page Renouf, 13 Nov. 1841, Pembroke College Archives, Oxford 63/9/1/232.
25. J. H. Newman to J. W. Bowden, 16 Jan. 1830, T. Gornall and I. Ker (eds), *Letters and Diaries of J. H. Newman* ii (1979), 189.
26. J. H. Newman to J. Newman, 17 Mar. 1829, ibid. 132.
27. J. H. Newman, *Apologia*, 108.
28. G. Moberly, *A Few Thoughts on the Proposed Admission of Dissenters into the University of Oxford* (Oxford 1834), 14. Cf. W. Sewell, *The Attack upon the University of Oxford in a Letter to Earl Grey* (Oxford 1834), 36.
29. J. H. Newman to H. J. Rose, 17 Mar. 1834, T. Gornall & I. Ker (eds), *Letters and Diaries of John Henry Newman* iv (1980), 209. Newman also contrasted 'the exemplary sobriety and decorum' of the Oxford Union Society with the apparent licence and rampant liberalism of its Cambridge counterpart. Ibid. 210.
30. For discussion of the more liberal intellectual tradition and ethos of Cambridge, see D. A. Winstanley, *Unreformed Cambridge* (London

1935); D. A Winstanley, *Early Victorian Cambridge* (London 1940); M. M. Garland, *Cambridge before Darwin: the Ideal of a Liberal Education, 1800–1860* (London 1980); J. Gascoigne, *Cambridge in the Age of the Enlightenment* (Cambridge 1989).

31. [L. Stephen], *Sketches from Cambridge* (1865), 13. Cf. E. P. S. Haynes, 'Oxford and Cambridge—a study in types', *Cornhill Magazine* xxi (November, 1906), 686–7; cf. *Early and late reflections of Clement Carlyon, M.D. late Fellow of Pembroke College, Cambridge* (London 1856) ii. 134. While F. D. Maurice considered that Cambridge provided for a freer cultivation of creative powers, he argued that Oxford was stronger 'in moral and intellectual discipline, in the cultivation of habits, in the exercise of the practical faculties'. F. D. Maurice, *Has the Church, or the State, the Power to Educate the Nation? A course of Lectures* (London 1839), 68. This same contrast between Cambridge and Oxford appeared to surface once more at the time of the later controversy over *Essays and Reviews*; see G. W. Kitchin, *Edward Harold Browne: A Memoir* (London 1895), 210.
32. *Christian Remembrancer* xxiii 'Memoir of Bishop Copleston' (Jan. 1852), 18.
33. D. Newsome, *The Parting of Friends: a study of the Wilberforces and Henry Manning* (London 1966), 62–70.
34. F. Oakeley, *Historical Notes*, 180; F. Oakeley, *Remarks on the Study of Aristotelian and Platonic Ethics, as a branch of the Oxford system of Education* (Oxford 1837), 26–9. Similarly, according to Peter Maurice, chaplain of Jesus College, Oxford, Tractarianism was 'the natural result' of Aristotelian studies 'pursued in our public schools and the University of Oxford in particular'. P. Maurice, *The Ritualism of Oxford Popery. A Letter to Dr. MacBride* (Oxford 1867), 111. Yet it would be wrong to suggest that the Tractarians found in Butler an alternative or antidote to the reasoning of the 'Noetics'—Copleston was a keen adherent of Butler; see Corsi, 77.
35. D. Newsome, *Two classes of men: Platonism and English Romantic Thought* (London 1972), 62–72. For discussion of how the Tractarians used Aristotle's concept of the mean to uphold their own particular model of the church as against that of some 'Noetics' and Evangelicals, see F. M. Turner, *The Greek Heritage in Victorian Britain* (New Haven 1981), 333–6.
36. M. Pattison, *Memoirs* (London 1885), 236–7; J. A. Froude, 'The Oxford Counter-Reformation', *Short Studies in Great Subjects* iv (London 1893), 231–60. Similarly, the radical university reformer, Goldwin Smith, argued that an early nineteenth-century 'movement of Academical Reform' was 'crossed' and thwarted by the Oxford Movement in the 1830s, *Oxford Essays, 1858* (Oxford 1858), 266. For modern expositions of this view, see Ward, *Victorian Oxford*, ch. vi; A. Engel, *From clergyman to Don: the rise of the academic profession nineteenth-century Oxford* (Oxford 1983), 22–7. Professor Ward has

recently restated this argument, 'Faith and fallacy: English and German perspectives in the nineteenth century', in R. J. Helmstadter and B. Lightman (eds), *The Victorian Crisis of Faith: Essay in continuity and change in Nineteenth-Century Religious Belief* (London 1990), 56.

37. *Tait's Edinburgh Magazine* New Series xvi (Aug. 1849), 530. Cf. *British Quarterly Review* iii (May 1846), 358–76.

38. R. W. Church, *The Oxford Movement: twelve years, 1833–1845* (London 1889), 407.

39. On the appearance of Hampden's controversial *Observations on Religious Dissent*, Newman wrote to him indignantly protesting that his pamphlet marked the 'beginning of hostilities in the University', and lamenting 'that by its appearance the first step has been taken towards interrupting that peace and mutual good understanding which has prevailed so long in this place, and which if once seriously disturbed will be succeeded by dissensions the more intractable because justified in the minds of those who resist innovation by a feeling of imperative duty'. J. H. Newman to R. D. Hampden, 28 Nov. 1834, *Letters and Diaries* iv, 371. Such had been the apparently broad and unifying basis of initial Tractarian support within Oxford, that even according to the hostile observer, Baden Powell, 'nearly the whole residue of the Church and University, older and younger . . . seemed for a while to be joined in the Puseyite movement', *Westminster Review* xvi (July 1859), 45. As late as 1834/5 a scheme had been discussed at Oxford for a new theological journal, whose proposed contributors were to include Pusey as well as Whately and Hampden, A. P. Stanley, *Essays on Church and State from 1850 to 1870* (London 1870), 49.

40. See [H. W. Wilberforce], *The Foundations of the Faith assailed in Oxford: A letter to His Grace the Archbishop of Canterbury* (Oxford 1835).

41. Corsi, 73. As John Kent has explained, Newman and the Tractarians could use the term 'liberal' in a non-pejorative and conservative sense, 'as referring to studies which freed the mind from the control of inherited prejudice and contemporary error by bringing in the Classics as well as theology to reduce the "modern" to order', J. Kent, 'Newman and Science', *Louvain Studies* xv (1990), 271.

42. Corsi, pts I and III; cf. R. Brent, *Liberal Anglican politics: Whiggery, Religion and Reform* (Oxford 1987), 148–9; P. Hinchliff, *Benjamin Jowett and the Christian Religion*, 10.

43. Corsi, 106–23.

44. W. J. Copleston, *Memoir of Edward Copleston, D.D. Bishop of Llandaff* (London 1851), 47. Copleston also regarded Arnold's views as 'rash and dangerous'. W. Tuckwell, *Pre-Tractarian Oxford* (London 1900), 45. Moreover, in private, Copleston would later admit to a much greater degree of agreement with the Tractarians than he avowed in public. As he confessed to his friend Hawkins as late as 1843, 'I am

no anti-Tractarian. I mean that I humbly consider those writings ['Tracts for the Times'], to have done in the main good service to the cause of true religion. I am sure they have been useful to myself—and as I believe to very many others'. E. Copleston to E. Hawkins, 27 Nov. 1843, Hawkins MSS. Oriel College Archives Oxford Letter Book i No. 9. For Davison's theological position, see note 118. None the less, Copleston did repeatedly complain about the iniquities of Tractarian tutors; Hinchliff, 10.

45. He was thus considered by the author of a biographical portrait of him, Dean Burgon. See J. W. Burgon, *Lives of Twelve Good Men* 'Edward Hawkins: The Great Provost' i (London 1889), 374–465.
46. Corsi, 9–11, 21–33. For further perceptive discussion of the development of Baden Powell's intellectual and theological position, see I. Ellis, *Seven Against Christ: a study of 'Essays and Reviews'* (Leiden 1980), 44–6, 218–20; Pusey appears to have overlooked Powell's pre-Tractarian High Church background, when he asserted, in 1861, that Baden Powell 'was a Rationalist of old, before the Tracts', E. B. Pusey to J. Jebb, 23 Oct. 1861, Pusey MSS, Pusey House Library, Oxford.
47. *Dublin Review* xvii no. 33 [H. Wilberforce], 'Dr. Hampden and Anglicanism' (July, 1871), 72–3. The High Churchman Hugh James Rose warned about an apparent intellectual shift taking place in the position of 'Noetics' such as Powell, in an article in the *British Critic* in 1834; Ellis, 219.
48. Dean Burgon put the moderate Tractarian case well. According to Burgon, Hawkins 'abhorred, as irreligious and revolutionary', the later secularizing 'liberal' movement for university reform. But Burgon poses the question whether or not Hawkins's connection with 'the liberalism of the old Oriel school' had not played a part in the 'disorganisation of the University which has subsequently prevailed'. For Burgon, principles 'were then surrendered, views were then strenuously advocated, which paved the way for yet larger demands and yet more fatal concessions. We know on the best authority that they that have "sown the wind shall reap the whirlwind". But men cannot see, and will not be shown, the end from the beginning', J. W. Burgon, i. 456. Dean Church later described Hawkins as 'the ablest and most hurtful' opponent of the Tractarian religious spirit in the university, R. W. Church, *Occasional Papers* (London 1896) ii. 346.
49. R. D. Hampden, *Observations on Religious Dissent* (1834), 38–9.
50. *Hansard* xxv. 641 (20 June 1834).
51. [Baden Powell], 'Principles and Prospects of University Reform', *Monthly Chronicle* (1838), 65–81.
52. Lord Holland to P. N. Shuttleworth, 7 Oct. 1834, BL Add MSS 51597, f. 133.
53. *Hansard* xxv (August 1, 1834); *The Universities and the Dissenters. A Letter to Sir R. H. Inglis* (Oxford 1834), 6.
54. E. Denison, *A Review of the State of the Question respecting the*

Admission of Dissenters to the Universities (Oxford 1835), 6; [E. Hawkins], *A Letter to the Earl of Radnor upon the Oaths, Dispensations and Subscriptions to the Thirty-Nine Articles at the University of Oxford* (Oxford 1835), 26.

55. Edward Bayley (as proctor he could sit in on Board meetings), along with Hampden (Principal of St Mary Hall) and the Whig Warden of New College, Shuttleworth, shamelessly broke the supposed secrecy of the Board of the Heads of Houses' deliberations by informing Lord Holland and even the Whig Prime Minister, Melbourne, of what was taking place, and even seeking advice as to the course of action the government wished them to take. See for instance, E. Bayley to Lord Holland, 1 June 1835, BL Add MSS 51597, f. 189; P. Shuttleworth to Lord Holland, 19 June 1835, BL Add MSS 51597, ff. 146–147; Brent, 215–6.
56. [Baden Powell], 'On the Admission of Dissenters to the University of Oxford', *Quarterly Journal of Education* viii (1834), 78–92.
57. R. D. Hampden, *Observations*, 38; R. D. Hampden to Lord Radnor, 2 June 1835, Radnor Ms. PH RAD 1/2/21.
58. [H. W. Wilberforce], *Foundations of the Faith assailed*, 14.
59. J. Blanco White to E. Hawkins, 28 June 1837, Hawkins MSS. Oriel College Archives Oxford Letter Book ii, no. 112.
60. [H. W. Wilberforce], *Foundations of the Faith*, 6. Cf. F. Oakeley, *A Letter to His Grace, the Duke of Wellington* (Oxford 1835) 15–16.
61. Newman to Perceval, 11 Jan. 1836, cited in Matthew, 210. In fact, Newman went so far in private as to refer to the Articles as countenancing 'a vile Protestantism'. J. H. Newman to R. H. Froude, 13 May 1835, T. Gornall (ed.), *Letters and Diaries of John Henry Newman* v (Oxford 1981), 70.
62. [B. Harrison], 'Universities of England', *British Critic* XXII (1837), 435.
63. H. A. Woodgate, *The Study of Morals Vindicated and Recommended in a Sermon Preached before the University of Oxford* (Oxford 1837).
64. W. Sewell, *Thoughts on the Admission of Dissenters to the University of Oxford: and on the establishment of a State Religion* (Oxford 1834), 7.
65. W. P. Neville (ed.), *Addresses to Cardinal Newman, with his replies, 1879–81* (London 1905), 184.
66. H. Tristram (ed.), *John Henry Newman: Autobiographical Writings* (London 1956), 91.
67. *Quarterly Review* lxvi (June 1840), 165.
68. J. H. Newman, *The Idea of a University, Defined and Illustrated* ed. I. Ker (London 1876), 138.
69. For a later sympathetic appraisal by Newman of the 'Oriel school' in this respect, see H. Tristram (ed.), *John Henry Newman*, 73.
70. *Christian Remembrancer* xxiii (Jan. 1852), 5.
71. In spite of some 'Romanising' excesses of Tractarianism, Copleston in 1843 insisted that he remained increasingly 'inclined towards the

revival of true Church Principles (identical in the minds of some ignorant people . . . with Popery) . . .' E. Copleston to E. Hawkins, 18 Nov. 1843, Hawkins MSS, Oriel College Archives Letter Book i, no. 8; E. Copleston to E. Hawkins, 27 Nov. 1843, OCA i, no. 9.

72. Church, 303.
73. [A. P. Stanley], 'The late Dr. Arnold', *Edinburgh Review* lxxvi (Jan. 1843), 375. Similarly, another liberal critic of Tractarianism, Bonamy Price, a disciple of Arnold's, recognized that the 'most distinguishing feature' of the Tractarians, 'and that on which they most pride themselves', was 'the great and almost exclusive prominence which they gave to the moral part of our nature' [B. Price], 'Newman's History of the Arians', *Edinburgh Review* lxiii (April 1836), 4. Even Baden Powell recognized as a basis of the appeal of Tractarianism, its advocacy of philosophical 'theories of morals' and its emphasis on 'the ethical and metaphysical elements of all human motives and grounds of conviction'; Baden Powell, *Tradition Unveiled: or an exposition of the pretensions and tendency of authoritative teaching in the Church* (London 1841), 13; cf. *Westminster Review* xvi (July 1859), 44.
74. *Report and Evidence upon the Recommendations of Her Majesty's Commissioners for Inquiring into the state of the University of Oxford. Presented to the Board of Heads of Houses and Proctors, December 1 1853* (Oxford 1853), 142.
75. J. H. Newman to W. Rickards, 7 Feb. 1840, Hawkins MSS. OCA Letter Book xi, no. 1012.
76. Wellington MSS. Southampton University Archives 2/249/52–62; Wellington to E. Cardwell, June 1837, SUA 2/248/105; R. Palmer, *Memorials. Part I. Family and Personal, 1766–1865* (1865) ii. 230–2.
77. It is true that initially there had been some Tractarian-inspired opposition to formal attempts at statute revision by the Board, but this was entirely owing to jealousy for the constitutional rights of Convocation *vis-à-vis* the authority of the Heads. See, 'Some Remarks by a Member of Convocation for Objecting to the Proposed Revision of the university Statutes, and to the Revised Portion of them which has just been published', Wellington MSS. SUA 2/248/140; E. Greswell, *A Letter to His Grace the Duke of Wellington, Chancellor of the University of Oxford* (Oxford 1837).
78. J. H. Newman to C. Anderson, 24 Jan. 1836, *Letters and Diaries* vi. 212–3.
79. Matthew, 211; moreover the 'Noetics' were also, with the exception of Baden Powell, generally conservative in curricular matters, Corsi, 123.
80. P. Slee, *Learning and a Liberal Education: the Study of Modern History in the Universities of Oxford, Cambridge and Manchester, 1800–1914* (Manchester 1986), 41–2.
81. For the involvement of 'Noetics' such as Nassau Senior in the foundation at Oxford of the Drummond Chair of Political Economy in1825, see R. Brent in K. Tribe and I. Hont, *Trade, Politics and*

Letters (forthcoming); see also B. Hilton, *The Age of Atonement: the influence of Evangelicalism on Social and Economic Thought* (Cambridge 1988), 42, 45–7. On the development of political economy in the 1830s see S. Rashid, 'Political economy and geology in the early nineteenth century: similarities and contrasts', *History of Political Economy* xiii (1981), 726–44.

82. J. H. Newman to J. F. Christie, 29 Jan. 1837, G. Tracey (ed.), *Letters and Diaries* vi (1984), 19; Hilton, 47.
83. E. Hawkins to R. Whately, 1 Mar. 1837, Hawkins MSS. OCA Letter Book v, no. 419. See Newman's cynical comment on Woodgate's withdrawal; 'we know that no man of good principles can be found to understand the study of political economy. Is this a slur upon good principles or political economy?' J. H. Newman to H. W. Wilberforce, 27 Feb. 1837, *Letters and Letters* vi. 37.
84. R. Palmer to W. Palmer Jun., 12 Dec. 1836, Selbourne MS. Lambeth Palace Library, MS. 2837 f. 227; Hugh James Rose also thought that Maurice would propound 'far more wholesome' views of political economy 'and its limits' than any liberal candidate, H. J. Rose to P. Bliss, 3 Dec. 1836, BL Add MSS 34572 f. 120.
85. J. H. Newman to J. Keble [12 Feb.] 1837, *Letters and Diaries* vi. 27–8. In the end, a liberal, Charles Merivale, was elected. Significantly, Merivale had not expected to be elected, partly because he was a Whig, 'and partly from some peculiar views respecting the subject prevalent among the high flyers at Oxford. They imagine the science as at present studied to be altogether delusive and dangerous, and that it ought to be rendered subordinate to their own High Church scheme of Christian Ethics', H. Merivale to Lord Napier, 16 Jan. 1837, BL Add MSS 34618 ff. 8–10; cf. A. H. D. Acland (ed.), *Memoirs and Letters of Sir Thomas Dyke Acland* (Privately printed London 1902), 81.
86. For examples of this view, see M. Pattison, *Memoirs*, 237–8; *British and Foreign Review* 'Oxford and Dr. Hampden' (1843), 170–2; *The Life and Correspondence of William Buckland, D.D. F.R.S.* (London 1894), 122.
87. G. L'E. Turner, 'Experimental Science in early nineteenth-century Oxford', *History of Universities* viii (1989), 125–31: N. Rupke, 'The natural sciences at Oxford during the early nineteenth century' (unpublished conference paper, 1987); cf. F. Sherwood Taylor, 'The teaching of science at Oxford in the nineteenth century', *Annals of Science* viii (1952), 82–112.
88. S. F. Cannon, *Science in culture: the early Victorian period* (London 1978) ch. ii. Cf. J. B. Morrell & A. Thackray, *Gentlemen of Science: early years of the British Association for the Advancement of Science* (London 1981), 225–6. Boyd Hilton disputes the view advanced by Cannon, Morrell and Thackeray that early clerical proponents of scientific ideas were confined to the so-called 'Liberal Anglicans', citing the example of William Vernon Harcourt (1789–1871), a founder-member of the BAAS; Hilton, 30.

89. G. L'E. Turner, 125. For evidence of an earlier decline in scientific-study prior to the Oxford Movement, see D. Brewster, 'Decline of Science', *Quarterly Review* xliii (Oct. 1830), 305–42; C. Babbage, *Reflections on the Decline of Science in England, and on some of its causes* (London 1830). Moreover, Baden Powell's complaints concerning the decline in mathematical and physical studies in Oxford University predated the rise of the Oxford Movement. See Baden Powell, *The Present State and Future Prospects of Mathematical and Physical Sciences in the University of Oxford, considered in a public lecture* (Oxford 1832), 7–8, 38–9. Furthermore, Powell himself admitted that, even in the seventeenth and eighteenth centuries, scientific pursuits had exercised little or no influence 'on the studies, especially of the junior part of the university'; ibid. 4.
90. Mozley insisted that 'no one ever received the least discouragement in 'the prosecution of scientific studies. Discoveries were welcomed freely. Buckland's lectures were always well attended. I went to several with Robert Wilberforce'. T. Mozley, *Reminiscences chiefly of Oriel College and the Oxford Movement* ii (London 1882), 429. Newman himself appears to have attended Buckland's lectures in 1819 and 1821, Kent, 'Newman and Science', 275. Both Hurrell Froude and W. G. Ward were mathematical scholars.
91. Ibid. ii. ch. c. A. D. Thackeray, *The Radcliffe Observatory, 1772–1972* (Oxford 1972), 9–12. I am indebted to J. B. Morrell for drawing my attention to this reference.
92. Cannon, 11–15.
93. [W. Sewell], 'Memorials of Oxford', *Quarterly Review* lxi (January, 1838), 232–3.
94. For an account of 'Hutchinsonianism' and its anti-Newtonian scientific theories, see E. Churton, *Memoir of Joshua Watson* (2 vols 1861) i. 39ff; R. Spearman, *Life of John Hutchinson prefixed to a Supplement to the Works of John Hutchinson Esq.* (1765), i–xiv. For Baden Powell the Tractarian repudiation of natural theology and stress on the limitations of natural reason, was in the tradition of the Hutchinsonians who 'derived the whole of physical science from the Bible', see Baden Powell, *Oxford Essays: the Bennet Prizes. The Study of Natural Theology* (Oxford 1857), 178–80. However, in reality, the Tractarians, while in many ways intellectual and spiritual heirs to the Hutchinsonians, were less narrow and circumscribed in their attitude to the physical sciences. Moreover, in contrast to the Tractarians, the Oxford Hutchinsonians had argued that it 'was unchristian to rely on Aristotle or his Arab translators in understanding nature', B. W. Young, ' "Orthodoxy assailed": an historical examination of some metaphysical and theological debates in England from Locke to Burke' (Oxford D.Phil. 1990), 329–30.
95. J. H. Newman to E. B. Pusey, 21 April 1858, C. S. Dessain (ed.), *Letters and Diaries* xviii (1968), 326.

96. E. B. Pusey, *Collegiate and Professorial Teaching and Discipline* (London 1854), 215.
97. E. B. Pusey, *Patience and Confidence the Strength of the Church. A Sermon preached on the fifth of November [1837] before the University of Oxford* (Oxford 1838), 1–2.
98. For an exposition of Newman's views on this, see J. H. Newman, 'Faith and Reason contrasted as habits of mind' [An Epiphany Sermon], *Fifteen Sermons preached before the University of Oxford, 1826–1843* (3rd edn, London 1872), 176–201. In a memorable passage in 'The Tamworth Reading Room', Newman made the point succinctly, 'science, knowledge, and whatever other fine names we use, never healed a wounded heart, nor changed a sinful one'. C. F. Harrold (ed.), *Essays and Sketches of John Henry Newman* ii (New Haven 1948), 185. See also the striking passage in the *Apologia*, where Newman speaks of looking into 'this busy, living world, and seeing no reflexion of its Creator'. As John Kent observes, in this sense, 'Newman has little practical theological use for science'; Kent, 'Newman and Science', 268.
99. W. Sewell, *An Inaugural Lecture delivered in the Clarendon Building, University of Oxford* (Oxford 1836), 4. Cf. H. A. Woodgate, *The Study of Morals Vindicated* (Oxford 1837), 24.
100. F. Nolan, *The Analogy of Revelation and Science* (Oxford 1833), vii–viii, 2–5; H. Cole, *Popular Geology subversive of Divine Revelation: A Letter to the Rev. Adam Sedgwick* (London 1834). Nolan has been wrongly identified in various sources, including the DNB as an Evangelical. Corsi describes him as 'a rather eccentric High Church intellectual' who opposed the reform plans of Copleston and Davison in the 1800s from a reactionary standpoint. He was to emerge as a bitter theological opponent of Tractarianism, but had been no less critical of Evangelicalism as politically subversive. P. Corsi, 132–3. However, on the issue of Science in relation to Revelation, Nolan was at one with the more extreme Evangelicals.
101. J. H. Newman to J. W. Bowden, 4 September 1838, *Letters and Diaries* vi, 313.
102. [J. W. Bowden], 'The British Association for the Advancement of Science'; *British Critic* xxv (Jan. 1839), 12. Even Baden Powell found the Tractarian attitude to be rather 'enlightened' when compared to that of most Evangelicals with their adherence to the narrowest biblical literalism; *Tradition Unveiled*, 14–15.
103. [J. W. Bowden], 14.
104. A. D. Orange, 'The idols of the theatre: the British Association and its early critics', *Annals of Science* xxxii (1975), 285–9. Cf. *Oxford University Magazine* i 'The British Association' (November 1, 1834), 407; [J. W. Bowden], 36–7.
105. Baden Powell, *Revelation and Science* (Oxford 1833), 4, 10–11.
106. [J. W. Bowden], 42. In 1874, Newman recalled, 'old Tractarians 30 or

40 years ago were the first to protest against the British Association then beginning. My dear friend, the late Mr. Bowden, wrote a strong article against it . . . our deep suspicion of it was, because, in spite of its being a scientific society, it would meddle with religion. It then undertook the office of patronising it by a mild, cold Deism'. *Letters and Diaries* vi, 215.

107. Keble complained about Oxford's 'bowing of the knee to Baal' by entertaining the British Association in the summer of 1832. J. Keble to E. B. Pusey, 17 July 1832, quoted in, H. P. Liddon, i, 219. Recalling the 'invasion' of Oxford by the BAAS, Tom Mozley commented that Newman 'could not but be stirred by the vulgarity of the triumphant "savants"'. T. Mozley, *Reminiscences* i, 179.
108. [J. W. Bowden], 42–3. For further discussion of Tractarian attitudes to science, see R. R. Yeo, 'Whewell's Philosophy of Knowledge', in M. Fisch and S. Schaffer (eds), *William Whewell: A Composite Portrait* (Oxford 1991), 177–9.
109. E. B. Pusey, *Collegiate and professional teaching*, 215. Cf. E. B. Pusey, *Un-Science, not Science, adverse to Faith. A Sermon preached before the University of Oxford* (Oxford 1878).
110. B. Harrison to W. Palmer Jun., 17 Sept. 1834, Selbourne MSS LPL Ms. 2837 f. 76.
111. J. H. Newman to W. Rickards, 7 Feb. 1840, Hawkins MSS OCA Letter Book xi, no. 1012.
112. Culler, 118. Cf. *Hints on the Formation of a Plan for the safe and effectual Revival of the Professorial System in Oxford. Addressed to the Rev. the Warden of New College* (Oxford 1839), 25–6.
113. [W. Sewell] 'Oxford Tutors and Professors', *Quarterly Review* lxvi (June 1840), 184.
114. A. T. Gilbert to Wellington, 8 June 1840, Wellington MSS SUA 2/251/140. Cf. Oxford University Archives, Bodleian Library, Oxford. N.W. 21.5 'Memoranda respecting the Professorships of Pastoral Theology and Ecclesiastical History and the Statute "De Disciplina Theologica"'.
115. J. H. Newman to A. P. Perceval, 11 Jan. 1836, quoted in H. P. Liddon, i, 301. Similarly, Oakeley argued that 'the less, in fact, divinity is studied here with a view to examinations and academic honours, the better . . . academic honours are sought, not as means of good, (which they are), but as ends (which they are not) and too often rested in as such', *Remarks upon the Study of Aristotelian and Platonic Ethics*, 21.
116. *British Critic* xxxii (July, 1842), 161–4.
117. *The New Examination for Divinity Degrees* (Oxford 1844), 13.
118. John Davison (1777–1834), one-time Fellow of Oriel and in the 'Noetic' circle, typically was claimed at a later date by both Liberals and Tractarians. His widow, who was sympathetic to the movement, indignantly denied Hampden's claim that her husband had approved of his Bampton Lectures. In fact, in the great polarization of the early-

1830s he remained on the 'conservative' side of the divide. Newman considered that he was really a High Churchman in principle, but owing to 'the peculiarity of his age', i.e. the defective mental climate of the Oxford of the 1800s and 1810s, one who at that date could but express his High Churchmanship very indistinctly. [J. H. Newman], 'The works of the late Rev. John Davison', *British Critic* xxxi (Apr. 1842). It is significant that Burgon cites Davison as part of his catalogue of pre-Tractarian High Church witnesses. See Burgon i. 154. For discussion of Davison as a link between the Oriel 'Noetics' and the High Church 'Hackney Phalanx'; see Corsi, 22–5.

119. [J. H. Newman], 'Memorials of Oxford', *British Critic* xxiv (July, 1838), 144.
120. [J. H. Newman], 'Memorials', 145.
121. [J. R. Hope-Scott], 'The statutes of Magdalen College, Oxford', *British Critic* xxvii (1840), 368–9.
122. Culler, 90.
123. J. T. Coleridge, *Memoir of the Rev. John Keble M.A.* (London 1869), 248.
124. J. Keble to J. T. Coleridge, 16 Oct. 1837, Coleridge MSS Bodleian Library, Oxford. Ms. Eng. Misc. d. 134.
125. 'Oxford tutors and professors', 175.
126. Culler, 91.
127. Tristram, *John Henry Newman*, 91.
128. Ibid. 96–7.
129. *Christian Remembrancer* xxiii 'Memoir of Bishop Copleston' (Jan. 1852), 5. None the less, the same writer qualified this by asserting that 'Copleston's success in forming a gentlemanly character is to be remarked as being the immediate parent of a great religious movement', ibid. 4.
130. E. G. W. Bill, *University Reform in nineteenth-century Oxford: a study of Henry Halford Vaughan, 1811–1885* (London 1973), 57. Hawkins strongly insisted that the Charter of the Foundation of Oriel and the original statutes laid down that the character of the College 'was to be Ecclesiastical: a School of Divinity; not for Education generally, but specially for Theology, and the training up of Christian Ministers'. J. W. Burgon, *Lives*, 'Edward Hawkins' i, 454.
131. Hawkins had little semblance of poetic feeling, and had an eighteenth-century horror of 'enthusiasm'. However, as with Copleston, the Tractarians probably underestimated his High Church spiritual inclinations. According to Burgon, 'his practice was so very much better than his theory', ibid. 433.
132. [W. Sewell], 'Oxford tutors and professors', 173–4.
133. R. Ornsby, *Memoirs of James Robert Hope-Scott* i (1884), 178–90.
134. [J. R. Hope-Scott], 'The statutes of Magdalen College', *British Critic* xxviii, 394.
135. B. W. Henderson, *Merton College* (London 1899), 167. According to

Hope-Scott's biographer, 'the Merton reform was perhaps, the only direct effort of the kind made by any college in its corporate capacity'. R. Ornsby, *Memoirs*, i, 179. On the implementation of Tractarian ideas in the college by the Fellows of Merton, see, M. Everett, 'Merton Chapel in the nineteenth century', *Oxoniensia* xlii (1977), 247–55.

136. Henderson, 168–9.
137. One of the keenest devotees of counter-revolution at Magdalen was its eccentric, neo-Tractarian Fellow, William Palmer. According to the liberal university reformer, Goldwin Smith, 'Don Quixote did not live in the age of chivalry more completely than did William Palmer in the age of medieval religion. As an inn was a castle to Don Quixote, to William Palmer the colleges were monasteries, only with a rule unhappily relaxed, the Fellows were monks, the scouts or college servants were lay brethren'. A. Haultain (ed.), *Reminiscences of Goldwin Smith* (London 1910), 57.
138. Liddon, i, 338–9. Some protestant High Churchmen regarded these gatherings in a subversive light and even thought them liable to the statute 'De Conventiculis illicitis reprimendis', G. V. Cox, *Recollections of Oxford* (2nd edn London 1870), 294.
139. A. Mozley (ed.), *Letters of J.B. Mozley* (London 1885), 78. Cf. M. Pattison, *Memoirs*, 180–1.
140. Culler, 94–5.
141. *An Apology for the Universities* (London 1846), 5–6, 61–2.
142. W. C. Lake to A. C. Tait 15 April 1842, Tait Papers, Lambeth Palace Library, vol. 77, f. 163.
143. C. Marriott, *Letter to the Rev. E.C. Woollcombe, Fellow and Tutor of Balliol College, on University Extension, and the Poor Scholar* (Oxford 1848). Cf. J. W. Burgon, *Lives of Twelve Good Men* 'Charles Marriot: the man of saintly life' i (London 1889), 359–62. For Marriott's efforts to engage support for new private halls, see his correspondence with Gladstone. BL Add MSS 44251, ff. 1–6. Cf. W. R. Ward, 137–41.
144. W. E. Gladstone to Sir R. Peel, 28 June 1845, BL Add MSS 44206, ff. 315–16. Cf. E. C. Woollcombe, *University Extension and the Poor Scholar Question: a Letter to the Provost of Worcester College* (Oxford 1848).
145. Bill, *University Reform in nineteenth-century Oxford*, 57.
146. J. Pycroft, *The Collegian's Guide: or, Recollections of College Days, setting forth the advantages and temptations of a University Education* (Oxford 1845), 269.
147. C. A. E. Moberly, *Dulce Domum: George Moberly, his family and friends* (London 1911), 31.
148. For further discussion of this theme, see H. W. Fulweiler, 'Tractarians and philistines: the "Tracts for the Times" versus Victorian middle-class values', *Historical Magazine of the Protestant Episcopal Church* xxxi (1962). Contemporaries made the same point. One writer observed in 1850 that 'during this reanimation of the Church on the

collegiate side, the tide of life has run in the opposite direction', *Westminster Review* liii (April 1850), 203.

149. *Quarterly Review* lxi, 232.
150. [J. H. Newman], 'Memorials of Oxford', *British Critic* xxiv, 134.
151. L. O. Frappell, 'The Reformation as a negative Revolution or obscurantist Reaction: the Liberal debate on the Reformation in Nineteenth Century Britain', *Journal of Religious Studies* xi (1980), 301–2. Even Baden Powell admitted the Movement's claims 'to a peculiar alliance with learning' and 'possession of the fountain heads of ecclesiastical erudition', *Tradition Unveiled*, 13. In 1859 Powell went further, arguing that it had been the Tractarians, following the initial inspiration provided by Charles Lloyd as Regius Professor in the 1820s, who had really restored to the university the study and application of a learned 'scientific theology'. Powell emphasized the contrast between Tractarian learning and an 'Evangelical want of learning', [Baden Powell], 'Jowett and the Broad Church', 44–5.
152. *Good Words* (October, 1895), 668.
153. H. C. G. Matthew, 'Edward Bouverie Pusey: From Scholar to Tractarian', *Journal of Theological Studies* NS xxxii (1981), 101–24.
154. R. W. Pfaff, 'The Library of the Fathers: the Tractarians as Patristic Translators', *Studies in Philology* lxx (1973), 329–44.
155. S. Gilley, *Newman and his Age* (London 1990), 112.
156. W. R. Ward, 'Oxford and the origins of Liberal Catholicism in the Church of England', *Studies in Church History* i (1964), 236–7.
157. Newman refused to accommodate Stanley's plea that in re-editing his *Apologia*, he should alter the remarks he had made in the first edition about the Liberals having driven him from Oxford. C. S. Dessain and E. Kelly (eds.), *Letters and Diaries of John Henry Newman* xxi (1971), 449–50. For Stanley's contrary view, see [A. P. Stanley], 'Subscription', *Macmillan's Magazine* xliii (Jan. 1881), 209–10.
158. Church, 391–2. The Tractarians lamented the 'natural repugnance to mystical divinity' characteristic of Copleston and his Oriel Noetic cohorts, see *Christian Remembrancer* xiii. 19. However, according to Church, the new liberals in contrast to the 'old latitudinarians', were 'interested in the Tractarian innovators and, in a degree, sympathised with them as a party of movement who had the courage to risk and sacrifice much for an unworldly end'. Church, 338. This analysis helps explain Baden Powell's surprisingly favourable notice of the Tractarians in some of his later writings.
159. J. H. Newman to E. B. Pusey, 11 Mar. 1854, quoted in H. P. Liddon, *Life of E.B. Pusey* iii, 394; I. Ellis, 'Pusey and University Reform', P. Butler (ed.), *Pusey Rediscovered* (London 1983), 326–7.
160. E. A. Knox, *Reminiscences of an Octogenarian, 1847–1934* (London 1935), 65–6; for the High Church revival in Oxford in the 1860s, see Ellis, *Seven Against Christ*, 230–2.
161. I. Williams to J. H. Newman, 5 June 1863, C. S. Dessain (ed.), *Letters*

and Diaries of John Henry Newman xx (1970), 459. See Newman's own comments at this time, 'I look with the most anxious interest at the state of Oxford—the more so because I anticipated the present perplexities', J. H. Newman to M. MacColl, 24 Mar. 1861, C. S. Dessain (ed.), *Letters and Diaries of John Henry Newman* xix (London 1969), 487.

162. For an example of this view, see *A Letter to the Rev. the Vice-Chancellor of the University of Oxford and the learned Doctors who assisted him on a late occasion, from Torquemada the younger* (Oxford 1843).
163. H. A. Woodgate, *Considerations on the Present Duty of the University of Oxford* (Oxford 1843), 20.
164. A. Ramm, 'Gladstone's Religion', *Historical Journal* xxviii (1985), 335–6.
165. F. Meyrick, *Memorials of life at Oxford* (London 1905), 27–9.
166. W. R. Ward, *Victorian Oxford*, xv.
167. F. H. Thicknesse, 'The Great Commission of the Great King' [1870], 10. Cf. T. G. Talbot, 'The Church and the Universities' in A. Weir & W. D. Maclagan (eds), *The Church & the Age: essays on the Principles and Present Position of the Anglican Church* second series (1872), 151–82. Cf. *Contemporary Review* lx, 'The nationalisation of Cathedrals' (September 1891), 363–4, 369. Cf. A. G. L. Haig, 'The Church, the Universities and Learning in later Victorian England', *Historical Journal* xxix (1986), 199.

Higher Education and the Emergence of the Professional Woman in Glasgow *c.* 1890–1914

Catherine M. Kendall

The purpose of this paper is to show how the effort and achievement of gaining higher education broadened the range of professional opportunity for women. In late Victorian Britain women's job opportunities increased as demand grew for clerks, shop assistants, nurses, and teachers, but middle-class women were restricted to occupations considered suitable for ladies. Higher education was a great outlet for these women since it channelled their energies into something worthwhile, and proved useful for future employment. Access to universities opened the way to professional training, not necessarily for paid work, but to the same standards attained by men. We will consider the campaign for women's higher education and how it affected three of the first professions open to women. Education, medicine, and social work were all caring professions with identifiable roots in woman's traditional role within the family. Of these, teaching was most important as it was the main destination of genteel women with a living to earn, and demand from this group hastened women's admission to universities; medicine involved a long and costly training and hence was restricted to those women with wealthy fathers or private incomes; social work found its roots as a profession in women's traditional charitable work through the women associated with voluntary bodies such as the Queen Margaret College Settlement in Glasgow.

Settlements of this kind were a characteristic development of late nineteenth century universities, both in Britain and the United States.[1] Inspired by T. H. Green's thinking about social service, men and women students from many universities established settlements in poor urban areas. Settlements developed in different ways which depended on the motivation of their workers and the local conditions. Nevertheless there was considerable cross-fertilization of ideas between settlements. For example the Queen Margaret Settlement had a strong link with the Women's University Settlement in Southwark and contacts with the North West Settlement in Chicago.

Queen Margaret Settlement was initiated under the auspices of Queen Margaret College, which was itself founded in 1883 by the Glasgow Association to promote the Higher Education of Women in the west of Scotland. Similar developments in the higher education of women took place concurrently in other major Scottish cities and university towns, mainly Edinburgh and St Andrews. Queen Margaret College was incorporated into Glasgow University as the Women's Department in 1892 as a consequence of legislation which finally admitted women to Scottish universities.

This study is based largely on women from the Queen Margaret Settlement. They form an interesting group in their own right although they are not representative of the general College population.[2] They include early campaigners for women's higher education in Glasgow and some of the supporters of Queen Margaret College in its earliest days. The desires which underlay the struggle for degrees were whetted rather than satisfied when higher education was won, and grew in new directions. Moreover most of the women came from those well-to-do professional, mercantile or manufacturing families which formed the elite of Glasgow society. Such women formed a powerful network through charitable societies, ladies' auxiliaries for hospital fund-raising, and from 1883 they attended Queen Margaret College in pursuit of higher culture. It was part of their background and upbringing to initiate and participate in worthy causes. Hence the College's Settlement for social work among the poor attracted support from old and new members of the College Students' Union. Finally, the training undertaken by these women caused them to analyse the conditions they met in Settlement work. They arranged lecture courses upon a variety of social issues, and within a few years these courses developed further in a university school for social study. A similar trend (of professionalizing women's practical expertise) has been noted among other university women.[3] In her study of women academics at the universities of Cambridge, Oxford, and London, Fernanda Perrone argues that the professionalization of social work in the early twentieth century led women naturally from their traditional role in philanthropy into study of social administration and sociology at universities. She also notes that while women found it difficult to enter the natural sciences because of lack of teaching resources and dearth of opportunities afterwards, in the social sciences they could develop their expertise into a professional training. (This also sheds an interesting light on the particularly practical focus of the early lecture courses in the Glasgow School of Social Study and the later empirical development of British sociology.[4])

The following is a study of the way in which the experience of being pioneers in higher education affected these particular Glasgow women and stimulated further change. It is not an exhaustive study of women's entry into professional life. The widened access to higher education was to revolutionize the career possibilities for genteel and educated women within two or three decades. An address to a teachers' meeting in Glasgow in 1896 acknowledged 'the New Woman ... arisen out of that great middle class which is now the backbone of the nation ... This middle class adopted a new standard—of extreme and conventional respectability. The life of women especially was narrowed by artificial restriction, against which there has been a revolt, taking sometimes an extreme form.'[5] In the mid-century the role of middle-class women was extremely circumscribed. Formerly women had managed businesses; now the zones of men and women's work were completely separated as families moved from the centres of economic activity to residential suburbs to the west of cities. Hard work was a virtue, yet the middle-class lady was demeaned by housework. A woman's place was in the home for her husband and family. 'The natural crown of woman's career is wedded life. There is no doubt about that.'[6]

Spinsters denied this fulfilment were constrained to a marginal life at home, only relieved by the church and good works. In 1859 Miss Jane Smith was '... disconsolate, because if the school goes, all my work in the world will seem to have gone too. I wish unmarried women could follow some trade or profession.'[7] A similar reaction motivated Miss Janet Galloway, first Secretary to Queen Margaret College. 'Finding by experience the disadvantages to which women were subjected by reason of the restricted character of their education and the consequent limitation of their activities, she became an ardent supporter of the movement for the removal of these limitations and for the provision for women of an education of the same character as that of men.'[8] Single women benefited most from new opportunities afforded by higher education by which they could gain independence and status outside the marital bond.[9]

The campaign for women's higher education in Glasgow was part of a nationwide movement which gained ground from the mid-century onwards. In England, Girton College was founded in 1869; in Scotland, St Andrews University began to award the 'Lady Literate in Arts' qualification in 1879. However the women's aim was to achieve equality and not simply equivalence in university teaching and qualifications. Women in several cities formed associations to work for women's admission to Universities. The Glasgow Association for Promoting the Higher Education of Women (GAHEW) was launched at a public meeting in April 1877. It is worth noting how the issue was regarded by both sexes at the time. Men's views can mainly be judged from a report of the 1877 meeting. Women were not called to speak at that meeting so their opinions have been drawn from other contemporary writings.

The main motivation for women was self-fulfilment; the terms 'higher education' and 'higher culture' were used interchangeably. Opening a lecture series, Professor Ramsay considered that 'a cultured person should have a fair knowledge of history . . . know something about all the great names of this country and western Europe. Culture doesn't know everything, it is an attitude towards true knowledge.'[10] It would be wrong to assume that greater job opportunity was the prime reason for women to seek higher education. Clearly some women graduates were ambitious, but generally the early supporters of higher education were wealthy enough not to justify the expense by future financial return. Indeed the Edinburgh Ladies' Association expressed their aim as 'not to train for a profession but to give women the advantages of a system already acknowledged to be well-suited for the mental training of the sex'.[11]

Higher culture for women was represented as benefiting woman's work with her family, not merely as an end in itself. Several speakers dwelt upon the benefits to men ('whose wives having resources within themselves might be something more than mere housekeepers—intelligent companions, wise counsellors to their husbands'[12]) and sons and daughters ('who is the first and greatest educator of all our future men and women? Woman does all this and should she not be educated?'[13]).

Outside the home, it was suggested that the elevation of women would benefit society as a whole. 'Educated women will tend to raise the morals of our country for it is well-known that education drives all that is foolish and false from the mind.' There was also a strong tendency in Glasgow to view higher education as excellent training for the mission field. 'When circumstances place girls above [working for their living] they should train themselves for doing the great unpaid work of the world where "the harvest is plentiful but the workers are few." '[14] The first woman graduate was challenged thus, 'I do not think, Miss Gilchrist, that you have any right to study medicine unless you are going to the mission field.'[15]

The arguments raised by women tended to emphasize how higher education was compatible with their existing role and would improve performance of their current work. These arguments were acceptable because they would not threaten the Victorian family balance of power. It is quite evident however that many of the women pioneers in higher education were ambitious, either for their own professional advancement, or that of their sex. They were not particularly social revolutionaries in a wider sense, they simply wanted to share fully in the benefits of their class.

Men who supported women's higher education brought forward other arguments. The women in Glasgow enjoyed support from a number of prominent men in the church, business, and university communities, who spoke at the GAHEW inauguration. The meeting was also reported seriously and in great detail in the major Glasgow daily newspapers. According to the Mistress of Queen Margaret College, the women's campaign encountered less hostility in Glasgow than in Edinburgh because Sophia Jex-Blake's struggle to enter Edinburgh University had already raised public awareness.[16] There was also a long-standing east/west coast rivalry between Edinburgh and Glasgow; Professor Nichol 'wouldn't wish it to be supposed that in a movement of this kind the city had fallen behind other places. Certainly it had not fallen behind Edinburgh . . .'[17]

Professional men particularly welcomed higher education for women, seeing in it a way to provide daughters with qualifications to earn their own living after their father's deaths. 'Money didn't flow like water into their pockets. They were glad and relieved that a way was being hewn through prejudice which would lead to careers for their daughters as well as their sons.'[18] Several speakers from the Church and the university sounded a more cautionary note. Principal Caird owned that 'it is impossible for any member of the University to be indifferent to a scheme for promoting the higher education of any class of persons in the community' but then qualified this acceptance. It seems that he was covering himself against possible future 'awkwardness'; 'when your scheme was matured it would come before the University authorities for approval'.[19] There was no question of the university taking the initiative in women's higher education; it was up to the GAHEW campaign to demonstrate the demand and establish the system. The Principal had supported lectures for women and now he exhorted the women to make the courses worthwhile; he warned against 'desultory and unconnected courses of lectures not arranged to any systematic plan of study' which were 'comparatively valueless as a means of education'. He raised briefly the question of women's intellectual ability to cope with study but appeared to dismiss it in the phrase 'no limitations have yet been proved'.

Men's concern about the suitability of higher education for women centred on fears that it would erode 'womanly' qualities; 'learned women could grow into mere pedantry and lose the grace and sweetness of womanhood and become painfully disagreeable'.[20] The subjects for study caused concern; there was felt to be 'something suitable in the artistic side of education as applied to ladies' whereas natural sciences were implicitly deemed 'unwomanly', 'although there were some women whose minds needed them'. There was something freakish and unattractive about an educated woman whose interest in her subject threatened her natural role in a family. One male speaker caused amusement by admitting this frankly; 'Certainly, if a lady found more interest in differential calculus than Beethoven, or more interest in the formation of a beetle than the study of Shakespeare, she should study calculus and the beetle . . . but he confessed he would rather be associated with the admirer of Beethoven and Shakespeare than the other lady.'[21]

GAHEW classes began in autumn 1877 and proved very popular. Support came mainly from wealthy mothers and daughters in Glasgow society, but such higher education was a luxury. Women with a living to earn could only afford it if it improved their employment prospects. GAHEW's ultimate aim was a university degree but they had to convince public and university opinion that they were serious. The greatest proof of commitment came in 1883 when a women's college was established through the gift of Mrs Isabella Elder, a wealthy Glasgow widow.

The foundation of Queen Margaret College spurred on the campaign. The Queen Margaret Diploma increased prestige in arts and science courses, and classes were raised to degree level in all subjects. Numbers increased rapidly at first, then levelled and dropped slightly. Yet the College's success only emphasized its limitations. Reliance upon the support of leisured ladies did not offer much security for the future, and was not helpful for its public image; Mrs Elder wrote of the 'impression of exclusiveness which exists in the public mind towards QMC'.[22] Moreover the demand from those requiring degrees for employment was still unsatisfied. However, little could be done until the passing of the Universities (Scotland) Act in 1889. To the disappointment of some, the Act did not allow for the immediate opening of the universities to women but required an enabling ordinance of the Commissioners and the 'will of the University'. The College was incorporated into the University as the Women's Department and the first female students matriculated in 1892.

What changes occurred as a result of the universities opening to women? In Glasgow entry to degree courses began almost immediately. Arts classes were opened to women in October 1892, followed shortly by science, and medicine in 1894. Numbers increased enormously, doubling during the first decade (in 1893/4 there were 176; in 1900/1, 334), and almost doubling again by 1913 (1912/13, 639).[23] Initially many students still came from upper middle class Glasgow families; they lived at home and some still took occasional courses rather than full degrees. The problems of finding accommodation and money for bursaries had to be tackled before the College could satisfy the growing demand from girls all over Scotland and beyond.

The reaction to women within the university was mixed. Most professors were happy to teach women students and some began co-educational courses at Gilmorehill immediately, although most teaching continued in the College. Some refused, saying it was outwith the terms of their contract to teach women whereupon special lecturers were appointed for the College.[24] In one instance a lecturer was reported to have apologized to his men students for the poor standard of his lectures, but said they had been prepared for the weaker intellects of QMC.[25]

Generally the novelty value caused most comment. The *Glasgow Herald* described the first intake of medical students 'from the stern female clad in severe navy blue serge to the little girl with ringlets who ought to have been eating chocolates in a drawing room'.[26] This reveals more about the popular perception of women in education than of typical women students because these two are reported to have failed. Even at graduation ceremonies several years later, a former student wrote that 'each woman was singled out for outbursts of wild catcalls and vociferous cheering as if she were something from another planet'.[27] The excitement affected the women too. The same student recalled 'the girls now hurried off more enthusiastically to QMC than their brothers. I think because it was novel and there was a challenge to be met.'

Apart from the excitement of pioneering higher education, the attainment of a degree conferred advantages. The teaching profession was the first to benefit, since it was the most common occupation for a genteel woman with a living to earn. Women taught mainly as governesses or in elementary schools and sought qualifications to enhance their employment prospects. 'If a governess got a certificate in languages or literature from an academic source it would go very far with regard to her reception into families.'[28] Demand from this group forced the pace of change in higher education because teachers offered the best potential source of student interest outside the leisured classes.

GAHEW tried to meet the need by co-operating with similar local associations to establish the Northern United Registry for governesses and the Governess Loan Fund to help with fees. More important was the 'Calendar of teachers holding University certificates' which reinforced both teachers and institutions: '... very useful in helping to give these examinations their proper value and as enabling heads of families and schools to find ladies who have qualified themselves for their profession by passing these examinations'.[29] Yet all efforts fell short of obtaining the university's MA degree qualification and Mrs Elder was exasperated that the College was missing a valuable opportunity to attract students. 'In Glasgow there are a large number of women preparing to be teachers who do not seem to be attracted to QM and for whom every encouragement ought to be provided ... Mothers requiring governesses will not take time to examine the value of different degrees even if they had the education to do so but they will invariably give the preference to governesses with the mystical letters after their names.'[30]

Following women's admission to the University, the College attracted aspiring teachers from all over Scotland. Indeed the principal use of an MA for women was as a qualification for teaching. Graduate status changed both emphasis and opportunity in the teaching profession; it enhanced women's view of teaching as a highly-qualified career, and it enabled them to compete on equal terms with men for posts in secondary schools and for senior posts in elementary schools. Many of the early graduates remained single and pursued their teaching careers with dedication, to the extent that they were regarded as slightly odd, like the woman interested in calculus and the beetle. The first woman graduate with first-class honours in mathematics taught at Laurel Bank School, in Glasgow; pupils recalled her with 'an abundance of fair hair in a bun right on top of her head and a pencil skewered through it—that's where she kept it'.[31]

Laurel Bank was one of the new girls' schools which offered possibilities of employment to women graduates; others in Glasgow included the Park and Westbourne schools. However Scottish opportunities were limited and a number of women left to go elsewhere. According to Louisa Lumsden of St Andrews, graduates were 'compelled to look almost entirely to England for a worthy professional career'.[32] However, in this group of Glasgow women, more travelled abroad than to England. A few took senior posts in South Africa; several more went out as missionaries to India, where one first-class honours graduate in modern languages spent thirty-two years training native teachers, 'teaching them in their own language within six months'.[33] Some moved into teacher-training and made original contributions to the development of Scottish education.[34]

There is evidence that graduate teachers carried something of the College ethos into their new job. The work of the College Settlement among the poor in Anderston was taken up in at least two schools in which former students taught. Girls from the Park school took part in entertainments for the Settlement before 1914, and Laurel Bank assisted the Hillside kindergarten school which took tubercular children from Anderston and Cowcaddens,[35] two of the city's most congested areas.

Degrees taken in early life proved valuable for employment later on. Some single middle-class women did not take a paid post after graduation but continued to live in the family home; their families were able and possibly preferred to support them. However a significant number moved into teaching after 1918, perhaps as family circumstances changed.[36] Teaching was therefore not a new field for women, but a degree facilitated their greater participation.

The opening of universities to women enabled them to qualify for other professions which had previously been exclusive to men. The first notable example was medicine. It was very difficult to overcome hostility to the idea of women as doctors, since this offended the notion of middle-class women's sensitivity. Women's physical and mental strength to cope was questioned. An article on careers for girls in medicine (published in 1908 when women doctors were not so unusual) warned sternly that the prime 'indispensable quality' was a 'thoroughly healthy constitution to enable her to stand the stress of both training and "practice". In addition, she must have a thoroughly healthy and well-balanced mind, free from the tendency to nerves and hysteria which characterise so many of her sex.'[37]

More significantly, the idea of women studying the human body contradicted contemporary ideas of 'delicacy' of the female sex. Queen Victoria expressed repugnance at the 'Awful idea ... to propose that they should study with Men things which could not be named before them, certainly not in a mixed audience.'[38] Clearly there was a social distinction here, since male doctors were not embarrassed by working with female nurses. Even after the Nightingale reforms though, nurses were recruited from the working classes, while female medical students were invariably middle-class because of the high educational standard required for entry, and the cost of the fees. Four years' medical study at Queen Margaret College including fees, instruments, and accommodation totalled four hundred pounds. A hundred pounds a year for a daughter's education was a considerable undertaking for most fathers.[39]

The women also had to face professional opposition from practising doctors and medical students, both in training and in the search for posts. The Glasgow medical school for women opened in Queen Margaret College in 1890, Mrs Elder meeting all expenses for the first two years. Dr Marion Gilchrist recalled that 'the dissecting room was the old kitchen in the basement; the anatomy lecture room was the small apartment adjoining'.[40] Two professors were appointed (one from the university) and nine students were accepted for the first year. Some classes were taught with men students but many remained unmixed beyond 1910, and there is evidence to suggest that this separate teaching hindered the women's academic attainment.[41] Gaining access to hospitals for clinical training proved even more difficult. Dr Gaffney recorded that 'the College application was refused outright by the Western Infirmary, shelved by the Victoria Infirmary and given very limited approval by the Maternal Hospital. The Royal Infirmary gave guarded approval but following protests from male medical students had to withdraw from the agreement, and from 1893 taught women in separate groups.'[42] Notwithstanding these problems, teaching at the College was of a sufficiently high standard that when medical degrees were opened to women, attendance at Queen Margaret College qualified students for the university examinations. Two medical graduates were the first women to be 'capped' by the University in 1894, only four years after the School started. By 1914, Dr Gaffney records that about seventy women doctors had graduated from Glasgow University.

The struggle to qualify then gave way to the battle for hospital access. The large voluntary hospitals offered the best training, but competition for places was fierce and women stood less chance of selection than men. After 1900 the Victoria and Royal Infirmaries began to appoint some women as house officers, perhaps because hospital boards were required to include two lady directors from 1899. It was somewhat easier for women doctors to obtain posts in hospitals specializing in women and children because the old arguments of modesty could not apply to them. In Glasgow such hospitals had large numbers of women directors, many of whom had links with the College.[43] These hospitals were the first to accept female students for training and to appoint onto the staff. The Samaritan Hospital for Women appointed its first women doctors in 1892 and two Junior Dispensary officers in 1897, both of whom were Settlement workers. Dr Gilchrist worked at Redlands Hospital for women, and the Victoria Infirmary; Dr Ethel Lochhead worked in maternity and child welfare for twenty years. Because of the difficulty of obtaining hospital work several women took posts in the growing field of public health. A few left for India, either for the mission field, or to take a post with the new Indian Women's Medical Service.[44] Most of the other women doctors in this study entered general practice. In 1911 the Careers Guide stated, 'nowadays the path of a woman who wishes to qualify for the profession is a comparatively clear one', but she still faced an uphill struggle after qualifying.[45]

A third important pre-war development was professional training in social work. In Glasgow this arose directly from Queen Margaret Settlement which was founded by the College Union in 1897, and hence owes its particular development to women's higher education. The Settlement idea arose in the 1880s and was symptomatic of the Progressive movement in the late nineteenth century which redefined thinking on social problems. The Progressive movement was very broadly based, encompassing the gradualist approach of Canon Barnett's Settlement and the more political Fabian society, but generally speaking, it embraced a view of society as an organic whole. R. H. Tawney was a prophet of the new thinking who described his own conversion from the strict individualist line taken by the Charity Organisation Society (COS) that each individual was responsible for his own survival and betterment, to a view of the state as a collection of individuals where salvation could only come through collective action.[46]

The Settlement idea attempted to cross class barriers and educate future leaders. Canon Barnett's original Settlement was established in a poor area of London where Oxbridge students lived and experienced at close quarters the life of the poor. It was simply a base for social interaction between Settlers and local people, as much for the education of the students as the uplifting of the rest. The idea took root and Settlements sprang up in other major cities, including Chicago where Jane Addams set up Hull House. However the ideal was criticized by the COS and others for being 'somewhat sentimental and unpractical'[47]: the Settlers were in the area but not of it; the need to draw local people meant that activities took over Settlement life.[48] Far from being unrealistic though, the Queen Margaret Settlement was highly pragmatic in its development, and its residence gave it an advantage over the COS when training expanded. In practice each Settlement developed along the lines set by dominant influences and local conditions. Queen Margaret Settlement was shaped by its origin in a women's college, by other women's settlements, and through co-operation with the Glasgow COS.

Indeed the Settlement was very much a creature of the College. It was founded in 1897 exclusively for College members, an activity which drew together old and new members of the College Union, especially after the enormous increase in student numbers from 1892. In practice a small activist group was dominant; the senior members of Settlement and Union at that time were practically identical. It was also a women's initiative for women. Janet Galloway countered the proposal that women students should help with the men students' Settlement at Possilpark with 'Why not have one of their own?'.[49] In 1896 the Queen Margaret Students' Union President Marion Gilchrist had declared that 'the Union should take special interest in all women's work, whatever branch, but especially the work of the labouring classes'.[50] The main work was among women and children who were popularly seen as the innocent victims of their drunken and profligate menfolk. Furthermore the Settlement provided a link between town and gown, 'a means of keeping the University in touch with the world outside,'[51] and rendered something back to the city. A memorial to Mrs Campbell of Tullichewan spoke of the 'great pleasure she took in seeing the former students of Queen Margaret College using the advantages they had received to help their poorer sisters'.[52]

Queen Margaret Settlement followed Barnett's original Settlement idea more closely than the two previous Glasgow Settlements. The London Women's University Settlement particularly had a strong impact on the development of its Glasgow sister because several Scotswomen trained and worked there before returning home to Glasgow to model the new one.[53] The restatement of the Settlement ideal with a strong strand of Christian motivation by Helen Story, a daughter of the Principal of the University, captured the Queen Margaret ethos very well. 'We must not dream of playing the Lady Bountiful now-a-days, that phase of charity has happily passed away. We go as man to man and try mutually to make our corner of the vineyard a pleasanter and more fruitful place.'[54]

The other great influence on the Queen Margaret Settlement was the COS. Again, there was a high degree of overlap between the organizations. The COS too laid great emphasis upon training workers thoroughly in the Society's principles before application to casework. 'The first object of anyone who is trained should be to help to train others, and he should consider this as even more a point of his work than dealing with the causes of distress. . . . the Committee would like to see in the Society the nucleus of a future University for the study of social science in which all those who desire to undertake philanthropic work desire to graduate.'[55]

However, the COS practice of close scrutiny into the affairs of other charities meant that it was mistrusted and could not fulfil this ideal on its own. At the same time the Settlement was well-placed to move into social work training. In 1901 Kathleen Bannatyne (a prominent figure in COS and Settlement circles) outlined 'why the Settlement was a natural outcome of College life and how many of the qualities developed by University education were precisely those demanded by that new view of charity and social work which was gaining ground. The training of its workers in this new way was not the least important of this Settlement's objectives.'[56]

The Settlement's later role in social work training was promoted by several factors from the outset. Its first work in Anderston was to run the COS district office to deal with needy cases, and to set up a Collecting Savings Bank to encourage thrift. Both these required the workers to visit the poor and grasp the difficulties of their situation. Simple panaceas were not enough; thrift, for example, was encouraged, but 'saving may be a crime. There may be a question whether a man earning less than a pound a week . . . ought to save his money rather than spend it on the bodies, souls and brains of his children.'[57]

From the start workers desired to learn more about the circumstances in which they worked. Occasional lectures were held on social and economic theories and in 1903 Miss Galloway proposed that they should form a regular part of Settlement work. In 1904 lectures were organized jointly with two representatives from the COS who were also members of the Settlement Council, and the following winter this Joint-Committee was augmented by two representatives from the Glasgow Union of Women Workers—again these two were members of both organizations. The Joint-Committee programme included short courses by local experts and lectures on a variety of topics by notable people, including Beatrice Webb, Professor and Mrs Bosanquet, and R. H. Tawney (a lecturer in the history department at the University from 1906 to 1908). The lecture programme gathered momentum from 1907, but like the progress towards higher education itself, required accommodation and money for students before it could offer serious training.

At the same time, the Settlement's search for new premises had important repercussions for its own future and that of training. The Council endorsed Barnett's ideal of a residential base but had been unsuccessful in attracting visitors. The rooms of the first residence were described as 'an odd shape and not very homely', the fee for board was quite high, and furthermore most of the workers lived in comfortable West End homes within a mile or two of the Settlement and were not tempted to Anderston. An enforced move in 1907 made the Settlement Council reconsider its priorities, and it decided that a residence should be maintained. Two tenement houses were purchased, one to be let as workmen's dwellings, and the other to be the Settlement's offices, meeting rooms, and residence.

The subsequent rise in resident numbers owed something to the lighter, airier building, but more to the growing number of posts with pay. The Warden and the Girls' Club Superintendent (who had to live in the Settlement under the terms of their contract) were joined first by additional paid Settlement staff and later by women seeking social work training. Internally there was a growing trend towards creating a management structure with a hierarchy of paid professional workers. This is most clearly demonstrated in the post of Warden.

The Warden's role increased in scope, status, and salary (from £50 to £80) in fourteen years. Under her original contract Miss Rutherfurd was really a glorified maid-of-all-work, 'housekeeping for herself and the residents, carrying on the work of the Settlement and training workers who may present themselves'.[58] She could take part only in service which had direct bearing on Settlement work. Thus it caused controversy on the Settlement Council when she was invited to stand as a candidate in the Parish Council elections in 1904 and again in 1907. The Council vetoed the first request saying 'it would interfere with her work as Warden,'[59] but in 1907 accepted an anonymous donation of £50 for the salary of a sub-warden to assist in the Settlement. Miss Rutherfurd was duly elected Parish Councillor and became involved in the administration of the Poor Law. In subsequent years the Warden was called to serve on national committees by civil servants who included former Settlement colleagues: she became a member of the Central Committee for Scotland on Women's Unemployment, and Convenor of the Sub-committee on Juvenile Employment. The 1907 election marked several significant changes: the use of the Warden's local knowledge and practical experience in service to a wider community than just the Settlement; an acceptance of the validity of the contributions made by the women of the Settlement; and especially that their opinions should be heard on official bodies.

The co-ordination of workers was one of the Warden's main concerns after 1907. Settlement work had grown enormously since

1897: the two original girls clubs had given rise to eight and a Scout troop, covering all ages from six to twenty; the Collecting Savings Bank extended over nineteen districts; about three hundred babies were visited by Settlement health visitors. Volunteers could be found for the more popular tasks but few took on more than two Settlement commitments, sometimes because they were involved in other organizations. Only a handful of very dedicated workers were involved across the range of activities. Reliance upon volunteers had its problems, as with the difficulty of attracting residents above. Year-round commitment also posed a problem. Women were prepared to give time to Settlement work from September to May (the Glasgow social season ran from December to the end of March) but not over the summer (when whole households moved north and westward to the coast, highlands, and islands). The Council tried to keep the Settlement open at first, but then had to close down completely over the summer months. The people of Anderston though, did not disappear for months to the seaside.

Single women were also still at the first call of their families, and had to interrupt their activities if summoned. Even paid staff were subject to this; Miss Lizzie Lochhead, the Superintendent, resigned her post in 1908 'as she was needed more at home,' and then negotiated a new contract by which she could live at home in Paisley over the summer and in Anderston for the Girls' Club over the winter.[60] Miss Annie Harrison, a very popular Sub-warden and the daughter of the Episcopal Bishop of Glasgow and Galloway, resigned in 1911 'as she was wanted at home'.[61] Quite a sizeable minority left Glasgow for an extended period to travel abroad with their families. Miss Alice Younger, who was appointed Convenor in 1909 after the death of Miss Galloway, spent three months in Canada later that year.

The vagaries of working with a volunteer workforce caused the Settlement to create a management structure with a hierarchy of paid professional workers. Executive decisions about direction and development remained firmly in the hands of the Settlement Council, but decisions about the running and improvement of existing services lay with the resident staff. Following the move to new premises, the Warden and Club Superintendent were joined by a Sub-warden, a trainee resident worker, and in 1911 by the holder of the Janet Galloway memorial scholarship. The number of residents also increased with a number of short-term women visitors and social work students after 1909.

Moreover the demand for training increased as a result of the Liberal welfare reforms from 1906 to 1911. A series of Acts of Parliament embodied some of the ideas of New Liberalism, which was part of the Progressive movement. The reforms were aimed at the more vulnerable members of society, the young and old, and at problems of work, including those who could not work through accident, illness, or unemployment in certain categories of work. The reforms increased demand for paid and unpaid workers trained in social welfare. Not a great many paid posts were created, although staff were required for labour exchanges, for national and health insurance schemes, the probation service, and welfare work in large firms. Other workers such as Poor Law and trade union officials, church and charity workers also needed to keep abreast of current developments. Hilda Cashmore of Manchester University's School of Social Study identified a wide variety of skills required by workers in social welfare, including administration, business and group organization, case work, superintendence of staff.[62]

The Settlement was ideally placed to answer this need. Under the leadership of Helen Story and Mrs Francis Charteris[63] the Joint-Committee became more ambitious. In May 1909 a resolution was passed 'urging the City authorities and the University to take steps to provide for education in the duties of citizenship and social service by the establishment of special classes'.[64] Gaining acceptance for social studies as a university discipline followed the same pattern as women's struggle for university education. The Joint-Committee had to prove that the demand for such courses existed and demonstrate their commitment by arranging lecture courses, with examinations for a diploma. Mr J. H. Jones from the men Students' Settlement joined the team and later became Director of Studies. Under his management the diploma course was developed and extended every year.

The first syllabus in 1909 stated the basis of the course. 'It is strongly felt by those who are engaged in any kind of public or social work that their practical training ought to be supplemented by some systematic instruction in the history and theory of social economics if the best results are to be obtained. The problems that such workers are called upon to face demand for their solution more knowledge than can be gained from practical experience alone. . . .'[65] The first year consisted of twenty-one lectures over three terms, and one conference. Lectures were held on Friday evenings at the university so that working men and women could attend, and the fees were kept low at six shillings for the whole series. Encouraged by the response, the Joint-Committee planned a similar course the following year incorporating tutorial classes, and pursued the idea of awarding a diploma for social work. In discussion with the university authorities, however, this was deemed to be 'premature'[66] so the Joint-Committee decided to hold their own theory examinations that winter and award a certificate signed by the lecturers. In the third session, 1911/12, practical work became an integral part of the training. A minimum of twelve hours per week was required at the Settlement or the COS.

Early in 1912 the Joint-Committee decided to set up in its place a Board of Studies incorporating representatives from various public bodies. This increased the breadth of support but the Settlement still held a dominant position. Of the twenty seven Board members, thirteen were also members of the Settlement Executive Council; three of these were ex-officio, two were nominated from the Settlement, two were co-opted, and the rest represented other organizations, the COS, GUWW, and the School Boards. The degree of overlap seems remarkable.

In April the Board launched the School of Social Study and Social Training. 'The demand for workers has been so great in recent years that men and women with no training have been called upon to assist in the administration of laws dealing with social conditions . . . They should be able to show some systematic training in social work and attained to a certain standard of efficiency, as would be assured by a certificate or diploma of a recognised School of Social Study.'[67] 'Training will be philosophical in a wider sense, intended to train the imaginative reason rather than to impart a detailed body of knowledge.'[68]

The School continued to organize thematic series of public lectures for general interest and further developed its formal training course. From 1913 the Glasgow University Ordinary Diploma was granted for theoretical study with sufficient practical work to illustrate it, and the Endorsed Diploma for study combined with a specific course of practical training at a named institution. The COS and the Settlement were the first to undertake to train students; the COS declined to charge for this, but the Settlement was short of funds and agreed a fee of £5. Despite this, more students chose to train at the Settlement.

The Settlement was a thorough training ground for students. COS training was valuable, but Settlement work was more diverse and so was chosen for the illustrative experience required for the Ordinary Diploma. A survey of women's Settlements for the *Englishwoman's Yearbook* indicates that Queen Margaret Settlement had a particularly extensive range of activities.[69] It also undertook investigations for other agencies; in 1910 all the students were engaged in research for Professor Noel Paton's dietary study on the working classes.[70] Trainee students were expected to take part in a cross-section of work; Miss E. R. Jamieson, resident in 1910, was involved in nine separate branches of service. The Settlement gave wide organizational experience in 'programme-making, expenses, committee minutes, records'. The residential experience gave an extra dimension to the training as well as being a convenient combination of home and work base for students. Miss Cashmore included among her 'essential methods', 'Every student should live in a working class or industrial district . . . should become familiar with the centres of working class life . . . No visiting can give the same training as residence. It is abundantly clear that unless a University Settlement can be so organised as to be adaptable . . . as a practising school for students, such a thorough training is impossible.'[71]

The Settlement regarded students' work as a separate concern from 1909 when the first women were accepted for residential training. Like the first generation of higher education students they were quite wealthy; grants were not available until 1917 from the Carnegie Trust, while board alone at the Settlement cost twenty-three shillings a week, which was equivalent to many working men's weekly wage. Most students were young Scotswomen, but not all had degrees. Once qualified, they went into established charity work, as COS secretaries or Parish Sisters, and one became Warden of the Presbyterian Settlement in Poplar.

From 1912 the School of Social Study and Social Training took men and women students, although women still predominated. The records of home addresses and future work are not complete, but it appears that most students came from Scotland and a few from England. Men were already employed and studied part-time, but the effect of the Liberal government's welfare reforms is clearly seen in the great variety of the women's work destinations, many of which were new. The majority of students took posts in the Labour (later Employment) Exchanges, or in manufacturing and commercial firms as welfare supervisors. A large minority went to work with children, becoming health visitors, teachers, or club leaders. A handful became hospital almoners or factory inspectors. Two long-serving Settlement workers took senior civil service posts: Dorothy Allan, a former Settlement Sub-warden, became a Chief Woman Inspector for the National Health Insurance; Alice Younger, Convenor of the Settlement Council, was appointed Organiser for Women's Labour Exchanges in Scotland. Until 1914 some women appear not to have worked after qualifying; by 1918 all those who gained diplomas were already employed. By this time the effects of war had increased the number of women in social work and raised demand for new courses, such as one for factory welfare supervisors from the Ministry of Munitions.

The Liberal welfare legislation took over a number of functions from voluntary agencies and caused some to question if their days were numbered. Several of the Settlement's 'babies' were transferred to the control of statutory bodies; the successful Invalid children's school, the first of its kind in Glasgow, passed to the Glasgow School Board in 1906; the Skilled Employment Committee was absorbed into the Juvenile Labour Exchange. The Settlement still had influence in these organizations but had to work to keep it.

In practice, 'there was no danger of the volunteer army becoming regular'.[72] The number of paid posts represented a tiny fraction of social work effort, and the state needed volunteers to supplement the official service. Many contemporary writers reaffirmed the need for continued and new efforts by voluntary workers. Sidney Webb wrote 'We need the voluntary worker to be the eyes and fingers of the Public Authority.'[73] Helen Story argued that voluntary agencies freed from their former tasks could extend their field to other needs. 'The volunteer ... brings a personal touch to bear ... can try schemes which need development before they are recognised by the state as deserving support, and bring pressure to bear on the state to amend existing or introduce new provision for social needs.'[74] The Settlement also had other work to do. 'The Council would emphasise that the main aim of the Settlement's existence is not to train professional workers. Settlements were founded to bring about between different members of the social world a more friendly relationship ... mutual understanding, based upon real knowledge gained at first hand.'[75] Many initiatives arose from the Settlement, but probably the training of social workers was of the most lasting significance for Scottish social welfare and for the Settlement's own future.

The total effect of all these changes was to encourage women's education to be taken seriously. 'Whether a girl marries or not, it is highly desirable that she should be able to take her place in the ranks of women workers should the need ever arise.'[76] The consequences raised standards because women could no longer afford a dilettante approach. 'A natural result of the extension of field of work for women is that . . . a high standard of proficiency is exacted. There is no place for the untrained worker.'

Professional progress preceded political freedom. Settlement members were among the first women elected to Parish Councils and School Boards in the 1900s, and most were active in the campaign for women's suffrage. The Women's Suffrage Society with its strong Liberal inclination gained most support from Settlement women. Some of the most dynamic Settlement members joined the more militant Women's Social and Political Union and another organized the 'Scottish scattered' for the Women's Freedom League.[77]

The revolutionary progress made by these women tempts one to overstate their original desire for reform. However original motivations should not be deduced from eventual results; indeed such an emphasis overlooks other significant aspects of their achievements. Not all women were in favour of political emancipation, even those who supported women's fulfilment through higher education. Janet Galloway worked unstintingly for women's higher education yet she was opposed to women's suffrage: 'the surprising thing . . . was her conservatism'.[78] On the other hand Marion Gilchrist was politically active within and without the College, but she was professionally ambitious rather than a radical feminist.

Despite the progress recorded above there was still a common perception that women's work was not essential. Even paid professionals were called away from the Settlement by family demands. The great catalyst to alter that perception and to prove the need for working women was the First World War. A sense of duty combined with new opportunities encouraged educated women to try new openings. In a letter to all Queen Margaret graduates in 1915 Frances Melville exhorted the women to utilize their university training to the full. 'At the moment, an opportunity, unsought and unwelcomed, offers itself for women to discover paths hitherto untrodden by them, occupations perhaps more congenial to the individual tastes of many'.[79] With men called away, women in the professions mentioned above gained new ground and proved their competence. Within one generation they had achieved equal qualifications with men. Gaining equal promotion took longer.

Catherine M. Kendall
53 Exminster Road,
Styvechale,
Coventry CV3 5NW

REFERENCES

1. M. E. Rose, 'Neighbours of the working poor' (paper delivered at the Economic History Conference, Liverpool, 1990).
2. The information upon this group is taken from my M.Litt. thesis in progress, 'The Queen Margaret Settlement: Glasgow women pioneers in social work 1897–1914'.
3. See F. Perrone, 'Women Academics at Cambridge, London, and Oxford: 1880–1930', and B. Svadbova, 'The genesis of the first women graduates of Charles University in Prague' (papers delivered at the university and society conference, Glasgow, 1990).
4. Glasgow University Archives (GUA) Glasgow School of Social Study and Social Training, lecture notes 1909–12.
5. GUA, 23407, *Glasgow Herald (GH)*, 25 Jan. 1896, Dr Wenley's address to Teachers' Guild.
6. GUA, 19982, *Glasgow News (GN)*, 4 Apr. 1877, Report of meeting to form Association for Promoting Higher Education for Women, speech by Revd F. L. Robertson.
7. Strathclyde Regional Archives (SRA), TD 1/905, Miss Jane Smith to Mrs A. Smith, July 1859.
8. Dr D. Murray, *Janet A. Galloway LL.D: A Book of Memories*, ed. Mrs Robert Jardine (Glasgow, 1914), 11.
9. Martha Vicinus, *Independent Women: work and community for single women 1850–1920* (London 1985), and Sandra Burman, *Fit Work for Women* (London 1979), 36–7.
10. SRA, TD 1/905, Margaret Smith to her mother, 3 Nov. 1891.
11. 'Memorial of Edinburgh Association for the University Education of Women to the Scottish University Commissioners', quoted in Rosalind K. Marshall, *Virgins and Viragos: A History of women in Scotland from 1080 to 1980* (London 1983), 259.
12. *GN*, 4 Apr. 1877, Revd F. L. Robertson.
13. GUA, 20280, 'BINA', 'Reminiscences of the Early Days of the Association for Higher Education of Women, by a former student'.
14. ibid.

15. GUA, 20618, Dr Marion Gilchrist, 'Some early recollections of the Queen Margaret Medical School', *Surgo* (Mar. 1948).
16. Frances H. Melville, 'Queen Margaret College', *Pass It On*, Nov. 1935.
17. *GN*, 4 Apr. 1877, Prof. Nichol.
18. GUA, 34375, *GH*, 19 Mar. 1955, 'Through College Windows'.
19. *GN*, 4 Apr. 1877, Principal Caird.
20. ibid. Revd F. L. Robertson.
21. ibid. Prof. Nichol.
22. GUA, Ure-Elder papers, letterbook, Mrs Elder to Mrs Campbell of Tullichewan, 18 Apr. 1891.
23. GUA, Queen Margaret College Matriculation Records.
24. GUA, 20580 Frances H. Melville to K. M. Atholl on women's education, 26 Sept. 1924.
25. Marshall, *Virgins and Viragos*, p. 261.
26. Gilchrist (above, n. 12).
27. *GH*, 19 Mar. 1955 (above, n. 15).
28. *GN*, 4 Apr. 1877, Sir Jas. Watson.
29. GUA, GAHEW Annual Reports, 1880/1, 1881/2.
30. Elder (above, n. 19).
31. Morven Cameron, *The Laurel Bank Story 1903–78* (Glasgow 1978).
32. R. D. Anderson, *Education and Opportunity in Victorian Scotland* (Oxford 1983), 255.
33. GUA, *College Courant*, IX no. 17 (1956), obituaries.
34. Noteworthy are Helen Rutherfurd, later Warden of Jordanhill College of Education, and Jenny McAra, who founded Hillside School for girls upon the Dalton Plan. The Settlement itself pioneered the Montessori technique in Scotland in its kindergarten before 1914.
35. Cameron, *Laurel Bank*.
36. GUA, General Council Registers can be used to chart career changes.
37. Florence B. Jack (ed.), *The Woman's Book* (London 1911), 633.
38. K. Hudson, *The Place of Women in Society* (London 1970), quoted in Rona Gaffney, *Health Care as Social History: the Glasgow Case*, eds O. Checkland and M. Lamb (Aberdeen 1982), 134–5.
39. Wendy Alexander, *First Ladies of Medicine* (Glasgow 1987) p. 18. I am grateful to Dr R. Trainor for bringing this book to my attention.
40. Gilchrist, QM Medical School (above, n. 12).
41. Alexander, *First Ladies*, 27–32.
42. Gaffney, *Health Care*, 135–6. Wendy Alexander also points out that the Western Infirmary's refusal to admit women students necessitated much more travelling for them, since the Royal Infirmary was in the centre of the city, well away from the QMC/Gilmorehill sites.
43. GUA, Greater Glasgow Health Board Archives, HB 10/1/1, Women's Private Hospital (Redlands), (1902–23), Samaritan Hospital for Women (1887–1900, 1905–1909), Royal Hospital for Sick Children (Annual Reports 1906–22), Glasgow Maternity Hospital (Annual Reports 1911–34).

44. Alexander, *First Ladies*, 61.
45. Jack, loc. cit.
46. P. F. Clarke, 'The Progressive Movement in England', *TRHS* 5th ser., 24 (1974), 170.
47. Sidney Webb, *Socialism in England* (London 1893), 75.
48. C. S. Loch, *Charity Organisation Review (COR)* ed. C. S. Loch, 2 (Dec. 1897), 317.
49. Marion Rutherfurd, *Janet A. Galloway*, ed. Jardine, 36.
50. GUA, 19696, Queen Margaret's Students Union Minute Book (1890–1908), 6 Nov. 1896, 67.
51. GUA, 49.22.144, Queen Margaret College Settlement Association (QMCSA) Annual Reports (AR) 1897–1913, 6th AR 1902/3, Principal Story.
52. GUA, 49.22.161, QMCSA Minute Book IV, 12 Feb. 1907.
53. Kathleen Bannatyne was onetime Warden of the Women's Univ. Settlement, Marion Rutherfurd trained there before returning to Glasgow as first Warden at QMCSA. Lizzie Lochhead also trained in London at the Canning Town Settlement prior to becoming the QM Girls' Club Superintendent.
54. G. E. R. Young, *Elma and Helen Story: A Recollection* (Glasgow 1948), 16.
55. COS Occasional Paper, 2nd ser. 11 (London 1898), 7–10.
56. GUA, 49.22.144, QMCSA 4th AR, 16 Nov. 1901, Miss K. Bannatyne.
57. Canon S. Barnett, *COR* ed. Loch, 9 (1895), 341.
58. GUA, 49.22.169, QMCSA Minute book I, 15 Jan. 1901.
59. GUA, 49.22.5, QMCSA Minute book III, 10 May 1904.
60. GUA, 49.22.6, QMCSA Minute book IV, 14 Apr. and 8 Dec. 1908.
61. ibid. 11 Jan. 1911.
62. Hilda Cashmore, *Notes on Training of Students in the Principles and Practice of Social Work* (Manchester, c. 1918).
63. Helen Story was a daughter of the former Principal of the University, and was later awarded the LL.D. for her work in social work training. Mrs Charteris, formerly Annie Kedie, was a daughter of a prominent Glasgow businessman, and she and her parents were extensively involved in charitable works in Glasgow. Her husband Francis became a professor at St Andrews University.
64. GUA, 49.22.6, QMCSA Minute book IV, 8 June 1909.
65. GUA, Glasgow School of Social Study and Social Training (GSSSST), Syllabi 1909–43.
66. GUA, 49.22.6, QMCSA Minute book IV, 15 Nov. 1910.
67. GUA, GSSSST, Syllabus 1912–13.
68. *GH*, 11 Oct. 1912, 'The Training of Social Workers'.
69. G. E. Mitton (ed.), *The Englishwoman's Yearbook and Directory* (London 1914), 275–8.
70. Dorothy E. Lindsay B.Sc., *Report upon a Study of the Diet of the Labouring Classes in Glasgow* (Glasgow 1913).

71. Cashmore, *Notes on Training*.
72. Burman, *Fit Work*, 57.
73. Sidney Webb, quoted in G. E. R. Webb, *Elma and Helen*, 19.
74. Helen Story, loc. cit.
75. GUA, 49.22.144, QMCSA 15th AR 1911–12.
76. Jack, *Woman's Book*, 615.
77. Dr Marion Gilchrist, Miss Florence McPhun were WSPU members, as was Dr Elizabeth Chalmers Smith, who was imprisoned after her conviction for her part in an arson attack on a Glasgow mansion. Miss Eunice Murray, daughter of Dr D. Murray above, wrote pamphlets exhorting all Scottish women to take part in the Women's Freedom League campaign for the vote.
78. Prof. J. L. Morison, *Janet A. Galloway*, ed. Jardine, 39.
79. GUA, 20678, letter from Frances H. Melville to all Queen Margaret graduates, 1915.

Universities and Elites in Modern Britain

R. D. Anderson

This paper discusses the relation of British universities to élites and élite formation in the light of some recent general theories about university development, notably those in the collective volume on *The Transformation of Higher Learning, 1860–1930* (1983) edited by Konrad Jarausch, and in Harold Perkin's *The Rise of Professional Society: England since 1880* (1989). From these books, and from other contributors to the debate like Fritz Ringer and Harmut Kaelble, four main points seem to emerge. One is that the years from the 1860s to the 1930s form a distinctive period, the middle phase of a transition, in Jarausch's words, 'from traditional elite higher learning to modern mass higher education'. Jarausch sees a 'seismic shift' within this period, as 'a small, homogeneous, elite and pre-professional university turned into a large, diversified, middle-class and professional system of higher learning'.[1] There was a substantial rise in enrolments, but (and this is the second point) the key to expansion remained middle-class demands. Working-class students were few, and some authors have claimed that in this period those poorer students whom tradition had formerly admitted were squeezed out as competition for middle-class positions intensified. Thus Kaelble sees this as the era of 'competitive opportunities', coming between those of 'charitable' and 'welfare' opportunities, with the last phase not starting before 1914. Jarausch too considers that 'only after World War One did conscious attempts to create equality of educational opportunity begin to have an impact on enrollments'. For England, Perkin would put the process a little earlier, seeing the period 1900–1920 as the 'critical turning point' both for the entry of talent from below, and for the process by which 'the university became the normal route to high status and income'.[2]

It is Perkin who discusses most fully the third point, the link between university expansion and the phenomenon of professionalization. In *The Origins of Modern English Society 1780–1880* (1969), Perkin examined the triumph of the 'entrepreneurial' over the aristocratic ideal, part of the struggle being to wrest control of education from the hands of the old élite; this was expressed in the two great middle-class university campaigns, for the foundation of the University of London, and for the reform of the ancient universities of Oxford and Cambridge. In this struggle the professional class, especially the intellectuals within it, figured as allies of the entrepreneurs. In Perkin's new book the professionals come to the front of the stage, and since 1880 their ideal of 'trained expertise and selection by merit' has had an ever-increasing grip on status and influence. Part of this story was the third wave of middle-class action, the creation of the provincial or 'civic' universities, with their distinctively scientific and vocational mission. As universities progressively took over the training of the professions, and formal qualifications replaced earlier systems of personal patronage or apprenticeship, universities became key social institutions. By 1930, Perkin argued in his contribution to the Jarausch volume, a 'revolution' had taken place in British higher education, transforming the university from a marginal institution, a 'finishing school for young gentlemen', into 'the central power house of modern industry and society'.[3]

The fourth point is one of the themes of Fritz Ringer's *Education and Society in Modern Europe* (1979): that this period of development (the 'high industrial' phase in his terminology) saw a marked incongruence between the actual needs of industrial society and the aristocratic or pre-industrial values which schools and universities transmitted to the bourgeoisie through the classics and the ideal of liberal education; the gentlemanly ideal gave the professions or public service higher prestige than business, and diverted talent away from the latter.[4] This phenomenon is a well documented one in France, Germany and other countries. Comment on it in Britain also has a long history, going back at least to Matthew Arnold, and both the ancient universities and the boarding 'public schools' which fed into them (for in Britain more than most countries, higher and secondary education cannot be discussed apart) have been praised or blamed, according to taste, for their efficacy in absorbing the new middle classes and their wealth. Recently this argument has been given a new twist by the 'Wiener thesis': Martin Wiener argued in 1981 that the British élite had adopted a set of anti-industrial, anti-urban values which were responsible for the 'decline of the industrial spirit' and the failures of the British economy in the twentieth century. By 1900, wrote Wiener, the 'nation possessed a remarkably homogeneous and cohesive élite, sharing to a high degree a common education and a common outlook and set of values . . . [which] marked a crucial rebuff for the social revolution begun by industrialization'.[5] Many scholarly commentators have been sceptical of Wiener's theory, but it has enjoyed great vogue in political, business, and journalistic circles in Britain. So have the views of Correlli Barnett, who argued in *The Collapse of British Power* (1972) and *The Audit of War* (1986) that the pursuit of an ethos of public service by Britain's governing élite led it first to cultivate imperial illusions instead of accepting the realities of power, and after 1945 to devote Britain's limited resources to the welfare state instead of industrial reconstruction.[6] For both Wiener and Barnett, the public schools were the chief villains of the piece; but the businessmen and neo-liberal politicians who have repeated their indictment of liberal education have directed it almost exclusively against the universities.

The aim here is not to argue that these theories are wrong, but rather to test and refine them. This essay addresses three main points. First, it argues that the chronology of development needs some subdivision, and that significant movement towards wider access and equality of opportunity can be seen well before 1914. Second, it suggests that until a quite recent period the link between universities and élite formation was selective: the university-educated professions were not necessarily those which enjoyed the highest prestige, while for many of the most powerful élites university education remained marginal. The two parts of Perkin's revolution should therefore be separated: democratization of the universities (of a limited kind) can be observed before 1914, but was chiefly associated with the rise of low-status professions like schoolteaching; while university education has become near-mandatory for the general range of middle-class careers only since the Second World War, and the process is not yet complete.

Thirdly, we shall seek to look at British higher education from the periphery rather than the centre, and to stress the element of national and cultural identity in 'élite formation'. It is a weakness of the Jarausch book that its essays—including the useful statistical material compiled by Roy Lowe—only cover England. Thus in a discussion of the social origins of students the 'British' figures for

1870, 1890, and 1910 are in fact those for Oxford which, not surprisingly, show few students from the lower social strata.[7] This parochially English approach is a particular weakness in comparative work, where it can lead to serious distortion, but it is common enough among historians, as is over-concentration on Oxford and Cambridge and the public schools. Michael Sanderson has pointed out, for example, that Wiener's thesis only seems plausible because it ignores the civic universities, which were 'the largest part of the university sector' and 'a prime expression of the industrial spirit, closely linked with industry, drawing their life-blood finance from it, and pumping back research and students to it'—as indeed Sanderson showed in his pioneering book of 1972 on universities and industry.[8] Again, in a recent article on 'The modern university and national values, 1850–1930', Reba N. Soffer swiftly narrows the subject down to the formation of the national élite in Oxford and Cambridge, and specifically to the role of history teaching.[9] But there were 'national values' of other kinds within the British Isles.

The relation between universities and nationalism, their role in the formation of national élites and the promotion or maintenance of distinctive national cultures, is a familiar theme in many parts of Europe. This kind of perspective has rarely been applied to Britain. Yet modern Britain is a multi-national state. Education, at both school and university level, has been central to definitions of national identity, and has been an early subject of the administrative devolution which has been combined, in the complex British political system, with unitary parliamentary representation. Ireland, the greatest problem and the greatest failure of the multi-national state, provides the most obvious example.

Only the briefest summary can be given here of the complex Irish university question. Originally there was only one university in Ireland—Trinity College Dublin, which, though open to students of all denominations since 1793, remained strongly Anglican in spirit. In 1849 the state founded three strictly non-denominational Queen's Colleges, which were intended to provide a university education acceptable to Catholics, and so bind the Catholic élite closer to British rule. These colleges were condemned by the Vatican and the Irish hierarchy, and only the college in Protestant Belfast flourished. This condemnation was followed in 1854 by the creation of a non-governmental Catholic University, which became after varying fortunes University College Dublin. These developments had religious motives, but undoubtedly contributed to the rise of national feeling among the Catholic middle class, and to the creation of a professional and intellectual élite alienated from British values. By the end of the century one cultural aspect of this was Gaelic revivalism. After many controversies, in which the significance of the colleges for the sense of identity and the professional ambitions of the different Irish communities became very clear, the settlement of 1908 combined University College Dublin with the Queen's Colleges at Cork and Galway in the National University of Ireland, while Queen's College Belfast became an entirely separate university. The National University met the longstanding demand of Catholics for a university which reflected their interpretation of Ireland's cultural traditions, and a few years later it duly made a knowledge of the Irish language compulsory for matriculation. As T. H. Moody points out, although the 1908 Act was opposed at the time by Ulster Unionists, and although Queen's University Belfast was to remain faithful to a tolerant and non-sectarian tradition, 'the university settlement of 1908 ... was in a profoundly significant sense the prelude to the partition of Ireland in 1921'.[10]

After that date, universities in southern Ireland pass outside our scope. But it is anachronistic to treat nineteenth-century Ireland as if it were not part of the British state. The religious implications of the Irish university question made it a centre of controversy in Westminster politics, especially in the 1870s, and both the Queen's University of 1850 (a federal university granting degrees for the Queen's Colleges) and its successor the Royal University of Ireland of 1879 (a purely examining university like the University of London) were taken as models in British university debates. For neither Irish nor Scottish universities existed in isolation: the influence of Scotland on the foundation of University College London and the English provincial colleges is well known, the state subsidies given in Ireland and Scotland were often cited enviously by proponents of university development in England and Wales, and academic staff circulated freely between the four countries. Students, too, competed for the same national positions, especially through competitive examinations like those for the Indian and administrative civil services, which gave a powerful impetus to the standardization of curricula. In medicine, schoolteaching, the clergy, and many other occupations, the outlying parts of the British Isles produced a quantity of trained brain-power which could not be absorbed locally, and which was exported both to England and to the British Empire.

In Wales, the university question was closely connected with the national revival of the late nineteenth century, and the university movement rested on a powerful 'democratic' myth. The University of Wales of 1893, incorporating the colleges founded at Aberystwyth in 1872 and at Bangor and Cardiff in the 1880s, was claimed to express a national reverence for learning which could be traced back to the days of the Celtic church, and was identified with the Nonconformist, rural, Welsh-speaking, 'peasant' side of Welsh life; it was a university of the people, which turned out schoolteachers and educationists, pastors and poets, rather than lawyers, doctors or businessmen.[11] This was a somewhat misleading image, for much of industrial Wales was also Nonconformist and Welsh-speaking. When the appeal for a Welsh university was first launched in the 1860s, it was the 'elevation' of the middle class and the need to form a native technical élite which were stressed:

> The material wealth and commercial importance of the Principality are every day increasing. Our mines and manufactures, our railways and shipping interests, are rapidly expanding. The demand for educated talent, for scientific acquirements, for engineering skill—in a word, for all the results of a liberal training—is becoming more and more imperative . . . The direction of our large and lucrative undertakings, the chief posts in the country which require superior skill and attainments, are monopolized by strangers.

But with university training, 'the enterprising Welshman, now almost always thrown into the rear, would soon be found successfully competing with the Englishman and the Scotchman for posts of lucrative employment'.[12] In practice, no doubt, the colleges did help to create a functional élite of the type hoped for, as well as a national political and cultural leadership which was well in evidence by 1914. And although Welsh was valued as an academic subject, teaching and social life were conducted in English, for one aim was to prepare Welsh graduates for posts in the wider British sphere.

Scotland had its own 'democratic' myth, well established by the end of the eighteenth century, which stressed the 'popular' character of the universities and the way in which the national élite was drawn from all social classes and parts of the country. Scots prided themselves on the distinctiveness of their universities, which were seen as a point of superiority over England, but because they were already in existence, and no battles for new foundations had to be fought, there was no university question to become the focus of nationalism. Scottish universities were funded relatively generously by the state, and their teaching was effectively remodelled to allow Scots to seize the prizes in British life.[13] This was probably one reason why the Scottish middle classes remained profoundly unionist in modern times. If the Irish universities were one of the irritants which led to the failure of the union of 1801, the Scottish ones maintained a balance of independence and integration which contributed to the success of that of 1707.

The Scots, like the Welsh, were attached to their cultural identity without seeking political separation from the United Kingdom. But unlike the Welsh, they had no major grievances over religion (the Scottish religious situation, though internally divisive, being free from English intervention) or language (Gaelic being marginal geographically, and long seen as a hindrance to social progress rather than an inheritance to be cherished). It would be wrong, however, to suggest that there was no debate about national identity. Scotland's cultural distinctiveness from England had long rested on its religion, but as secularization weakened the force of this, some Scottish intellectuals sought substitutes, whether in philosophy, history or literature. This debate is the subject of G. E. Davie's influential but controversial books *The Democratic Intellect* (1961) and *The Crisis of the Democratic Intellect* (1986). Elite formation is one of Davie's specific themes, for he argues that the Scottish tradition of philosophical education once created, and could create again if it were revived, a national leadership of an organically democratic kind. However, these ideas have not prevailed in official university culture, where assimilation to 'British' norms has generally been preferred.

It would be interesting to explore questions of cultural identity within England itself. Has the role of religion as a divisive force been underestimated? Did the London colleges have an identifiable urban or metropolitan character?[14] Did the civic universities represent a distinctive 'bourgeois', provincial, or entrepreneurial culture, as asserted by many of their historians,[15] or were the new universities captured by the values of the old and assimilated to a national pattern?[16] Here, however, we shall confine discussion to some quantifiable criteria which illustrate the significance of differences within Britain.

The first of these is the rate of expansion. According to Lowe's figures, students in English universities and university colleges rose from 3,385 in 1861 to 26,414 in 1911, and then to 37,255 in 1931.[17] In the nineteenth century, there was a latent demand for university education which the new colleges, locally accessible and cheaper than Oxford and Cambridge, were able to tap. But in 1861, England still had fewer students than Scotland (3,399), with ten times the population. Scottish totals rose to 7,770 in 1911 and 11,072 in 1931.[18] However, these increases were accompanied by general demographic growth, and also covered the period when women were admitted; since women students were generally of the same social class as men, this did not involve any downward social penetration. If women students are left out of account, and university enrolments are related to total population, there was still a large 'real' increase in England. But in Scotland, as Table 1 shows, there seems to have been no fundamental change in the balance between the universities and society between 1800 and the Second World War. Here Jarausch's 'seismic shift' registered low on the Richter scale. Moreover, if the key to the 'modern' university is its relationship with the professions and its service of middle class needs, the Scottish

Table 1. Scotland: male university students per 1000 population

	Total	Ratio
1800	*c.* 2850	1.8
1825	*c.* 4250	1.8
1861	3399	1.1
1881	6604	1.6
1911	5924	1.2
1931	7674	1.6
1951	11149	2.2

Sources. For 1800: R. L. Emerson, 'Scottish Universities in the Eighteenth Century, 1690–1800', *Studies on Voltaire and the Eighteenth Century*, 167 (1977), 473. For 1825: R. D. Anderson, *Education and Opportunity in Victorian Scotland: Schools and Universities* (Oxford 1983), 346–7. For 1861–1951: R. D. Anderson, 'Education and Society in Modern Scotland: a Comparative Perspective', *History of Education Quarterly*, 25 (1985), 467.

universities became modern well before the 1860s. The combination of general education with vocational training for church, law and medicine was established in the late eighteenth century, and W. M. Mathew's work on Glasgow shows that students from the landed aristocracy declined from thirty-two per cent in the 1740s to seven per cent in the 1830s; by then half the students came from 'industry and commerce' (including many from the working as well as the middle class), and seventy per cent of them were absorbed by the three learned professions.[19]

The proportion of student places to population continued to vary nationally, as is shown in Table 2, which gives the situation in 1910–11. England lagged behind the less industrialized parts of Britain, and this tendency is confirmed by the ratio for 'Northern England', which compares student numbers at Liverpool, Manchester, Leeds and Sheffield with the population of Lancashire, Cheshire and Yorkshire. These counties had a population of 9.6 million, larger than many European countries, and together formed one of the greatest concentrations of wealth and industry in the world. In their four university colleges there were 3246 students, only about two-thirds of whom were taking a full course leading to graduation. Were these really the power-houses of an industrial society?

The figures in Table 2 correspond to age-cohort participation

Table 2. U.K.: full-time university students per 1000 population, 1910–11

	Total	Ratio
England	19617	0.58
Northern England	3246	0.34
Wales	1375	0.68
Scotland	6736	1.4
Ireland	*c.* 3000	0.69

Sources. For England, Wales, and Scotland: *University Grants Committee. Report for the Period 1929–30 to 1934–35* (London 1936), 52–3. For Ireland, estimate based on: *The National University Handbook, 1908–1932* (Dublin 1932), 69, 127; T. W. Moody and J. C. Beckett, *Queen's, Belfast 1845–1949: the History of a University* (2 vols London 1959), ii, 663; R. B. McDowell and D. A. Webb, *Trinity College Dublin, 1592–1952: an Academic History* (Cambridge 1982), 500; Annual Reports of Queen's Colleges, for 1908–9, in PP 1909, XX.

ratios of around one per cent, rising to perhaps two per cent in Scotland.[20] This was considerably less than the 'middle-class' share of the population, and in this sense universities were highly élitist. But this did not mean that their student body was drawn exclusively from the higher social strata. The social origins of Scottish students are well documented, and Table 3 gives data for Glasgow and Aberdeen in 1910. Here thirty to forty per cent of the students came from below the 'bourgeois' level, their parents being members of the 'intermediate' group, including shopkeepers and clerks, or engaged in manual labour. Comparison with data from other periods shows a significant democratization since the 1860s, but little further change in the 1920s and 1930s.[21] The composition of the manual-worker group also changed: in the nineteenth century, these parents were predominantly traditional artisans, but by 1910, especially at Glasgow, they included skilled factory and engineering workers. At no period did unskilled workers or labourers make much of a showing. But perhaps twenty per cent of Scottish university students could properly be described as 'working class'.

Table 4 shows that in Wales the proportions were even higher. Aberystwyth and Bangor were small towns, with an important slate-quarrying industry at Bangor, while Cardiff was the commercial centre of the South Wales coalfield, and over a third of the Welsh manual-worker fathers listed in this 1910 source were miners or

Table 3. Scotland: parental occupations of students, 1910 (%)

	Glasgow		*Aberdeen*	
	Male	Female	Male	Female
Professional	26	27	20	24
Businessmen	25	27	13	14
Farmers	3	7	13	20
Intermediate*	20	19	16	12
Manual workers	24	18	14	15
Not known	3	1	26	15
N=	229	88	152	93

*small business, shopkeepers, white collar

Source. Anderson, *Education and Opportunity*, 310–15.

Table 4. Wales: parental occupations of students, 1910 (%)

	Aberystwyth	Bangor	Cardiff
Professional	24	18	24
Businessmen	7	3	9
Farmers	14	18	6
Intermediate	31	17	30
Manual workers	24	44	32
N=	393	222	388

Source. PP 1913, XVIII, *Royal Commission on the Civil Service. Appendix to Third Report* [Cd. 6740], 309–10.

quarrymen. Much depends on definitions, but Jarausch's conclusion that down to 1930 it was only in post-revolutionary Russia that more than ten per cent of the students were 'recruited from the bottom half of the population' surely needs modification.[22]

The evidence suggests that the Welsh and Scottish 'democratic myths' had some substance, and that members of the British élite recruited there may have had broader social origins than their English colleagues. In practical terms, access to universities was regulated by four factors: the structure of the school system, and its ability to prepare students to university entrance standard; the cost of a university education; the financial aid available to individuals; and the occupational advantages which a university training brought—or, to put it another way, the degree to which entrance to an occupation was still possible at the age of twenty-one or twenty-two. The precocity of the Scottish universities was helped by favourable conditions in all these respects. They were accessible without formal entrance requirements, and fed by a network of rural parish schools, while in the towns the middle classes had access to cheap and efficient day schools; fees were kept low by state endowment; bursaries to support poorer students were quite widely available, and often awarded by open competition; and the careers for which university training was thought desirable included schoolteaching as well as the traditional professions. From about 1890, however, England began to move in the same direction.

Although the middle class had access to effective day schools which could compete with the public schools well before 1902, it was not until the Education Act of that year that public organization and subsidy of secondary schools began, followed in 1907, as part of a conscious policy of educational opportunity, by the provision of free places for scholars from elementary schools. Outside England, however, systematic state aid began earlier. In Ireland, an Act of 1878 distributed subsidies on the basis of examination results, allowing secondary schools of all denominations a share. In Wales, the 'intermediate' schools created in 1889 were notable for putting an academic education within easy reach of students in small country towns, and remarkably high levels of access to secondary schooling underlay the success of the Welsh university colleges.[23] In Scotland, state grants to secondary schools began in 1892, and meant that there was no loss of democratic access when a university entrance examination was introduced, the age of entry rose, and university preparation was abandoned by the smaller schools. All these developments in secondary education, incidentally, greatly increased the demand for graduate teachers.

The state subsidy which universities had always received in Scotland, and which supported the Queen's Colleges in Ireland, allowed fees to be kept low. In Scotland a university education cost as little as £10–12 in arts and science (fees for medicine were always higher everywhere), and after 1901 fees ceased to be a real barrier, as the Carnegie endowment paid them for all Scottish-born students who applied. In Wales, fees were kept near the Scottish level, and state subsidy began in 1882. Annual state grants for English university colleges began in 1889, and by 1910 less than a third of university income in England and Wales was derived from fees.[24] They were thus well below the market rate, and the cost of an arts degree in English provincial universities was usually about £15–20 a year, though University and King's Colleges in London were considerably more expensive. Moderate fees put university education within reach of the reasonably prosperous middle class. Lodgings, or a place in one of the still uncommon student residences, were likely to cost £40–50 per annum. But the total cost was still well below the £200 or so needed to cover fees, college residence and the necessary lifestyle at Oxford or Cambridge, or indeed the £80–100 and upwards charged by public schools.

Even so, university education would normally be beyond the reach of the lower middle or working classes. Few of the new colleges were well enough endowed to offer scholarships. It was local authorities (county and borough councils) which came to fill this gap in England and Wales. Under Acts of 1889 and 1890, they were able to aid 'technical' education, a term which was interpreted broadly. Large industrial towns saw the development of higher technical schools, which usually had some work of degree standard and developed links with the local university, sometimes being formally affiliated or incorporated with it. Many councils also gave significant amounts for the general support of their local universities. For individuals, there were university scholarships in technical or scientific subjects, and after 1902, when the English local authorities took over schools of all levels from the former school boards, they were able to develop integrated scholarship systems leading from the elementary school via the council grammar school to the university. In 1910, the royal commission on the civil service, which carried out a systematic inquiry into educational opportunities, found that 366 boys and 143 girls left state secondary schools in England and Wales with university scholarships, 134 and twenty-seven respectively going to Oxford or Cambridge; 253 of the boys and seventy of the girls had started their careers in elementary schools. In England, local authorities maintained 1327 university scholarships, equivalent to about seven per cent of the total number of students.[25] This might not seem a high proportion, and of course these students were a tiny handful compared with the mass of working-class children in elementary schools. Yet several of the witnesses to this commission, including those from Scotland and Wales, claimed that the ladder of educational opportunity was already almost complete; their conception was the limited one of the time, under which only the exceptionally 'bright' children of the working class were expected to progress beyond elementary schooling.

The final significant development was the establishment from 1890 of 'day training colleges' for elementary teachers within the universities. The demand for elementary teachers with basic qualifications had previously been met by non-university colleges, recruited from elementary schools via the 'pupil-teacher' system. This had itself provided a significant channel of social mobility, especially for women, and in Scotland male students at the colleges were allowed to attend university classes as early as 1873. Now the state was prepared to subsidize this training within universities, and although at first the day training students might not stay long enough to graduate, a new range of experiences and potential opportunities was opened to them. New social strata were being tapped, and fears were expressed that the presence of the day training students would frighten away those from more affluent families.[26]

Generalization about the social role of the English provincial universities is hampered by the absence of systematic information about their students' backgrounds. The sources usually describe them as essentially middle-class, but this does not take us far. It is also clear that, though most students were drawn from the immediate locality, the development of specialities not offered elsewhere could make a wider appeal to students of high social status. This was especially true of the applied sciences: when Ludwig Wittgenstein wished to continue his studies in engineering, it was to Manchester that he came from Berlin in 1908.[27] It was said that the public-school men at the provincial universities were especially likely to study vocational subjects like engineering, medicine or architecture—and in the 1890s twenty-six per cent of the students at the Victoria University (Manchester, Liverpool and Leeds) came from public schools.[28] Arts and pure science were left to the less privileged students and the prospective teachers; in several civic universities, the day training students formed a third or a half of the arts and science faculties. This was indeed a swing away from technology or applied science, but one which could hardly have less to do with the adoption of 'aristocratic' or gentlemanly values.

Some fragmentary data for the years after 1890 are in Table 5. The figures for Birmingham come from Sanderson, and show limited working-class participation: many of the 'intermediate' group here were small businessmen. For Nottingham, however, the figures are interesting because they distinguish the day training students from the rest, and clearly show their modest origins—the miner's son D. H. Lawrence was among these students in the 1900s. This source also reveals that while nearly a third of the general students had fathers earning over £300 a year (a comfortable middle-class income), this was the case for only one of the day training students. Nottingham was exceptional because the city council was the direct sponsor of the college, and was able to make it

> the coping stone of an educational edifice based on the broadest and most democratic principles. Nine-tenths of the regular students of the College, we were informed, commence their education in the public elementary schools;

Table 5. English provinces: parental occupations of students (%)

Mason College, Birmingham, 1893	
Professional	37
Businessmen	17
Intermediate	34
Manual workers	13
N=	270

University College, Nottingham, 1911	*General*	*Day TC*
Professional	29	5
Businessmen	27	6
Farmers	4	5
Intermediate	19	41
Manual workers	5	32
Not known	16	11
N=	75	63

Sources. For Birmingham: M. Sanderson, *The Universities and British Industry, 1850–1970* (London, 1972), 98–9. For Nottingham: PP 1913, XL, *Royal Commission on University Education in London. Appendix to Final Report* [Cd. 6718], 173.

from these they pass to the large and well-organised municipal or high schools, and thence with the aid of scholarships to the College.

So reported the Treasury inspectors in 1907. Their predecessors in 1902 had found that 'the majority of the students belong to the artisan and lower middle classes, and many of them are very poor', and that 'though the students are drawn from all classes, the opportunities specially afforded to young working men of ability and promise are thus very considerable, and from this point of view we think that the College exhibits the nearest approach, of all the Colleges which we visited, to a People's University.' It was true that 'there are many grades between the extreme types of a People's University ... and the ideal towards which the largest and best endowed of the Colleges are striving, of carrying Oxford and Cambridge into populous centres'.[29] But there were other universities like Liverpool, Sheffield or Leeds where the local authorities took a similar benevolent interest, and Leeds told the civil service commission that 'there is in Yorkshire a complete system of scholarships by which the children of poor parents are assisted to pass from the elementary schools to the Universities and to secure in after life positions suitable to their capacities'. It was 'well known' at Leeds that many 'of its most distinguished alumni have been the sons and daughters of working men, assisted by scholarships from the elementary stage upwards'.[30]

It is unnecessary to discuss Oxford and Cambridge at length. Stone on Oxford, and Jenkins and Jones on Cambridge, have established their social exclusiveness and their close links with the public schools.[31] The establishment of day training colleges, the attempt to reduce living expenses by founding cheaper colleges and introducing 'non-collegiate' students, and the ability of state secondary schools to compete for college scholarships must have had some democratizing effects before 1914. But these universities retained a special 'national' role in several ways: their recruitment, like that of the public schools, was not localized; they were the universities normally chosen by the landed aristocracy and the wealthiest of the middle class; they had a connection with the highest reaches of national power in law and politics; and academically or socially ambitious students came to them from the Scottish or provincial universities.

Studies of the educational background of specific élite groups usually show the predominance of Oxford and Cambridge over other universities. One such study, of over 3000 élite members between 1880 and 1970, lies behind Perkin's recent work. Whereas in *The Transformation of Higher Learning* Perkin placed the 'revolution' in higher education before 1930, elsewhere he has acknowledged that the tight connexion between universities and professionalization is more recent, and that many powerful élites previously did without higher education. Nevertheless, Perkin provides convincing evidence that the nineteenth-century emphasis on educational qualifications did shift influence from the traditional élite to the middle classes.[32] W. D. Rubinstein, using the same data as Perkin, has pushed this argument further, arguing that attendance at a public school or an ancient university should not be seen as evidence of privileged status, and that British élites were recruited from comparatively wide social backgrounds. It is certainly true that the public schools and universities helped the sons of clergymen, army officers, colonial civil servants and other relatively modest members of the middle class to improve their social status through education. But one may question Rubinstein's description of these families as the 'lower middle classes', and although he uses the term 'meritocracy', it was only middle-class merit which could benefit, for public schools (and the preparatory schools which became an essential preliminary) remained expensive.[33]

If Oxford and Cambridge did draw on a wider middle class, graduation often led to positions of useful obscurity rather than power. In Compton Mackenzie's novel *Sinister Street* (1913), the hero Michael Fane spends four years at Oxford, with no particular occupation in mind, for he has a private fortune in prospect. He meets an old school-fellow:

> 'I'm just down from Oxford,' Michael informed him.
> 'Pretty good spree up there, eh?'
> 'Oh, yes, rather,' said Michael.
> 'Well, I had the chance to go,' said Drake. 'But it wasn't good enough. It's against you in the City, you know. Waste of time really, except of course for a parson or a schoolmaster.'[34]

Oxford and Cambridge had a glamorous role as finishing schools for a life of leisure, and gave a serious intellectual preparation to those whose wealth and family background were likely in any case to secure them an influential position in business or a profession. But their strictly meritocratic function was more humdrum, and training parsons and schoolmasters was not so different from what less famous universities were doing. This is illustrated by Table 6, which shows the career destinations of students from Aberdeen and Bangor. Aberdeen had an important medical school, but otherwise it is the predominance of teaching as a university outlet, especially for women, which is most striking. The detailed data also show that teaching and the church were classic 'transitional' professions: the ones most likely to be chosen by students with modest social backgrounds, with low continuity from one generation to the next.[35]

Few students from Aberdeen or Bangor went into business. The background of business élites has attracted a good deal of recent historical work, which has generally shown both that businessmen had less higher education than other élite figures, and that British businessmen had less than their continental or American counterparts.[36] In a preliminary analysis of business leaders between 1860 and 1980 included in the *Dictionary of Business Biography*, David Jeremy found that twenty-nine per cent went to a university, though the proportion rose in the twentieth century.[37] A similar analysis of the *Dictionary of Scottish Business Biography, 1860-1960* shows that

Table 6. Occupations of former students, Aberdeen and Bangor (%)
Occupations of graduates of Aberdeen, 1901–25, and of students at Bangor *c.* 1884–1904

	Aberdeen *Men*	Aberdeen *Women*	Bangor
Education	27	68	59
Church	9	0	16
Medicine	42	11	3
Civil service	5	1	0
Law	3	0	1
Business	4	2	1
Engineering			3
Science	3	1	1
Agriculture	3	0	14
Miscellaneous	3	2	2
None, married, died	2	16	
N=	2912	1627	1303

Sources. For Aberdeen: T. Watt, *Roll of the Graduates of the University of Aberdeen, 1901–1925* (Aberdeen 1935), 943. For Bangor: J. G. Williams, *The University College of North Wales: Foundations, 1884–1927* (Cardiff 1985), 214.

eighty-three (twenty-two per cent) of the 381 men included attended a university or higher technical school. None went to Oxford, only ten to Cambridge. The commonest pattern was study at a Scottish university, sometimes in science or engineering, more often in the general arts course, though many stayed for only a year or two and did not graduate. Higher technical training was most likely to be found among men in mining, steel or shipbuilding, and was acquired at the Royal School of Mines in London, at English provincial universities chosen for their specialization in applied science, or at the college which is today Strathclyde University. On the whole, the choice of higher education was a pragmatic one, and revealed little movement away from business values.

The same was true of secondary education, where Scottish habits differed from English. The founders of businesses often had a rudimentary education, but later generations were sent to the best local day schools, including some which had a technical bias like Allan

Glen's in Glasgow. Only twenty-three (six per cent) went to English public schools. If they were not destined for higher education, the sons of business families usually left school at fifteen or sixteen to enter the family business or to take up an apprenticeship. This habit of early school leaving persisted even after several generations of wealth.[38] Thus if Scottish industry failed to adapt to the challenges of the twentieth century—and some of the men in this dictionary presided over spectacular entrepreneurial disasters—it would seem to be due less to the absorption of anti-industrial values through education, than to rejection of theoretical training, and outdated adherence to the mystique of learning on the job. G. W. Roderick, in a study of Welsh industrialists, comes to rather similar conclusions.[39]

It is also striking that all the Scottish business leaders who went to a university, with one exception, were of the second or later generations, and owed their positions to inheritance, not to managerial careers based on trained expertise. The exception, Donald Matheson, general manager of the Caledonian Railway between 1910 and 1922, was trained as an engineer at Watt College, Edinburgh and Owens College, Manchester.[40] As a gardener's son, he was also the only one of these 381 men whose career resembled that of the classic 'lad of parts' rising through education: the men of humble origin among the business élite usually left school at the earliest opportunity and reached the top through qualities of character and practical experience. This probably changed later with the decline of family control—the *Dictionary* is confined to those whose business careers were completed by 1960—but Paul Robertson has concluded from his study of Scottish universities and industry that 'on balance, except for Glasgow and Edinburgh engineering graduates, businessmen appear to have had almost no interest in the products of Scottish university education before 1914.'[41] There were few salaried posts in industry, and in commerce, which absorbed the bulk of the boys who left secondary schools, educationists were still trying to persuade employers to accept entrants at seventeen rather than the traditional fourteen or fifteen. For these very important careers, which certainly led to positions of wealth and power, universities were decidedly marginal institutions.

This leads to our first conclusion: that the categories of 'graduates' and 'élites' overlapped, but did not coincide. On the one hand, university graduates ranged from cabinet ministers to village schoolteachers; on the other, it was quite normal—not only for businessmen—to reach élite positions without attending a university. Universities were important for the endorsement of élite status based on birth or wealth, but their role in élite *formation* was limited. Medicine was virtually the only profession which concentrated its training in degree-granting institutions. Other 'graduate' professions (sometimes with professional training elsewhere) included the higher civil service, the Scottish clergy, the Anglican clergy in England and Ireland, barristers in England and Ireland and advocates in Scotland, university and secondary teachers, and professional scientists. The main new professions to develop university training before 1914 were engineering and architecture, but still only in conjunction with the traditional apprenticeship system. Other professions or semi-professionalized occupations used either apprenticeship, or specialized colleges which might or might not have university affiliations. Trainee solicitors, bankers or accountants might attend university lectures without graduating; but for commerce and most family-run enterprises university education was the exception. For the army and navy—professions of high prestige which attracted the aristocracy—it was both unnecessary, and difficult to combine with the usual modes of entry.

What mattered more was schooling. The choice of secondary school accurately reflected social status, and above a certain level to send sons to a public school (or a day school of equivalent status in Scotland) was *de rigueur*. After that, whether a son was sent to a university would depend on the planned career. If business was aimed at, he would normally not be. This tends to invalidate the argument that universities diverted talent away from entrepreneurial careers: for every businessman's son who went to Oxford and became a civil servant, there may well have been a civil servant's son who did not go to Oxford and became a businessman. A Scottish aristocratic example to illustrate this is that of the second and third marquesses of Aberdeen, brothers born in 1879 and 1883. Both went to Harrow, but while the eldest son was then sent to St Andrews and Oxford, and duly inherited the title, his brother was apprenticed to an Aberdeen shipyard, and went on to an English industrial career, ending as chairman of a Sheffield steel firm, and serving as president of the Federation of British Industries. He inherited the marquessate at the age of 81; his own son was at Harrow and Oxford, then apprenticed as a land agent in preparation for managing the family estate. It was Harrow School which was the common educational element for this family.[42]

The same perspective may be applied to the education of women. The admission of women is surely the most significant single development in European universities before 1914, yet the élites/professionalization approach has little to say about it; the question is almost ignored in the Jarausch book. The prominence of women from the leisured upper middle classes in the early years of the women's education movement makes it difficult to explain in terms of career demands, and the main occupation for which universities did prepare women, teaching, was neither fully professionalized nor of high status. Apart from medicine, the main professions were closed to women until after the First World War, and this put a limit on the expansion of student numbers.[43]

It perhaps makes sense to think of a 'middle-class leaving age' for full-time education. In the mid-nineteenth century (when working-class children left school at ten or eleven) this was commonly fifteen or earlier, and only the small élite who used the old public schools stayed till eighteen. By 1914, it was the accepted pattern that middle-class children of both sexes were kept at school until between sixteen and eighteen. But after that, university education was an option, in which three broad patterns may be discerned. First, there were the leisured or wealthy classes, who were likely to choose Oxford or Cambridge for social reasons, with a career decision postponed until later. Second, there was the broad mass of the professional and business middle class, especially in the provinces. Only a minority of their sons was likely to be sent to a university, and the expense had to be justified by a clear intention to enter a profession, or to acquire specialized scientific or engineering skills. This class was more likely to give its daughters a higher education than the wealthy upper class, and cases can certainly be found where a daughter went to university, to become a teacher, while her brothers went straight into business. Thirdly, there were the lower middle and working classes, small numbers of whose children reached a university through luck or talent, and whose choice of occupation thereafter was limited by lack of resources or family influence.

Although most of the evidence in this paper comes from before 1914, there was no fundamental change after the First World War. The extension of secondary education continued to work itself out, more scholarships were available from local authorities and after 1920 also from the state, and the value of a university education was more widely appreciated. Enrolments rose after 1918, and remained on a new plateau. Access ratios increased—though only to 1.7 per cent of the age-group in 1938.[44] By the 1930s numbers were stagnant, and there were few symptoms of an imminent breakthrough to a new era. That only came after the Second World War, due partly to spontaneous and unanticipated demand, and partly to the series of educational reforms which ran from the Education Act of 1944 via the Robbins report of 1963 to the introduction of comprehensive secondary education.

It is as part of this process, and only since the 1950s, that the 'middle-class leaving age' has been raised to twenty-one or twenty-two. As university training has become necessary for a much wider range of careers, including those in business, competition for posts has forced the middle classes to use the universities far more than before; one outcome is that a large expansion of enrolments has taken place without a fundamental shift in the social composition of the student body. Motivation towards university attendance continues to vary by class, and to some extent by gender, and Britain remains a country where higher education is thought of as something for the privileged or the especially able rather than as a standard aspiration. It is also a country where, according to recent surveys, only a minority of business managers have any sort of higher education, a situation illustrated in David Lodge's latest academic novel *Nice Work* (1988), and relevant too to Perkin's interpretation of recent British politics as a conflict between the public-service professionals with university training and the corporate professionals committed to entrepreneurial values.[45]

A further post-1945 development was the system of mandatory state grants, which made it no more expensive to attend a distant university than a local one. Combined with the centralized system of selection required by the new competition for places, this produced for the first time something like a homogeneous university system recruited on a national basis. The distinctiveness of Scottish, Welsh and civic universities, subject to powerful assimilative influences ever since the late nineteenth century, and undermined by a more general decline of regional cultures and societies in the face of broad economic forces, seemed destined to wane into insignificance. In the 1950s and 1960s, when new universities were being founded, the

Oxford and Cambridge-derived model of the residential, character-forming university, once vigorously challenged by rival ideals, had acquired an extraordinary ascendancy. Whether this model inhibited a genuine transition from élite to mass higher education in Britain, and whether the ideal of liberal education associated with it led to a new incongruence between the curriculum and the wide range of occupations for which universities now prepared, are among the many questions which there is no space to pursue here.

Department of History
University of Edinburgh
William Robertson Building
George Square
Edinburgh EH8 9JY
United Kingdom

REFERENCES

1. K. H. Jarausch, 'Higher Education and Social Change: some Comparative Perspectives', in *The Transformation of Higher Learning, 1860–1930: Expansion, Diversification, Social Opening, and Professionalization in England, Germany, Russia, and the United States* (Chicago 1983), 10, 36.
2. H. Kaelble, 'Educational Opportunities and Government Policies in Europe in the Period of Industrialization', in P. Flora and A. J. Heidenheimer (eds), *The Development of Welfare States in Europe and America* (New Brunswick 1981), 239–68; Jarausch in *Transformation*, 17; H. Perkin, 'The Pattern of Social Transformation in England', ibid., 218.
3. H. Perkin, *The Rise of Professional Society: England since 1880* (London 1989), xiii; Perkin in Jarausch, *Transformation*, 218.
4. F. Ringer, *Education and Society in Modern Europe* (Bloomington 1979), 6–12.
5. M. Wiener, *English Culture and the Decline of the Industrial Spirit, 1850–1980* (Cambridge 1981), 11–12. Cf. J. Raven, 'British History and the Enterprise Culture', *Past and Present*, 123 (1989), 178–204.
6. C. Barnett, *The Collapse of British Power* (London 1972), 19–43; C. Barnett, *The Audit of War: the Illusion and Reality of Britain as a Great Nation* (London 1986), 201–33.
7. Jarausch, *Transformation*, 24.
8. M. Sanderson, 'The English Civic Universities and the "Industrial

Spirit", 1870–1914', *Historical Research*, 61 (1988), 103; M. Sanderson, *The Universities and British Industry, 1850–1970* (London 1972).

9. R. N. Soffer, 'The Modern University and National Values, 1850–1930', *Historical Research*, 60 (1987), 166–87.
10. T. W. Moody, 'The Irish University Question of the Nineteenth Century', *History*, 43 (1958), 109. For a fuller account, see T. W. Moody and J. C. Beckett, *Queen's, Belfast 1845–1949: the History of a University* (2 vols London 1959).
11. W. C. Davies and W. L. Jones, *The University of Wales and its Constituent Colleges* (London 1905), xi–xiii, 160, 197–8.
12. Ibid., 74, 82. For the Welsh university question generally, see K. O. Morgan, *Rebirth of a Nation: Wales 1880–1980* (Oxford 1981), 106–11.
13. R. D. Anderson, *Education and Opportunity in Victorian Scotland: Schools and Universities* (Oxford 1983).
14. S. Rothblatt, 'London: a Metropolitan University?', in T. Bender (ed.), *The University and the City, from Medieval Origins to the Present* (New York 1988), 119–49.
15. E.g. Sanderson, cited above, and D. R. Jones, *The Origins of Civic Universities: Manchester, Leeds & Liverpool* (London 1988).
16. E.g. Barnett, *Audit of War*, 222–3. A more nuanced view is that of R. Lowe, 'The Expansion of Higher Education in England', in Jarausch, *Transformation*, 53–4, and 'Structural Change in English Higher Education, 1870–1920', in D. K. Müller and others (eds), *The Rise of the Modern Educational System: Structural Change and Social Reproduction, 1870–1920* (Cambridge 1987), 163–78.
17. Jarausch, *Transformation*, 13. Most new foundations in Britain started as 'university colleges', unable to award their own degrees; but for convenience the generic term 'universities' has been used in this article.
18. R. D. Anderson, 'Education and Society in Modern Scotland: a Comparative Perspective', *History of Education Quarterly*, 25 (1985), 467.
19. W. M. Mathew, 'The Origins and Occupations of Glasgow Students, 1740–1839', *Past and Present*, 33 (1966), 78, 85.
20. Ringer, *Education and Society*, 229; Jarausch, *Transformation*, 16, 52.
21. Anderson, *Education and Opportunity*, 148–53; R. D. Anderson, *The Student Community at Aberdeen, 1860–1939* (Aberdeen 1988), 138–41; I. J. McDonald, 'Untapped Reservoirs of Talent? Social Class and Opportunities in Scottish Higher Education, 1910–1960', *Scottish Educational Studies*, 1 (1967), 52–8; A. Collier, 'Social Origins of a Sample of Entrants to Glasgow University', *Sociological Review*, 30 (1938), 161–85, 262–77.
22. Jarausch, *Transformation*, 36.
23. G. E. Jones, *Controls and Conflicts in Welsh Secondary Education, 1889–1944* (Cardiff 1982), 45, 80, 82–3.
24. In 1912–13, fees were 28% of income in institutions receiving Treasury grants: *Board of Education. Reports for the Year 1912–13 from those*

Universities and University Colleges in Great Britain which are in Receipt of Grant from the Board of Education (2 vols London 1914), i, pp. xiv–xv.

25. Parliamentary Papers (hereafter PP) 1914, XVI, *Royal Commission on the Civil Service. First Appendix to Fourth Report* [Cd. 7339], 47, 55, 86.
26. PP 1902, LXXX, Parliamentary Return of 2 July 1902 incorporating inspectors' reports, 15.
27. B. McGuinness, *Wittgenstein, a Life: Young Ludwig, 1889–1921* (paperback ed. London 1990), 61.
28. PP 1897, LXX, Parliamentary Return of 17 June 1897 incorporating inspectors' reports, 7, 31; PP 1902, LXXX, Parliamentary Return of 2 July 1902, 31, 64, 74; T. Kelly, *For Advancement of Learning: the University of Liverpool, 1881–1981* (Liverpool 1981), 92, 136. For the percentage of public-school students, see PP 1895, XLIX, *Royal Commission on Secondary Education. Vol. IX. Appendix. Statistical Tables* [C. 7862–VIII], 426–7.
29. PP 1907, LXIV, Parliamentary Return of 23 July 1907 incorporating inspectors' reports, 93; PP 1902, LXXX, Parliamentary Return of 2 July 1902, 16, 94, 96.
30. PP 1913, XVIII, *Royal Commission on the Civil Service. Appendix to Third Report* [Cd. 6740], 315–16.
31. L. Stone, 'The Size and Composition of the Oxford Student Body, 1580–1910', in L. Stone (ed.), *The University in Society. Volume I. Oxford and Cambridge from the 14th to the Early 19th Century* (Princeton, 1975), 66–7, 93, 103; H. Jenkins and D. C. Jones, 'Social Class of Cambridge University Alumni of the 18th and 19th Centuries', *British Journal of Sociology*, 1 (1950), 93–116. For Cambridge, see also S. Rothblatt, *The Revolution of the Dons: Cambridge and Society in Victorian England* (London 1968), 280–1.
32. H. Perkin, 'The Recruitment of Elites in British Society since 1800', *Journal of Social History*, 12 (1978–9), 222–34, and *The Structured Crowd: Essays in English Social History* (Brighton 1981), 151–67. Cf. *Rise of Professional Society*, 87–91.
33. W. D. Rubinstein, 'Education and the Social Origins of British Elites, 1880–1970', *Past and Present*, 112 (1986), 163–207.
34. C. Mackenzie, *Sinister Street* (new ed., London 1949), 652.
35. R. K. Kelsall, 'Self-Recruitment in Four Professions', in D. V. Glass (ed.), *Social mobility in Britain* (London 1954), 308–20; for the Aberdeen case, see also Anderson, *Student Community*, 11, 139–40.
36. H. Kaelble, 'Long-Term Changes in the Recruitment of the Business Elite: Germany compared to the U.S., Great Britain, and France since the Industrial Revolution', *Journal of Social History*, 13 (1979–80), 404–23; F. K. Ringer, 'The Education of Elites in Modern Europe', *History of Education Quarterly*, 18 (1978), 159–72.
37. D. J. Jeremy, 'Anatomy of the British Business Elite, 1860–1980', *Business History*, 26 (1984), 12.

38. A. Slaven and S. Checkland (eds), *Dictionary of Scottish Business Biography, 1860–1960* (2 vols Aberdeen 1986–90). Cf. editors' conclusion, ii, 430.
39. G. W. Roderick, 'South Wales Industrialists and the Theory of Gentrification, 1770–1914', *Transactions of the Honourable Society of Cymmrodorion*, 1987, 65–83.
40. Slaven and Checkland, *Dictionary*, ii, 302–4.
41. P. Robertson, 'Scottish Universities and Scottish Industry, 1860–1914', *Scottish Economic and Social History*, 4 (1984), 49.
42. A. Gordon, *A Guide to Haddo House* (Edinburgh 1981), 18–19.
43. Cf. J. Howarth and M. Curthoys, 'The political economy of women's higher education in late 19th and early 20th-century Britain', *Historical Research*, 60 (1987), 208–31.
44. Ringer, *Education and Society*, 229.
45. Perkin, *Rise of Professional Society*, 505, 517–19.

Conference Reports

Seventh Centenary of the University of Coimbra: Coimbra 5–9 March 1990.

In 1990, the University of Coimbra, for many centuries the only one existing in Portugal, faced an important turning point: for the first time in its history, an assembly formed by representatives of all bodies of the university drew up new statutes, thus giving birth to an era of autonomy, hopefully real and creative. This major event was almost simultaneous with the celebration of the seventh centenary of the foundation of the university. The planning of the university's future demanded a look backwards, in order to better define the identity of the institution: this realization led to the organization of a conference on Coimbra's history.

The intention of the organizers (the *Instituto de História e Teoria das Ideias* and the *Instituto de História Económica e Social* of the Faculty of Arts, and the department of History of Education of the Faculty of Psychology) was to achieve a large and multidisciplinary participation. Thus, some 130 communications, besides the initial and final lectures, were presented, mainly devoted to the history of the university but also focusing on present problems and perspectives. The large group of contributors included university historians, some of them coming from other Portuguese universities or from abroad (Brazil, Spain, France, Italy, and Germany), specialists in other fields, teachers, librarians, and students. The publication of all these contributions is already under way.

As the University of Coimbra has been primarily a teaching institution it is no wonder that this aspect of its history was paid special attention. Of the three moments traditionally considered as the most significant in the university's life (1537, when the university was finally settled in Coimbra, and the following years, in which the Arts College became a renowned centre of humanist studies; the reformation imposed by the government, through the Marquis de Pombal in 1772; the changes caused by the coming of the republican regime in 1910), the second was the one which inspired the most interest. Several papers stressed the importance of the new faculties (Natural Philosophy and Mathematics) created by the 1772 reform, the consequent and overall redefinition of the plan of studies which imposed attendance in those faculties before entering the higher faculties, and the foundation of supporting institutions such as the Museum of Natural History, the Botanical Garden, the Physics and Chemistry Laboratories, the

Pharmaceutical Dispensary, and the Astronomical Observatory. Thereby was planted the roots of the modern Faculty of Sciences and Technology. Since 1772 a 'scientific mentality' has dominated the activities of many of the university's researchers and some of them were remembered for their important role in the development of their branches of knowledge. It was also this reformed university that trained the pre-liberal élite both in Portugal and Brazil and thus had a strong influence on the political upheavals of the 1820s. Brazilian historians were well aware of this fact while the Spanish concentrated on comparing the events of 1772 with similar enlightened reforms in several universities of their own country. The specialist tools of intellectual labour—archives and libraries—including those belonging to the university colleges and those created after the 1772 reforms (such as the libraries of the faculties of Philosophy and Medicine) received particular attention.

As crucial a milestone as this reformation might have been, it did not monopolize the attentions of the participants and other subjects were dealt with. They fall into two main categories: the university within its walls and, in contrast, its relationship with the surrounding society. Papers given on the economic life of the university and the problems faced in this particular field by the university administration, the role of the rectors and professors, and the architectural and artistic importance of the university's buildings fall under the first head. Papers falling into both categories were those which considered the geographical and social origins of the students, their way of living and dressing, their societies, and their participation in popular festivities. The dialogue between the university and society was examined in its cultural aspect (and here the University's humanist era received particular attention) but more intensely in its political and religious facets. The peculiarity of Portuguese society, where the Inquisition exercised an important hold, was reflected in the university's life. On the other hand, the institution was frequently involved in political changes and volte-faces (from the seventeenth-century restoration of national independence to the twentieth century 'Estado Novo') and this was one of the aspects which received the attention of several researchers.

As a result of the conference decisive steps have been made towards the solution of some classical problems (the precise date of the foundation of the university in Lisbon, for example). Others have been enriched by a novel theoretical approach, such as the relationship between universities and political power and the philosophical basis of the nature and autonomy of the university.

No restrictions—chronological or thematic within the general subject—were placed on the contributors. The result was a wide variety of papers making a synthesis a difficult task and naturally creating a certain imbalance between periods and themes. But it can be said that the main intention of feeling the pulse of contemporary research on the University of Coimbra was successfully fulfilled. The conference was at the same time a point of departure for the idea germinated of producing a new history of the university of Coimbra, a history based on the convergence of different branches of research. The possibility of successfully accomplishing this desideratum was demonstrated by the conference.

Fernando Javiera da Fonseca
Faculdade de Letras
3049 Coimbra
Portugal

Researchers and Practitioners: Aspects of French Medical Culture in the Eighteenth and Nineteenth Centuries: Virginia Polytechnic and State University, Blacksburg, VA, 19–22 April 1990.

This conference was primarily devoted to the study of medical research and medical practice in eighteenth- and nineteenth-century France. To the extent, however, that medical practitioners were trained in medical faculties and medical research was increasingly organized in university-affiliated institutes and hospitals, many of the papers inevitably touched directly or indirectly on problems of interest to historians of higher education.

Several papers were informative about the early history of the Paris medical school. Founded by the revolutionaries in 1795 (the old faculty was closed in 1793) the Paris school quickly became renowned throughout the world as a centre of teaching thanks to its pioneering emphasis on clinical and anatomical instruction. The broad history of the school in the early nineteenth century is now well known through the work of Ackerknecht (1967), but its genesis and subsequent development as an educational archetype in Europe and the United States remain largely unexplored. Caroline Hannaway addressed the first question in a paper devoted to the state of anatomy teaching in pre-Revolutionary Paris. The position, she revealed, was far healthier than has usually been thought thanks to the plethora of private courses existing outside the Faculty. Comparative anatomy was particularly promoted and in the hands of Vicq d'Azyr moved from an interest in form to an interest in structure. The second question was addressed by John Warner who examined the reactions of English and American visitors to the Paris school in the early-nineteenth century. Anglo-Saxon visitors, it seems, were highly impressed by the clinical bias of the course, but they were disturbed by the impersonal and callous nature of patient/professor relations. Now that a greater emphasis was placed on the observation of the patient than on the patient's own account of his malady, the sick were on the way to becoming statistics. It is possible, however, that the Anglo-American observers were misreading the situation. Clinical patients were always the poor. Another paper given by Jackie Duffin on the medical practice of the great Laennec revealed that private, 'quality' patients continued to be treated deferentially. Indeed, Laennec even treated his hospital patients sensitively, having bedside discussions conducted in Latin to avoid undue stress and ensuring that Bretons were addressed in their own tongue.

A second set of papers threw fresh light on the eventual 'decline' of the Paris school. In the early decades of the century the school was famed as a centre of research not just of teaching, but its reputation supposedly fell in the mid-nineteenth century when its neophytes spurned the aid of microscopy and chemical analysis and continued to emphasize the primacy of clinical observations. Ann La Berge's paper on the Paris microscopy community of the late 1830s and 1840s showed that the traditional picture in the first instance needs revising. A microscopy thesis was sustained by Donné as early as 1831 and the faculty quickly permitted private courses to be given under its auspices where the medical possibilities of the instrument were displayed. It remains true, on the other hand, that the Paris school contributed relatively little to the development of the anti-humoral medicine of the late nineteenth century which the new technology and chemical analysis helped to develop. Bacteriology was the creation of the Pasteur circle at the Ecole normale, the brainchild of scientists not physicians. Moreover, as Ann-Marie Moulin convincingly demonstrated in a paper on bacteriological research there was stubborn resistance to the new ideas among the medical fraternity. Even by the turn of the twentieth century the Pasteurians had had little impact on official circles. If Bouchard integrated germ theory into the leading French medical textbook of the period, he did so while insisting that parasites were only one of four different causes of disease. At the same time, the Paris school's continued devotion to clinical research led their professors up some unsavoury alleys. In a disturbing paper Toby Gelfand showed how J. B. Charcot, the renowned student of psychological disorders who influenced Freud, became a firm believer in racial degeneracy and albeit unwittingly helped to fuel French anti-Semitism on the eve of the Dreyfus Affair.

Unfortunately the papers added little to our knowledge of the social history of the student body and professoriate, another aspect of the nineteenth-century Paris medical school which cries out for attention. Mention, however, must be made of Joy Harvey's paper on the Paris sojourn of Mary Putnam Jacobi. Mary Putnam was yet another American who crossed the Atlantic to taste the delights of Paris medicine. As a woman she inevitably found access more difficult and the paper became a peg on which to discuss the eventual collapse of the male monopoly of the French medical profession.

The other five papers of the conference which had no bearing on the history of higher education were all of high quality. Historians of medicine, even more than historians of higher education, will be pleased to know that the papers will eventually be published in a conference volume. For further information, readers are asked to write to Professor Mordechai Feingold, Centre for the Study of Science in Society, Virginia Polytechnic and State University, Blacksburg, VA, 24061–0247 USA.

L. W. B. Brockliss
Magdalen College
Oxford OX1 4AU

Education et diffusion scientifique en France à la veille de la Révolution française: Institut national de recherche pédagogique, Paris, 17 May 1990.

This colloquium was organized by Luce Giard and Jean Dhombres, two historians of science and philosophy of the CNRS (Laboratoire d'histoire des sciences et techniques UPR 21). The major part of the day was given over to the critical examination of recent studies of mathematical and scientific education in eighteenth-century France. Until a few years ago the standard account of science education before the Revolution was provided by the volume of essays edited by René Taton in 1963, but this has now been supplanted by the appearance of a number of detailed studies on specific institutions. The colloquium addressed the work of four educational historians: L. W. B. Brockliss, on the colleges and universities (Oxford, 1987); A. Picon, on the Ecole des Ponts et Chaussées (in press); B. Belhoste, on the predecessors of the Ecole polytechnique (*Histoire de l'Education* no. 42, 1989); and D. Julia on the schools of the *gardes de la marine*.

Each work was subjected to the critical scrutiny of another expert in the field, then the author was allowed to reply before the discussion was thrown open to the other participants. The discussion particularly concentrated on three areas: access, course content, and examinations. This reflected the commitment of the participants to a sociological study of science education on the eve of the Revolution. Many acute observations were made in the course of the day. In particular speakers continually drew attention to the paradox of government educational policy at the end of the ancien regime. Access to the new technical schools was largely by competitive examination. In this respect they were very different institutions from the colleges and universities. On the other hand, they were also socially selective for recruitment was restricted to nobles. Where this was not the case (viz the *Ecole des Ponts et Chaussées*), then there was no entrance examination and the school resembled a workshop where the pupils taught each other. The one issue which firmly divided speakers was over the nature of eighteenth-century geometry teaching. Jean Dhombres, an expert on the Ecole polytechnique, argued forcibly that the colleges and technical schools taught a synthetic geometry which treated problems as 'closed'. It was only with the foundation of the Ecole polytechnique that an analytical course was introduced which thereby made possible the great flowering of French science and mathematics after 1800. Piers Bursill-Hall disagreed totally, insisting that geometry was already taught analytically in eighteenth-century France but not eighteenth-century England; hence the relative weakness of English mathematics at this date. No conclusion was reached.

Bursill-Hall belongs to the Cambridge University Department of Pure Mathematics. He is an expert on eighteenth-century mathematics teaching whose work deserves to be much better known. At present he is working on the diffusion of the calculus in eighteenth century France and part of the afternoon was given over to an exposition of his research. Drawing on hitherto unknown or little known evidence, he was able to show convincingly that a knowledge of calculus was widely diffused on the eve of the Revolution: even women could attend the many private courses. On the other hand, calculus seems to have been learnt as a social accomplishment: certainly classroom physics had no need of its aid. Bursill-Hall's paper was in some respects the high point of the colloquium. Interesting though it was to explore the implications of statements on which the ink is now well dried, there is no better intellectual stimulant than a dose of 'hot' research.

L. W. B. Brockliss
Magdalen College
Oxford OX1 4AU

The Scottish Universities System: Distinctiveness and Diversity: Aberdeen, 26–9 June 1990.

The conference began with a paper from Sheldon Rothblatt (Berkeley) who enlarged his already published views on the federal principle in higher education. His talk was followed by a lively discussion which set the tone for the conference.

On Wednesday, John Fletcher (Aston) spoke about the college-university, discussing the later history especially of Aberdeen and Trinity College, Dublin, as northern examples of this interesting experiment. James Cameron (St Andrews) traced the lives of Netherlands' students at St Andrews in the late sixteenth and early seventeenth centuries through their lively correspondence, and Christine Shepherd (Edinburgh) showed how attempts to impose at least a common course in philosophy in the Scottish universities failed in the seventeenth century. Returning to the situation in Aberdeen, Colin McLaren (Aberdeen) gave a detailed analysis of the very informative seventeenth-century statutes for King's College which suggested a perhaps over-enthusiastic effort by the authorities to regulate almost every hour of the student's day. Deborah Brunton (Edinburgh) indicated that the Edinburgh medical school of the eighteenth century attempted successfully to provide for both the high-flyer and the less academic student by good teaching and well organized lectures. Carol Pennington (Aberdeen) demonstrated how the teaching of physiology at Aberdeen in the late nineteenth century, after somewhat eccentric beginnings, absorbed and transmitted approaches earlier made in Germany, while, for Edinburgh, Lawrence Williams (Dundee) stressed the relative tolerance of the divine faculty in the years of the late Enlightenment, but saw some changes later perhaps as fears of possible repercussions from the French Revolution spread to Scotland. The response of the professions to the Industrial Revolution in Scotland was the theme of the paper presented by Allan MacLaren (Strathclyde); he saw no one set response by the different groups to this change. Both myth and reality were treated in the final session of the day when David Forrester (Strathclyde) looked at some fictional representations of the 'lad o'pairts' and Marjorie-Ann Harper (Aberdeen) give a very detailed and very stimulating report on investigations into the careers of Aberdeen students 1860–1880 at the university and afterwards.

The final day began with David Withrington (Aberdeen) again returning to the discussion concerning a possible national university for Scotland, but now considering the middle decades of the nineteenth century, and with Winifred Horner (Texas) emphasizing the reliance placed on Scottish teaching matter by the early American universities. Jan Rupp (Utrecht) discussed the views of Ringer and Jarausch concerning modern European education and examined the Dutch experience in this context. Two different aspects of modern Scottish university history were surveyed by Lindy Moore (Wales), who chronicled the different responses of the different institutions to the demand for female higher education, and by Iain Hutchison (Stirling), who portrayed the Scottish Office as preferring to support local colleges and local authorities against attempts by the universities to expand their control of course programmes. Finally and appropriately, Robert Anderson gave a wide ranging but incisive survey of the past, present, and future possibilities for Scotland, asking how far any specific native contribution to university development could be isolated. This impressive paper again stimulated much discussion and ended a conference notable both for the excellence of the papers presented and for the readiness of participants to question and discuss. The organizers,

Jennifer Carter and Donald Withrington, provided smooth administration and much-appreciated catering facilities.

It is hoped to publish the proceedings of the conference and readers interested may contact Dr Jennifer Carter, Department of History, University of Aberdeen, Aberdeen AB9 2UB for further details.

John M. Fletcher
Department of Modern Languages, Aston University
Aston Triangle
Birmingham B4 7ET

University and Society: Glasgow, 29 June–1 July 1990.

It was fitting that Glasgow 1990—European City of Culture—should have been the venue for a conference that was essentially European in content, particularly if the UNESCO definition is adopted, which includes both North America and Israel. The conference, which was organized under the auspices of this journal, was divided into six themes: (1) Origins and Patterns of Attendance; (2) the Church and the Medieval University; (3) the State and the Modern University; (4) Universities and Vocational Training; (5) Universities and Elite Formation; (6) The Professoriate.

The conference opened on Friday 29 June as it was to end, with a *tour de force* by Professor Willem Frijhoff of Erasmus University in Rotterdam, who arrived bearing tables and charts describing, according to the title, patterns of attendance at the Dutch universities from 1575–1814. In fact they presented the results of meticulous research so characteristic of Frijhoff's work into the relationship between schooling and Universities in Holland from, in some cases, the late middle ages to the beginning of the nineteenth century. Like many other sources in Northern Europe, the detail that was presented in the tables was remarkable, particularly the grading of students' intellectual attainments at the grammar school at Zutphen from 1687 to 1722 down to grade V '*leger (utcumque), non scribere/mediocriter legere, vix scribere*'. Overall, Frijhoff identified a secular decline in grammar school attendance and a consequent fall in demand for arts courses at universities, compensated for by a growth in demand after the Reformation for training in theology, medicine and law. Unfortunately, owing to family bereavement, Professor Rainer Mueller was unable to attend to present his paper on the international origins of the students of the University of Ingolstadt in Bavaria. His contribution showed how the University drew students from the Catholic Holy Roman Empire, but made little impact on Northern Europe with the exception of a few strays.

The sessions resumed on the Saturday with a further discussion of patterns of attendance in more recent times. Dr Harald Heppner reviewed the origins of the students of the University of Graz coming from Slovene countries, showing how children from rural areas were disadvantaged and Slovenes appear to have been discriminated against in favour of Germans and Italians. Discussing choice of faculty, he identified a clear preference for vocational courses holding out the promise of social advancement amongst ethnic groups. This was followed by a contribution from Peter Lauf examining the Jewish students at the University of Cologne from 1919 until the Nazis came to power. Cologne had one of the largest Jewish communities in Germany and the University could have been expected to attract a large number of Jewish students when it re-opened at the beginning of the Weimar Republic in 1919. Altogether Lauf identified 1,390 Jewish students, roughly 4 per cent of all the students, in his database created as part of the celebrations to mark the 600th anniversary of the University in 1988. In a very detailed analysis, he reviewed the characteristics of both male and female Jewish students, emphasizing the persistence of the tradition of the *peregrinatio academica*—over 58 per cent attended other Universities before their first enrolment. The paper ended on a sombre note with a discussion of the fate of these students under the National Socialists. Last in this section was Dr Richard Trainor, batting for the home team with a paper on the student population at Glasgow between 1890 and 1940, in which he sought to dispel some of the commonly held assumptions about the home-based character of the University. He illustrated the significance of women students up to the end of the 1920s and their decline during the 30s slump, arguing that families chose to educate their boys rather than their girls when funds were tight. He referred to the large proportion of part-time students, the vital role of fee income in Glasgow's finances, and the adverse staff/student ratio of around 1:20 until the outbreak of the Second World War.

The section on the 'Church and the Medieval University' opened with a scholarly paper by Dr Julia Barrow on the decline of the oblate system among secular clergy in Western Europe in the 11th and 12th centuries. She explained the working of the system in monastic and secular houses, whereby parents would present a son as a child to God along with a hefty endowment or entrance gift, as a way of reducing the number of heirs entitled to share in a family's patrimony at a time when partible inheritance was commonplace. She reviewed the paucity of the evidence for the working of the system in secular houses and made reference to the various rules to be observed in the treatment and training of *pueri*. She argued that the decline in oblation was due to a combination of circumstances, the rise of the higher schools, the development of a monied economy, and the termination of partible inheritance. The theme of cost of education was picked up by Jean Dunbabin in her contribution on 'meeting the costs of university education in Northern France in the thirteenth century'. She suggested that cost constraints made it unlikely that universities offered a 'career ladder' to boys from peasant or lower middle class origins. Occasionally families would club together to help a son through university; more commonly, poor boys could obtain an education by entering the service of wealthy scholars as *beneficarii*. Although the papal authorities tried to force cathedral chapters to provide benefices for scholars, she explained that these were normally only open to boys from aristocratic families. The questions of funding and access to higher education by poor students were central to Antonio García y García's discussion of the University of Salamanca before 1500. Salamanca was founded by King Alfonso the Wise in 1218/19 and in the fourteenth century developed a collegiate structure with provision for poor students. García y García emphasized the importance of benefices in supporting the students.

The section on the State and the Modern University led the discussion away from the mundane but necessary issues of finance to matters of policy. Professor Notker Hammerstein described the clash of cultures when the British Control Commission sought to revamp the Johann Wolfgang Goethe-University in Frankfurt after the National Socialist period. He explained how the British, with no concept of the Humboldtian ideal, sought to dilute *wissenschaft* with practical subjects more commonly taught in Germany in *technischen hochschules*. It was easy to imagine the regular conversations at cross purposes that must have taken place between German scholars and young British educationalists. The effects of a changed political regime was the theme of Dieter Halbwidl's paper on the career of Thun-Hohenstein, Minister of Education and Culture following the disturbances in 1848/49, which brought the Catholic reactionary, Emperor Franz Joseph to power. He showed how Thun, a bitter opponent of the 1848 revolution and a close confidant of the new Emperor, managed to implement lasting reforms in Austrian higher education, particularly the emphasis on the study of history, in a period characterized by Catholic conservatism. Professor Yaacov Iram concluded this section with a spirited account of the hotly contested debate about curriculum and structural reform at the Hebrew University in Israel from 1929–1948. After recounting the long pedigree of proposals for a Jewish university dating back to Sicily in 1466, he concentrated on the Hebrew University founded in 1925 in Jerusalem. The arguments about the structure of the administration centred on the fundamental issue of academic and administrative control—should they be separated or not? The protagonists were distinguished intellectual members of international Jewry, including Professor Joseph Horowitz of the University of Frankfurt am Main, the great physicist Albert Einstein, and the influential Zionist Dr C. Weizmann. Eventually in 1935 the separatists won. The curricular debate was less contentious and more pragmatic. Was the University to be research or teaching orientated? Those with origins in Eastern Europe, where educational opportunities for Jews were very limited, wanted teaching across the disciplines *ab initio*. This was too expensive and flew in the face of accepted orthodoxy of research going hand-in-hand with teaching. Those who believed the emphasis should be on research gained the upper hand and were strengthened by the massive influx of professionally trained Jews into Israel in the 1930s, obviating the need for undergraduate teaching. A broadly based degree structure was not introduced until after the Second World War.

Over-subscription to the session on vocational training first thing on Sunday morning, necessitated a division between medieval and early modern and the modernists. The medieval and early modern session began with a paper by Maria Denley on the late vocation of graduates to the Bridgettine Order in England. She stated that there was only one Bridgettine house in England, Syon House, established in the late fifteenth century at Twickenham on the outskirts of London, which later moved to Isleworth. She showed how the order became a centre of influence in English intellectual and religious life, attracting men and women in later life to take vows. Many of the men had a variety of previous careers and some were distinguished scholars, like Richard Whitford, the friend of More and Erasmus. She explained how the brothers published a range of influential spiritual works right up to the Dissolution. Dr Claudia Fascione's paper, which followed, was concerned with the secular careers of university graduates in Tuscany in the age of Medici, particularly the relationship between social origins and destinations. She focused on graduates from rural backgrounds, where she identified a high level of school attendance and scholastic achievement, explained in part by the willingness of families to fund the education of a gifted son. Employment and career prospects was the subject of Dr Jiří Pešek's investigation into the teaching activities of graduates of the University of Prague from 1570–1620. This excellent contribution, which dispelled any doubts about the state of historical scholarship in Czechoslovakia, challenged many commonly held assumptions about graduates' prospects and the function of teaching in the Latin schools, controlled by the University's Rector. Pešek showed that these positions, far from being dead-end jobs, were in fact first steps on a career ladder leading to lucrative appointments in local government. Without the aid of a computer Dr Pešek based this conclusion on the careers of 900 graduates whose biographies are to be found in the *Echriridion renatae poesis Latinae in Bohemia et Moravia cultae*.

The modern session on vocational training considered contributions on the education of women at Glasgow and Prague Universities by Catherine Kendall and Dr Blanka Svadbova, both of whom were prevented from attending. The theme of both these papers was the beginning of the education of women at the end of the nineteenth century or early twentieth century. Catherine Kendall described the resistance to educating women from men who believed a woman's place was in the home, and barriers to career opportunities. She referred to the emergence of social work training within the University of Glasgow as a consequence of the involvement of women in various voluntary associations. Dr Svadbova's paper emphasized the very small number of women students at Prague University, in a society where hostility to women working was if anything greater than in Scotland. She ended her discussion on the eve of the First World War, when a small group of Czech women broke through into academic careers, led by Milanda Paulova and Albina Dratvova. From women, the session turned to the legendary German *technischen hochenschule* with a paper by Professor Klaus E. Pollman on the *hochschule* at Brunswick, the oldest in the Kaiser-Reich. To those familiar with the nineteenth century debate over the quality of technical training in Britain compared with that available in Germany, Professor Pollman's description of the Brunswick *technischen hochschule* was a surprise. Although it was being over-taken by the end of the century by the celebrated *hochschules* at Berlin and Carlsruhe, it was remarkable to learn that the majority of civil engineering graduates found their way into government or public service, and in those specialities where there were no openings in government service, there was graduate unemployment by the end of the century as they were thought to be over-qualified for industry, which drew mostly from the *mittelschules*. It was tempting to speculate that British engineering professors, who drew invidious comparisons, did so in order to frighten university authorities and industry into funding new laboratories.

The conference re-assembled for the next session on élite formation opened by Dr Robert Anderson with a thought-provoking discussion of universities and élites in modern Britain. He challenged the assumption that there was a link between universities and the formation of a professional élite, suggesting that for the most powerful élites, university education remained marginal while schooling was all important. Related to this theme, he considered the role of the universities in the formation of national élites and cultural identity in the United Kingdom—in England, Ireland, Scotland and Wales. He concluded with a review in this context of access to higher education from lower social classes, noting that the 'democratic myth' in Scotland and Wales had some substance in reality. Professor Heinrich Best of the Social Sciences Information Centre in Bonn developed the cultural role of universities in his paper 'Kulturnation' to the 'Staatsnation': 'Universities and National Integration in mid-nineteenth century Germany', an outcome of his inquiry into the members of the Reichstag in the Kaiser Reich. The paper focused on the members of the Frankfurt National Assembly of 1849, 87 per cent of whose members had an academic background. He showed that there was scanty evidence to link eventual political orientation with university curriculum, sweeping aside as uncritical the conceived wisdom of scholars like Dahrendorf and Siemann. Although he singled out the *peregrinatio academica*, one of the striking features of the

German educational system until the 1930s, as contributing to the formation of supra-regional networks, the great variety of subjects and places of study prevented the emergence of a homogenous élite, at least within the university system. Dr Daniel Greenstein's paper—'Broadening out from a central core which remains unchanged; Oxford University Recruitment 1900–1970', was the first presentation of the results from another large-scale prosopographical enquiry—in this case into the Oxford graduate population in the twentieth century as part of the history of the University of Oxford project. His thesis was largely familiar, identifying a watershed in 1945 when the widespread availability of local government student awards made it possible for colleges' admission policy to break way from consideration of means of subsistence. As he explained, this in turn led to the accusation that Oxford was creaming off the best to the disadvantage of the rest of the university system with the exception of Cambridge. This was much more than a sophisticated head count. Daniel Greenstein argued that the whole process of recruitment was mediated from the beginning of the century by competition, political pressure, and Government policy or the lack of it. The session concluded with an engaging paper by Dr J. F. A. Mason titled 'One House and Another: Christ Church Members of Parliament', in which he explained that despite the number of this Oxford college's MPs on both sides of the House of Commons, little direct use was made of them to further the College's interests.

After lunch the last session was devoted to the Professoriate—the teachers themselves. It opened with a discussion by Fernanda Perrone of women academics at Cambridge, London, and Oxford 1880–1930. She showed how the number of women academics in the British university system as a whole had reached 5 per cent by 1912, climbed to 10 per cent by 1930 and then failed to progress until the 1970s. At Oxford she explained the poverty of the new women's colleges imposed enormous teaching burdens on the dons, the majority of whom came from well-to-do backgrounds. She contended that the women's colleges played an important role in sustaining the development of an academic career for women until they could be assimilated into the male-dominated profession. Lack of material rewards was an element in Dr Peter Denley's paper on 'Career, Springboard or Sinecure? University teaching in fifteenth century Italy'. In a university founded on the model of Bologna which still has a rector elected by the students but at which like other Scottish universities there are pressures to abolish, it was refreshing to learn that the practice in Italy did not survive the medieval period. Dr Denley went on to explain that a university system driven by the consumers soon became a system driven by the providers, the teachers whose names are found on *rotoli*, the university lecture lists. From these he concluded that a large number of so-called lecturers only held their posts as sinecures as means of achieving more financially lucrative professional careers in private practice in, for example, law and medicine.

Professor Willem Frijhoff brought the conference to close on a high note touched with personal sadness as this paper was to have been delivered by his research associate Harry de Vries, who died of a brain haemorrhage at Christmas 1989—a much loved village schoolmaster. In his presentation Professor Frijhoff described the remarkable academic dynasties that dominated the Dutch university system from the sixteenth to the nineteenth century with tentacles that stretched into Germany.

Without the financial support of the European Cultural Foundation, the British Academy, House of Fraser plc, and Robertson & Baxter Ltd, the conference would not have attracted such a diversity of speakers, whose contributions left me at least, as organizer, full of new ideas and insights. For the organizer of a conference, it is always difficult to tell if the outcome has been a success. One certain touchstone is the absence of complaint—there were none, except about the weather but as Professor Hammerstein says 'In Scotland it is always raining!' The third conference in this series will be held at the University of Aberdeen where the local organizer will be Dr Jennifer Carter of the Department of History. The theme will be the University and its Urban Environment, not the city of politics and intellectual life but the city of buildings, builders, booksellers, students lodgings, landladies, brothels, riots, sickness, poverty, and litigious professional groups defending their privileges. Aberdeen, on the east coast, is nearer the European homeland, let us hope the sun shines.

Michael S. Moss
University of Glasgow

Political Powers and the University: Madrid, 26 August–2 September 1990.

At the seventeenth International Congress of Historical Sciences a symposium on the theme 'Political Powers and the University' was jointly organized by the *Commission internationale d'historie des universités* (International Standing Committee for the History of the Universities) and the *Association internationale d'histoire du droit et des institutions* (International Society for the History of Law and the Institutions), both affiliated to the International Committee of Historical Sciences. The symposium took place from Tuesday 28 to Thursday 30 September and was attended by some 50 or 60 participants. Unfortunately, several speakers did not show up, and speaking English or French proved to be too difficult for some non-Western orators. Hence a somewhat curtailed symposium, that suffered in addition from the rather institutional and empirical approach advocated by the organizing committees. The speakers had been asked to examine the relations between political powers, in the broadest sense of the word (sovereigns and territorial princes, cities and states, pope and bishops, etc.), and the universities, defined as the institutions of the world of learning and higher education. In fact, most of the participants laid considerable stress on state intervention in university life, much less on the university's own role in policy-making and politics. The questions of the university's (supposed) autonomy or its relations with ecclesiastical authorities were touched only in some of the papers.

In fact, three types of papers may be distinguished. Several lectures addressed an inventory of the various forms of relations between state and university. The participants dealing with the French universities (J. Gaudemet—who was not present at the symposium but whose paper had been distributed in advance—J. Verger, P. Gerbod, and M. Alliot), for instance, sketched together a sometimes lively and always very detailed picture of the ups and downs of the French state's interventions into the university's life and structure from the Middle Ages to the reform era following 1968. Similarly, M. Peset Reig outlined a typology of the Spanish universities and their relations with the Spanish crown, the church and the religious orders in the early modern period. A second series of papers was more explicitly devoted to the chronological evolution in the countries concerned. J. Fletcher and A. Manchester sketched the lines of influence and the forms of control exerted by the English crown, then the British government on the universities in that country from the Middle Ages to the present. The same was done for early modern Denmark by D. Tamm, for tsarist and soviet Russia by Y. Kukushkin, and for modern Italy by L. Berlinguer, whereas M. Heinemann examined the transformation of the German universities after the Second World War under the active control of the Allied Forces. Finally, a third series of communications was centred around a specific problem or a thesis. Thus A. de Benedictis placed her paper on late medieval and early modern Italy under the heading of the forms of interaction between the political powers (such as professional corporations) and university education. N. Hammerstein asked the question whether in the early modern German Empire the territorial rulers or the Emperor were really representative of the state or the nation, and whether the great number of universities and other schools of academic level was adequate for early German society. J. Herbst examined the impact of modern nationalism—in his view a central agency of the contemporary state—on university policy in six geographical areas: France, Prussia, Britain, North America, Latin America, and (Black) Africa. In his concluding remarks W. Frijhoff tried to sum up the results of the symposium. He emphasized some major lacunae—little attention was paid, for example, to the great turning points: the rise of the centralized state in the Renaissance period and the enlightened university reforms—and briefly discussed some desiderata. The publication of the papers is presently under consideration.

Willem Frijhoff
Erasmus University
Rotterdam

Les Jésuites et l'enseignement dans l'Europe de la Renaissance (XVIe et XVIIe siècles): Paris, 23 November 1990.

On the initiative of Luce Giard, the French Ministère de la Recherche is currently funding a project at the CNRS (Laboratoire d'histoire des sciences et des techniques UPR 21) entitled 'Les jésuites producteurs et circulateurs intellectuels dans l'Europe de la Renaissance'. One of the project's aims is to bring together scholars in France and Europe currently working on different aspects of Jesuit education in a series of colloquia. The Paris meeting in November 1990, held appropriately in the city's Jesuit university, was the first in the envisaged series. The colloquium consisted of eight papers.

Luce Giard opened the morning session with an account of the development of Jesuit educational policy in the letters of Loyola, an extremely fruitful but hitherto neglected source. Her paper was followed by an analysis of the administrative structure of the Jesuits' colleges, given by Adrien Demoustier. Father Demoustier's paper was notable for unlocking the secrets of the personal dossiers that the Jesuits kept on their college personnel. Unfortunately, as yet we do not know in what way, if at all, the information in the dossiers was used in making college appointments: the computer age, however, makes such a study a possibility. After Father Demoustier's general account, the next paper by Gian Paolo Brizzi looked at the specific case of the Society's Italian colleges. Brizzi's research into the pace and character of the collegiate foundations south of the Alps offered many points of fruitful comparison and contrast with the history of the Society's foundations in France, already well known thanks to the work of Dominique Julia. As a result this paper was followed by a lively discussion. The morning's session closed with a paper by Paul-Richard Blum on the role of metaphysics in the Jesuits' educational programme. Using as his starting point the *Ratio Studiorum* Dr Blum argued convincingly that in theory metaphysics was intended to dominate and control the Jesuit philosophy curriculum and that in Germany at least (the focus of his paper) this was definitely so.

Laurence Brockliss began the afternoon session with an account of Jesuit physics teaching in the mid-seventeenth century. He attempted to show that the Jesuit professors paid far closer attention to contemporary developments in the experimental philosophy than other physics teachers in France. On the other hand, they were far more reluctant to discuss and engage with mechanist or hermetic alternatives to neo-scholastic Aristotelian natural philosophy. The next paper was delivered by Jean Cassinet on the mathematician, Jacques de Billy. The latter was shown to be an interesting figure, peculiar among Jesuit mathematicians in his interest in number theory, but important to the history of mathematics through his association with and influence on Fermat. The penultimate paper was given by Pierre-Antoine Fabre who examined the Jesuit methods of textual expurgation by comparing and contrasting in particular the editions of Terence by Jouvancy and the Jansenist, Sacy. The colloquium was closed by a paper on Jesuit geography which Daniel Nordman used as a vehicle to analyse the contribution of the late Father de Dainville to the study of Jesuit education. Dainville, he reminded us, did most of his detailed research into the Jesuit curriculum in the 1930s, yet his work has still not been superseded.

This was a lively and informative colloquium and bodes well for its successors in the series. It is intended that the papers will be published. Further information about the series can be obtained from the project organizer: Luce Giard (9 rue Eugène-Gibez, 75015 Paris).

L. W. B. Brockliss
Magdalen College
Oxford 0X1 4AU.

Future Projects and Conferences in the Field of University History

i. Educational Selection and Society in Modern Europe: Sixteenth to Nineteenth Centuries.

In the next few years a group of international scholars interested in the role of higher education in professionalization are working on a collaborative project with the intention of better understanding the emergence of the diploma society. The aims of the project and the direction of the research in progress is set out below.

As the machinery of State and Church grew progressively more complex, occupational functions diversified and became more technical, and intellectual requirements grew more rigorous. Numerous developmental processes which until then had taken place within the family, guild, or corporate body now took on an academic form. This applied to professions as diverse as surgery, engineering, architecture, or the various technical branches of the military (navy, artillery, engineering corps). Our intention is to enquire into the modalities by which processes of selection founded upon the meritocratic supposition that a privileged position should be given to the intellectual capacities of each individual insinuated themselves into the heart of societies where the primary means of defining individuals was by the 'order' or 'estate' to which they belonged, or the title or rank they held. Can we succeed in determining how classification according to ability—or specific abilities—was progressively substituted for family networks, the bond of fidelity between master and client, and the class of corporate bodies? What relationships arose between these different methods of classification? To what extent did various bodies and orders resist the introduction of a meritocracy alien to them by taming or disfiguring it to their own advantage? Or were they eroded from within by its operation?

It goes without saying that the chronological development of the modern mechanisms of selection is not identical in all countries. One of the aims of this project will be to pinpoint the origins of differences between countries.

Our chronological boundaries are set at 1750 and 1900. By the latter date we may surmise that, for a whole range of professions, the modern methods of classifying individuals according to educationally defined abilities were very widely established in the various countries of Europe. However, this project does not intend to undertake the construction either of global statistics or of tables of the educational requirement for different careers compiled nation by nation. Instead, we have given the preference to extensive case studies established upon the prosopographical reconstruction of individual careers allowing us to correlate social and family origins, educational experience and academic performance, and eventual career orientation. A special attention will be given to selection procedures and criteria for classification used to establish distinctions between candidates taking the same examination, or competing for the same prize or post, by perusal of the transcripts of vivas or pupils' scripts for example.

There is no intention of examining specific professions or the pattern of training required for a particular qualification. We intend rather to enquire into the manner by which methods of academic classification fostering meritocracy were able to erode the established hierarchies from within, to such an extent that those who gained from privileges of birth, or privileges of quasi-hereditary transmission within corporations, were constrained to yield to them. In other words we are interested in the social usage of definition according to academic qualifications: what transformations did they produce in existing functions? How flexible or inflexible was the new system based on holding a diploma in comparison to systems of recommendation or patronage? To what extent was it taken on board or even assimilated by these systems seizing it for their own advantage?

These reflections do not preclude the possibility of studies of comparable professional fields. At a conference in Florence in February 1990 which brought together several specialists it was concluded that several professions offered fruitful fields for research: the Catholic clergy or Ministers of the Reformed Churches; civil engineers; army officers and military engineers; surgeons; primary school teachers and secondary school teachers; civil servants. Perhaps the professions at the boundaries of the traditionally defined fields of knowledge would be the most fruitful to study, because in order to emerge they had to assert the specific features that defined their identity against the dominant categories, e.g. engineers vis-à-vis traditional military hierarchy, surgeons vis-à-vis doctors.

We envisage a conference on this theme in early 1992. All proposals or requests for information should be addressed to Dominique JULIA, Instituto Universitario Europeo, 9, via dei Roccettini, 50016 San Domenico di Fiesole, Italy.

ii. The University in its Urban Setting

An international conference is to be held at the University of Aberdeen in July 1993 in collaboration with the journal *History of Universities*. Papers are invited on any aspect of this subject, historical or modern, relating to any part of the world. Subject to the normal conventions of refereeing, papers may be published in the journal *Histories of Universities*.

The relationship of town and gown, or the city and the university, has commanded the attention of social historians and of cultural historians for many years. A distinguished contribution to the genre was Thomas Bender, *The University and the City* (Oxford, 1988). But the theme is inexhaustible. It is a particularly fruitful one for comparative studies, and for extending into such less familiar areas as the economic relationships between universities and their urban host communities, the architectural challenges and results of university building in towns, and the political connections between universities and their surrounding communities. It is interesting to observe that, whereas in early modern Europe universities were often regarded by city fathers as a very dubious blessing, in Britain today leading citizens of Lincoln and Inverness consider the creation of a local university a civic prize well worth capturing.

The occasion for holding this conference in Aberdeen is the 1993 quatercentenary of the founding of Marischal College, one of the two colleges of the university. Marischal College was often called the 'Town's College', to distinguish it from the older but less urban King's College and because it was so closely connected with the City of Aberdeen. It enjoyed some celebrity in the century as a leading Enlightenment University in Scotland, and its building is of architectural interest, or at least curiosity, as the second largest granite building in the world.

Proposals for papers should be sent to the local organizer of this conference, *no later than 31 January 1993*: Dr J. J. Carter, Department of History (QHP), King's College, Aberdeen AB9 2UB, Scotland.

Essay Review

Giovanni Santinello, *Storia delle storie generali delle filosofia,* vols i and ii Brescia: Editrice La Scuola, 1981 and 1979, vol. iii, parts 1 and 2 Padua: Editrice Antenore, 1988.

There can be no doubt that the historical description of the history of philosophy in a comprehensive handbook is a great and deserving enterprise, far outstripping the account of Lucien Braun in his Strasbourg dissertation (Lucien Braun, *Histoire de l'histoire de la philosophie*, Paris, 1973). A group of Italian philosophical historians has set about the task of tracing the history of philosophy for the sixteenth to nineteenth centuries, and treating it as a serious philosophical discipline in its own right. Five sections have been planned:

i. Dalle origini rinascimentali alla 'historia philosophica'
ii. Dall'età Cartesiana a Brucker
iii. Il secondo illuminismo e l'età Kantiana
iv. L'età Hegeliana
v. Il secondo Ottocento

Sections i–iii have appeared in four volumes. The first two in Brescia, in 1981 and 1979 and section iii in two volumes, in Padua, 1988.

To consider the most important result first, a completely new canon of significant philosophical authors is created here. Johann Jacob Brucker's (1696–1770) *Historia critica philosophiae* of 1742–1767 emerges as the central and focal work of historical philosophical research in the eighteenth century. Moreover, the Enlightenment writer Christian Thomasius (1655–1728) appears together with his father Jacob (1622–1684), nominally a Protestant metaphysician, in the vanguard of philosophical historians. It emerges that English philosophy of the seventeenth century cannot be considered without the philosophical history of Thomas Stanley (1625–1678). And alongside the great systematic thinkers of German Idealism, the historical studies of Dietrich Tiedemann (1748–1804) and Johann Gottlieb Buhle (1763–1821) were a formative influence on philosophical discussion.

An even more significant finding emerges from these volumes. They show that the history of philosophy was a central and determinant factor in education and training in seventeenth and eighteenth century schools, indeed without exception in Protestant colleges and universities, and that from the Renaissance onwards it acquired an increasingly important place beside Logic and Metaphysics.

The authors have sub-divided their *Storia delle storie generali della filosofia* such that we may trace the development of national characteristics in the seventeenth century.

Volume i contains first a description of the Renaissance foundations of the history of philosophy, which concentrates naturally on Italy in particular. This is followed by the historical development of 'Historia Philosophica' at the turn of the 16th–17th centuries. This type of *historia philosophica* is clearly conceived as a general, taught discipline, going far beyond the scope of the modern concept of philosophy. The authors have intelligently chosen to divide the chapters into polyhistory and the history of philosophical schools, although there arise some difficulties of relationship in the chapter on Anti-Aristotelianism, as polyhistory certainly has an element of anti-aristotelianism.

After these introductory chapters, the history of historical philosophy itself begins, categorized according to nations, authors, and works. The first part deals with England and the Netherlands. A special place is reserved naturally for Thomas Stanley and his influential *History of Philosophy* of 1655 (although this only deals with Antiquity). But problems with the categories and subdivisions used already begin to emerge in dealing with the Dutch philosophers. It is not clear why the classical philological polyhistorians G. J. Vossius (1577–1649), Georg Horn (1620–1670), and Abraham de Grau (1632–1683) do not trade under the name of 'Polyhistory', in that chapter of the first volume. There is a similar problem with the Renaissance *philosophia perennis*, whereby all philosophy is conceived as wisdom unified in God and proceeding from Him. The Cambridge School—Smith, Moore, Ralph Cudworth—represents this same conception, as is also true of the philosophical histories of Theophile Gale (1628–1678) and Thomas Burnett (1635–1715). The grid formed by national histories of philosophy and the universal science of Renaissance philosophy may not really be separated out at this stage.

Something similar is true of the German tradition: the great Jacob Thomasius, for example, is certainly not adequately characterized as an historical philosopher; he is a school philosopher in his own right, and as such an historical philosopher too.

Overall, volume i demonstrates that it is extremely difficult, at least in tracing the history of a single discipline, to do proper justice to the national components of scholarly history where these are measured on a European scale. But it also becomes clear that such national distinctions are in existence at the end of the century, particularly after the Edict of Nantes was repealed (1681), after the Netherlands became francophone, and following the hegemony which developed in matters of literary history in the Protestant universities, and did not in the Catholic ones.

Volume ii goes on to demonstrate this: in the eighteenth century, the history of philosophy was written on a predominantly national level, often in the native language. This is true of the French-speaking region of the

Netherlands, as is exemplified by Pierre Bayle's (1647–1706) *Dictionnaire historique et critique* (1691), and may also be said, with characteristic tardiness in France, of A. F. Boureau-Deslandes' (1689–1757) *Histoire critique de la philosophie* of 1737. This development is characterized in the German-speaking area by Christian Thomasius, but especially by Gottfried Arnold (1666–1714), whose monumental *Kirchen- und Ketzerhistorie* (1701) is not dealt with in the present handbook, despite being the most significant account in the field of philosophical and theological mysticism. Brucker's *Kurtze Fragen aus der philosophischen Historie* is an example of the history of philosophy in the native language. But the same is not true of his major work (and this was the reason why he was able to gain international influence at all), the monumental *Historia critica philosophiae*, to which are devoted the last hundred pages of volume ii of the *Storia*.

The tradition of polyhistory extending over many disciplines is especially marked in the German-speaking area. This is evident from the fact that Arnold's great *Kirchen- und Ketzerhistorie*, which is simply fundamental to the early Enlightenment conception of history, is treated as a theological theory of the history of science, not as a philosophical one, and therefore does not appear in the *Storia*. This is regrettable and inexplicable, particularly in the light of the fact that Pietist accounts of the history of philosophy are treated in a special chapter together with the eclectic school (Chapter v: 'La storia della filosofia tra eccletismo et pietismo'). Fortunately, the work includes the literary-historical tradition of Hamburg philology with Johann Albert Fabricius which is indispensable to an understanding of the available sources of the eighteenth century.

The polyhistorical tradition in all areas of learning is much stronger in Germany than in France, Italy, and England, something which manifested itself in the 'eclectic' school of the eighteenth century with Christian Thomasius and Johann Franz Budde (1667–1729) (who, incidentally, receives adequate space in Mario Longo's account, but is treated in inadequate depth, as it fails to deal with the relationship of eclecticism to the history of philosophy). In the case of the chief philosophical author of the eclectic school, Brucker, it becomes clear that his eclecticism depends on Budde and Christian Thomasius, and that his achievement consists above all in having described the *historia vitarum et doctrinarum*, which serves but to open the treasure-chest of historical study.

Volume iii treating in part one the history in France, Italy, and England of the history of philosophy, and in part two the German tradition up to the age of Kant, indicates how the tradition of a coherent *historia doctrinarum* was maintained in the area of Protestant Enlightenment. Such consideration of the historical development of thought in its contexts cannot be found to exist in comparable form in the French tradition of encyclopaedic and/or essay literature, nor in Scottish philosophy with its economic and practical orientation. At the same time, Brucker's philosophical eclecticism is of influence especially in Diderot's *Encyclopédie*. Diderot goes beyond Boureau-Deslandes in using Brucker's *Historia critica philosophiae* in his Encyclopédie, infecting it with materialism. But precisely this infection is indication of the fact that Diderot was not concerned with *historia doctrinae* itself, but with Enlightenment as he practised it—and so he exemplifies the French tradition, insofar as it is not apologetic in kind. Voltaire too utilizes the history of philosophy as an arsenal for his ideological aims for Enlightenment, and not as a collection of genuine or important doctrines, as Brucker had.

Academic treatment of the history of philosophy is carried over into teaching of originally scholastic courses. The scholastic tradition lasted particularly long in Catholic countries, Italy being the foremost, and now text-books were being written with a historical-philosophical element, as is shown in the chapter on the history of philosophy in eighteenth-century Italy. In the Anglo-Saxon Enlightenment, particularly the Scottish, on the other hand, the history of philosophy did not play any major role. Adam Smith used it purely as a source of historical examples. The only real history of philosophy from this time in the Anglo-Saxon area, William Enfield's (1741–1797) *History of Philosophy*, is an abstract of Brucker's.

The philosophical school which continued the historical study of philosophy with a clearly practical intent was the Göttingen school, which inherited eclecticism: Christopher Meiners (1747–1810), Johann August Eberhard (1739–1809), and Johann Georg Heinrich Feder (1740–1821) (Johann Lorenz Mosheim (1693/4–1755) is notably absent, being a theologian also). This school is completed and supplanted by Dietrich Tiedemann's (1748–1804) *Geist der spekulativen Philosophie* (1791–1797). In this work Tiedemann first tries to infer the history of philosophy from the arguments of its individual authors, thereby departing from the eclectic conception of Brucker, Budde, and Thomasius. He is concerned to discover innovative thinking in the great philosophical authors (vol. iii, p. 820f.), not solely in order to uncover the treasures of historical study and to ensure their continuing availability. The decisive thing with Tiedemann, and something not considered in the present handbook, is that he gives to the history of philosophy its sense of time. Of course, for the neo-platonist Tiedemann, the goal of the history of philosophy remains that of Divine Wisdom, so that he is at the same time historicist and one of the last representatives of *philosophia perennis*.

Tiedemann comes from the historical and philological tradition of Göttingen, embodied in Christoph Gottlieb Heyne (1729–1812). In his history of philosophy Tiedemann combines pre-Kantian philosophy with neo-platonic speculation. By contrast, the other great historiographer of philosophy at the end of the eighteenth century, Johann Gottlieb Buhle (1763–1821), who also has his origins in the famous philology seminar of Heyne in Göttingen, documents the history of the Kantian conception of the history of philosophy. With him, German Idealism begins to assimilate the history of philosophy for itself: Tiedemann's *Geist der spekulativen*

Philosophie describes the pre-Romantic conception of a neo-platonicizing history of philosophy, which arose out of the discussion stirred up by the conflict with Spinozism (a point not made in the handbook), and pays particular attention to Pythagoras, Plato, Plotinus, Lullus, and the neo-platonic tradition of the Modern period. On the other hand, Buhle's *Geschichte der neueren Philosophie* (1800–1805) begins only with the 're-creation of science' since the Reformation, and takes the modern philosophical era to be a decisive phase for German Idealism as regards the history of philosophy.

These are the main features of canon of the history of philosophy which is set up in Santinello's *Storia delle storie generali della filosofia.* It is impossible not to value highly the biographical and bibliographical achievement of this work. The account of many authors who are unknown even to specialists, of the biographical connections and the interrelation of the schools makes this an indispensable handbook.

There remain none the less certain problems, predominantly ones of method. First, no use at all is made of the tools of conceptual history. This means that the historical conception of history, which changes considerably in the course of the seventeenth century, but above all in German Idealism, is not employed productively. This is particularly true because there is no consideration of the most significant historical philosopher of the eighteenth century, Herder. Moreover, concepts such as Eclecticism, Polyhistory, Encyclopaedia are used quite without taking into account their contemporary historical situation and context. Secondly, there is no treatment of the changing significance of the history of philosophy in the overall conception of philosophy. It should surely have been a matter for consideration that in the course of the seventeenth century the history of philosophy largely takes the place of metaphysics, especially in the eclectic school; that the course in school philosophy was supplanted, first in Protestant areas, then in Catholic, by the history of philosophy. Thirdly, it would have been useful, above all to determine what the role of history was: (a) in Renaissance polyhistory and encyclopaedia, particularly in the wake of Ramistic philosophy; (b) the relation of history to theological history should have been elucidated more precisely (this is especially true for Gottfried Arnold); (c) it would have been extremely useful to determine the link between philology and the history of philosophy as constituents of this type of philosophy.

It is quite clear however that this *Storia delle storie generali della filosofia* is an indispensable and worthwhile handbook. We may look forward to part iv 'Hegel', and part v 'The Nineteenth Century' with great interest.

W. Schmidt-Biggemann
Freie Universität Berlin
Königin-Luise-Strasse 34
1000 Berlin 33

Book Reviews

William J. Courtenay, *Schools and Scholars in Fourteenth-Century England*. Princeton, New Jersey: Princeton University Press, 1987. xix + 436 pp.

Until comparatively recently, the history of late medieval English education was a desert overlooked by a few antique Ozymandian monuments. Now the desert has burst into life; we have substantial studies of both universities and new surveys of the grammar schools that produced most of their students. Scholars have begun with learned articles to probe into many details of school and university life and organization, and to investigate the vast amount of unpublished manuscript material produced by Oxford and Cambridge graduates.

Prof. Courtenay, both in his books and in his articles, has shown the close links between Oxford and continental schools in the fourteenth century, and has emphasized how well received abroad were English writings in logic, science, and theology. These interests also dominate this present volume, which is somewhat misleadingly titled: there is, for example, no proper discussion of the English contribution to the study of medicine or law; Cambridge, perhaps understandably, does not attract much attention. Although he has much of interest to summarize, Prof. Courtenay does not inspire confidence in his survey of the English schools, which forms part one of this volume. His descriptions of the Oxford academic year and of the curriculum of the Oxford faculty of arts, for example, must be used with caution. Nor, as he himself recognizes, is his account of the 'schools' of England anywhere near complete. Perhaps part one deserved separate and more extensive treatment by some scholar with greater sympathy for organizational matters.

Once Prof. Courtenay turns, however, in part two to a survey of the 'Golden Age of English scholasticism' we are under the leadership of an experienced and thoughtful guide. For the general reader no better summary of the intricate history of the activities of the members of the Oxford faculties of arts and theology exists. The changing concerns of Oxford graduates as the century progressed are carefully traced from their surviving works: the characteristic Oxford 'mathematical' approach to theology is described and its reception on the continent discussed. The important role of foreign mendicants sent to Oxford for study in spreading English usages, especially in Italy, is clearly shown.

Finally Prof. Courtenay asks what became of this great ferment of activity in the later part of the century. He suspects that the growing attraction of law, removing some talent from the faculty of theology, and the apparent concern of the Church for more devotional, pastoral and 'preaching' guidance from scholars reduced the production of scholastic work at Oxford at the close of the century. These seem rather inadequate explanations for what, as Prof. Courtenay notes, may well be a misconception. In fact, his stimulating work leaves us with the important question of what happened afterwards. Quite frankly we do not know, and may never know, such was the extent of the later destruction of English manuscript material. Perhaps this will be the great field for investigation by scholars of the next generations. If so, Prof. Courtenay has given them a sound basis and many stimulating suggestions as an encouragement to their future work.

John M. Fletcher
Department of Modern Languages
Aston University
Birmingham B4 7ET

Michael H. Shank, *'Unless You Believe, You Shall Not Understand': Logic, University, and Society in Late Medieval Vienna.* Princeton, New Jersey: Princeton University Press, 1988. xviii + 257 pp. $35.00.

Michael Shank's pioneering study opens the late medieval world of the University of Vienna to view. His tale begins with the exodus in 1383 of scholars from Paris after the Great Schism, and the subsequent arrival of Henry of Langenstein and Henry Totting of Oyta at the fledgling University of Vienna in 1384. He ends with the burning of the Jews in Vienna in 1421, a horror fuelled by the Council of Constance and the Hussite wars. Shank describes the university as open at first and optimistic. The student notebook of Johannes Bremis recorded principal debates from the year 1388–1389 of four protagonists. Their sharp differences of opinion and examination of theological *sophismata* indicate that theology students felt free to debate and press their logical skills to the limit. Shank explores the increasingly negative fate of this attitude through an examination of how key figures at the university regarded the question of whether the doctrine of the Trinity proved an exception to the principles of Aristotelian logic.

Following a survey of debates over the Trinitarian question at Oxford and Paris during the first half of the century, Shank outlines the positions of

Oyta and Langenstein, both of whom adopted traditional devices for dealing with Trinitarian paralogisms: the formal distinction (restricted to God) and the fallacy of accident. Oyta expanded a suggestion from Adam Wodeham that the logic of Platonism obtained in God and developed an analysis of the suppositional distribution of terms to cope with the Trinitarian cases. Both men firmly declared the compatibility of Aristotelian logic with Trinitarian doctrine.

However, faith in the compatibility of logic and theology began to come unravelled for Langenstein during the last years of his life. Whereas the students of Bremis's generation in the 1390s exhibited the same optimism as Oyta and Langenstein, by 1396 Langenstein himself had come to a different conclusion. Exploration of the reasons for his change of mind constitute the crux of Shank's book. Both Langenstein and the students of the early fifteenth century who cite his views, ascribed his change of heart to a counter-example that he argued had no remedy. But the production of counter-examples was stock-in-trade for scholastics, and Shank argues that Langenstein's new pessimism over the compatibility of Aristotelian logic and Trinitarian doctrine stemmed from the opposition he encountered among the learned Jews of Vienna. A teacher's moral authority replaced demonstrative argument in defending the faith against Jews and heretics.

Significant change is evident in the generation of students (including Nicholas Prunczlein of Dinkelsbül, Peter Czech of Pulkau, Arnold of Seehausen, and Johann Berwart of Villingen) who followed. Their discussion of the Trinitarian dilemma shows a remarkable conformity. Moreover, when they disagreed, they now accused each other to the university authorities, rather than deal with differences through debate as before. When Peter of Pulkau and Nicholas of Dinkelsbül attended the Council of Constance, they were primed to accept the arguments of Jean Gerson used against Jerome of Prague, that although he had argued well and even said what was true, he had not understood that rhetorical logic obtained in matters of faith and that only in natural philosophy did Aristotle's logic apply. On his return to Vienna, Dinkelsbül defended killing those who opposed the faith. The destruction of the Viennese Jewish community soon followed and along with it the vitality of the University of Vienna.

Few flaws mark this intricate and valuable book. The anti-fideism of a previous generation of scholars sometimes enters the text. A subtler story about the Parisian background of Oyta and Langenstein goes unrecognized. But the book is a splendid addition to our understanding of the late medieval university.

Hester Goodenough Gelber
Stanford University
Stanford
California 94305

Raimondo Turtas, *La nascita dell'università in Sardegna. La politica culturale dei sovrani espagnoli nella formazione degli Atenei di Sassari e de Cagliari (1543–1632)*. Sassari: Dipartmento di Storia-Università degli Studi di Sassari, 1988. 201 pp. Lire 25,000.

From the period of the late fifteenth century there certainly existed in Sardinia's most densely populated city some kind of grammar school. Its early history and also its consequent development can be reconstructed only with difficulty since much of the source material has been lost. It is easily understandable that from such beginnings there was some concern to see an expansion of educational facilities. To this end in the 1530s the local Parliament, responsible and answerable to the Viceroy, determined to obtain from its imperial overlord, Charles V, an increase in provision.

From 1543 Sardinia was part of the Spanish dominions, the young Philip II ruling through his Viceroy. From now on negotiations were, therefore, conducted with Madrid. The 'povera isola', menaced in the second half of the century by Turks and Saracens, might appear indeed to lie at the end of the world—'sequestrata da tutto il mondo', but to the Spaniards it was an important strategic outpost. So it was understandable that Spanish kings from Philip II to Philip IV first permitted the erection of a Jesuit college which immediately provided the usual instruction in the philosophical and theological faculties. Following successful pressure in Cagliari, always a rival city, for the establishment of a university there, Sassari itself eventually obtained a recognized university in 1632.

The history of the establishment of the two Sardinian universities has not been often properly treated. Turtas here sets out carefully and clearly the problems of financial support, the difficult arguments with the Spanish Crown and the need to co-operate with the higher clergy, incited by the decisions of the Tridentine Council. In an appendix which occupies almost half the length of the book a profusion of previously unedited documents, supplementing this study, is presented. All interested in the history of the development of these two universities will find something of value in this short book. It must be hoped that in a further volume, the composition of the teaching staff and the student body will be described and the socio-historical development of the universities be considered.

Notker Hammerstein
University of Frankfurt am Main

Arthur Field, *The Origins of the Platonic Academy of Florence*. Princeton, New Jersey: Princeton University Press, 1988. xvi + 302 pp. $47.50.

Arthur Field's ambitious and important first book marks a significant revision of our understanding of the role of Marsilio Ficino and Cosimo de' Medici in the founding of the Platonic Academy in Florence. Reversing the causation established over several generations and especially argued by Eugenio Garin, Field convincingly demonstrates that the study of Platonism arose in Florence before Cosimo's patronage of Ficino and the founding of the Academy at Careggi. Thus, to put Field's thesis in its most simple form: the Platonic doctrine of friendship provided a useful ideology for the Medici party at the end of the decade following the Peace of Lodi (1454); only later did Cosimo, and particularly Lorenzo, adopt the Platonic concept of the philosopher-king to buttress their rule over Florence.

Field's detailed argument from manuscript sources falls into three parts: discussion of the historiographical problem and the relations of Florentine intellectuals to the Medici party, treatment of the teachings and pupils of John Argyropoulos in the Studium, and sketching the scholastic and philosophical background of the first members of the Platonic Academy, focusing on the interests, lectures and works of Marsilio Ficino, Donato Acciaiuoli, and Cristoforo Landino. In this account of the transition from Poggian humanism to Ficinian Platonism, minor figures, such as Francesco da Castiglione, Lorenzo Pisano, Niccolò Tignosi, Antonio and Pellegrino degli Agli, become major forces. The turning-point came in the dispute of 1455 over the replacement for the chair held at the University by the recently deceased Carlo Marsuppini, seen as the last Florentine humanist of Bruni's circle and interests. With the aid of Piero de' Medici, the single chair was divided into three, with Argyropoulos appointed to lecture on natural and moral philosophy (teaching mainly Aristotle, not Plato), Castiglione on Greek literature, and Landino on the *ars oratoria* and *poesis*. From this matrix emerged Ficino as an eager and talented student of Greek letters and philosophy, using Platonic doctrines in his own quest for human perfection and genuine truth, at precisely the moment when a Medici party in disarray would have been incapable of promoting institutionalized Platonism. By 1466, to be sure, Platonic ideas of harmony, friendship and unity, already made current by Ficino, were adopted by the Mediceans as an ideology for their rule and party.

Field's account of these basic changes in Florentine values and institutions in the mid-Quattrocento is certain to generate controversy. Founded on extensive research in archival and manuscript collections, presented in an urbane, often witty, style, buttressed by extensive quotation (in English) with the Latin originals given in the notes, this study is serious, significant, and, for me, convincing. Lapses and misprints are very few: but the 'mystifying' reference to 'garlic' and 'chicken' in Tignosi's commentary on Aristotle's *Ethics* (p. 139, fn. 37) should probably be understood as a pun on scholars from the Agli and Capponi families.

Benjamin G. Kohl
Department of History
Vassar College
Poughkeepsie, New York 12601
U.S.A.

R. A. Houston, *Literacy in Early Modern Europe. Culture and Education 1500–1800*. London & New York: Longman. 1988. ix+266 pp.

I am always somewhat suspicious (and envious) of the author who identifies a market before writing the book. Rab Houston has done precisely that. Recognizing the vast and amorphous array of books and articles on the subject of literacy, education and printing, and the lack of a single volume that ranges freely across it, he has synthesized the lot into 250 pages. His target reader is the undergraduate, though the latter will hardly thank him for it, for the student will surely be reprimanded if he or she trots out Houston's generalized judgements without recourse to the original works upon which they are based.

It follows from this that Dr Houston is not, at least in this book, an original theorist. One looks in vain for the kind of profound leaps of a Walter Ong or a Marshall McLuhan. The author is content to present us with a resumé of where our knowledge stands, and the kinds of research that are advancing it. The canvas is remarkably wide, ranging from the end of the Middle Ages to the Industrial Revolution, from Finland to the Mediterranean. Indeed, in introducing Scandinavian research into the frame, Houston has usefully re-introduced that evidence into a European context.

Only the sub-title of the book indicates the author's scope: he is interested not only in the occurrence of literacy, but also in its uses. The latter inevitably leads into the wider field of employment patterns, educational practice and achievement, and the impact of print. Here surely the parameters of the subject matter and time-span covered are too great. On the issue of wage-levels, for example, no figures in a variety of European currencies are of much value without detailed and continuous reference to average earnings, rates of exchange and comparative urban and rural inflation. Such evidence would muddy the clarity of Houston's analysis, but it is of little worth without. The inclusion of early industrial societies into the coverage is too ambitious, for it introduces issues such as provision for education within the poor law and the appearance of Sunday schools and vocational training, beyond the scope of so general a study.

It might seem surprising that a book on literacy should contain a chapter on the universities. One wonders whether it was worth devoting fifteen pages to higher education, when they contain suggestions of the kind that theology was part of the arts faculty at Oxford and Cambridge, and that no other disciplines could be studied there. Here again the breadth of the book has left it hazardously thin on individual specialist areas. The work is well organized, easy to find one's way around, and efficiently indexed. It is perhaps a shame that the publisher could not be induced to provide some illustrations: that lack of concrete detail is perhaps its greatest disadvantage.

Christopher A. Upton
Birmingham University

G. A. van Gemert, J. Schuller tot Peursum-Meijer, and A. J. Vanderjagt, *'Om niet aan onwetendheid en barbarij te bezwijken'. Groningse geleerden 1614–1989*. Verloren: Hilversum, 1989, 287 pp.

Groningen University, founded in 1614, was the third establishment of its kind in the Dutch Republic, after Leiden and Franeker. The intention expressed by the founding-fathers 'to prevent the world from succumbing to ignorance and barbarity' now serves as the title of a commemorative book. In reality, the prospects were far from bleak, and the motives rather less noble. As a foster child of proud provincialism, the University, after experiencing a brilliant infancy and a rather dowdy adolescence, developed into a mature institution of research and higher education.

Part of the articles edited by Van Gemert *et al.* are basically papers read to a wide student audience. They deal with the broad outline of the development of the university and its scholarly activities, without adding very much to our present knowledge of Dutch university history. But the other contributions are meant to focus on individual scholars who are not widely known now, but who have in some way or other influenced the intellectual tradition of their own university. Since Groningen University has nearly always had its fair share of excellent or at least interesting professors, the result is a wide variety of valuable short biographies.

Among the scholars treated in this way are the eighteenth century Swiss mathematician Johann Bernouilli and the professor of Law Frederik Adolf van der Marck. But the contributions on the nineteenth and twentieth centuries are the core of the book. I. J. Botke shows how Jacobus Uilkens and Herman van Hall introduced agronomy as a science in Groningen, according to the law of 1815 which intended theologians and their future parishioners to benefit from this subject. F. R. J. Knetsch argues that Romantic passion was the most important new element in the teaching of the theologian Petrus Hofstede de Groot. With Hartog Hamburger the physiologist, introduced by H. Beukers, and Gerard Heymans, we reach the present century.

P. J. van Strien discusses Heymans, the founder of psychology in the Netherlands, and I. E. de Wilde Jantina Tammes, the first professor of genetics in our country and the first woman to hold a professorship in the University of Groningen. The liberal church historian Johannes Lindeboom has found a biographer in W. Nijenhuis. People of truly international standing are the archaeologist Albert van Giffen, the inventor of the quadrant method (H. T. Waterbolk); Helmuth Plessner, one of the founding fathers of philosophical anthropology (H. Redeker); Horst Gerson, the art historian and documentalist (H. W. van Os); and the criminologist B. V. A. Röling, who was a judge in the International Military Tribunal for the Far East and the writer of a famous textbook on International Law (H. W. Tromp).

Johanna Roelevink
Instituut voor Nederlandse Geschiedenis
The Hague

Kölner Universitätsgeschichte vols i–iii: vol. i, E. Meuthen, *Die alte Universität*; vol. ii, B. Heimbuchel and K. Pabst, *Das 19 und 20 Jahrhundert*; vol. iii, E. Meuthen, *Die neue Universität—Daten und Fakten*. Boehlau: Cologne/Vienna 1988.

The modern German university history, apart from selective monographs and editions of source materials and matriculation records, has appeared in four basic forms: first, in the form of extensive jubilee anthologies (such as the recent histories of Tübingen, Heidelberg, and Göttingen); secondly, in the shape of reports on long-term research (as for Freiburg, Tübingen, Munich, etc.); thirdly, in the form of general works or those covering a particular period of time (such as C. McClelland, S. Turner, N. Hammerstein, K. Jarausch, F. Ringer, R. C. Schwinges); fourthly, in the form of extensive compendiums of general topics (e.g. Kluge, Prahl, Steiger, Ellwein, Boehm-Mueller). An example of those belonging to the first category are the three volumes published under the auspices of the Senate Commission for the History of Cologne University, to celebrate the sixth centenary of that university. This is work of a high standard, whose 1,800 pages more or less replace the older works (Franz Joseph v. Bianco, *The Old University of Cologne and the Later Colleges in the Town*, Cologne 1855, and Hermann Keussen, *The Old University of Cologne. Basic Elements of its Conception and History*, Cologne 1934), and is structured around the hiatus in the university's history—it ceased to exist during the nineteenth century—being divided into two parts, the first in one volume, the second in two.

Without doubt the first part of E. Meuthen's account of *Die alte Universität*, covering the period from its foundation in 1388 to its dissolution by the French in 1798, is a masterpiece of German university history, which can be equated in quality with the standard works and classics from Denifle, Kaufmann, Lexis, and Paulsen (H. Denifle, *The Establishment of Medieval Universities*, Berlin 1885; G. Kaufmann, *The History of German Universities*, 2 vols Stuttgart 1885–96; W. Lexis, *The Universities*, Berlin 1904; Fr. Paulsen, *The History of Scholarly Teaching* 2 vols Berlin/Leipzig 1919–21). Meuthen's work can be regarded as authoritative for three basic reasons: firstly, because of its wide scope, which brings in the essential contours and interconnections of European university history—less so in the early modern than in the medieval period; secondly, because of the effective combination of institutional and social history, and the history of science; and finally, on account of the clear style in which it is written. The author deals with the concept of a 'university' from European models, and illustrates his discussion by using 'The German Syllabus at Cologne' as his example. Those who read the first fifty pages of this study have a more than satisfactory 'sandwich course' in medieval European university history. The descriptions of early modern universities, even though the majority of examples given are German, offer valuable insights into complex problems.

The same compact and homogeneous account by a single author is not attempted in the coverage of the modern university. Instead, the diversification of universities and specialization in the sciences during the nineteenth and twentieth centuries—Cologne University reopened in 1919—are traced by several authors. The first part follows chronologically the 'thought in Cologne University between the French Revolution and the Prussian reaction 1794–1818' (Klaus Pabst) as well as the 'self-perception, ideas, and realization' of the new university (Bernd Heimbuchel), and the second part, 'Data and Facts' (K. H. Hansmeier, Fr. W. Henning, M. Kops, B. Branski, P. Lauf, H. Ludwig, P. Peil), containing a list of the institutes' rectors and deans, the directors, student statistics, and teaching bodies. The attempt to sketch these two centuries had only previously been done in three jubilee pamphlets (1929, 1938, 1969).

If one criticism might be made, it would be the lack of illustration in the works. This omission, however, is remedied by the exhibition catalogue, *The Oldest Town University in North West Europe* (Cologne 1988), from Cologne's Historical Archives, with a commentary by Manfred Groten.

R. A. Müller
Katholische Universität Eichstätt
Ostenstrasse 26–28
D–8078 Eichstätt
Germany

J. N. D. Kelly, *St Edmund Hall. Almost Seven Hundred Years.* Oxford: Oxford University Press, 1989. x + 155 pp. £22.50.

When a series of histories of the Oxford and Cambridge colleges was published at the turn of the twentieth century to cater for an enlarged readership of old members, St Edmund Hall was not among the societies accorded a volume. Its independent future looked bleak, for the statutes made by the 1877 Oxford University commissioners had provided for the Hall's absorption into its collegiate neighbour, Queen's, upon the retirement of the sitting Principal. The Hall managed to survive, however, and Dr Kelly has now written the first full history of one of Oxford's oldest academic societies, a survival from the pre-collegiate era in the university's history.

In 1927 Dr Kelly's predecessor, A. B. Emden, produced an account of the medieval hall, on which the early chapters of this history are based. There is a brisk survey of the Hall's origins and early history. The most significant episode in the Hall's early years was its association with Lollardy at the beginning of the fifteenth century; William Taylor (Principal *c.* 1405) became a Lollard preacher and was subsequently executed as a heretic, and one of his successors (Peter Payne, *c.* 1410) fled to Prague. In 1768 the Hall was once again involved in a celebrated religious controversy when six students were expelled for dabbling in Methodism. The treatment of religious issues is a strong feature of Dr Kelly's account; in the early nineteenth century, the Hall was notable as a stronghold of evangelical Anglicanism, but in 1854 a Principal of Tractarian leanings was appointed. Within six years of the Hall assuming an Anglo-Catholic complexion, 'disaster struck' as the Principal, who had used Newman as a confessor, took refuge in Boulogne in the wake of 'a most painful report' concerning his excessive intimacy with a student.

Unendowed and not acquiring a full corporate character until 1957, the Hall lacks the wealth of archival material found in many of the colleges, so Dr Kelly has had slender institutional materials to work from. This deficiency is well compensated for, however, by biographical sources, ranging from the caustic gossip of Thomas Hearne, who was admitted to the Hall in 1695 and lived there until 1735, to the pious diaries—'crowded with devout exclamations and reflections'—of the early nineteenth-century Vice-Principal, John Hill. Surviving letters from undergraduates to their families supply important evidence of the working of the tutorial system showing the extent of the pastoral care which Principals extended to their pupils.

About half the book is allotted to an account of the last two centuries of the Hall's history and—unusually for college histories—the twentieth century is given particularly detailed treatment, carrying the story up to the admission of women in the 1970s. It is this part of the history which will be of particular value to university historians. Having been Principal for nearly 30 years, Dr Kelly is a uniquely well-informed witness to the changes which the Hall underwent in the mid-twentieth century. To historians familiar with the colleges, the Hall in the early twentieth century presents some strikingly unusual features. In the colleges, tutors enjoyed full constitutional powers of self-government; in St Edmund Hall, until the 1950s, they were virtually hirelings of the Principal, lacking even a common room or the dignity of high table at dinner. The story of the Hall's incorporation is essentially one of growing approximation to the common collegiate pattern, a process mirrored elsewhere in Oxford.

As an unendowed foundation, the Hall was entirely reliant on student fees to pay its way, and Dr Kelly illustrates the varying strategies of the Principals to maintain its viability. In the sixteenth century its links with Queen's ensured a North country connection. From the 1650s an attempt was made to cultivate Wiltshire county families and for a period the Hall attracted gentry patronage. But subsequently it became the resort of students of more moderate means for, paradoxically, it was possible to obtain a cheaper education in an unendowed Hall than in one of the lavishly-funded colleges. The nuances of the English education system are well conveyed in Dr Kelly's observation that in the 1930s the Hall was popular with undergraduates from grammar and direct grant schools and 'minor to middling public schools'. The Hall was particularly successful in generating a corporate feeling among its students through a range of clubs and societies, well illustrated by extracts from the diary kept by an undergraduate in 1885. From the late nineteenth century sport was important, and seems to have been developed as a matter of official policy. In the 1870s Hertford and Keble colleges, both new foundations, used sporting success as a means of gaining institutional acceptance; it is striking therefore, to read that two years after St Edmund Hall acquired its charter, in 1957, it carried away the rugby, football, and athletic cups. The other option open to a smaller foundation was to develop teaching in newer disciplines not covered by the larger colleges and St Edmund Hall took up English and modern languages noticeably earlier than many of the colleges.

Mark Curthoys
Clarendon Building
Bodleian Library
Oxford OX1 3BG

M. Peset (ed.) *Universidades Españolas y Américanas*. Valencia: Generalitat de Valencia, 1987. 551 pp.

Inspired by the example of a seminar at the University of Valencia, M. Peset has brought together thirty-one essays on Spanish universities on both sides of the Atlantic in the colonial era. Naturally Valencia University has been specially attended to (eight essays); but a wide range has been achieved. Mexico, Argentina, Chile and Peru are all represented. One of the main themes of the collection is the extent to which the Enlightenment in Spain in the reign of Charles III percolated through to America. The expulsion of the Jesuits was certainly effective on both sides of the Atlantic. The one Jesuit university to survive (Córdoba, Argentina), was transferred to the Franciscans. But successive colonial governors dragged their feet where university reform was concerned.

In an interesting essay on the replacement of Latin by the vernacular in Spanish universities in the eighteenth century, J. Gutiérrez Cuadrado shows how the position of Latin as the language of communication was weakened firstly because the humanists disapproved of the traditional scholastic so-called 'barbaric' Latin received from the Middle Ages. Then Latin came to be seen as a defensive bulwark by supporters of the absolute monarchy of Ferdinand VII. The vernacular was naturally championed by the liberals, though they had to wait for the king's death in 1833 before they could consolidate the victory which they first won in 1813.

Dámaso de Lario offers a valuable wide-ranging survey of the role of the *colegios mayores* in the fifteenth and sixteenth centuries in order to go beyond the basic work of Kagan and to place their achievement in a European context as they trained up bureaucrats for the Spanish state.

Of the essays on the colonial universities that by M. Baldó Lacomba on the university of Córdoba in the face of the Enlightenment (1767–1810), stands out. Córdoba is a good example for showing how unwillingly after 1767 colonial governors allowed the ideas of Aranda and Floridablanca to influence the course of studies in America. The university was first of all transferred from the Jesuits to the Franciscans and not to secular clergy who were anxious to control it. When in 1778 there was a royal instruction to secularize the university the viceroy, Vértiz, and bishop (San Alberto) resisted it. One practical reason lay in the fact that the Franciscans gave their services free whereas a secular university would have to be funded. A visitation in 1783 by the bishop did little more than modify the constitutions of Rada drawn up in 1664. It is true that two chairs of law were instituted and the university subsequently was able to give degrees in law. But the chairs were very poorly endowed. A reform of 1800 put the emphasis on Latin, law, the arts and theology. It took no notice of the needs for mathematics, experimental physics or botany. Moreover the institution continued to be starved of funds. In such circumstances it could not flourish. This was a disappointing fruit for the Spanish Enlightenment.

J. R. L. Highfield
Merton College
Oxford

George W. Pierson, *The Founding of Yale: the Legend of the Forty Folios*. New Haven: Yale University Press, 1988. xii + 275 pp.

This study addresses the uncertainty surrounding the founding of Yale College, the second institution to provide higher education in British America. The school was definitely chartered in October 1701, when the General Court of Connecticut granted ten ministers the authority to erect and operate such an institution. The uncertainty lies with whether these ministers had met previously and donated some forty folios with the intention of founding a college, or if such a meeting took place afterwards, as a consequence of the charter. In the former case, Yale would be a public foundation; in the latter, its origins would be private. This symbolism is significant to so venerable an institution (by American standards), and has in fact played a role in the university's history.

The story of the private founding of Yale by the donation of the folios was given wide currency, and some embellishment, by Yale President Thomas Clap (1745–1766) in a history of the college published in 1766. This was hardly a disinterested account. Clap's zeal to keep the college in an orthodox Puritan mould embroiled the institution in continual controversy. At that time he was campaigning to avoid being held accountable to the colony's governors. He accordingly portrayed the college as a private undertaking that had only subsequently sought public sanction and support. His version of events was not contradicted by contemporaries and subsequently jibed well with the private character of the institution. Only when original documents were published in this century did doubt surface. Not only were Clap's ulterior motives transparent, but it then became apparent that he had altered minor facts to suit his purpose. Could the legend of the forty folios be a fabrication?

The question warrants our historical curiosity. The author, emeritus historian of Yale University, has done far more than clarify this small matter of chronology. Writing in the first person, he conducts the reader through the detective work required to shed new light on the issue: he reviews existing documents; scrutinizes what other historians have surmised from them; and finally, through some imaginative use of ancillary materials, weighs a variety of what might be called the circumstantial evidence. This last process provides the distinctive value of this study—the sustained and ingenious historical reasoning by which the author sorts out what can be known about these remote and uncertain events. Even more than the founding of Yale, then, this study is about the craft of history. Moreover, this is a detective story that any reader can enjoy.

But what does Professor Pierson conclude? He gives us good reason to believe that something like the giving of the folios antedated the chartering of the college. Like other colonial colleges, Yale was a 'quasi-public, quasi-independent institution' (p. 258). But if public authorization and subsidization were necessary for its existence, he places even greater importance on the independent and voluntary actions of the Connecticut ministers, which began long before the charter and persisted thereafter to make the founding a success.

Roger L. Geiger
Pennsylvania State University

C. Bruneel and P. Servais (eds), *La Formation du médecin: Des Lumières au laboratoire*. Louvain-La-Neuve: Travaux de la Faculté de Philosophie et Lettres de l'Université catholique de Louvain XXXVII; Centre d'histoire des Sciences et des Techniques, sources et travaux IV, 1989. 109 pp.

This book consists of six papers primarily devoted to different aspects of Belgian medical education in the late eighteenth and nineteenth centuries. The papers were originally delivered at a colloquium held in December 1988.

The first paper, by V-P. Comiti, gives a brief and unexceptional account of the development of clinical medicine in eighteenth century Europe. The second, by C. Bruneel, looks specifically at the attempt to reform the medical faculty of Louvain in the late 1780s. This is a novel and very important contribution to the history of medical teaching in the Age of the Enlightenment. Had the reform been consolidated (unfortunately it was cut short by the Brabantine Revolution) the official curriculum of the faculty would have contained a compulsory year of clinical study in the hospitals at Brussels. No other faculty in Northern Europe had at such an early date envisaged so momentous innovation. The paper is a useful corrective to the common belief that clinical medicine enters the official curriculum only with the foundation of the Paris school in 1795. The article is also important for the information it provides about the pattern of graduation in the Louvain faculty of medicine over the eighteenth century, a hitherto unresearched field. The third paper, by M. Debiève, explores the development of pharmaceutical education in Belgium. Towards the end of the ancien régime Belgian reformers were in the forefront of attempts in Northern Europe to make pharmacy a university profession. During the French occupation their wishes were achieved, but the establishment of the new state of Belgian-Holland saw a regression. Pharmacists once more no longer had to have compulsory university education. The fourth paper by Cl. Dickstein-Bernard is the most informative in the collection. In a surprisingly short space of time the author describes the history of medical education in Belgium between 1795 and 1876. The French occupation saw an end to the traditional division between medicine and surgery and the legalization of two types of medical practitioner: those certified by a medical faculty and those (of inferior standing) who were certified by a departmental jury after only a rudimentary theoretical training. This division was abolished in 1835 (it was to be another fifty years before the French followed suit) and thereafter all medical doctors had to be faculty trained. The law of 1835, however, took away the faculties' right to qualify doctors and gave this to a governmental body. This was one of the reasons why Belgian medical education thereafter stagnated, plus the absence of enough beds for proper clinical teaching, and the failure to develop institutions of research. The penultimate article by P. Servais looks at clinical medicine at the University of Louvain towards the end of the nineteenth century. This is a pioneering article for the way it uses the surviving dossiers of patients to build up a pathological and sociological portrait of a clinical ward. As the author points out himself, it is a pity that the information in the dossiers is not more complete. The final paper by C. Havelange concerns the medical press, which first becomes important in Belgium after 1850. The author makes out a good case for regarding the medical press as the fundamental organ of post-faculty education.

All but the introductory paper in this volume are considerable additions to our knowledge and should be compulsory reading for any historian of nineteenth century medicine. It is a pity, however, that the authors confine their attentions so exclusively to Belgium, apparently unaware of the work on medical education being done in other countries. The paper by C. Bruneel, for instance, is to be applauded for demonstrating that Louvain by the end of the eighteenth century was awarding more degrees in medicine than Leiden. Nevertheless, there is no mention of the information that is available for other faculties, such as the figures for attendance at Montpellier and Paris. It is a pity, too, that other aspects of nineteenth-century medical education are not explored. In particular, a paper on the Belgian medical societies would have helped to complete the volume.

L. W. B. Brockliss
Magdalen College
Oxford OX1 4AU

James C. Albisetti, *Schooling German Girls and Women: Secondary and Higher Education in the Nineteenth Century*. Princeton, New Jersey: Princeton University Press, 1988.

This is not only the pioneering study of secondary school education for girls in the German states before 1918, but a fascinating analysis of the uphill struggle fought by women after 1865, the year the first successful organization devoted to the pursuit of the rights of women was founded in Leipzig, to gain access to higher education: the passport to the liberal professions in Germany. This book exhibits the learning, clarity of style, and bold conclusions which marked Albisetti's earlier prize-winning, *Secondary School Reform in Imperial Germany* (1983).

Albisetti charts a seachange between 1815 and 1914, which does credit to several German states, notably Prussia, in this novel comparison with women's education and entry to the professions in other European nations. From a schoolscape with few two- or three-class schools offering secondary education there emerged, particularly after 1880, a system where thousands of German women were able to pursue higher education and a professional career. This was achieved in a series of forceful and remarkably successful petition compaigns between 1885–95, which demanded in particular, admission to the overcrowded fields of medicine and secondary teaching. Albisetti modifies the conclusions of previous feminist historical analysis in stressing the important role played by 'moderate' feminists like Helene Lange, who believed in an 'equality of difference' which allowed for the development of specifically female talents and virtues, and the way that her work and agitation by like-minded upper middle-class women really affected the seemingly hardboiled male educational establishment personified by the two Prussian ministers of education of the period 1892–1907, Robert Bosse and Konrad von Studt. They were largely responsible for Albisetti's conclusion that, 'the admission of women to the *Arbitur*, to matriculation and degrees at the universities, to certification as physicians, and to the examination *pro facultate docendi*, along with the creation of numerous *Studienanstalten* supported by city and state governments, may well, in fact, have constituted the greatest successes achieved by feminists in Imperial Germany. Albisetti also stresses the important input made by supportive city and state governments to higher girls' schools and the training of women teachers. This combined work resulted in a wide variety of institutions preparing girls for the universities and admission of women to all institutions of higher education after 1900. This was not done, however, without a struggle excellently told in chapter 6 over the question of women's capacities by the male establishment, which, softened by the passage of time, has its funny moments amidst its post-Darwinian physiological crudity. These were cruder men and cruder times, possibly because much was already medically measurable, than that of German upper-class enlightened figures who conducted an idealistic debate about the '*Bestimmung*' of mankind in general and women in particular a century earlier. Bebel, for instance, facetiously pointed to an autopsy showing the tiny brain of Theodor von Bischoff, the professor of medicine at Munich, who had published an influential pamphlet in 1872, which alleged that the lightness and much smaller size of the female to the male brain proved that men should always be preferred to do the job.

Albisetti has less to say on regional variation, and on the important differences between Protestant, Catholic, Jewish, and interdenominational schools (on which he does contribute a few informative pages assessing the positive effects of *Kulturkampf* legislation on Prussian girls' schools), but as he admits, there is just so much one can put into an admirably clear and pioneering overview as is given in this excellent book.

Nicholas Hope
University of Glasgow

Christophe Charle and Eva Telkes, *Les Professeurs de la Faculté des Sciences de Paris: Dictionnaire Biographique (1901–1939)*. Paris: Editions du CNRS, 1989. 271 pp. F180.

This is a further instalment in the valuable series of academic prosopographies sponsored by the *Centre National de la Recherche Scientifique*. As in previous volumes, the data are given fully in the 113 individual biographies, with a brief introductory analysis by the editors. This shows that scientists shared the general characteristics of the centralized French academic world: a quarter were born in Paris, nearly all studied there at some stage (especially at the *Ecole Normale Supérieure*), and the provincial science faculties played a very subordinate part in the *cursus honorum*. Although there was one professor from the old aristocracy (Louis de Broglie), scientific careers did not appeal widely to the wealthy bourgeoisie, and most had backgrounds in small business, teaching, the bureaucracy, or the lower middle class. Few had direct connections with industry: the Paris faculty, where pure science ruled, differed from the provincial ones, whose industrial links have been studied by George Weisz. Another sign of the self-contained nature of French academic science is that only two of the 113 professors spent any period of study or research abroad—surely a remarkable difference between France and other countries, or perhaps between the twentieth century and the nineteenth.

Among the many points which can be followed up from the individual biographies are the use of scientists in the First World War, their religious and political allegiances (practising Catholics were as common as militant anticlericals, but where scientists were politically active it was usually on the left), and the malign influence of the Vichy regime. All the Jewish professors lost their posts, and two died in Auschwitz; one member of the faculty was dismissed because he was a freemason, another because she was a woman. The latter was the chemist Pauline Ramart-Lucas, the only woman appointed in this period apart from Marie Curie. Ramart-Lucas, a blacksmith's daughter, was also remarkable for having learnt her science in evening classes, after a purely elementary education. Most of her colleagues, though often of modest origin, had at least benefited from secondary schools and scholarships, and this volume further documents both the openness to talent and diversity which underlay the strength of French intellectual life, and the limitations on that openness in a society which retained its traditional bourgeois character.

R. D. Anderson
University of Edinburgh

Antonio García y García (ed.), *La Universidad Pontificia de Salamanca. Sus Raices. Su Pasado. Su Futuro.* Salamanca: Universidad Pontificia de Salamanca, 1989. 413 pp.

The Pontifical University of Salamanca, founded in 1940, is, of course, not to be confused with the ancient and famous secular University of Salamanca. The original purpose of the Pontifical University's foundation under General Franco's régime was to make good the nineteenth-century suppression of Salamanca University's theology faculty and the cessation then of all teaching there of canon law in the law faculty and of scholastic philosophy in the philosophy faculty. These limited aims have long been left behind. There are now, *inter alia*, also faculties of Education, Information, Politics and Sociology, and Psychology. At the end of the last decade there were some 3,000 matriculated students. Though the new university's headquarters in the imposing seventeenth-century former Jesuit Colegio Real are almost within a stone's throw of those of the older university, each institution tends to keep the other at arm's length. In the 1940s and again in the 1960s attempts were made to integrate them (pp. 100–1) but these failed largely, one is left to suppose, because of the resistance of the secular university to what must have then looked like a potential takeover by the Church. Nevertheless the Pontifical University sees itself as the legitimate heir to the theological and canonical teaching traditions of ancien régime Salamanca. The present volume therefore begins with a succinct historical study (pp. 21–80) of the work in those areas carried out by the so-called 'School of Salamanca', particularly in the sixteenth century. These pages, specially those written by distinguished scholars of the calibre of J. I. Tellechea Idígoras and A. García y García, can be recommended to enquirers without the inclination to look at the many more specialized historical studies there are in this field.

The rest of the volume is really a handbook which describes in detail the development of the University since 1940, the work and programmes of its individual faculties and dependent institutes and so on. Tables are used to demonstrate that a considerable proportion of the students are non-practising Catholics and that not a few, specially in the Philosophy Faculty in 1988/9, were prepared to proclaim themselves indifferent or unbelievers. Be that as it may, the Pontifical University, whatever the private religious or political attitudes of its students and though a majority of those who study there now are lay men and women, makes no bones about the fact that it is a confessional institution. A fact that will surprise some is that its numerically most flourishing faculties and institutes are these days to be found not in Salamanca at all but in Madrid. Though the tone of the volume is optimistic, reading between the lines one is left with the impression that, despite having successfully surmounted many financial crises and reorganizations in the last fifty years, the Pontifical University still has identity problems. These are perhaps inevitable given the original decision to locate it in Salamanca.

P. E. Russell
Oxford

John D. Hargreaves and Angela Forbes (eds), *Aberdeen University 1945–1981: Regional Roles and National Needs* Aberdeen: Aberdeen University Press, 1989. x + 146 pp.

The second publication of the Aberdeen Quincentennial Studies makes for the most distressing reading. Not because the material is badly compiled or written, but because the subject matter strikes a resonant and too familiar note with anyone connected with university education in the United Kingdom over the last 15 or so years. It is distressing too because the crisis in higher education is shown to reflect administrative breakdown of the highest order. The university, the UGC, and central government are simply seen as having been incapable of devising and implementing effective long-term planning which might have saved Aberdeen from its roller-coaster ride through rapid expansion followed by precipitous decline. One cannot read through this book without wondering whether the relevant administrative agencies today are any better equipped to avoid the traumatic mistakes of the past.

The work represented in this book, however, is incomplete. It represents the tentative (although clearly well-researched) musings of those who contributed to public seminars held at the University of Aberdeen in 1989.

The first of these by John Hargreaves (Professor of History, 1962–85) sets the tone of the book. In the post-war years, Aberdeen was encouraged by the UGC to expand its facilities and increase student numbers at a rate which was hitherto inconceivable to a university principally serving the north of Scotland and recruiting its intake on a more or less meritocratic basis. Despite latent fears that rapid expansion governed by national need and central funding would dilute Aberdeen's local character, its academic quality and its intimate community, UGC offers of more buildings, more teaching staff and new academic departments proved irresistible. By 1960, undergraduate numbers had increased more than 50% from a post-war figure of nearly 1,300 to 1,903. In the flush of the immediate post-Robbins era, Aberdeen was encouraged to plan for a total student population of closer to 6,000 by 1970 and 10,000 by the close of the subsequent decade. Why, the contributors seem to cry out in a collective voice, was Aberdeen targetted firstly for far more rapid expansion than other UK universities, and then secondly so devastated by the squeeze on central funding which began to be felt in the early 1970s? Surprisingly, the bitterness which one might expect is hardly apparent. Instead, one senses the mood of an adolescent who has been inexplicably and perhaps unjustly chastized by an otherwise encouraging parent, turning inward on itself and asking 'was it something I did?'.

As if to seek reassurance from past achievements, chapters 2, 3, and 4 attempt to measure the university's impact on the region which it has traditionally served. In the first of these, Alex Kemp and Sandra Gailbraith provide a sophisticated measure of the university's financial input into the local economy. Roy Weir explores the relationship between the medical faculty and the local health service which improved regional health care but nearly destroyed the medical school when success was measured in the 1980s in terms of research output. Lastly in this section, John Sewel presents the early results of a survey showing the extent the university contributed to the local élite. In every respect, the university checks out with a clean bill of health. Despite its recent discouragement by the UGC, it is still a dynamic institution which is vital to its region. Throughout these chapters, the chronic tensions between national and local needs is fully in view. So too is the fact that in providing for the former, national policy-making bodies too readily overlook the latter.

The final three chapters similarly seek re-assurance by looking even more closely at the university itself. University archivist Colin McLaren uses student magazines and oral evidence to provide an engaging account of changes in student life from 1945 to the present. Students' persistent parochialism and political apathy stand out in stark contrast to the expansionist policies which derived from the UGC's desire to see Aberdeen make an ever-increasing contribution to the nation's higher education needs. None the less, the university clearly served its students well, fostering loyalty and a sense of community amongst them while, at the same time, preparing most for professional positions within the region.

Jennifer Carter, co-ordinator of the QHP's prolific efforts looks at the university's governmental structure to determine whether it may be held responsible for denying the university a long-term strategy in the expansionist years when it most needed one. I. G. C. Hutchison expands on this theme and claims that if the university administration had its weaknesses with respect to planning, it is not alone responsible for the dramatic events of the last 17 years. According to Hutchison, the UGC could only act as an effective mediator between central government and the universities when their interests converged in the years of expansion. When central government changed its policy, the UGC proved unable to provide rational direction to the universities. Central government, too, does not escape from blame as its assumptions about how quickly universities could change whatever long-term strategies they had devised by 1973 may have been unrealistic.

If the work has shortcomings they are only those which are normally associated with publications based on preliminary findings. The reader is constantly shown potentially fruitful areas of investigation which are left under-developed by their authors. Tantalizing titbits drawn from interviews, and surveys, are held up which can only support the most tentative conclusions. Indeed, the subject of every chapter demands book-length treatment. Only by enhancing our understanding of the recent failures in higher education will we ensure that they are not repeated.

Daniel I. Greenstein
Glasgow University

Burton R. Clark (ed.), *The Academic Profession—National, Disciplinary and Institutional Settings*. Berkeley, Los Angeles, London: University of California Press, 1987. xii + 404 pp.

This is a book to depress any university president who is foolish enough to believe that his institution is anything more than a loose federation of departments eternally squabbling over car parking. The contents are themselves a product of changing academic environment in the Western world that the authors seek to describe a collection of conference papers, presented, not I should hasten to add at any old conference, but at a seminar at the prestigious Villa Serbelloni, Bellagio in Italy in 1984. This is not a hasty rushing into print but a considerable over-view of the winds of change that have swept the groves of academe since the Second World War. As in all tempests, the authors discovered that much endured and has recovered to threaten the luxurious growth that sprang up in the new dawn of the 1960s. The first four chapters deal with the national settings, providing much of the context for the rest of the work, Harold Perkin on the United Kingdom, Wolfgang J. Mommsen on the Federal Republic of Germany, Enhard Friedberg and Christine Musselin on France, and Walter P. Metzger on the United States. Their theme is common, greater or lesser expansion of university education after 1945, fuelled by the rising birth rate and paid for by rising prosperity; the consequent increase in the middle grades of university teaching staff and resulting promotion bottlenecks; student unrest in the late 1960s and early 1970s supported by the dissatisfied middle ranks of the academic community who called for universities to be more responsive to the ambitions and aspirations of the taught; the abolition, at least in Europe, of academic ceremony—the symbols of authority and the weakening of the authority and leadership of the professoriate; and concluding with crisis in the 1980s declining roles, tightening budgets, hostile political and public attitudes, pressures to win private revenue, and the reassertion of the authority of the professoriate. Throughout this period, governments have treated universities as corporations with a structure (apparently made more coherent by successive reforms) able to respond deftly to external pressures. The second section of this book, disciplinary and institutional settings sweep away such assumptions. All four chapters, Guy Neave and Gary Rhoades 'The Academic Estates in Western Europe', Tony Becher 'The Disciplinary Shaping of the Profession', Sydney and Ann Halpern 'Professional Schools in the American University', and Kenneth Ruscia 'Many Sectors, Many Professions', confirm what every academic knows, that there is no such thing as a common academic profession. This is not the judgement of cynics but a statement of the obvious, that scholars' principal allegiances are to their subjects and not to their institution. They point out that some of these subjects are professions with powerful vested interests and institutions, notably law and medicine. Others by their nature take the academic outside the university, not as a practitioner as in medicine, but as an interested spectator as in economics and business studies. They also agree that the nature of knowledge is not unitary, research in applied sciences demands teamwork, whereas research in pure science, in both science proper and the humanities, is a personal activity, reinforcing the lack of homogeneity of the employing institutions. This questions efforts to make research, particularly in the humanities, look more like that in the science laboratory with teams of academics inter-acting with each other. The reassertion of the authority of the professor in the 1980s is apparent not in terms of academic leadership but in terms of revenue raising and their patronage; but, has it not always been thus? The weakness of the book is that it is repetitive and at times overwritten. It would have been refreshing to have had the added dimension of a spectator from Japan or a

Third World Country, where, at the top and the bottom of the economic league of nations there have been equivalent and dramatic expansions of the university systems in the belief that further education holds the key to riches untold. With this caveat it is an excellent book with statutory advice for academic policy-makers who have ambitions to make universities into something which they can never be—business corporations.

Michael Moss
University of Glasgow

Michael Moffatt, *Coming of Age in New Jersey: College and American Culture*. New Brunswick and London: Rutgers U.P., 1989. xvii + 355 pp., $35.00 (cloth), $12.95 (paper).

Now that the rain forests are vanishing and their remaining denizens charging doctoral students in anthropology fixed rates for showing them their totems and explaining their taboos, very few wild places remain in which intrepid professionals can study untainted primitives in their natural habitats. Consequently, Professor Moffatt deserves our sincere congratulations for discovering a latter-day Eden not a hundred miles away fron down-town Manhattan, and our unreserved admiration for daring, Kurtz-like, to look into the heart of darkness which he encountered while living as one of the natives over a period of years in Rutgers College, a large, state-financed institution in New Jersey. The result of his decade of safaris is an account of adolescent mores and behaviour in relation to some of the larger issues in American culture in the 1970s and 1980s which, while a serious academic study, is written with as much insight, understanding, and humour as many a campus novel. During the initial period (Chapters 1 and 2), the author enters the tribe and is subjected to initiation rites by elders and novices alike, discovering in the process that the faculty members 'were very much offstage in the consciousness of the undergraduates' (p. 14); that there were large differences between the idiolects of staff and students; that many student attitudes and expectations had changed since his own undergraduate years in the 1960s; and that the 'friendly fun' and 'social learning' aspects of tribal life were, especially during the first year, much more important than the academic ones—not least because American college life is far more about socialization, the cultivation of socially acceptable 'friend*li*ness' (p. 43), than its British counterpart. In Chapter 3, the author recounts a series of hair-raising experiences during the year when he spent a day and a night per week in one of the long-houses to which the younger tribespersons are consigned: the complex dances by which prohibitions surrounding the consumption of alcohol are circumvented (a classic case of 'tabooze or not tabooze'); the ritual incursions by bands of marauding males known as 'wedgie patrols', whose main cultic purpose was to shred the undergarments of other, coeval males while the owners were still wearing them (p. 86); the unwritten sanctions applied to the 'unfriend*ly*'; the obscure local dialect ('Undergraduate Cynical'), fluency in which apparently requires a developed ability to say what one does not mean; and the quaint, carnivalesque practices (involving traditional rubber penis-sheaths, exhibitionism, and cross-dressing) which went on during the (forbidden) 'Secret Santa Week' (pp. 104–11). Chapter 4 is the book's most sober section, documenting the tensions between black and pinko-grey undergraduates and coming to the sad and somewhat shame-faced conclusion that the 'students' pervasive individualism' was unable to account for the 'failure of friendliness between persons of different races' (p. 166). But it is Chapters 5 and 6 which constitute the book's core, dealing as they do with the topic which is 'arguably at the heart of the pleasure-complex that was college life as the students understood it in the 1980s' (p. 124)—SEX. Despite Professor Moffatt's initial methodological disclaimers (pp. 192–5), his findings, based on some pretty steamy raw data, explain very graphically just how the rut got into Rutgers: not only is sex an autonomous zone of experience for his subjects, referring to nothing outside itself (p. 251), their whole existence seems to be governed by the maxim 'I bonk therefore I am'. Indeed, the author asserts that it was difficult for the students of the pre-AIDS mid-1980s 'to choose *not* to consider sexuality to be at the core of their beings and their identities', adding that this was 'a cultural dictate that the students shared with their elders of course' (p. 230). Consequently, it comes as no small relief for the reader who is a university teacher to discover, in the final chapter, that Professor Moffatt's subjects found the intervening periods of enforced detumescence when they actually had to do some academic work valuable, beneficial, and 'an intellectually broadening experience'. In contradiction to Allan Bloom's charge that massive universities like Rutgers are responsible for the USA's cultural decline, Professor Moffatt argues that for his subjects, such an institution was in many cases a good deal more stimulating than the backgrounds from which they had come.

For the British reader, especially a non-anthropologist like myself, the book is possibly of most interest because of the contrasts it inevitably generates between the situations in this country and the USA: on the negative side, the impersonality and anonymity of the teaching and the triviality of some of the 'gut' courses (p. 286); and on the positive side, the openness of the students and, most importantly, the general acceptance by large swathes of the population that tertiary education is valuable as much because of what happens outside as because of what happens inside the formal teaching situation. Had anyone dared to publish such a book in

Thatcher's Britain (where I was once taken to task in public for suggesting that education could be an enjoyable experience), the demands for the abolition of state subsidization of student immorality would have echoed up and down the land, and the author would have probably been forced to resign (if not taken to court for seditious libel, witchcraft, or infringing one of the murkier paragraphs of the Official Secrets Act). But that lenten era is over, and books such as Professor Moffatt's can perhaps help us to re-learn a more generous, tolerant, and catholic understanding of the experience of higher education.

Richard Sheppard
Magdalen College
Oxford OX1 4AU

William G. Bowen and Julie Ann Sosa, *Prospects for Faculty in the Arts & Sciences: A Study of Factors Affecting Demand and Supply, 1987 to 2012*. Princeton: Princeton University Press, 1989. xvi + 225 pp.

Demand–supply analyses of any commodity—university faculty to pork bellies—is fraught with difficulties. It simply isn't possible to determine with one hundred per cent confidence what factors are likely to influence supply and demand. Neither is it always possible to measure precisely the contributions of those factors deemed to be influential in determining either supply or demand. Consequently, any such analysis is bound to be subject to criticism for excluding factors deemed by others to be important and for avoiding measurements where they are most difficult. *Prospects* is not exceptional in this respect. None the less, its analysis of factors which are seen as most likely to affect the demand for arts and sciences faculty members at US universities in the next 22 years, provides a gold mine of aggregate measures and conjecture which should influence strategies of higher education in the US in the near future.

According to Bowen and Sosa, the factors affecting the demand for university faculty in the next twenty years far outnumber those affecting their supply. Projected demand is calculated through measures of the age distribution and exit probabilities of current staff, population trends which will effect enrolment figures, relative growth and decline of various subjects areas, and staff–student ratios. On the supply side, only the likely production of new PhDs is measured. In the final analysis, however, it is the supply side which will be more determinate of the labour market in the immediate future. Put quite simply—too simply given the sophistication of the analysis—competition among universities for faculty appointments will intensify in the near future. Contrary to widespread opinion, however, increased competition will not result from any mass exodus from university teaching caused by the bunching of retirements among faculty over-represented in a particular age group. Nor will it be caused by the demands on university places made by the products of a miniature baby boom. Instead, it will intensify because of the dwindling supply of PhD candidates who are likely to choose academic careers.

Although the analysis may be read as good news by those hanging on by their fingernails to the lowest rungs of the professional ladder, some of its detailed points have distressing implications. The swing away from arts subjects, for example, which is far more pronounced outside the narrow sphere of liberal arts colleges and the so-called Research I universities may herald the emergence of a two- or three-tiered system of higher education in the United States. In it, a broad spectrum of universities will provide the vocational education required by future middle managers, technologists, and by members of the lesser professions. In the meantime, a small number of exclusive centres will provide the liberal education required by intellectual and professional élites, and the facilities and support required for advanced research in almost any discipline. As distressing is the fact that the educational institutions occupying the broader segments of the pyramid are already responsible for producing the lion's share of PhDs. Consequently, a more élitist system of higher education seems to become all the more likely.

It is perhaps only natural that a work which concentrates on national trends and aggregate measures will understate the important contributions that individuals (in this case individual institutions) make in determining their own future. Here, the authors insist that policy decisions taken at the level of individual universities—decisions about subject balance, teaching strategies which will effect staff–student ratios, and salary awards—can have only the most marginal impact on the future of the academic labour market. The conclusion is borne out by the evidence. But the evidence is drawn from a period when strictly local developments were insignificant in determining universities' educational and staffing policy when compared with national demographic changes and governmental funding of truly awesome proportions. Had the analysis been extended further back in time, the authors might have discovered that the period during and immediately after the universities had to absorb the baby boom generation may have been rather exceptional. At other times, when the demand for university places was constant or increasing only at an incremental rate, indeed at times like those which the authors forecast for the 1990s and beyond, university-level decisions were all important. So were the different developmental patterns of the various academic disciplines and the competition between universities for students important in determining both the demand and supply for university faculty. It may be that neither of these quantities are measurable, but an historical perspective would have brought their relative importance more sharply into focus.

Works which attempt to predict or model the future will always provoke some measure of scepticism from their readership. Those which do so without the benefit of an historical perspective, may be hard pressed to deflect it.

Daniel I. Greenstein
Glasgow University

Publications on University History since 1977: A Continuing Bibliography

Edited by John M. Fletcher
With the assistance of Christopher A. Upton

Produced with the co-operation of the International Commission for the History of Universities

---

Preface

Political changes have slightly altered the arrangement of this Bibliography; Germany in future will have one entry only. Our task in collecting material is being made more difficult as the growing practice of publishing collections of essays under general titles often conceals the fact that relevant material is included in such volumes. We ask all readers to keep us informed of any items published since 1977 that have not appeared in our lists. We have benefited greatly from such advice in the past year and are most grateful for it. Readers are reminded that lists for 1977–81 were published in *History of European Universities: Work in Progress and Publications* in five volumes available from the address below; lists for 1982–90, with additions to the earlier lists, have been published in volumes 7–9 of this Journal.

The following have contributed reports for this issue; membership of the International Commission is indicated by an asterix. A. Kernbauer (Austria), H. de Ridder-Symoens* and J. Paquet* (Belgium and the Netherlands), C. A. Upton (British Isles), J. Verger* (France), W. Smolka (Germany), L. Szögi (Hungary), D. Maffei*, P. Maffei and G. Minnucci (Italy), J. Basista (Poland), D. Tamm and P. A. Knudsen (Scandinavia), A. García y García*, A. M. Carabias Tores, D. L. M. Gutierrez Torrecillo and M. Augusto Rodrigues (Spain and Portugal), W. Rother (Switzerland) and G. A. Tishkin (USSR) (trans by S. Holland and C. A. Upton). Copy has been prepared by Pauline A. Fletcher. We are most grateful to all for their assistance.

Databases relating to university history

During the past years, many research workers have established or are establishing databases relating to the history of universities, and especially of their staff and students. We propose to publish in the next issue of the journal details of such databases. Requests for information are being distributed; a special form on which to submit details has been prepared. We would like to hear from anyone able to supply information about databases at the address below.

Dr Werner Fläschendräger

18 November 1936–31 August 1990

We have received the sad news of the death of Werner Fläschendräger of the University of Leipzig. Werner was a familiar figure at conferences concerning university history held in Eastern Europe where he delivered scholarly papers with great enthusiasm and a nice sense of humour and irony. He published regularly on the identification of the contributors to the *Acta Eruditorum*, the progress of the Reformation and especially on the history of his own university and others in East Germany. His early death has prevented his personality and his works becoming more widely appreciated as the barriers between eastern and western Europe are removed. Until recently, he contributed full and authoritative lists of publications in the DDR to this journal; it was my great pleasure to know him as a scholar, a colleague and a friend. He leaves a wife, Hannelore, to whom we send our condolences.

Dr John M. Fletcher
Department of Modern Languages
Aston University
Aston Triangle
Birmingham B4 7ET, England

Austria

Additions to Earlier Lists

For 1980

Oberkofler, G.: Der Kampf d. Univ. Innsbruck um d. Einheit d. Landes Tirol 1918–20, *Tiroler Heimatblätter*, 55: 78–89.

——— *Die Matrikel der Universität Innsbruck. Dritte Abteilung. Matricula Universitatis. 3. 1773/74–1781/82*, Innsbruck.

For 1981

Oberkofler, G.: Deutschnat. u. Antisemitismus in d. Innsbrucker Studentenschaft um 1920, *Der Föhn*, 9: 34–7.

——— Ber. über d. Opfer d. Nationalsoz. an d. Univ. Innsbruck, *Zeitgesch.*, 9: 142–9.

——— Die Bulgarischen Studenten an d. Univ. Innsbruck in d. Jahren 1918–28, *Tiroler Heimat*, 45: 39–72.

Uiblein, P.: Beziehungen d. Wiener Medizin zur Univ. Padua im Mittelalter, *Römische hist. Mitt.*, 23: 271–301.

For 1982

Oberkofler, G.: Der Fall Kastil. Acad. Antisemitismus u. d. Innsbrucker Karl Kraus-Vorlesung, *Kraus-Hefte*, 21: 2–6.

——— Die 'Entnazifizierung' eines österr. Nazigelehrten (Ferdinand Weinhandl). Eine Fallstudie, *Weg u. Ziel*, 41: 289–92. (F.W. prof. of philos. at univ. of Graz.)

For 1983

Huter, F.: Studenten aus Oberösterr. an d. Univ. Innsbruck von 1918, *Tiroler Heimat*, 46/47: 158–96.

——— *Professoren und Dozenten aus Oberösterreich an der Universität Innsbruck 1818–1918*, Linz.

——— Der Fall Bacchetoni. Von d. Anfängen d. Chirurgielehrkanzel an d. Univ. Innsbruck, *Domus Austriae*: 224–38.

Kollmann, J.: *Die Matrikel der Universität Innsbruck. Zweite Abteilung. Matricula Theologica. 3. 1735/36–1754/55*, Innsbruck.

Mair, W. N.: Die romanische Philol. an d. Univ. Innsbruck bis 1918, *Tiroler Heimat*, 46/47: 111–24.

Oberkofler, G.: Der Plan zur Errichtung einer Hochschule f. Leibesübungen in Innsbruck 1935, *Tiroler Heimat*, 46/47: 137–44.

——— Carl Stumpf (1848–1936) an Franz Hildebrand (1863–1926). Briefe 1894–1920, *Tiroler Heimat*, 46/47: 145–57. (Both eminent philosophers.)

——— Österr.-Sowjet. Wissenschaftsbeziehungen 1917–45, *Innsbrucker Beitr. zur Kulturwiss.* Sonderheft 55.

Schmutz, J.: Beiträge zur Geschichte des Lehrkörpers der theologischen Fakultät von 1623 bis 1700 an der Wiener Universität. Thesis. Vienna.

Publications 1984

Adamek, S.: Der Lehrkörper der Philosophischen Fakultät von 1800 bis 1848. Thesis. Vienna.

Oberkofler, G.: *Die Matrikel der Universität Innsbruck. Dritte Abteilung. Matricula Universitatis. 4. 1782/83–1791/92*, Innsbruck.

——— *Dokumente zur Geschichte der indogermanischen und allgemeinen Sprachwissenschaft sowie der altindischen Geschichte (Philologie) und Altertumskunde an der Universität Innsbruck. Von den Anfängen (1861) bis 1945*, Innsbruck.

Zeillinger, K.: Das erste Roncaglische Lehensgesetz Friedrich Barbarossas: das Scholarenprivileg (Authentica 'Habita') u. Gottfried von Viterbo, *Römische hist. Mitt.*, 26: 191–217.

For 1985

Bichler, R. ed.: *Hundert Jahre Alte Geschichte in Innsbruck. Festschrift für Franz Hampl*, Innsbruck.

Huter, F.: *Hieronymus Leopold Bacchetoni. Professor der Anatomie und Chirurgie an der Universität Innsbruck. Ein Beitrag zur Verselbständigung der Chirurgie als Lehrfach an den Universitäten nördlich der Alpen*, Innsbruck.

Maleczek, W.: Das Papsttum u. d. Anfänge d. Univ. im Mittelalter, *Römische hist. Mitt.*, 27: 85–143.

Oberkofler, G.: Die österr. Schule d. hist. Hilfswiss. im Urteil d. deutschen Hist. Albert Brackmann 1922, *Tiroler Heimat*, 48/49: 207–16.

——— Berufungen von Naturwissenschaftlern d. Univ. Innsbruck an d. Univ. Berlin. Dokumente, *Tiroler Heimat*, 48/49: 141–56.

——— Wiss.-Tech. Zusammenarbeit zwischen Österr. u. d. Sowjetunion in d. Zwanziger u. Dreissiger Jahren, *Zeitgesch.*, 12: 189–97.

——— and Rabofsky, E.: Zum Transfer österr. Wiss. u. Technol., *Weg u. Ziel*, 43: 5–7.

——— *Verborgene Wurzeln der NS-Justiz. Strafrechtliche Rüstung für zwei Weltkriege*, Vienna/Munich/Zurich.

Steibl, M.: Frauenstudium in Österreich vor 1945. Dargestellt am Beispiel der Innsbrucker Studentinnen. 2 vols. Thesis. Innsbruck.

For 1986

Fally, C.: Studenten aus den böhmischen Ländern an der Universität Innsbruck 1848–1918. Thesis. Innsbruck.

Oberkofler, G. and Rabofsky, E.: Das NS-Programm u. d. Römische Recht in Österr., *Zeitgesch.*, 13: 289–301.

For 1987

Gehler, M.: Die Studentenschaft an der Universität Innsbruck 1918–1938 unter Berücksichtigung der Korporationen und ihrer Verbände. 2 vols. Thesis. Innsbruck.

Grimm, G.: *Promotionen von Studenten aus Böhmen, Mähren und aus der Slowakei an der bayerischen Landesuniversität von 1472–1945*, Vienna.

Oberkofler, G.: Berliner Besetzungsvorschläge f. österr. Geographen, *Tiroler Heimat*, 50: 285–91.

——— and Rabofsky, E.: *Studien zur Geschichte der österreichischen Wissenschaft zwischen Krieg und Frieden*, Vienna.

Steibl, M.: Die Univ. als 'Vorschule f. d. verschiedenen Berufszweige d. männlichen Geschlechtes' 1877. Darstellung von Problemen d. Frauenstudiums auf d. Grundlage bisher unveröffentlicher Dokumente d. Univ. Innsbruck (19. Jh.), *Tiroler Heimat*, 50: 219–48.

Uiblein, P.: *Mittelalterliches Studium an der Wiener Artistenfakultät. Kommentar zu den 'Acta facultatis artium universitatis Vindobonensis' 1385–1416*, Vienna.

For 1988

Gehler, M.: Die Studentenschaft an d. Univ. Innsbruck u. d. Anschlussbewegung 1918–38, in T. Albrich ed.: *Tirol und der Anschluss. Voraussetzungen. Entwicklungen, Rahmenbedingungen 1918–38*, Innsbruck: 75–112.

——— Studenten im Freikorps Oberland. Der 'Sturmzug Tirol' in Oberschlesien 1921, *Tiroler Heimat*, 51/52: 219–52.

Goller, P.: Philosophie an d. Univ. Innsbruck 1918–45. Zwischen Humanismus, Katholizismus u. Nationalsozialismus, *Tiroler Heimat*, 51/52: 167–90.

Grass, N.: Claudius Martin Ritter von Scherer. Universitätsprof. u. Protomedicus in Innsbruck u. Graz, in H. Valentinitsch ed.: *Recht und Geschichte*, Graz: 183–218.

Publications 1989

Gehler, M.: Vom Rassenwahn zum Judenmord. Am Beispiel d. student. Antisemitismus an d. Univ. Innsbruck von d. Anfängen bis in d. 'Anschluss'-Jahr 1938, *Zeitgesch.*, 16: 263–88.

Goller, P., *Die Lehrkanzeln für Philosophie an der Philosophischen Fakultät der Universität Innsbruck 1848–1945*, Innsbruck.

Hirschegger, M.: *Geschichte der Universitätsbibliothek Graz 1918–45*, Vienna.

——— Ein Jh. aus d. Bibliotheksgesch. Die UB Graz seit d. Jahr 1895, in *Festgabe für Franz Kroller zum 65. Geburtstag*, Graz: 6–12.

Heiss, G. etc. eds: *Willfährige Wissenschaft. Die Universität Wien 1936–45*, Vienna.

Höflechner, W.: *Die Baumeister des künftigen Glücks. Fragment einer Geschichte des Hochschulwesens in Österreich vom Ausgang des 19. Jahrhunderts bis 1938*, Graz.

Holasek, A. and Kernbauer, A. eds: *Fritz Pregl an Karl Berthold Hofmann. Briefe aus den Jahren 1904–1913*, Graz. (F.P. biochemist of Graz and Innsbruck. K.B.H. his teacher at Graz.)

Oberkofler, G.: Über d. Einfluss d. österr. Schule d. hist. Hilfswiss. in Berlin. Die Berufung von Michael Tangl (1861–1921) nach Berlin (1897) u. seine Wahl zum ordentlichen Mitglied d. Preussischen Akad. d. Wiss. (1918), *Tiroler Heimat*, 51/52: 233–9.

——— and Reinalter, H.: *Naturrecht und Gesellschaftsvertrag im österreichischen Vormärz. Ein 'Promemoria' von Sebastian Jenull und ein 'Versuch' von Anton Freiherr von Hye-Glunek*, Innsbruck.

Weitensfelder, H.: Studium und Staat. Biographische Untersuchungen zur österreichischen Bildungspolitik um 1800. Thesis. Graz.

Publications 1990

Gehler, M.: Studenten u. Nationalsozialismus an d. Univ. Innsbruck 1918–38, *Skolast*, 34: 14–20.

Goller, P. and Oberkofler, G.: *Mineralogie und Geologie an der Leopold-Franzens-Universität Innsbruck 1867–1945*, Innsbruck.

Heider, M. etc.: Pol. zuverlässig-rein arisch-Deutscher Wiss. verpflichtet, *Skolast*, 34: 22–117.

Meixner, W.: '. . . . eine wahrhaft nat. Wiss. d. Deutschen . . .', *Skolast*, 34: 126–33.

Preglau-Hämmerle, S.: Univ. u. Nationalsozialismus—Überwältigung von ausser oder Anschluss von innen? *Skolast*, 34: 4–8.

Steibl, M.: 'Lernen Sie kochen, gnädige Frau!. . . . : Man hat lieber d. Mund gehalten', *Skolast*, 34: 118–25.

Walser, H.: Die Gesch. d. Innsbrucker Univ. in pol. Spannungsfeld d. Ersten Repub., *Skolast*, 34: 9–13.

Weinert, W.: Entnazifizierung an d. Univ. Innsbruck, *Skolast*, 34: 134–41.

Belgium and the Netherlands

Additions to Earlier Lists

For 1985

Kennedy, L. A.: Late-14th-cent. philos. scepticism at Oxford, *Vivarium*, 23(2): 70–102.

For 1986

Batllori, R. P.: Las obras de Vives en los cols jesuiticos del s. 16, in J. IJsewijn and A. Losada eds: *Erasmus in Hispania. Vives in Belgio*, Louvain: 121–46.

For 1988

Bernès, A.-C. ed.: *Libert Froidmont et les résistances aux révolutions scientifiques*, Haccourt. (L.F. 1587–1653 prof. at univ. of Louvain.)

Muzslay, I. P.: Magyar diákok a Leuveni Katolikus egyetemen (Hungarian students at the Cath. Univ. of L.), *A Sziv*: 461–2.

Nave, F. de: Franciscus I. Raphelengius 1539–97, grondlegger van de Arabische studiën in de Ned. (F.I.R. fnder of Arabic studies in the Neths), in M. de Schepper and N. de Nave eds: *Ex officina Plantiniana. Studia in memoriam Christophori Plantini* (c. *1520–89*), Antwerp: 523–53.

Otterspeer, W. and Poelgeest, L. van: *Willem III en de Leidse universiteit* (W. III and L. univ.), Leyden. (Cat. of an exhibition.)

Vermeersch, A. J. ed.: Een cultuuranalyse door L.A. Warnkönig: *Gedanken. . . . Belgien entgegenstehen. Begonnen in Anfang Juni 1825, beendigt im December 1825* (An analysis of culture by L.A.W. . . .), *Handelingen van de konink. commissie voor gesch.*, 154: 91–158. (Pp. 121–6 consider universities.)

For 1989

Acker, L. van: Westvlaamse promotieblazoenen (West Flemish graduation coats-of-arms), *Biekorf*, 89(3): 201–218.

Berg, R. van den, Deurwaarder, I. and Kuipers M.: *Bijzondere studenten. 40 jaar studentenbeweging aan de Vrije Universiteit* (Special students. 40 yrs of student activity at the Free Univ. of Amsterdam), Amsterdam.

Bezemer, C. H.: Style et langage dans les répétitions de quelques romanistes médiévaux, ou: sur l'importance de reconnaître les répétitions, in G. van Dievoet, P. Godding and D. van den Auweele eds: *Langage et droit à travers l'histoire. Réalités et fictions*, Louvain/Paris. (Discusses univ. lecturing methods.)

Bockstaele, P.: Astrologie te Leuven in de 17e eeuw (Astrol. at L. in the 17th cent.), *De 17e eeuw*, 5(1): 172–81.

Bruneel, C.: Au coeur des réformes: la fac. de méd. de Louvain dans le dernier quart du 18e s., in C. Bruneel and P. Servais eds: *La formation du médecin: des Lumières au laboratoire*, Louvain-la-Neuve (henceforth noted as *Formation du médecin*): 13–41.

Dickstein-Bernard, C.: Panorama de l'enseignement méd. au 19e s., in *Formation du médecin*: 59–75.

Dustin, P.: Les débuts de l'anat. pathologique en Belgique, *Acta Belgica hist. medicinae*, 2(4): 149–54.

Engels, M. H. H.: Een briefwisseling tussen Saeckma en Barlaeus 1630 (An exchange of letters between S. and B. 1630), *De vrije Fries*, 69: 45–56. (S. curator of Franeker; B. prof. at Leyden and Amsterdam.)

François, L. ed.: *Les mémoires d'un orangiste: L. A. Reyphins, ex-président de la Seconde Chambre des Etats généraux 1835*, Brussels. (Pp. 194–9 discuss universities.)

Gemert, G. A. van, Schuller tot Peursum-Meijer, J. and Vanderjagt, A. J.: '*Om niet aan onwetendheid en barbarij te bezwijken*'. *Groningse geleerden 1614–1989* ('So as not to succumb to ignorance and barbarism'. G. scholars 1614–1989), Hilversum.

Groen, M.: *Het wetenschappelijk onderwijs in Nederland van 1815 tot 1980. Een onderwijskundig overzicht. 3. Diergeneeskunde. Economische Wetenschappen. Sociale Wetenschappen. Interfaculteiten. Nabeschouwing. Bijlagen* (Scholarly teaching in the Neths 1815–1918. A survey of teaching skills. 3. Veterinary med. Econs. Soc. sciences. Interdisciplinary studies. Epilogue. Appendices), Eindhoven.

Henssen, E. W. A.: Enige opmerkingen over het schrijven van een contemp. univ. gesch. (Some remarks on writing contemp. univ. hist.), *Batavia acad.*, 7(1): 13–16. (Considers univ. of Groningen.)

——— *Rijksuniversiteit Groningen 1964–68* (The state univ. of G. 1964–68), Groningen.

Isaac, M.-T. etc.: *L'Ecole Centrale du Département de Jemappes—Les Mathématiques à l'école de la Révolution*. Mons. (Cat. of an exhibition.)

Keulen, J. van and Stienstra, H.: De archieven van de Groninger univ. in het Rijksarchief (The archives of G. univ. in the State Archives), *Batavia acad.*, 7(1): 17–22.

Kingma, J., Koops, W. R. H. and Smit, F. R. H.: *Universitair leven in Groningen 1614–1989. Professoren en studenten/Boek en uitgeverij* (Univ. life in G. 1614–1989. Profs and students/Publishing and printing), Groningen.

Makkink, H. K.: Ontkiemd met natuurkunde, geënt op werktuigbouwkunde. Ontstaan en profilering van de opleiding tot elektrotech. ingenieur in Neds. (Germinated from physics, grafted to mech. engineering. Origins and outline of the training of elect. engineers in the Neths), *Batavia acad.*, 7(2): 25–43.

Obert, C.: Les lectures et les oeuvres des pensionnaires du coll. St-Bernard, *Cîteaux*, 40(1–4): 245–91. (Concerns Paris coll. in middle ages.)

Otterspeer, W.: De kwestie Lievegoed of het eerste lectoraat in de journalistiek te Leiden (The L. question or the first lect. in journalism at L.), *Leids jb.*: 155–69.

Peeters, M.: De vrijmetselarij te Leuven (Freemasonry in L.), *Jb. van de gesch.- en oudheidkundige kring voor Leuven en omgeving*, 29: 14–28. (Inform. about L. in late 18th–early 19th centuries.)

Raes, R.: *De bladen van de Vlaams-Nationale Studenten Unie Gent 1957–81* (The papers of the VNSU of G. 1957–81), Ghent. (With an inventory of the VNSU archive.)

Ridder-Symoens, H. de: La nouvelle hist. des univs, *Cahiers de Clio*, 100: 79–87.

Schuller tot Peursum-Meijer, J. and Knoops, W. R. H. eds: *Petrus Camper 1722–89. Onderzoeker van nature* (P.C. 1722–89. Researcher from nature). Groningen. (P.C. prof. at G. Cat. of exhibition.)

Servais, P.: La clinique à l'univ. de Louvain au 19e s., in *Formation du médecin*: 77–97.

Simon-Van der Meersch, A. M.: François Laurent, hoogleraar (F.L. Prof.), in J. Erauw etc. eds: *Liber memorialis François Laurent 1810–87*, Brussels: 165–99. (F.L. prof. at Ghent 1836–80.)

Smeyers, M.: Studentencursussen uit de 17e en de 18e eeuw. Een tijdsbeeld van prof. en studenten (Coursebooks from the 17th and 18th cents. A portrait of profs and students), *Acad. tijdingen K.U. Leuven*, 23(2): 6–8.

Tiggelen, B. van: *Chronique de la Faculté des sciences de Louvain: l'institution et les hommes*, Louvain-la-Neuve. (Covers period from 1834.)

——— *La Faculté des sciences au fil des jours: héritages et métamorphoses*, Louvain-la-Neuve. (Cat. of exhibition.)

Tuin, B.: Het archief van de curatoren *c.* 1930–60 als bron voor de gesch. (The curators' archives *c.* 1930–60 as a hist. source), *Batavia acad.*, 7(1): 5–12.

Vanderjagt, A. J.: De intellect. achtergrond van de stichting van de Groningse Acad. (The intellect. background to the fndation of the G.A.), *Batavia acad.*, 7(1): 1–4.

Vanpaemel, G.: Kerk en wetenschap: de strijd tegen het cartesianisme aan de Leuvense univ. (Church and science: the struggle against cartesianism at the univ. of L.), *De 17e eeuw*, 5(1): 182–9.

Verpoest, L.: 125 jaar ingenieursopleiding aan de Kath. Univ. te Leuven. De tweede halve eeuw 1914–64: van Speciale Scholen tot Fac. der Toegepaste Wetenschappen (125 years of engineering educ. at the Cath. Univ. of L. The 2nd half cent. 1914–64: from Special Schls to the Fac. of Engineering), *Onze Alma Mater*, 43(4): 383–97.

Vries, H. de: Centralisatie van beleid. De Colls van Curatoren aan de Ned. univ. van 1815–1940 (Centralisation of pol. The colls of Curators at the Dutch univs 1815–1940), *Jb. centraal bureau voor geneal.*, 43: 221–49.

Publications 1990

Berting, J.: Over het bestaan en voortbestaan van soc.-wetenschappelijke disciplines sedert de 18e eeuw en de rol die de univ. daarbij speelden (On the existence and continuation of soc. science disciplines since the 18th cent. and the role played by the univs in this), in *Wetenschapsbeoefening binnen en buiten de universiteit*, Rotterdam (henceforth noted as *Wetenschapsbeoefening*): 73–91.

Bezemer, C. H.: Les *Quaestiones disputatae* orléanaises dans les commentaires de Jacques de Révigny, *Tijdsch. voor rechtsgesch.*, 58: 5–38.

Frijhoff, W.: Geleerd genootschap en univ.: solidair of complementair in de wetenschapsontwikkeling? Ned. en de omringende landen tot in de 19e eeuw (Learned soc. and univ.: amalgamated or complementary in the development of learning? The Neths and adjoining countries before the 19th cent.), in *Wetenschapsbeoefening*: 6–19.

Lambers, H. W.: Rotterdamse belangstelling voor de econ. wetenschappen 1848–1913 (Rotterdam's concern for econs), in *Wetenschapsbeoefening*: 20–45. (The early hist. of R.'s business school.)

Lieburg, M. J. van: De acad. van het medisch beroep en de ontwikkeling van het genootschapswezen in Ned. gedurende de 19e eeuw (The 'academicalisation' of the med. profession and the devel. of socs in the Neths in the 19th cent.), in *Wetenschapsbeoefening*: 92–102.

Ridder-Symoens, H. de: Hoe middeleeuws is onze univ. (How medieval are our univs?), in R. Harp, E. Mantingh and M. Rappoldt eds: *De Middeleeuwen in de 20e eeuw. Middeleeuwse sporen in de hedendaagse cultuur*, Hilversum: 85–98.

——— Reizende studenten in de late Middeleeuwen (Travelling students in the late middle ages), *Fibula*, 31(2): 5–11.

Soetermeer, F. P. W.: De *pecia* in juridische handschriften (*Pecia* in legal MSS). Thesis. Leyden.

Thomassen, K. : *Alba Amicorum. Vijf eeuwen vriendschap op papier gezet: het Album Amicorum en het Poëziealbum in de Nederlanden* (A.A. 5 cents of friendship put down on paper. The A.A. and Verse-albums in the Neths), Maarssen/ 's Gravenhage. (Many collections are from students.)

British Isles

Additions to Earlier Lists

For 1979

Cross, A. G.: Konstantin Bal'mont in Oxford in 1897, *Oxford Slavonic papers*, NS 12: 104–16. (K.B. gave Ilchester lectures at Oxford.)

For 1980

Morrish, P.S.: The Brotherton Library, its Judaica and Cecil Roth, *Univ. of Leeds rev.*, 23: 218–33. (Inform. about teaching of Hebrew at Leeds.)

For 1981

Ker, N. R.: The books of phil. distributed at Merton Coll. in 1372 and 1375, in P. L. Heyworth ed.: *Medieval studies for J. A. W. Bennett*, Oxford: 347–94.

Mackenna, R. O.: *Glasgow university athletic club. The story of the first 100 years*, Glasgow.

For 1982

Catto, J. I.: The acad. career of Thomas Cantilupe, in M. Jancey ed.: *St Thomas Cantilupe, bishop of Hereford: Essays in his honour*, Hereford: 45–55. (T.C. studied at Paris, Orléans and Oxford in 13th century.)

Heyck, T. W.: *The transformation of intellectual life in Victorian England*, London. (Considers role of universities.)

Rothblatt, S.: Failure in early 19th-cent. Oxford and Cambridge, *Hist. of educ.*, 11: 1–21.

For 1983

Hoffman, J. G.: The Puritan revoln and the 'beauty of holiness' at Cambridge, *Procs of the Cambridge Antiquarian Soc.*, 72(1982–83): 94–105.

Leader, D. R.: Grammar in late-medieval Oxford and Cambridge, *Hist. of educ.*, 12: 9–14.

For 1984

Anderson, R. D.: Brewster and the reform of the Scott. univs, in A. D. Morrison-Low and J. R. R. Christie eds: *'Martyr of Science': Sir David Brewster 1781–1868*, Edinburgh: 31–4.

For 1985

D'Avray, D. L.: *The preaching of the Friars: Sermons diffused from Paris before 1300*, Oxford. (Considers role of univ. in encouraging preaching.)

Stewart, M. A.: Berkeley and the Rankenian Club, *Hermathena*, 139: 25–45. (Activities in the most important Edinburgh univ. student club.)

Thomson, A.: *Ferrier of St Andrews. An academic tragedy*, Edinburgh.

For 1987

Anderson, R. D.: Scott. univ. profs 1800–1939: Profile of an elite, *Scott. econ. and soc. hist.*, 7: 27–53.

——— Sport in the Scott. univs 1860–1939, *The internat. jnl of the hist. of sport*, 4/2: 177–88.

Corsten, S.: Univs and early printing, in L. Hellinga and J. Goldfinch eds: *Bibliography and the study of 15th-century civilization*, London: 83–123.

Davie, G.: *The crisis of the democratic intellect: the problem of generalism and specialization in 20th-century Scotland*, Edinburgh. (Considers debate within Scott. universities.)

Jones, C.: Montpellier med. students and the medicalisation of 18th-cent.

France, in R. Porter and A. Wear eds: *Problems and methods in the history of medicine*, London: 57–80.

Stewart, M. A.: John Smith and the Molesworth Circle, *18th-cent. Ireland*, 2: 89–102. (Concerns Irish radicals at Glasgow univ. in 1720s.)

For 1988

Ditchfield, G. M.: The subscription issue in British parliamentary pols 1772–79, *Parliamentary hist.*, 7: 45–80. (Discusses requirement that univ. members should declare their allegiance to Anglican Church.)

Henderson, G. P.: *The Ionian Academy*, Edinburgh.

For 1989

Bradshaw, B. and Duffy, E. eds: *Humanism, Reform and the Reformation. The career of Bishop John Fisher*, Cambridge. (J.F. involved in the refndations of Christ's Coll. and St John's Coll., Cambridge.)

Fletcher, J. M. and Upton, C. A.: The Merton College library roof 1502–1503, *Library hist.*, 8/4: 104–9.

Fraser, A. G.: *The building of Old College: Adam Playfair and the University of Edinburgh*, Edinburgh.

Heyworth, P. L.: *Letters of Humfrey Wanley: Palaeographer, Anglo-Saxonist, librarian 1672–1726*, Oxford. (H.W. for some yrs assistant at Bodleian Library, Oxford.)

Owen, D. M.: *Cambridge university archives: a classifed list*, Cambridge.

Rorabaugh, W. J.: *Berkeley at war: The 1960s*, Oxford.

Publications 1990

Barfoot, M.: Hume and the cult. of science in the early 18th cent., in M. A. Stewart ed.: *Studies in the philosophy of the Scottish Enlightenment*, Oxford (henceforth noted as *Scott. Enlightenment*): 151–90. (Discusses nat. phil. curriculum and the class library at Edinburgh.)

Carter, I.: *Ancient cultures of conceit: British university fiction in the post-war years*, London.

Emerson, R. L.: Science and moral phil. in the Scottish Enlightenment, in *Scott. Enlightenment*: 11–36. (Considers role of universities.)

Kenny, A.: *The Oxford diaries of Arthur Hugh Clough*, Oxford. (A.H.C. Poet. Student at Balliol. Fellow of Oriel. Early Victorian period.)

Maesschalck, E. de: The relationship between the univ. and the city of Louvain in the 15th cent., *Hist. of univs*, 9: 45–71.

Matthew, H. C. G.: Noetics, Tractarians, and the reform of the univ. of Oxford in the 19th cent., *Hist. of univs*, 9: 195–225.

McLaughlin, R. E.: Univs, scholasticism and the origins of the German Refn, *Hist. of univs*, 9: 1–42.

Moore, J.: The 2 systems of Francis Hutcheson: On the origins of the Scottish Enlightenment, in *Scott. Enlightenment*: 37–59. (Considers Glasgow curriculum and continental comparisons.)

Pellistrandi, B.: The univ. of Alcalá de Henares from 1568 to 1618: Students and graduates, *Hist. of univs*, 9: 119–65.

Price, D. T. W.: *A history of Saint David's University College Lampeter. 2. 1898–1971*, Cardiff.
Reid, D. M.: *Cairo University and the making of modern Egypt*, Cambridge.
Sher, R. B.: Profs of virtue: The soc. hist. of the Edinburgh moral phil. chair in the 18th cent., in *Scott. Enlightenment*: 87–126.
Ultee, M.: The pols of prof. appoint. at Leiden 1709, *Hist. of univs*, 9: 167–94.
Wood, P. B.: Science and the pursuit of virtue in the Aberdeen Enlightenment, in *Scott. Enlightenment*: 127–49.
Wright, J. P.: Metaphysics and physiology: Mind, body and the animal econ. in 18th-cent. Scotland, in *Scott. Enlightenment*: 251–301. (On the Edinburgh med. schl with some ref. to Leyden.)

Canada

Additions to Earlier Lists

For 1982

Grendler, P. F.: The univ. of Florence and Pisa in the high Renaissance, *Renaissance and Refn*, 6: 158–65.
Tachau, K.: The problem of *Species in medio* at Oxford in the generation after Ockham, *Mediaeval studies*, 44: 394–443.

For 1984

Levitt, C.: *Children of privilege: Student revolt in the 1960s*, Toronto.

France

Additions to Earlier Lists

For 1986

Antier, J.: La bibl. du Coll. de Navarre au 18e s., *Mél. de la Bibl. de la Sorbonne*, 7: 105–24.
Bienvenu, J.-J.: Recherches documentaires, *Annales d'hist. des facs de droit et de la sc. juridique*, 3: 243–8. (Discusses position of facs of law at Lille and Nice in 19th and 20th centuries.)
Demier, F.: Avant-gardes écon. et diffusion de l'écon. pol. en France de 1815 à 1914, *Econs et socs*, 20: 103–42.
Etner, F.: L'enseignement écon. dans les grandes écs au 19e s. en France, *Econs et socs*, 20: 159–74.
Gilles, H.: La fac. de droit de Toulouse au temps de Jean Bodin, *Annales d'hist. des facs de droit et de la sc. juridique*, 3: 23–37.
Hecht, J.: Une héritière des Lumières, de la physiocrat. et de l'idéologie: la première chaire fr. d'écon. pol. 1795, *Econs et socs*, 20: 5–48.
Laissus, Y. and Torlais, J.: *Le Jardin du roi et le Collège royal dans l'enseignement des sciences au 18e siècle*, Paris.

Le Van-Lemesle, L.: De la Soc. d'écon. pol. aux facs de droit: caractères et paradoxes de l'institutionnalisation de l'écon. pol. en France au 19e s., *Econs et socs*, 20: 223–37.

Ribault, J. Y.: Des médecins. 1. Les profs de la fac. de méd. de Bourges au 18e s., *Cahiers d'archéol. et d'hist. du Berry*, 84: 65–6.

Steiner, P.: J.-B. Say et l'enseignement de l'écon. pol. en France 1816–32, *Econs et socs*, 20: 63–95.

Thomann, M.: A l'origine d'une discipline univ.: le complot 'pour l'hist.' à la fac. de droit de Strasbourg au 19e s., in *L'Europe, l'Alsace et la France. . . . Etudes réunies en l'honneur du doyen Georges Livet pour son 70e anniversaire*, Colmar: 39–46.

Tuilier, A.: Un conflit entre un étudiant croate et l'univ. de Paris au 15e s., *Mél. de la Bibl. de la Sorbonne*, 7: 37–104.

Ventre-Denis, M.: La première tentative en France d'un enseignement de l'écon. pol. dans une fac. 1819–22, *Econs et socs*, 20: 97–102.

For 1988

Bompaire-Evesque, C.: *Un débat sur L'Université au temps de la Troisième République: la lutte contre la 'Nouvelle Sorbonne'*, Paris.

Chevalier, B.: La vie dans un coll. parisien au début de la Renaissance. Le coll. de Tours 1463–1541, in *L'intelligence du passé. Les faits, l'écriture et le sens* (*Mélanges J. Lafond*), Tours: 21–32.

Schang, P. and Livat, G.: *Histoire du Gymnase Jean Sturm. Berceau de l'Université de Strasbourg 1538–1988*, Strasbourg.

For 1989

Charle, C. and Telkes, E.: *Les professeurs de la Faculté des sciences de Paris. Dictionnaires biographique 1901–39*, Paris.

Jolly, C. ed.: *La Bibliothèque de la Sorbonne*, Paris. (Considers period 1762 until today.)

Tuilier, A. etc. eds: *L'Université de Paris, La Sorbonne et la Révolution: célébration du Bicentenaire de la Révolution française en Sorbonne, 20 juin—14 juillet 1789*, Paris. (Cat. of an exhibition.)

Vulliez, C.: Les étudiants dans la ville: l'hébergement des *scolares* à Orléans au Bas Moyen Age, in *Villes, bonnes villes, cités et capitales* (*Mélanges B. Chevalier*), Tours: 25–35.

Publications 1990

Calvignac, J.-P.: La bibl. de la Sorbonne et les dons étrangers 1840–1914, *Mél. de la Bibl. de la Sorbonne*, 10: 179–89.

Chedozeau, B.: La fac. de théol. de Paris au 17e s.: un lieu privilégié des conflits entre gallicans et ultramontains 1600–1720, *Mél. de la Bibl. de la Sorbonne*, 10: 39–102.

Devaux, O.: *L'enseignement à Toulouse sous le Consulat et l'Empire*, Toulouse. (Ch. 3 considers the revival of higher education.)

Farge, J. K.: *Registre des procès-verbaux de la Faculté de théologie de Paris 1524–36*, Paris.

Jacq, F.: Göttingen à l'orée du s. Survol de la vie d'une fac. allemande 1890–

1925, *Bull. d'inform. de la Mission hist. Fr. en Allemagne*, 21: 7–53. (Concerns the fac. of sciences.)

Jolly, C.: La bibl. de la Sorbonne de 1762 à 1987, *Mél. de la Bibl. de la Sorbonne*, 10: 152–77.

Ouvarov, P. Y.: L'univ. de Paris et les intérêts locaux à la limite des 14e–15e s.: 'Les états généraux en miniature?' in *Actes du 11e colloque des historiens français et soviétiques (18–21 septembre 1989). 1. L'administration centrale et le pouvoir local en France et en Russe (13e–15e siècle)*, Paris: 137–64.

Verger, J.: Les étudiants méridionaux à Paris au Moyen Age: quelques remarques, *Annales du Midi*, 102: 359–66.

Germany

Additions to Earlier Lists

For 1977

Bellone, E.: Cult. e studi nei progetti di reforma presentati al concilio di Vienne 1311–1312, *Annuarium hist. conciliorum*, 9: 67–111.

Hartmann, F. and Vierhaus, R. eds: *Der Akademiegedanke im 17. und 18. Jahrhundert*, Bremen/Wolfenbüttel.

Liermann, H.: *Die Friedrich—Alexander—Universität Erlangen 1910–20*, Erlangen.

For 1978

Baumann, A.: Die Erneuerung d. Leipziger Burschenschaft nach 1833 im Zusammenspiel von liberalem Bürgertum u. Schülerschaft, *Darstellungen u. Quellen zur Gesch. d. deutschen Einheitsbewegung im 19. u. 20. Jh.*, 10: 105–52.

Baumgart, P.: Die deutsche Univ. d. 16. Jhs. Das Beispiel Marburg, *Hessisches Jb. f. Landesgesch.*, 28: 50–79.

Feige, H.-U.: Zum Beginn der antifaschistisch—demokratischen Erneuerung (April 1945–5.2.1946). Thesis. Leipzig. (Re-opening of univ. of Leipzig.)

Heimpel, H.: Scheltrede eines Prof. d. Bürgerlichen Rechts, d. Kölner Dr legum Iohannes 'vam Hirtze' an Papst Gregor XII. (Brixen, am 11. Nov. 1407), in *Festschrift für Franz Wieacker*, Göttingen: 245–60.

Hentschel, V.: Die Staatswiss. an d. deutschen Univ. im 18. u. frühen 19. Jh., *Ber. zur Wissenschaftsgesch.*, 1: 181–200.

Hömig, H.: Jean Ignace Roderique u. d. Anfänge d. Geschichtswiss. an d. Kölner Univ., *Annalen d. Hist. Vereins f. d. Niederrhein*, 180: 146–68.

Krafft, F.: Der Weg von d. Physiken zur Physik an d. deutschen Univ., *Ber. zur Wissenschaftsgesch.*, 1: 123–62.

Stelzer, W.: Zum Scholarenprivileg Friedrich Barbarossas (Authentica 'Habita'), *Deutsches Archiv zur Erforschung d. Mittelalters*, 34: 123–65.

For 1979

Grau, C. etc.: *Die Berliner Akademie der Wissenschaften in der Zeit des Imperialismus. 3. Die Jahre der faschistischen Diktatur 1933–45*, Berlin.

Kahle, E.: *Hochschulschriften zur Geschichte der Medizin, Pharmazie und Naturwissenschaften der Julius—Maximilians—Universität Würzburg 1865–1970*, Erlangen.

Wendehorst, A.: *Aus der Geschichte der Friedrich—Alexander—Universität*, Erlangen. (F.-A.-U. = univ. of Erlangen.)

For 1980

Giessler-Wirsig, E.: Univ.- u. Hochschulmatrikeln, in W. Ribbe and E. Henning eds: *Taschenbuch für Familiengeschichtsforschung*, Neustadt a. d. A.: 141–80.

Matheus, M.: Das Verhältnis d. Stadt Trier zur Univ. in d. zweiten Hälfte d. 15. Jh., *Kurtrierisches Jb.*, 20: 60–139.

Riesinger, W. and Marquardt-Rabiger, H.: Die Vertretung d. Faches Gesch. an d. Univ. Erlangen von d. Gründung (1743) bis zum Jahre 1933, *Jb. f. fränkische Landesforschung*, 40: 177–249.

Schinkel, E.: Studenten aus Westfalen an d. Univ. in Köln zwischen 1388/89 u. 1559, in *Köln Westfalen 1180–1980. Landesgeschichte zwischen Rhein und Weser 1. Beitrage*, Münster: 377–83.

Weisert, H.: Univ. u. Heiliggeiststift. Die Anfänge d. Heiliggeiststifts zu Heidelberg, *Ruperto Carola*, 32(64): 55–77. (See also under 1981, Weisert.)

For 1981

Corsten, S.: Univ. u. Buchdruck in Köln. Versuch eines Überblicks f. d. 15. Jh., *Wolfenbütteler Abhandlungen zur Renaissanceforschung*, 2: 189–201.

Gaweda, S.: *Die Jagellonische Universität in der Zeit der faschistischen Okkupation 1939–45*. (Trans. by B. Schweinitz), Jena.

Jeudy, C. and Schuba, L.: Erhard Knab u. d. Heidelberger Univ. im Spiegel von Handschriften u. Akteneinträgen, *Quellen u. Forschungen aus it. Archiven u. Biblioth.*, 61: 60–108.

Matheus, M.: Zum Einzugsbereich d. 'alten' Trierer Univ. 1473–77, *Kurtrierisches Jb.*, 21: 55–69.

Schmidt, R.: Kräfte, Personen u. Motive bei d. Gründung d. Univ. Rostock (1419) u. Griefswald (1456), in R. Schmidt ed.: *Beiträge zur pommerschen und mecklenburgischen Geschichte*, Marburg: 1–33.

Weisert, H.: Die ältesten Statuten d. Medizin. Fak. Heidelberg (1425), *Ruperto Carola*, 33(65/66): 57–71.

——— Univ. u. Heiliggeiststift. Die Anfänge d. Heiliggeiststifts zu Heidelberg, *Ruperto Carola*, 33(65/66): 72–87. (See also under 1980, Weisert.)

For 1982

Bräuer, H. etc. eds: *Materialen zur Geschichte der Slavistik in Deutschland*, Berlin. (Considers role of univ. departments.)

525 Jahre Albert-Ludwig-Universität Freiburg im Breisgau, Freiburg.

Sottili, A.: Wege d. Humanismus: Latein. Petrarchismus u. deutsche Studentenschaften it. Renaissance-Univ., in *From Wolfram and Petrarch to Goethe and Grass. Studies in Literature in honour of Leonard Forster*, Baden-Baden: 125–49.

For 1983

Alston, P. L.: The dynamics of educ. expansion in Russia, in K. H. Jarausch ed.: *The transformation of higher learning 1860–1930*, Stuttgart/Chicago (henceforth noted as *Higher learning*): 89–107.

Angelo, R.: The soc. transform. of American higher educ., in *Higher learning*: 261–92.

Brower, D. R.: Soc. stratification in Russian higher educ., in *Higher learning*: 245–60.

Bruch, R. vom: Forschungen u. Arbeiten zur pol. u. soz. Gesch. d. deutschen Bildungsbürgertums im 19. u. frühen 20. Jh. mit besonderer Berücksichtigung d. Hochschullehrerschaft, in *Jahrbuch der historischen Forschung 1982*, Munich etc.: 36–41.

Burke, C. B.: The expansion of American higher educ., in *Higher learning*: 108–30.

Classen, P.: *Studium und Gesellschaft im Mittelalter*, Stuttgart. (Papers ed. by J. Fried after death of P. C. Separate items noted below under *S.u.G.*)

——— Die ältesten Universitätsref. u. Universitätsgründungen d. Mittelalters, in *S.u.G.*: 170–96.

——— Die Hohen Schulen u. d. Gesellschaft im 12. Jh., in *S.u.G.*: 1–26.

——— Die königlichen Richter d. Common Law: Rechtswiss. u. Rechtsstudium ohne Univ., in *S.u.G.*: 197–237.

——— *Libertas scolastica*-Scholarenprivilegien—Acad. Freiheit im Mittelalter, in *S.u.G.*: 238–84.

——— Richterstand u. Rechtswiss. in it. Kommunen d. 12. Jhs., in *S.u.G.*: 27–126. (Considers univ. teaching of law in Italy.)

——— Rom u. Paris: Kurie u. Univ. im 12.u.13. Jh., in *S.u.G.*: 127–69.

——— Zur Bedeutung d. mittelalterlichen Univ., in *S.u.G.*: 285–92.

Craig, J. E.: Higher educ. and soc. mobility in Germany, in *Higher learning*: 219–44.

Engel, A.: The Eng. univs and professional educ., in *Higher learning*: 293–305.

Heinemann, M. and Schneider, U.: Akten zur Gesch. d. Hochschulwesens in Westdeutschland nach 1945. Eine quellenkundliche Übersicht, *Bildung u. Erziehung*, 36: 77–89.

Herbst, J.: Diversification in American higher educ., in *Higher learning*: 196–206.

Jarausch, K. H.: Higher educ. and soc. change: some comparative perspectives, in *Higher learning*: 9–36.

Kiene, M.: Die Grundlagen d. europ. Universitätsbaukunst, *Z. f. Kunstgesch.*, 46: 63–114.

Light, D. W.: The devel. of professional schls in America, in *Higher learning*: 345–66.

Lowe, R.: The expansion of higher educ. in England, in *Higher learning*: 37–56.
Lundgreen, P.: Differentiation in German higher educ., in *Higher learning*: 149–79.
McClelland, C. E.: Professionalization and higher educ. in Germany, in *Higher learning*: 306–20.
McClelland, J.: Diversification in Russian-Soviet educ. in *Higher learning*: 180–95.
Mertens, D.: Die Anfänge d. Univ. Freiburg, *Z.f. Gesch. d. Oberrheins*, 131: 289–308.
Rothblatt, S.: The diversification of higher educ. in England, in *Higher learning*: 131–48.
Thielbeer, H.: *Universität und Politik in der deutschen Revolution von 1848*, Bonn.
Timberlake, C. E.: Higher learning, the state and the professions in Russia, in *Higher learning*: 321–44.
Titze, H.: Enrollment, expansion and acad. overcrowding in Germany, in *Higher learning*: 57–88.

For 1984

Finkenstaedt, T.: Humboldts Erben. Zu Gesch. u. Struktur d. deutschen Univ., *Mitt. d. Hochschulverbandes*, 32: 311–19.
Fries, A.: Hat Albertus Magnus in Paris studiert? *Theol. u. Philos.*, 59: 414–29.
Kundert, W.: *Katalog der Helmstedter juristischen Disputationen. Programme und Reden 1574–1810*, Wiesbaden.
Müller, R. A.: Gymnasial- u. Hochschulwesen d. frühen Neuzeit in personalgesch. Sicht. Forschungsstand–Methodische Probleme–Quellen, in R. Lenz ed.: *Leichenpredigten als Quelle historischer Wissenschaften*, Marburg: 125–38.
Oexle, O. G.: Alteurop. Voraussetzungen d. Bildungsbürgertums: Univ., Gelehrte u. Studierte, in W. Conze and J. Kocka eds: *Bildungsbürgertum im 19. Jahrhundert. 1. Bildungssystem und Professionalisierung*, Stuttgart: 29–78.
Quarg, G.: *Universitäts- und Stadtbibliothek Köln. 200 Jahre Kölner Vorlesungsverzeichnisse*, Cologne. (Cat. of an exhibition.)
Toellner, R.: Die medizin. Fak. unter d. Einfluss d. Ref., in A. Buck ed.: *Renaissance-Reformation. Gegensätze und Gemeinsamkeiten*, Wiesbaden: 287–97.

For 1985

Berliner Historiker. Die neuere deutsche Geschichte in Forschung und Lehre an der Berliner Universität, Berlin.
Die Afrika-, Nahost- und Asienwissenschaften in Leipzig, Leipzig.
Gaukel, K.: Die Haltung der Studenten der Universität Leipzig zur Arbeiterbewegung in der Zeit des Sozialistengesetzes 1878–90. Thesis. Berlin.
Hardtwig, W.: Krise d. Univ., student. Reformbewegung (1750–1819) u. d.

Sozialisation d. jugend. deutschen Bildungsschicht. Aufriss eines Forschungsproblems, *Gesch. u. Gesellschaft*, 11: 155–76.

Lorenz, S.: 'Libri ordinarie legendi'. Eine Skizze zum Lehrplan d. mitteleurop. Artistenfak. um d. Wende vom 14. zum 15. Jh., in W. Hogrebe ed.: *Argumente und Zeugnisse*, Frankfurt a. M./Berne/New York: 204–58.

Maier, H.: *Politik und Rechtswissenschaft an den deutschen Universitäten*, Passau.

Quarg, G.: Dummer Mensch u. Tölpel. Eine Kölner Vorlesungsübersicht von 1791, *Jb. d. Kölnischen Geschichtsvereins*, 56: 195–8.

Schneider, U.: Berlin, d. Kalte Krieg u. d. Gründung d. Freien Univ. 1945–49, *Jb. f. d. Gesch. Mittel- u. Ostdeutschlands*, 34: 37–95.

For 1986

Belloni, A.: *Professori giuristi a Padova nel secolo 15. Profili bio-bibliografici e cattedre*, Frankfurt a. M.

Die Universität zu Prag, Munich.

Döring, D.: Die Bestandsentwicklung der Bibliothek der Phil. Fakultät der Universität Leipzig von ihren Anfängen bis zur Mitte des 16. Jh. Ein Beitrag zur Wissenschaftsgeschichte der Leipziger Universität in ihrer vorreformatorischen Zeit. Thesis. Leipzig.

Gantzl, K. J. ed.: *Wissenschaftliche Verantwortung und politische Macht. Zur Entwicklung des Instituts für Auswärtige Politik (Hamburg) 1923–45*, Berlin.

Heydemann, G.: Der Attentäter Karl Ludwig Sand. 20 Briefe u. Dok. aus d. Erlanger u. Jenaer Studienjahren, *Darstellungen u. Quellen zur Gesch. d. deutschen Einheitsbewegung im 19. u. 20. Jh.*, 12: 7–77.

Kahle, E.: *Bibliographie der Hochschulschriften zur Geschichte der Medizin, Pharmazie und Naturwissenschaften der Universität Breslau 1811–1945*, Erlangen.

Kunitzsch, P.: *Peter Apian und Azophi: Arabische Sternbilder in Ingolstadt im frühen 16. Jahrhundert*, Munich.

Meyer-Bahlburg, H. and Wolff, E.: *Afrikanische Sprachen in Forschung und Lehre. 75 Jahre Afrikanistik in Hamburg 1909–84*, Berlin.

Müller, R. A.: Die Univ.—eine 'soz. Erfindung' d. Scholastik, *Mitt. d. Hochschulverbandes*, 5: 272–3.

Namhafte Hochschullehrer der Karl-Marx-Universität Leipzig. 7, Leipzig.

Oehler, J.: Der akademische Austausch zwischen Köln und England/Schottland zur Zeit der ersten Kölner Universität. Thesis. Cologne.

Schroeder, H.-D.: *Das Hauptgebäude der Ernst-Moritz-Arndt-Universität Griefswald*, Leipzig.

Seebass, G.: Heidelberg-Universitätsgründung im Spannungsfeld d. Spätmittelalters, *Ruperto Carola*, 74: 15–21.

Tewes, G.-R.: Die Studentenburse d. Mag. Nikolaus Mommer von Raemsdonck. Ein Konflikt zwischen Rat u. Univ. im Spätmittelalter, *Gesch. in Köln*, 20: 31–66.

Wolgast, E.: *Die Universität Heidelberg 1386–1986*, Heidelberg.

Zur Geschichte der ökonomischen Lehre und Forschung an der Berliner Universität von 1810 bis 1945, Berlin.

For 1987

Czok, K.: *Wissenschafts- und Universitätsgeschichte in Sachsen im 18. und 19. Jahrhundert: nationale und internationale Wechselwirkung und Ausstrahlung*, Berlin.

Feenstra, R.: Die Leydener jurist. Fak. im 17. u 18. Jh. Einige neuere Forschungsergebnisse, *Leipziger Beitr. zur Universitätsgesch.* 1: 43–53.

Fläschendräger, W.: 'Dass eine Universitätsgesch. in Zukunft noch herausgegeben werde'. Gescheiterte Bemühungen um eine Gesch. d. Alma mater Lipsiensis zur 500—Jahr—Feier 1909, *Leipziger Beitr. zur Universitätsgesch.*, 1: 15–30.

——— 'Do mythe d. univ. gemehrt u. gebessert solde werden', *Beitr. zur Hochschul- u. Wissenschaftsgesch. Erfurts*, 21: 53–62. (Luther's view on ref. of univ. of Leipzig.)

——— Lomonossows Marburger Lehrer Christian Wolff u. seine Beziehungen zur Univ. Leipzig, *Leipziger Beitr. zur Universitätsgesch.*, 1: 54–61.

Gaukel, K.: Der Student Walther May 1868–1926. Eine biograph. Skizze, *Leipziger Beitr. zur Universitätsgesch.*, 1: 66–74.

Hammerstein, N.: Schule, Hochschule u. Res publica litteraria, in *Res publica litteraria. Die Institutionen der Gelehrsamkeit in der frühen Neuzeit*, Wolfenbüttel: 93–110.

Hoyer, S.: Gedanken zur weiteren Erforschung d. Gesch. d. Karl-Marx-Univ. Leipzig, *Leipziger Beitr. zur Universitätsgesch.*, 1: 5–14.

Kanthak, G.: *Der Akademiegedanke zwischen utopischem Entwurf und barocker Projektmacherei*, Berlin.

Katsch, G.: 30 Jahre Universitätszeitung d. Karl-Marx-Univ. Leipzig-Gedanken über ihre Gesch. u. deren Erforschung, *Leipziger Beitr. zur Universitätsgesch.*, 1: 83–92.

——— and Schwendler, G.: Der Marxist Alfons Goldschmidt als Lehrbeauftragter an d. Leipziger Univ. nach bisher unbekannten Dok. aus Universitätsarchiv u. -bibliothek, *Leipziger Beitr. zur Universitätsgesch.*, 1: 75–82.

Miethke, J.: Marsilius von Inghen als Rektor d. Univ. Heidelberg, *Ruperto Carola*, 76: 110–20.

Oberkofler, G. and Rabofsky, E.: Juristen-Romanistik im NS-Staat, in H. Hürz ed.: *Pflicht der Vernunft für Manfred Buhr*, Berlin: 44–61.

Salve Academicum. *Festschrift der Stadt Schweinfurt anlässlich des 300. Jahrestages der Privilegierung der Deutschen Akademie der Naturforscher Leopoldina durch Kaiser Leopold I*, Schweinfurt.

Steiger, G. and Ludwig, H.-J.: Gaudeamus igitur. *Lasst uns fröhlich sein. Historische Studentenlieder*, Leipzig.

Steinmetz, M.: Müntzer u. Leipzig, *Leipziger Beitr. zur Universitätsgesch.*, 1: 31–42.

Wolgast, E. ed.: *Die Sechshundertjahrfeier der Ruprecht-Karls-Universität Heidelberg. Eine Dokumentation*, Heidelberg.

For 1988

Biskup, M.: Die Bedeutung d. Leipziger Univ. f. d. intellekt. Leben d. polnischen Staates im 15. bis zur Mitte d. 16. Jhs., *Leipziger Beitr. zur Universitätsgesch.*, 2: 5–16.

Dix, R.: Frühgeschichte der Prager Universität. Graduierung, Aufbau und Organisation 1348–1409. Thesis. Bonn.

Döring, D.: Die Leipziger Univ. in d. Zeit d. Vormärz im Spiegel d. Akten d. Rektorats von Moritz Wilhelm Drobisch 1840–41, *Leipziger Beitr. zur Universitätsgesch.*, 2: 27–36.

Feige, H.-U.: Zur Traditionspflege am Franz-Mehring-Instit. (Leipzig) 1948–86, *Leipziger Beitr. zur Universitätsgesch.*, 2: 69–77.

Gaukel, K.: Die Studentensektion d. Sozialdemokratischen Arbeiterpartei in Leipzig, *Leipziger Beitr. zur Universitätsgesch.*, 2: 37–48.

Häfele, R.: *Die Studenten der Städte Nördlingen, Kitzingen, Mindelheim und Wunsiedel bis 1580. Studium, Berufe und soziale Herkunft*, Trier.

Hanslick, J. A.: *Geschichte und Beschreibung der Prager Universitätsbibliothek*, Aalen.

Henning, E. and Kazemi, M.: *Chronik der Kaiser-Wilhelm-Gesellschaft zur Förderung der Wissenschaften*, Berlin.

Katsch, G.: Zur Vorgesch. d. Instit. f. Deutsche Gesch. an d. Karl-Marx-Univ. Leipzig u. zu d. Voraussetzungen seiner Gründung, *Leipziger Beitr. zur Universitätsgesch.*, 2: 78–92.

Klimt, U. P.: *Max Hofmeier. Leben und Werk*, Würzburg. (M.H. (ob. 1927) prof. of med. at Giessen and Würzburg.)

Krammer, O.: *Bildungswesen und Gegenreformation. Die Hohen Schulen der Jesuiten im katholischen Teil Deutschlands vom 16. bis zum 18. Jahrhundert*, Würzburg.

Miethke, J.: Die Welt d. Prof. u. Studenten an d. Wende vom Mittelalter zur Neuzeit, in K. Andermann ed.: *Historiographie am Oberrhein im späten Mittelalter und in der frühen Neuzeit*, Sigmaringen: 11–33.

Szeskus, R.: Bach u. d. Leipziger Universitätsmusik, *Leipziger Beitr. zur Universitätsgesch.*, 2: 17–26.

For 1989

Binder, D. A.: *Politischer Katholizismus und Katholisches Verbandswesen. Am Beispiel des Kartellverbandes der Katholischen nichtfarbentragenden Studentenverbindungen Österreichs*, Schernfeld.

Bussche, H. van den: *Im Dienste der 'Volksgemeinschaft': Studienreform im Nationalsozialismus am Beispiel der ärztlichen Ausbildung*, Berlin/Hamburg.

——— ed.: *Medizinische Wissenschaft im 'Dritten Reich'. Kontinuität, Anpassung und Opposition an der Hamburger Medizinischen Fakultät*, Berlin/Hamburg.

Calder III, W. M. and Kosenina, A. eds: *Berufungspolitik innerhalb der Altertumswissenschaft im wilhelminischen Preussen. Die Briefe Ulrich von Wilamowitz-Moellendorffs an Friedrich Althoff 1883–1908,* Frankfurt a. M.

Gröger, J.: *Schlesische Priester auf deutschen Universitätslehrstühlen seit 1945*, Sigmaringen.

Hudemann, R. and Heinen, A. eds: *Universität des Saarlandes 1948–88*, Saarbrücken.

Jeismann, K. E.: *Bildung, Staat, Gesellschaft im 19. Jahrhundert. Mobilisierung und Disziplinierung*, Stuttgart.

Kamp, N. and Levi, A.: *Exodus professorum. Akademische Feier zur Enthüllung einer Ehrentafel für die zwischen 1933 und 1945 entlassenen und vertriebenen Professoren und Dozenten der Georgia Augusta am 18. April 1989*, Göttingen. (Prints essays and documents.)

Kiene, M.: Die it. Universitätspaläste d. 17. u 18. Jh., *Römisches Jb. f. Kunstgesch.*, 25: 329–80.

Klose, W. ed.: *Stammbücher des 16. Jahrhunderts*, Munich. (Considers many univ. students.)

Koolmann, E.: *Die Kollegnachschriften der Landesbibliothek Oldenburg*, Oldenburg.

Meyer, G.: *Zu den Anfängen der Strassburger Universität. Neue Forschungsergebnisse zur Herkunft der Studentenschaft und zur verlorenen Matrikel*, Hildesheim etc.

Schiesser, M.: *Alois Geigel (1829–87). Leben und Werk*, Würzburg. (A.G. prof. of med. at Würzburg.)

Schindling, A.: Die kath. Bildungsref. zwischen Humanismus u. Barock. Dillingen, Dole, Freiburg, Molsheim u. Salzburg. Die Vorlande u. d. benachbarten Univ., in H. Maer and V. Press eds: *Vorderösterreich in der frühen Neuzeit*, Sigmaringen: 137–76.

Steiner, J.: *Die Artistenfakultät der Universität Mainz 1477–1562. Ein Beitrag zur vergleichenden Universitätsgeschichte*, Stuttgart.

Publications 1990

Barmann, J.: *Zur Geschichte des Mainzer Universitäts-Fonds 1781–1822. Ein Archiv-Bericht. 1. Text. 2. Anlagen zu Band 1*, Stuttgart.

Blättermann, P.: *Die Universitätspolitik August des Starken 1694–1733*, Cologne/Vienna.

Broser, W.: *Chemie an der Freien Universität Berlin. Eine Dokumentation*, Berlin.

Bruch, R. vom and Müller, R. A. eds: *Formen ausserstaatlicher Wissenschaftsförderung im 19. and 20. Jahrhundert. Deutschland im europäischen Vergleich*, Stuttgart.

Conrady, K. O.: *Völkisch-nationale Germanistik in Köln. Eine unfestliche Erinnerung*, Schernfeld.

Eisenmann, P. and Schmirber, G. eds: *Deutsche Hochschulen und Europa. Das Zusammenwachsen der deutschen Hochschulen im Rahmen der europäischen Einigung*, Regensburg.

Fischer, H.: *Völkerkunde im Nationalsozialismus. Aspekte der Anpassung, Affinität und Behauptung einer wissenschaftlichen Disziplin*, Berlin/Hamburg.

Fleckenstein, J. etc.: *In memoriam Hermann Heimpel. Gedenkfeier am 23.*

Juni 1989 in der Aula der Georg-August-Universität, Göttingen. (Prints also speech of H.H. of 1953.)

Golücke, F.: *Lebensbilder aus der Würzburger Studentenschaft*, Schernfeld.

Heinen, E.: Aspekte d. Gesch. d. Erziehungswiss. Fak. d. Univ. zu Köln, in C. A. Lückerath ed.: *Von den Generalstudien zur spezialisierten Universität*, Cologne (henceforth noted as *Von d. Generalstudien*): 73–94.

Henning, F.-W.: *Handelsakademie—Handelshochschule—Wirtschafts- und Sozialwissenschaftliche Fakultät. Der Weg von der Handelsakademie und Handlungswissenschaft des 18. Jahrhunderts zur Wirtschafts- und Sozialwissenschaftlichen Fakultät und Betriebslehre des 20. Jahrhunderts*, Cologne/Vienna.

Krokotsch, B.: *Tierhaltung und Veterinärmedizin im Berlin des 19. und 20. Jahrhunderts*, Berlin.

Krönig, W. and Müller, K. D.: *Nachkriegssemester. Studium in Kriegs- und Nachkriegszeit*, Stuttgart.

Miethke, J.: *Die mittelalterlichen Universitäten und das gesprochene Wort*, Munich.

Mildner-Mazzei, S. and Tröhler, U.: *Die Göttinger Medizinischen Promotionen im 18. Jahrhundert*, Göttingen.

Mühlberger, K. and Schuster, W. eds: *Die Matrikel der Universität Wien. 6. 1689/90–1714/15*, Cologne/Vienna.

Müller, R. A.: *Geschichte der Universität. Von der mittelalterlichen Universitas zur deutschen Hochschule*, Munich.

——— Kirche, Orden u. Univ. im späten Mittelalter, in *Von d. Generalstudien*: 3–28.

Oberkofler, G. and Rabofsky, E.: *Wissenschaft in Österreich 1945–60. Beiträge zu ihren Problemen*, Frankfurt/Berne/New York/Paris.

Rössler, M.: *Wissenschaft und Lebensraum. Geographische Ostforschung im Nationalsozialismus. Ein Beitrag zur Disziplingeschichte der Geographie*, Berlin.

Rotta, J. C.: *Die Aerodynamische Versuchsanstalt in Göttingen–ein Werk Ludwig Prandtls. Ihre Geschichte von den Anfängen bis 1925*, Göttingen.

Scheler, M. ed.: *Berliner Anglistik in Vergangenheit und Gegenwart 1810–1985*, Berlin.

Schindling, A.: Univ. im 16. u. 17. Jh. Bildungsexpansion, Laienbildung u. Konfessionalisierung nach d. Ref., in *Von d. Generalstudien*: 29–52.

Studier, M.: *Der Corpsstudent als Idealbild der Wilhelminischen Ära*, Schernfeld.

Titze, H.: *Der Akademikerzyklus. Historische Untersuchungen über die strukturellen Bedingungen und sozialen Mechanismen der periodischen Wiederkehr von Überfüllung und Mangel in akademischen Karrieren*, Göttingen.

Trabant, J.: *Beiträge zur Geschichte der romanischen Philologie in Berlin*, Berlin.

Vierhaus, R. and Brocke, B. vom eds: *Forschung im Spannungsfeld von Politik und Gesellschaft. Geschichte und Struktur der Kaiser-Wilhelm/Max-Planck-Gesellschaft*, Stuttgart.

Wagner, A.: *Forschungstransfer klassischer Universitäten*, Tübingen.
Windolf, P.: *Die Expansion der Universitäten 1870–1985. Ein internationaler Vergleich*, Stuttgart.
Wolff, K.: Univ. Bayreuth. Universitätsgründungen nach 1945—Beispiel Univ. Bayreuth, in *Von d. Generalstudien*: 53–71.

No date
Hahmann, W.: *Wie die Technische Universität Berlin entstand. Chronik der Zeit vom 2. Mai 1945 bis zum 9. April 1946*, Berlin.

Hungary

Additions to Earlier Lists

For 1986
Fehér, G.: A hohenheimi mezőgazdasági akad. magyar hallgatói 1818–93. Sorsok, életpályák (Hungarian students of the Agricult. Acad. of Hohenheim: their careers), in *Magyar Mezőgazdasági Múzeum Közleményei 1984–85*: 537–67.

For 1987
Cach, J.: The work of the first profs of philos. of the Charles Univ. in Prague, in S. Komlósi ed.: *History of international relations in education. Conference papers for the 9th session of the International Standing Conference for the History of Education. Pécs. 31 August–3 September 1987*. 3 vols, Pécs (henceforth noted as *International relations*). 1: 84–95.
Carpenter, P.: Kurt Hahn and the scholarships to Cambridge Univ., in *International relations*. 1: 105–16.
Giles, G.: 'Oxbridge in jackboots?' The attraction of Oxford and Cambridge for univ. reformers in Nat. Soc. Germany, in *International relations*. 1: 192–201.
Jones, D. R.: Transporting the univ.: the transmission of heritage and habits, in *International relations*. 1: 343–9.
Lowe, R.: Europ. influences on American univ. planning: the case of Berkeley, in *International relations*. 2: 70–81.
Lüth, C.: The impact of the American higher educ. system on the concept of a 'Gesamthochschule' in the Fed. Repub. of Germany, in *International relations*. 2: 81–91.
Meek, L.: The transportation of higher educ.: brief notes from Melanasia, in *International relations*. 2: 91–101.

For 1988
Herner, J. ed.: *Batthyány Kristóf európai utazása 1657–58* (K.B.'s travels in Europe 1657–58), Szeged. (Notes his visit to various universities.)
——— ed.: *Széchenyi Zsigmond itálai körútja 1699–1700* (Z.S.'s tour of Italy 1600–1700), Szeged. (Notes his visit to various universities.)

For 1989

Bank, J.: Kinek a Jogán tanitanak a hittudományi karokon a professzorok? (By whose authority do the profs of the fac. of theol. lecture?), in A. Uzsoki ed.: *Magyar Egyháztörténeti Vázlatok*, Budapest (henceforth noted as *Egyháztörténeti*). 1: 177–94.

Herner, J. ed.: *Kérészi István omniáriuma* (I.K.'s diary), Szeged. (Notes his visit to various universities.)

Keserű, B. ed: *Teleki Pál külföldi tanulmányútja. Levelek, számadások, iratok 1695–1700* (P.T.'s study-tour abroad. Letters, statements, documents 1695–1700), Szeged. (Notes his visit to various universities.)

——— ed.: *A Thurzó-család és a wittenbergi egyetem. Dokumentumok és a rektor Thurzó Imre írásai 1602–24* (The T. family and the univ of W. Documents and papers of I.T. rect. of the univ.), Szeged.

Mészáros, I.: A magyarországi római katolikus tanügyigazgatás torténeti áttekintése (Hist. survey of the Roman Cath. educ. admin. in Hungary), in *Egyháztörténeti*, 1: 221–56.

Ujváry, G.: Egyetemi ifjuság és katolicizmus a neobarohk társadalomban (Univ. youth and Cath. in neobaroque soc.), *Levéltari Szemle*, 4: 51–63.

'Vitéz-e avagy ájtatos?' I. Batthyány Ádám sajátkezű bűnlajstroma s némely fontos kicsiseg (Valorous or devout? A.B.'s record of his travels), Szeged.

Publications 1990

Barabás, B. and Joó, R. eds: *A Kolozsvári magyar egyetem 1945-ben. A Bolyai Egyetem szervezésének válogatott dokumentumai* (The Hungarian univ. of K. in 1945. Selected docs on the organis. of B. univ.), Budapest.

Judit, B.: *Magántanárok a pesti egyetemen 1848–1952* (Privatdozent at Budapest Univ. 1848–1952), Budapest.

Szögi, L.: Katolikus egyetemalapítási törekvések Magyarországon (Attempts to found Cath. univs), *Vigilia*, 5: 328–36.

——— ed.: *Az Eötvös Loránd Tudományegyetem Jubileumi emlékkönyve 1635–1985* (The Jubilee Album of the L.E. univ. 1635–1985), Budapest.

Zsoldos, A. ed.: *Matricula Universitatis Tyrnaviensis 1635–1701*, Budapest.

Italy

Additions to Earlier Lists

For 1978

Ashworth, E. J.: A note on Paul of Venice and the Oxford Logica of 1483, *Medioevo*, 4: 93–9.

For 1982

Dumoulin, M.: Hommes et cultures dans les relations Italo-Belges 1861–1915, *Bull. de l'instit. hist. Belge de Rome*, 52: 271–567. (Inform. about academics.)

Field, A.: The inaugural oration of Cristofero Landino in praise of Virgil, *Rinascimento*, 21 (1981): 235–45. (Inform. about univ. of Florence in 15th century.)

Maierù, A. ed.: *English logic in Italy in the 14th and 15th centuries*, Naples. (Several essays on connections between Eng. and Ital. universities.)

Tamba, G.: In margine all'ed. del 14 vol. del *Chartularium Studii Bononiensis, Atti e memorie della Deputazione di storia patria per le prov. di Romagna*, 33: 151–68.

For 1983

Movia, G.: Struttura logica e consapevolezza epistemologica in alcuni trattatisti padovani di med. del sec. 15, in A. Poppi ed.: *Scienza e filosofia all'Università di Padova nel Quattrocento*, Trieste/Padua (henceforth noted as *S.F.*): 375–94.

Schmitt, C. D.: Aristotelian textual studies at Padua: the case of Francesco Cavalli, in *S.F.*: 287–314.

Zanier, G.: Ricerche sull' occultismo a Padova nel sec. 15, in *S.F.*: 345–72.

For 1984

Montecchi, G.: Le antiche sedi univ., in O. Capitani etc. eds: *Le sedi della cultura nell'Emilia Romagna*, Milan: 117–29.

For 1985

Ciliberto, M.: Giordano Bruno 1582–83. Da Parigi a Oxford, *Studi storici*, 26: 127–60.

Classen, P.: Ital. Rechtsschulen ausserhalb Bolognas, in S. Kuttner and K. Pennington eds: *Proceedings of the 6th International Congress of Medieval Canon Law, Berkeley, California 28 July–2 August 1980*, Vatican City (henceforth noted as *Proceedings, Berkeley*): 205–21.

Herberger, M.: Dialettica e giurisprud. all'Univ, di Padova nel Cinquecento, in K. Nehlsen von Stryk and D. Nörr eds: *Diritto comune, diritto commerciale, diritto veneziano*, Venice: 141–54.

Piergiovanni, V.: Il primo sec. della scl. can. di Bologna, in *Proceedings, Berkeley*: 241–56. (Also pub. in *Annali della fac. di giurisprud. di Genova*, 20 (1984–85): 174–92.)

For 1986

Gehler, M.: Studentenischer Antisemitismus an d. Univ. Innsbruck, in *Die Geschichte der Juden in Tirol. Von den Anfängen im Mittelalter bis in die neueste Zeit*, Bolzano: 73–87.

Grumo, R.: La 'questione scol.' in Puglia e Basilicata in età giolittiana. Un' analisi della stampa soc., *Annali del dipart. di scienze storiche e soc.-Univ. di Lecce*, 4 (1985): 407–66.

Piana, C.: Postille al Chartularium Studii Bononiensis S. Francisci, *Arch. franciscanum hist.*, 79: 78–141, 449–99.

Tomasini, I. P.: *Gymnasium patavinum*, Bologna.

For 1987

Cecchi, D.: Il liceo napoleonico del Dipart. del Musone 1808–1815, *Riv. di storia del diritto ital.*, 60: 139–78. (Also published in *Studi in memoria di Mario E. Viora*, Rome, 1990: 199–238.)

Festorazzi, L.: Proposta di una Scl. Normale a Chiavenna nel 1797, *Clavenna*, 26: 203–9.

Greci, R.: Note sul commercio del libro univ. a Bologna nel Due e Trecento, *Studi di storia medievale e di diplom.*, 9: 49–97.

Rizzo, M.: L'univ. di Pavia tra potere centrale e comunità locale nella seconda metà del Cinquecento, *Boll. della soc. pavese di storia patria*, 39: 65–125.

Salandin, G. A. and Pancino, M.: *Il 'teatro' di filosofia sperimentale di Giovanni Poleni*, Trieste/Padua. (G.P. of univ. of Padua.)

Zen Benetti, F. ed.: *Acta graduum academicorum gymnasii patavini ab anno 1601 ad annum 1605*, Padua.

For 1988

Baldini, U.: La teoria della spiegazione scientifica a Bologna e a Padova 1680–1730: influenze e differenze, in L. Rossetti ed.: *Rapporti tra le Università di Padova e Bologna. Ricerche di filosofia medicina e scienza*, Trieste/Padua (henceforth noted as *Rapporti*): 191–254.

Del Negro, P.: 'L'univ. della ragione spregiudicate, della libertà e del patriotismo'. Melchiorre Cesarotti e il progetto di riforma dell'Univ. di Padova del 1797, in *Rapporti*: 375–402.

Feenstra, R.: Les juristes de l'ancienne Univ. de Franeker et leurs recueils de *disputationes* (période de 1635 à 1735), *Studi senesi*, 100, suppl. 2: 604–29. (Also pub. in *Estudios jurídicos en homenaje al maestro Guillermo Floris Margadant*, Mexico, 1988: 137–53.)

Intini, V.: Un' istit. educ. nella storia cittadina: il Seminario di Monopoli nei sec. 17 e 18, *Monopoli nel suo passato*, 4: 233–60.

La fondazione fridericiana dell'Università di Napoli, Naples. (Reprint of essays by Torraca and Arnaldi, with ed. of docs by Marti.)

Maierù, A.: L'insegnamento della logica a Bologna nel sec. 14 e il MS antoniano 391, in *Rapporti*: 1–24.

Malagola, C.: 'I rettori dell'Univ. di Bologna': rivisto e accresciuto da G. P. Brizzi, *Annuario dell'anno accad. 1987–88*, 1: 7–75.

Ongaro, G.: Morgagni a Bologna, in *Rapporti*: 255–306.

Piovan, F.: *Per la biografia di Lazzaro Bonamico. Ricerche sul periodo dell'insegnamento padovano 1530–52*, Trieste/Padua.

Poppi, A.: Il prevalere della 'vita activa' nella paideia del Cinquecento, in *Rapporti*: 97–125.

Powitz, G.: 'Modus scolipetarum et reportistarum'. Pronunciatio and 15th-cent.-univ. hands, *Scrittura e civiltà*, 12: 201–11.

Premuda, L.: Sul flusso reciproco di insegnanti tra lo Studio med. di Bologna e di Padova dopo l'unità nazionale, in *Rapporti*: 403–16.

Riondato, E.: Giudizi di G. Zabarella su maestri dell'Ateneo bolognese: P. Pomponazzi, L. Boccadiferro, A. Achillini, in *Rapporti*: 71–96.

Rosino, L.: Geminiano Montanari astronomo della seconda metà del Seicento a Bologna e a Padova, in *Rapporti*: 173–89.

Rossetti, L. ed.: *Rapporti tra le Università di Padova e Bologna. Ricerche di filosofia medicina e scienza*, Trieste/Padua. (Relevant items noted separately.)

Seneco, F.: Un fallito tentativo di Girolamo Mercuriale di tornare nell' Ateneo patavino, in *Rapporti*: 161–72.

Soppelsa, M. L.: Gli scienziati veneti e l'Istit. delle Scienze di Bologna, in *Rapporti*: 325–73.

Zutshi, P. N. R.: Some uned. papal docs relating to the Univ. of Cambridge in the 14th cent., *Archivum hist. pontificiae*, 26: 393–409.

For 1989

Bellomo, M.: Scuole giuridiche e univ. studentesche in Italia, in L. Gargan and O. Limone eds: *Luoghi e metodi di insegnamento nell'Italia medioevale (secoli 12–14)*, Galatina (henceforth noted as *Luoghi e metodi*): 121–40.

Belloni, A.: Iohannes Heller e i suoi libri di testo: uno studente tedesco a Padova nel Quattrocento tra insegnamento giuridico ufficiale e 'natio theutonica', *Quad per la storia dell' Univ. di Padova* (=*Q.U.P.*), 20 (1987): 51–100.

——— L'insegnamento giuridico nelle univ. ital., in *Luoghi e metodi*: 141–52.

Bucci, O.: Gli studi giuridici nello *Studium Curiae* dal trasferimento all' Apollinare fino alla Accad. delle conferenze storico-giuridiche, in A. Ciani and G. Diurni eds: *'Lex et Iustitia' nell'utrumque ius: radici antiche e prospettive attuali*, Rome: 147–98.

Cherubini, P. ed.: *Roma e lo Studium Urbis. Spazio urbano e cultura dal quattro al seicento*, Rome. (Cat. of an exhibition.)

Colao, F.: 'La ragione non conviene a quant'altri che non la giurisprud.' Alcune idee sul diritto naturale nella Siena del 18 sec., *Studi senesi*, 91: 361–406.

Cremascoli, G.: La fac. di teol., in *Luoghi e metodi*: 179–200.

Dolezalek, G.: La pecia e la preparazione dei libri giuridici nei sec. 12–13, in *Luoghi e metodi*: 201–17.

Frova, C.: Città e 'studium' a Vercelli (sec. 12 e 13), in *Luoghi e metodi*: 83–99.

Gallo, D.: Lauree ined. in diritto civ. e can. conferite presso lo Studio di Padova 1419–22, 1423, 1424, 1428, *Q.U.P.*, 20(1987): 1–50.

Garfagnini, G. C.: Città e studio a Firenze nel 14 sec.: una difficile convivenza, in *Luoghi e metodi*: 101–20.

Gargan, L.: Libri, librerie e bibl. nelle univ. ital. del Due e Trecento, in *Luoghi e metodi*: 219–46.

——— and Limone, O. eds: *Luoghi e metodi di insegnamento nell'Italia medioevale (secoli 12–14)*, Galatina. (Relevant items noted separately.)

Geld, P. F.: Latin readers in 14th-cent. Florence. Schoolkids and their books, *Scrittura e civiltà*, 13: 387–440.

Grossato, E.: Ancora sugli allievi dell'Univ. di Padova appartenenti ai Mille, *Q.U.P.*, 20(1987): 137–43.
Maierù, A.: Gli atti scol. nelle univ. ital., in *Luoghi e metodi*: 247–87.
Manno Tolu, R.: *Scolari italiani nello Studio Parigi. Il 'Collège des Lombards' dal 14 al 16 secole ed i suoi ospiti Pistoiesi*, Rome.
Montironi, A. ed.: *Università di Macerata 1290–1990*, Jesi.
Nardo, D.: Giovanni Antonio Volpi fil., latinista, edit. 1686–1766, *Q.U.P.*, 20(1987): 101–15. (G.A.V. prof. at univ. of Padua.)
Paravicini Bagliani, A.: La fondazione dello 'Studium Curiae': una rilettura critica, in *Luoghi e metodi*: 57–81.
Pesenti, T.: Arti e med.: la formazione del curriculum med., in *Luoghi e metodi*: 153–77.
——— La med. scol. padovana in alcuni studi recenti, *Q.U.P.*, 20 (1987): 151–66.
Piovan, F.: Gli studi padovani di Bartolomeo Panciatichi, *Q.U.P.*, 20(1987): 119–22.
Preziosi, A. M.: L'Univ. di Padova nella Resistenza: una lettere di Egidio Meneghetti a Fermo Solari (9 ottobre 1944), *Q.U.P.*, 20(1987): 145–50.
Ricuperati, G.: Linee program. per il Centro per la storia dell' Univ. di Torino, *Q.U.P.*, 20(1987): 223–6.
Soffietti, I.: L'insegnamento della Diplom. presso la Scl. torinese fino agli anni '70', *Arch. per la storia*, 2: 283–6.
Soppelsa, M. L.: *Leibniz e Newton in Italia. Il dibattito padovano 1687–1750*, Trieste/Padua.
Sottili, A.: Il palio per l'altare di Santa Caterina e il 'dossier' sul rettorato di Giovanni di Lussemburgo, *Annali di storia pavese*, 18–19: 77–102.
Veronese Ceseracciu, E.: Codici superstiti dell' arch. del sacro coll. dei teol. dall' inventario del 1619, *Q.U.P.*, 20(1987): 123–31.
Zaramella, I.: Laureati e licenziati dallo Studio di Padova dal 1719 al 1747 e provenienze degli studenti: dati statistici, *Q.U.P.*, 20(1987): 133–6.

Publications 1990

Confessore, O.: *Le origini e l'istituzione dell'Università degli Studi di Lecce*, Galatina.
Kaluza, Z.: Un manuel de théol. en usage à l'univ. de Cracovie: le commentaire des Sentences dit *Utrum Deus gloriosus*, in *L'église et le peuple chrétien dans les pays de l'Europe du centre-est et du nord (14e–15e siècles)*, Rome (henceforth noted as *L'église et le peuple*): 107–24.
Maffei, D.: Fra Cremona, Montpellier e Palencia nel sec. 12. Ricerche su Ugolino da Sesso, *Riv. internaz. di diritto comune*, 1: 9–30.
Natio Polona. Le università in Italia e in Polonia (secc. 13–20). Mostra documentaria, Perugia.
Nicolosi Grassi, G.: 'Audiencia' e 'quietitudine' alle lezioni di Cosimo Nepita nello Studio di Catania, *Riv. internaz. di diritto comune*, 1: 183–91.
Pace, G.: Cosmas de Veronisiis de Sicilia studente a Pavia, *Riv. internaz. di diritto comune*, 1: 193–9.

Verger, J.: Les étudiants slaves et hongrois dans les univs occidentales (13e–15e s.), in *L'église et le peuple*: 83–106.

Poland

Additions to Earlier Lists

For 1979

Mai, J.: Der preussische Staat u. d. polnischen Studenten in Greifswald 1870–1919, in S. Kubiak and L. Tricciakowski eds: *Rola Wielkopolski w dziejach narodu polskiego*, Poznań: 241–54.

For 1985

Spunar, P.: *Repertorium auctorum Bohemorum provectum idearum post Universitatem Pragensem conditam illustrans*, Wrocław.

For 1989

Bolewski, A. etc.: *Trudne lata Akademii Górniczej* (Difficult yrs of the Univ. of Mining), Cracow. (Considers hist. of Univ. of Mining, Cracow, in 20th century.)

Hajdukiewicz, L. ed.: *Wyrok na Uniwersytet Jagielloński 6 listopada 1939* (A verdict on the Jag. univ. 6 Nov. 1939), Cracow.

Zygmunt, A. ed.: *Kaźń profesorów lwowskich, lipiec 1941* (The execution of the Lwow profs, July 1941), Wrocław. (Descriptive chapter also in Russian, Germ. and English.)

Wrzesińska, W. ed.: *Studia nad przeszłością i dniem dzisiejszym Uniwersytetu Wrocławskiego* (Studies on the past and present of the univ. of W.), Warsaw/Wrocław.

Publications 1990

Banach, A.: *Bułgarzy na studiach w Uniwersytecie Jagiellońskim (do 1970)* (Bulgarians studying at the Jag. univ. before 1970), Cracow.

Bieńkowski, W.: UJ w latach 1870–1914 i jego kontakty z nauką austriacką (The Jag. univ. 1870–1914 and its contacts with Austrian science), *Studia hist.*, 33: 225–34. (Summary in English.)

Dybiec, J.: Rozwój badań nad stodunkami naukowymi polsko-austriackimi w latach 1945–89 (The state of research on Polish-Austrian scientif. ties 1945–89), *Studia hist.*, 33: 479–92. (Summary in English.)

Jadczak, R.: Wojenny rektorat Kazimierza Twardowskiego (K.T.; rect. of the war years 1914–17), *Studia hist.*, 33: 423–42.

Perkowska, U.: *Uniwersytet Jagielloński w latach I wojny światowej* (The Jag. univ. during the First World War), Cracow.

Pilch, A.: *Prasa studencka w Polsce 1918–39: Zarys historyczny; Bibliografia* (The student press in Poland 1918–39: Hist. sketch; Bibliog.), Cracow. (Summary in German.)

Płunka-Syroka, B.: *Recepcja doktryn medycznych przełomu 18 i 19 wieku w*

polskich ośrodkach akademickich w latach 1784–1863 (The reception of med. doctrines of the turn of the 18th–19th cent. in Polish acad. centres), Wrocław/Warsaw/Cracow. (Summary in Germ. and English.)
Stoksik, J.: Dzieje katedry geometrii praktycznej w Akademii Krakowskiej 1631–1778 (Hist. of the chair of practical geom. at the Cracow Acad. 1631–1778), *Zeszyty Naukowe UJ, Prace hist.*, 93: 21–37. (Summary in French.)
Stróżewski, W.: Idea uniw. (An idea of a univ.), *Res publica*, 7/8: 51–61.

Scandinavia

Additions to Earlier Lists

For 1977

Bahr, G. von: *Medicinska fakulteten i Uppsala: Professorer och läroämnen 1613–1976* (The fac. of med. in U.: Profs and chairs 1613–1976), Stockholm.
Bender, H.: *Københavns Universitets historie: Oversigt over arkivmaterialet og vejledning i deres benyttelse* (The hist. of the univ. of C.: Survey of docs and guide to their use), Copenhagen.
Bergman, M.: *Nationshusen i Uppsala: En beskrivning tillägnad* (The Houses of the Nations in U., with a description), Uppsala.
Blix, G.: *Festskrift till Nationens 150-årsjubileum d. 7. maj 1977* (Festschrift for the Nation's 150 yrs jubilee 7 May 1977), Uppsala.
Fog, M.: *Efterskrift: 1946 og resten* (Epilogue: 1946 and afterwards), Copenhagen. (Hist. of univ. of Copenhagen.)

For 1978

Albeck, G. ed.: *Århus Universitet 1928–78* (A. univ. 1928–78), Aarhus.
Bedoire, F.: *Stockholms Universitet 1878–1978* (The univ. of S. 1878–1978), Stockholm.
Hoel, A.: *Universitetet under okkupasjonen* (The univ. (of Oslo) during the Occupation), Oslo.
*Københavns Universitets Arkiv 1479–*c.*1910* (The archives of the univ. of C. 1479–*c.*1910), Copenhagen.
Møller, C. F.: *Århus Universitets bygninger* (The buildings of A. univ.), Aarhus. (English summary.)
Segerstedt, T. T. ed.: *The frontiers of human knowledge*, Uppsala. (Concerns univ. of Uppsala.)
Slottved, E.: *Laerestole og Laerere ved Københavns Universitet 1537–1977* (Chairs and teachers at the univ. of C. 1537–1977), Copenhagen.
Strömholm, S. ed.: *Universitetet i utvikling: Uppsala Universitet under Torgny T. Segerstedts rektorat 1955–78* (The univ. progresses: U. univ. during the rectorship of T.T.S. 1955–78), Uppsala.

For 1979

Eegholm-Pedersen, S.: *Utrykte Holbergiana i universitets Arkivet* (Unpublished Holbergiana in the univ. archives (of Copenhagen)), Copenhagen.

Kristensen, M. S. ed.: *Egmont H. Petersens Kollegium 25 år 1954–79* (The hall of residence of E. H. P. in 25 yrs 1954–79), Copenhagen.

Slottved, E.: *Universitetsjubilaeet: Universitetets 500 års jubilaeum* (The univ. jubilee: the 500 yrs jubilee of the univ. (of Copenhagen)), Copenhagen.

Student i Århus (Students in A.), Copenhagen. (15 examples of reminiscences collected by Gustav Albeck.)

For 1980

Wassard, E. ed.: *10 år af Studenterforeningens historie 1970–80* (10 yrs of the hist. of the Student Society (of Copenhagen) 1970–80), Copenhagen.

For 1981

Edlund, B.: *Ofrälse studenter i Lund utanför Nationsinddelingen 1710–1814* (Students in L. outside the classification of Nations 1710–1814), Lund.

Lindroth, S. A.: *Svensk lärdoms historia, 4. Gustavianska tiden* (The hist. of learning in Sweden. The age of Gustavus), Stockholm.

Modeer, K. A.: *Några Gestalter i den juridiske Fakultetens Historia* (Some personalities in the hist of the fac. of law (of Lund univ.)), Lund.

Studentsångarna i Lund 150 År (Student singers in Lund: 150 yrs), Lund.

For 1986

Lind, I.: *Vår egen lille verden: Studentersamfundet i Trondhjem 1910–85* (Our own little world: The Student Society in T. 1910–85), Trondhjem.

Thingrud, L.: *50 år for Universitets laererne: Foreningen af tjenestemenn ved Universitetet i Oslo 1936–86* (50 yrs for the teachers of the univ. The union of acad. employees of the univ. of O. 1936–86), Oslo.

For 1988

Schepelern, H. D.: Den laerde verden: 'Intet er så farligt for Stat og Kirke som ulaerd teol.' (The learned world: 'Nothing is as dangerous for state and church as unscholarly theol.'), in S. Ellehøj ed.: *The World of Christian IV*, Copenhagen: 276–301.

Publications 1982

Göteborgs Nation i Lund 1682–1982 (The Nation of G. in L. 1682–1982), Lund.

Håstad, T.: *The importance of tradition*, Uppsala. (Concerns univ. of Uppsala.)

Hult, G.: *Värmlands Nation i Lund 1682–1982* (The Nation of V. in L. 1682–1982), Lund.

Kleppe, I. A. ed.: *Kvinner ved Universitetet i 100 år–hvorlangt har vi nådd?* (Women at the univ. during 100 yrs—how far have we progressed?), Oslo.

Lunds Universitets Historia. 2. 1710–89 (The hist. of the univ. of L. 2. 1710–89), Lund.

Lundström, S.: *Gustav II Adolf och Uppsala Universitet* (Gustavus Adolfus II and the univ. of U.), Uppsala.

Skaerbaek, H. T.: *Roskilde Universitetscenter gennem 10 år* (The univ. centre of R. during 10 yrs), Roskilde.

Thimon, G.: *Stockholms Nations studenter i Uppsala 1649–1800: Vinculum Stockholmense* (The students of the Nation of S. in U. 1649–1800: V.S.), Stockholm.

Publications 1983

Jansen, F. J. B.: *Eksamen og Embede i det 18. århundrede* (Examination and Office in the 18th cent.), in F. J. Billeskov Jansen ed.: *Liv og Laerdom*, Copenhagen: 121–5.

Liedgren, J.: *Sixtus IV's bulla 1477 för Uppsala Universitet: i 1600-talsradering* (Sixtus IV's bull 1477 to the univ. of U.: in Swedish 17th-cent. etching), Uppsala.

Nilehn, L. H.: *Peregrinatio Academica: det svenske Sämhället och de utrikes Studieresorna under 1600-tallet* (P.A.: The Swedish Society and study tours abroad in the 17th cent.), Lund.

Nygren, S.: *Ur Uppsala Studentkårs Historia: från revolution till revolt* (From the hist. of the condition of students in U.: from revolution to revolt), Uppsala.

Segerstedt, T. T. ed.: *Universitetet i Uppsala 1852 till 1977* (The univ. of U. 1852–1977), Uppsala.

Publications 1984

Fehrman, C.: *Lärdommens Lund: Epoker, episoder, miljöer, människor* (Scholarship at L.: Eras, episodes, milieus, people), Malmo.

Kvinner på Universitetet 100 år (Women in the univ.: 100 yrs), Oslo.

Nilson, A.: *Studiefinansiering och social rekrytering til högre Utbildning 1920–76* (Student financing and soc. recruitment to higher educ. 1920–76), Lund.

Stigbrand, T. ed.: *Läkarutbilding och medicinsk forskning i Umeå 25 år* (Med. educ. and med. research in U.: 25 yrs), Umeå.

Wilner, P. ed.: *Lunds Universitets Matrikel 1667–1732* (The matric. records of the univ. of L. 1667–1732), Stockholm.

Publication 1985

Malmström, Å.: *Juridiska Fakulteten i Uppsala. Studier i fakultetens historia. 2. Den juridiska fakulteten under 1600-tallet och början av 1700-tallet* (The fac. of law in U. Studies in the hist. of the fac. 2. The fac. of law in the 17th and the beginning of the 18th cent.), Uppsala/ Stockholm.

Publications 1987

Gottschau, J.: *Rebeller og Medløbere* (Rebels and opportunists), Copenhagen.

Haedersdal, E.: Københavns Univ.: Oeconomi, residens og professorbolig (The univ. of C.: Economy, accommodation and prof. housing), *Bygningsarkaeol. studier*: 104–39.

Helk, V.: *Dansk-norske studierejser: fra reformationen til enevaelden 1536–1660: Med en matrikel over studerende i udlandet* (Danish–Norwegian study tours: from Refn to Absolutism 1536–1660, with a register of students in foreign countries), Odense.

——— Supplement til magisterpromotioner i København 1544–85 (Supplement to master's degrees in C. 1544–85), *Personalhist. Tidsskrift*, 107(1): 41–4.

Jexlev, T.: Kvindernes adgang til univ.: Et eksempel på sagsbehandling i 1870'erne (Women's access to the univ.: an example of treatment in the 1870s), in K. Hjort ed.: *Spor: Arkiver og Historie*, Copenhagen: 115–29.

Publication 1989

Breindahl, K. M.: *Valkendorfs Kollegium 1939–89* (The V. hall of residence 1939–89), Copenhagen.

Spain and Portugal

Additions to Earlier Lists

For 1979

Gallego Salvadores, J. and Felipo Orts, A.: Grados concedidos por la Univ. de Valencia durante la prima mitad del s. 16, *Analecta sacra tarraconensia*, 51/52: 323–80.

For 1980

Escolano Benito, A., García Carrasco, J. and Pineda Arroyo, J. M.: *La investigacion pedagógica universitaria en España. Estudio históricodocumental 1940–76*, Salamanca.

Veríssimo Serrão, J.: *A Universidade Técnica de Lisboa. 1. Primórdios de sua história*, Lisbon.

For 1983

Canellas, A.: *El Archivo de la Universidad de Zaragoza en 1770*, Saragossa.

Veríssimo Serrão, J.: *História das universidades*, Porto.

For 1984

Cardó Guinaldo y Horacio Santiago-Otero, M. T.: *Las instituciones juridicas en algunas escuelas medievales de la Península Ibérica*, Madrid.

For 1985

Alaustre, I.: Fiestas de la Universidad de Alcalá en los siglos 16 y 17. Thesis. Madrid.

Cuart, B. and Hinojo, G.: *Nonnulla memoratu digna. Memorias de D. Bernardino de Anaya, rector del Colegio San Clemente de los Españoles de Bolonia 1512–1513*, Salamanca.

Núñez Muñoz, M. F.: La Univ. de La Laguna: una reflexión sobre su evolución hist., *Bol. Millares Carlos*, 4: 163–97.

For 1986

Almuiña Fernández, C. and Martín González, J. J.: *La Universidad de Valladolid. Historia y patrimonio*. 2nd ed. expanded, Valladolid.

Esteban Pendas, M.: Estudio histórico del ceremonial de la Universidad de Alcalá de Henares: festejos reales, s. 16 y 17. Thesis. Alcalá.

Lahuert, M. J.: *Liberales y universitarios. La Universidad de Alcalá en el traslado a Madrid 1820–37*, Alcalá.

Sáenz de la Calzada, M.: *la Residencia de estudiantes 1910–36*, Madrid.

For 1987

Ballesteros Torres, L.: Bibliog. Complutense, *Anales Complutenses*, 1: 337–54.

Barrio Moya, J. L.: El col. de San Agustín en Alcalá de Henares, *Anales Complutenses*, 1: 19–48.

Bernabeu Mestre, J.: Pedro Miguel de Heredia, catedrático de med. de la Univ. de Alcalá de Henares, *Anales Complutenses*, 1: 49–64.

Casado Arbonies, M.: Un col. menor de la Univ. de Alcalá en el s. 17: Santos Justo y Pastor o de Tuy, *Anales Complutenses*, 1: 65–76.

Gil García, A.: Cátedras univ. complutenses en el s. 17, *Anales Complutenses*, 1: 113–34.

Gonzalez Navarro, R.: Nuevas aportaciones a medio s. de construcción univ. en Alcalá de Henares 1510–60, *Anales Complutenses*, 1: 135–66.

Martínez Gomis, M.: *La Universidad de Orihuela 1610–1807. Un centro de estudios superiores entre el Barroco y la Ilustración*. 2 vols, Alicante.

Sanz, F. J.: *Historia de la Facultad de Medicina de la Universidad de Sigüenza*, Guadalajara.

For 1988

Albinaña, S.: *Universidad e Ilustración. Valencia en la época de Carlos III*, Valencia.

Alvarez de Morales, A.: Tiene sentido hist. que la Univ. de Madrid se reclame Complutense? *Anales Complutenses*, 2: 17–20.

Alvarez Márquez, M. C.: El card. Cisneros y la Univ. de Alcalá, in *Actas del i encuentro de Historiadores del Valle del Henares*, Guadalajara (henceforth noted as *Encuentro de historiadores*): 33–48.

Augusto Rodrigues, M.: *Actas da Assembleia Geral da Universidade de Coimbra*, Coimbra.

——— *A Universidade de Coimbra nos seus Estatutos*, Coimbra.

Casado Arbonies, F. J. and M. and Gil Blanco, E.: Estudiantes alcalaínos y seguntinos en los arzobispados de Nueva España en la época de los Austrias, in *Encuentro de historiadores*: 121–30.

Catálogo de tesis doctorales sobre geografía e historia, que se conservan en el Archivo de la Universidad Complutense de Madrid 1900–87, Madrid.

García, M. M.: Bermejo Giner, un estudiante de Burbáguena en Salamanca, *Studia Zamorensia*, 9: 291–6.

García Oro, J.: El primitivo solar Acad. Complutense, *Anales Complutenses*, 2: 65–70.

——— La doc. pontificia de la Univ. Complutense en el periodo fundacional, in *Encuentro de historiadores*: 275–88.

García y García, A.: La diócesis de Mondoñedo y la Univ. de Salamanca, *Estudios Mindonienses*, 4: 501–506.

Gil García, A.: Estudio comparativo de las cátedras de la Univ. de Alcalá de Henares y de la Univ. de Salamanca en la primera mitad del s. 17, in *Encuentro de historiadores*: 309–18.

González Navarro, R.: Las acads de jurisprud. en la Univ. de Alcalá, in *Encuentro de historiadores*: 327–36.

Gutiérrez Lorenzo, P. and Casado Arbonies, F. J.: Fundaciones univ. españ. libres de patronato regio o ecles. Los cols autónomos de Alcalá de Henares fundados en el s. 16: San Cosme y San Damián o de Mena y Santa Catalina Mártir de los Verdes, in *Encuentro de historiadores*: 351–60.

Gutiérrez Torrecilla, L. M.: El municipio y la Univ. de Alcalá de Henares: dos instits trad. enfrentadas, in *Encuentro de historiadores*: 361–70.

Pradillo, P. J. and Caballero García, A.: Programa iconológico en el col. menor de San Ciriaco y Santa Paula (Alcalá de Henares), in *Encuentro de historiadores*: 553–62.

Puelles Benítez, M. de: *Textos sobre la educación en España (siglo 19)*, Madrid.

Rogent, J., Casassas, J. and Fontbona, F.: *Elias Rogent i la Universitat de Barcelona*, Barcelona.

Sáez García, C.: 868 referencias bibliog. y doc. sobre Alcalá de Henares, *Anales Complutenses*, 2: 161–79.

Sánchez Molto, M. V. and Casado Arbonies, F. J.: El Col. de San Lucas Evangelista o de Magnes de la Univ. de Alcalá de Henares 1593–1843, in *Encuentro de historiadores*: 597–610.

Soterraña Martin Postigo, M. de la: Col. de la diócesis de Pamplona en el Col. Mayor de Santa Cruz de Valladolid, *Príncipe de Viana*, 49: 165–74.

Zamorano Rodríguez, E.: Nuevos aspectos en torno a la figura de la Doctora de Alcalá, in *Encuentro de historiadores*: 657–63.

For 1989

Albiñana, S.: Leyes y cánones en la Valencia de la ilustración, in *Claustros y Estudiantes*, Valencia, 2 vols (henceforth noted as *C. y E.*), 1: 1–16.

Alvarez de Morales, A.: El Col. Mayor de san Ildefonso y la configuración del poder col., in *C. y E.*, 1: 17–24.

Augusto Rodrigues, M.: *Actas da Faculdade de Letras 1911–25. 1*, Coimbra.

——— *Actas do Senado 1911–1916. 1*, Coimbra.

Baldó, M.: Las 'luces' atenuadas: la ilustración en la Univ. de Córdoba y el col. de San Carlos de Buenos Aires, in *C. y E.*, 1: 25–54.

Cabezas, J. A.: Manjón y Giner de los Ríos, los dos grandes de la moderna pedagog. españ., *Cuadernos de pensamiento*, 3: 83–99.

Casado Arbonies, F. J. and M. and Gil Blanco, E.: *Diccionario de universitarios en la administración Americana: arzobispos y obispos de Nueva España 1517–1700*, Guadalajara.

Claustros y Estudiantes. Congreso internacional de historia de las universidades americanas y españolas en la edad moderna. Valencia noviembre de 1987, Valencia. (Relevant items noted separately.)

Correa Ballester, J.: Unas consultas al consejo de Indias sobre la Univ. de México 1595–97, in *C. y E.*, 1: 91–101.

Cortes Vázquez, L.: *La vida estudiantil en la Salamanca clasica*, Salamanca.

Esteban, L.: Filología humanismo en la univ. españ. del s. 15 y mediados del 16, in *C. y E.*, 1: 103–27.

Felipo Orts, A.: Los salarios de la univ. de Valencia durante el s. 17. Cátedras y pavordías 1611–1700, in *C. y E.*, 1: 129–56.

Ferreira Gomes, J.: *A Escola Normal Superior da Universidade de Coimbra*, Lisbon.

Ferrero Micó, R.: Rentas de la univ. de México hasta 1615, in *C. y E.*, 1: 157–81.

Gallego Barnés, A.: El impacto de la Carta Real de 1612 en el presupuesto del *Studi general*, in *C. y E.*, 1: 183–97.

Gallego Salvadores, J. and Felipo Orts, A.: La fac. de med. de Valencia desde 1499 hasta 1525, in *C. y E.*, 1: 199–219.

García Trobat, P.: El patrimonio del Col.-univ. de Gandía, in *C. y E.*, 1: 235–53.

García y García, A.: De las escuelas catedralicias a las univs, *Historia 16*, 14: 37–46. (Also pub. in *Cuadernos de Historia 16*, 175: 4–11.)

——— Las cátedras de lenguas indígenas en Indias, in *C. y E.*, 1: 221–33.

Gómez, T.: La batalla de la univ. pub. de Santafé de Bogotá 1768–1803, in *C. y E.*, 1: 255–64.

González González, E.: Una ed. crítica de los estatutos y constituciones de México, in *C. y E.*, 1: 265–78.

González Prieto, J.: *La Universidad de Alcalá en el s. 17*, Alcalá.

Graullera Sanz, V.: La enseñanza y práctica del derecho en la Valencia foral, in *C. y E.*, 1: 279–93.

Hernández, T. M.: La univ. di San Marcos de Lima felicita a las cortes por la abolición de la inquisición, in *C. y E.*, 1: 295–318.

Hernández Sandoica, E.: Poder colonial y dinámica de la reproducción cultural: la univ. de La Habana 1842–98, in *C. y E.*, 1: 319–42.

Lamarca Langa, G.: Lecturas y élites intelectuales: la bibl. de Vicente Casaña, in *C. y E.*, 1: 343–62. (V.C. prof. at Valencia in 18th century.)

Leal, I.: La recepción tardía de la ciencia en la univ. de Caracas y la labor del dr José María Vargas 1786–1854, in *C. y E.*, 1: 363–78.

Lértora Mendoza, C. A.: La enseñanza de la física en el Río de la Plata: tres ejemplos sobre la situación en el s. 18, in *C. y E.*, 1: 379–410.

Lluch Adelantado, M. A. and Micó Navarro, J. A.: Los grados en med. concedidos por la univ. de Valencia durante la primera mitad del s. 18, in *C. y E.*, 2: 11–28.

López Piñero, J. M.: La trad. anatómica de la univ. de Valencia y su hundimiento durante el primer tercio del s. 19, in *C. y E.*, 1: 411–32.

Luna Díaz, L. M.: Las ceremonias de fundación de la univ. de México 1553. Una propuesta de análisis, in *C. y E.*, 2: 1–9.

Mancebo, M. F.: Unas cartas del obispo Juan de Palafox al rey sobre las constituciones de México, in *C. y E.*, 2: 29–43.

Martínez Gomis, M.: Gandía ante la ref. carolina el proyecto de plan de estudios de 1767, in *C. y E.*, 2: 45–68.

Melcon, J.: *La enseñanza de la geografía y el profesorado de las escuelas normales 1882–1915*, Barcelona.

Menegus Bornemann, M.: La real y pontificia univ. de México y los expedientes de limpieza de sangre, in *C. y E.*, 2: 69–81.

Molero Pintado, A. and Pozo Andrés, M. C.: *Un precedente histórico en la formación universitaria del professorado español. Escuela de Estudios Superiores del Magisterio 1901–32*, Alcalá.

Mora Cañada, A.: Atisbos de ilustración en la real univ. de Santiago de Chile, in *C. y E.*, 2: 99–120.

Navarro, J.: La med. clínica valenciana durante la etapa final de la ilustración, in *C. y E.*, 2: 121–33.

Nieto Nafria, J. M.: *Los estudios de biología en las universidades de España: cuatro décadas de cambios*, León.

Orts i Hurtado, P.: Los estudiantes de med. en la Valencia de la segunda mitad del s. 17, in *C. y E.*, 2: 135–63.

Palacios Bañuelos, L.: El mundo de los valores de la Instit. Libre de Enseñanza, *Estudios de Deusto*, 37: 193–206.

Palao Gil, F. J.: Real patronato y legitimidad canónica de la Univ. de México, in *C. y E.*, 2: 165–76.

Pérez-Prendes y Muñoz de Arraco, J. M.: Para la hist. de una univ. sin nombre, in *C. y E.*, 2: 177–98.

Peset, M.: La primeras oposiciones en México, in *C. y E.*, 2: 213–36.

Peset Mancebo, M.: Provisión de una cátedra de med. en México 1598, in *C. y E.*, 2: 237–59.

Pilar Valero, M. del: *Documentos para la historia de la Universidad de Salamanca 1500–50*, Cáceres.

Prats, J.: La univ. de Cervera ante el ambiente de ref. de principios del reinado de Carlos III: corporativissmo y tradicionalismo, in *C. y E.*, 2: 261–78.

Ramírez González, C. I. and Pavón Romero, A.: De estudiantes a catedráticos. Un aspecto de la real univ. de México en el s. 16, in *C. y E.*, 2: 279–89.

Reis Torgal, L.: Univ., ciência e 'conflito de fac.' no iluminismo e nos primórdios do liberalismo português, in *C. y E.*, 2: 291–9.

Risueño Paniagua, J. I.: La formación univ. como valor en alza en nuestros días, *Estudios de Deusto*, 37: 237–51.

Rodríguez Cruz, A.: La ref. ilustrada de José Pérez Cabama en Quito, in *C. y E.*, 2: 301–20.

Rodríguez-San Pedro Bezares, L. E. etc.: Econ. agraria y hacienda de la univ. de Salamanca en el s. 17, in *C. y E.*, 2: 321–51.

Ten, A. E.: Trad. y renovación en la univ. de San Marcos de Lima. La ref. del virrey Amat, in *C. y E.*, 2: 353–64.

Torremocha Hernández, M.: Feuro y delincuencia estudiantil en el Valladolid del s. 18, in *C. y E.*, 2: 365–91.

Valero Garcia, P.: *Documentos para la historia de la Universidad de Salamanca 1500–50*, Cáceres.

Varela, I.: Aprox. al estudio de la población univ. de Santiago. S. 18, in *C. y E.*, 2: 393–8.

Vera de Flachs, M. C.: La univ. como factor de ascenso a la élite de poder en la América hispana: el caso de Córdoba 1767–1808, in *C. y E.*, 2: 399–426.

Zamora Sanchez, G.: *Universidad y filosofia moderna en la España ilustrada. Labor reformista de F. de Villalpando 1740–97*, Salamanca.

Publications 1990

Alvarez Villar, J.: *La Universidad de Salamanca, 3. Arte y Tradiciones*, Salamanca.

Augusto Rodrigues, M.: *A Universidade da Coimbra e os seus Reitores—Para uma história da instituição*, Coimbra.

——— ed.: Livro Verde *(Cartulário do séc. 15). Edição fac-similada*, Coimbra.

Barrientos García, J.: *Lucha por el poder y por la libertad de enseñanza en Salamanca. El estatuto y juramento de la universidad 1627*, Salamanca.

Carabias Torres, A. M.: Excol. mayores en la admin. de las Indias 1500–1750, in *17 Congreso Internacional de Ciencias Historias. Rapports*, Madrid. 2: 570–1.

Casado Arbonies, F. J.: *Indice de los documentos del Archivo Municipal de Alcalá de Henares*, Alcalá. (Section on univ. and colls of A.)

Escandell Bonet, B.: *Estudios Cisnerianos*, Alcalá (C. fnder of univ. of A.)
Fernandez Alvarez, M.: *La Universidad de Salamanca, 2. Docencia e Investigación*, Salamanca.
Ferreira Gomes, J.: *A Universidade de Coimbra durante a primeira República*, Lisbon.
Mendez Sanz, F.: *La Universidad Salmantina de la Ilustración. Hacienda y reforma*, Salamanca.
Rodriguez Cruz, A. M.: *Historia de la Universidad de Salamanca*, Salamanca.
Sáez, C. ed.: *Annales Complutenses: sucesión de tiempos desde los primeros fundadores griegos hasta estos que corren (s. 17)*, Alcalá.

Switzerland

Additions to Earlier Lists

For 1977

Maissen, F.: Bündner Studenten in Innsbruck 1671–1900, *Bündner Monatsblatt*: 355–76.
——— St. Galler Studenten an d. Univ. Innsbruck 1671–1900, *St. Galler Kult. u. Gesch.*, 7: 319–48.

For 1979

Arnold, K. and Maissen, F.: Walliser Studenten an d. Univ. Innsbruck 1679–1976, *Blätter aus d. Walliser Gesch.*, 17/2: 189–258.
Higman, F. M.: *Censorship and the Sorbonne*, Geneva.
Maissen, F.: Schweizer Studenten am Coll. Germanicum in Rom 1552–1900, *Z. f. Schweiz. Kirchengesch.*, 73: 256–305.

For 1980

Töndury, G.: Anatomie in Zürich, *Gesnerus*, 37: 271–87. (Hist. of the teaching of anatomy from 1833 to the present.)

For 1981

Maissen, F.: Bündner Studenten an d. Univ. München, *Bündner Monatsblatt*: 241–70.
——— Innerschweizer Studenten an d. Univ. Innsbruck 1671–1900, *Der Geschichtsfreund*, 134: 87–133.
——— St. Galler Studenten an d. Univ. Ingolstadt–Landshut–München, *St. Galler Kult. u. Gesch.*, 11: 277–313.
Mani, N.: Johann Jakob Wepfers Doktordisputation über d. Herzklopfen (1647), *Gesnerus*, 38: 143–7. (Inform. about the Basle fac. of medicine.)
Rintelen, F.: Zur Gesch. d. Basler Med. Fak. im ersten Drittel dieses Jh., *Gesnerus*, 38: 93–104.

For 1983

Jenny, B. R.: Die Musikprof. an d. Univ. Basel im zweiten Drittel d. 16. Jh. Eine personen- u. institutionsgesch. Untersuchung, *Basler Z. f. Gesch. u. Altertumskunde*, 83: 27–83.

For 1984

Maissen, F.: Schweizer Studenten an d. Univ. Innsbruck 1671–1900, *Z. f. Schweiz. Kirchengesch.*, 78: 129–69.

For 1985

Maffei, D.: Un privilegio dottorale perugino del 1377, in J. A. Ankum, J. E. Spruit and F. B. J. Wubbe eds: *Satura Roberto Feenstra*, Freiburg i. Ue: 437–44.

For 1987

Batts, M. K.: Germanistik in Kanada, *Jb. f. Internat. Germanistik*, 19/1: 148–63.

Bujanda, J.-M. de: *Index des livres interdits. 2. Index des livres de l'université de Louvain 1546, 1550, 1558*, Geneva.

For 1988

Beauregard, E. E.: *History of academic freedom in Ohio. Case studies in higher education 1808–1976*, Berne.

Bonner, T. N.: Pioneering in women's med. educ. in the Swiss univs 1864–1914, *Gesnerus*, 45: 461–73.

Dreifuss, J. J.: Charles Chossat 1796–1875, physiologiste, méd. et homme pol. genevois, *Gesnerus*, 45: 239–61. (Inform. about the Geneva fac. of medicine.)

ETH-Bibliothek Zürich ed.: *Albert Heim 1849–1937, Professor für Geologie an ETH und Universität Zürich, Katalog zur Gedenkausstellung 1987*, Zurich.

Fatio, O.: 450e anniv. de l'Univ. de Lausanne, *Biblioth. d'humanisme et renaissance*, 50: 121–3.

Grau, C.: *Berühmte Wissenschaftsakademien. Von ihrem Entstehen und ihrem weltweiten Erfolg*, Thun.

Herren, P. ed.: *Ohne Zukunft hat die Vergangenheit keinen Glanz. 150 Jahre Seminar Thun 1838–1988*, Thun/Leipzig.

Keel, O.: Les rapports entre méd. et chirugie dans la grande éc. anglaise de William et John Hunter, *Gesnerus*, 45: 323–41. (Hist. of the teaching of med. in 18th and 19th-cent. London.)

Kimura, N.: Die jap. Germanistik im Überblick, *Jb. f. Internat. Germanistik*, 20/1: 138–54.

Maissen, F.: Tessiner Studenten u. d. Univ. Ingolstadt–Landshut–München, *Boll. storico della Svizzera ital.*, 100: 180–90.

Müller, P.: Gabriel Gustav Valentin, Pionier d. Berner Physiol., *Gesnerus*, 45: 191–9. (Teaching of med. in 19th-cent. Berne.)

Saudan, G.: La physiologie à la Haute-Ec. de Lausanne: Le premier demi-siècle 1881–1932, *Gesnerus*, 45: 263–70.

Sauthoff, S.: *Adliges Studentenleben und Universitätsstudium zu Beginn des 16. Jahrhunderts. Darstellung anhand des Ausgabenbüchleins von Conrad zu Castell*, Berne.

Staatliches Lehrer- und Lehrerinnenseminar Langenthal ed.: *25 Jahre Seminar Langenthal 1963–88*, Langenthal.

Université de Neuchâtel ed.: *Histoire de l'Université de Neuchâtel. 1. La première Académie 1838–48*, Neuchâtel.

Publications 1989

Bissegger, P.: Etudiants suisses à l'Ec. polytech. de Paris 1798–1850, *Schweiz. Z. f. Gesch.*, 39: 115–51.

Burckhardt-Biedermann, T.: *Geschichte des Gymnasiums zu Basel 1589–1889*, Basle.

Collège Sainte-Marie, Martigny ed.: *Le 100e anniversaire du Collège Sainte-Marie, Martigny 1889–1989*, Martigny.

Ecole d'études sociales et pédagogiques, Lausanne ed.: *L'Ecole d'études sociales et pédagogiques. 25 ans, 1964–89*, Lausanne.

Gisiger, P. H.: Dissertationen von Zahnmedizinern an der Medizinischen Fakultät der Universität Zürich 1915–90, 3: 1953–69. Thesis. Zurich.

Huber, D.: *Das Kollegienhaus der Universität Basel*, Berne.

Iseli, J.: *Geschichte der Studentenverbindungen an der Kantonsschule Solothurn*, Berne.

Kunz, W.: Dissertationen von Zahnmedizinern an der Medizinischen Fakultät der Universität Zürich 1915–90, 5: 1978–85. Thesis. Zurich.

Leimgruber, S.: *Ethikunterricht an katholischen Gymnasien und Lehrerseminarien in der Schweiz. Analyse der Religionsbücher seit Mitte des 19. Jahrhunderts*, Freiburg i. Ue.

Marti, S. ed.: *Universität Freiburg 1889–1989*, Freiburg i. Ue.

——— *Université de Fribourg 1889–1989*, Freiburg i. Ue.

Meyer, F.: *Das Humanistische Gymnasium Basel 1889–1989*, Basle.

Mörgeli, C. and Blaser, A.: Henry E. Sigerist: Die Gestaltung d. medizinhist. Unterrichts. Ein unpubliziertes MS im Zürcher Medizinhist. Inst., *Gesnerus*, 46: 45–53. (Inform. about the beginnings of the teaching of hist. of med. at Zurich.)

Niederer, H.-M.: *Alfred Vogt 1879–1943. Seine Zürcher Jahre 1923–43*, Zurich. (Inform. about the teaching of med. at Zurich.)

Polivka, H. ed.: *75 Jahre Abstinente Burschenschaft. Eine Chronik mit zeitgenössischen Liedern und Gedichten*, Basle.

Steiner, A. A.: *Der Schweizerische Studentenverein und die Politik*, Berne.

Wäspi, M. C.: *Die Anfänge des Medizinhistorikers Henry E. Sigerist in Zürich*, Zurich. (Inform. about the teaching of hist. of med. at Zurich.)

The United States

Additions to Earlier Lists

For 1977

Beecher, H. K.: *Medicine at Harvard*, Hanover, N.H.

For 1978

MacLeod, R.: Breadth, depth and excellence: sources and problems in the hist. of univ. science educ. in Eng. 1850–1914, *Science educ.*, 5: 85–106.

For 1979

Lopez, E. H.: *The Harvard mystique*, New York.

Synnott, M. G.: *The half-opened door: Discrimination and admission at Harvard, Yale and Princeton 1900–70*, New York.

For 1980

Ash, H. G.: Acad. pols in the hist. of science. Experimental Psychol. in Germany 1879–1941, *Central europ. hist.*, 8: 255–68.

Paul, C. B.: *Science and immortality. The éloges of the Paris Academy of Sciences 1699–1791*, Berkeley, Calif.

Powell, A. G.: *The uncertain profession*, Cambridge, Mass. (Hist. of the Harvard schl of education.)

Story, R.: *The forging of an aristocracy: Harvard and the Boston upper class 1800–70*, Middletown, Conn.

For 1981

Brucker, G.: A civic debate on Florentine higher educ. 1460, *Renaissance quarterly*, 34: 517–33.

Hamlin, A. T.: *The university library in the United States. Its origins and development*, Philadelphia.

For 1982

Baldwin, J.: Masters at Paris from 1179 to 1215, in R. L. Benson and G. Constable: *Renaissance and renewal in the 12th century*, Cambridge, Mass.: 138–72.

Keller, P.: *Getting at the core: Curricular reform at Harvard*, Cambridge, Mass. (Hist. of debates leading to changes of 1979.)

Our Harvard: reflections on college life by 22 distinguished graduates, New York.

For 1983

Boyle, L. E.: The beginnings of legal studies at Oxford, *Viator*, 14: 107–31.

For 1984

Becker, H. W.: The soc. origins and post-grad. careers of a Cambridge intellect. elite 1830–60, *Victorian studies*, 28: 97–127.

Burstyn, J.: *Victorian education and the ideal of womanhood*, New Brunswick, N.J.

Giles, G. J.: German students and higher educ. pol. in the Second World War, *Central europ. hist.*, 17: 330–54.

For 1985

Anderson, R. D.: Educ. and soc. in modern Scotland: A comparative perspective, *Hist of educ. quarterly*, 25: 459–81.

Bunting, B.: *Harvard, an architectural history*, New York.

Harran, M. J. ed.: *Luther and Learning. The Wittenberg University Symposium*, Selinsgrove, Pa.

Logan, F. D.: The Cambridge can. law fac.: a late medieval encomium, *Bull. of medieval can law*, 15: 117–18.

Principe, W. H.: Bishs, theols and philos in conflict at the univs of Paris and Oxford: The condemnations of 1270 and 1277, in *Proceedings of the 40th annual conference of the Catholic History Society. San Francisco, June 5–6, 1985*, New York: 114–26.

For 1986

Dobson, R. B.: Recent prosopog. research in late medieval Eng. hist.: Univ. graduates, Durham monks and York canons, in N. Bulst and J.-P. Genet eds: *Medieval lives and the historians. Studies in medieval prosopography*, Kalamazoo, Mich. (henceforth noted as *Medieval lives*): 181–99.

Evans, R.: An analysis by computer of A. B. Emden's Biographical Registers of the Universities of Oxford and Cambridge, in *Medieval lives*: 381–94.

Schwinges, R. C.: Zur Prosopographie student. Reisegruppen im 15. Jh., in *Medieval lives*: 333–41.

Verger, J.: Prosopographie et cursus univ., in *Medieval lives*: 313–32.

For 1988

Brucker, G.: Renaissance Florence, Who needs a univ.? in T. Bender ed.: *The university and the city: from medieval origins to the present*, New York (henceforth noted as *The univ. and the city*): 47–58.

Ferruolo, S.C.: *Parisius Paradisus*, The city, it schls and the origins of the univ. of Paris, in *The univ. and the city*: 22–43.

Glazer, N.: Facing 3 ways: city and univ. in New York since World War 2, in *The univ. and the city*: 267–89.

Grafton, A.: Civic humanism and scientif. scholarship at Leiden, in *The univ. and the city*: 59–78.

Heyd, M.: The Geneva acad. in the 18th cent.: A Calvinist seminary or a civic univ.? in *The univ. and the city*: 79–99.

Hollinger, D. A.: The NYUs and 'The obligation of univs to the soc. order' in the Great Depression, in *The univ. and the city*: 249–66.

Hyde, J. K.: Univs and cities in medieval Italy, in *The univ. and the city*: 13–21.

Jay, M.: Urban flights. The world of soc. research between Frankfurt and New York, in *The univ. and the city*: 231–48.

McClelland, C. E.: 'To live for science'. Ideas and realities at the univ. of Berlin, in *The univ. and the city*: 181–97.

Phillipson, N.: Commerce and cult. Edinburgh, Edinburgh univ. and the Scott. Enlightenment, in *The univ. and the city*: 100–16.

Rothblatt, S.: London: A metropolitan univ., in *The univ. and the city*: 119–49.

Schorske, C. E.: Science as vocation in Burckhardt's Basel, in *The univ. and the city*: 198–209.

Shils, E.: The univ., the city and the world: Chicago and the univ. of Chicago, in *The univ. and the city*: 210–30.

Stevenson, L. L.: Preparing for public life: the coll. students at New York univ. 1832–81, in *The univ. and the city*: 150–77.

For 1989

Frängsmyr, T. ed.: *Science in Sweden: The Royal Swedish Academy of Sciences 1739–1989*, Canton, MA.

Gabriel, A. L.: Universities, in *Dictionary of the Middle Ages*. 12, New York: 282–300.

Leonardi, S. J.: *Dangerous by degrees: Women at Oxford and the Somerville College novelists*, New Brunswick, NJ.

Oshinsky, D. M., McCormick, R. P. and Horn, D.: *The case of the Nazi professor*, New Brunswick, NJ.

Wilson, L. G.: *Medical revolution in Minnesota: A history of the university of Minnesota medical school*, St Paul, Minn.

Publications 1990

Schafer, R. G.: *A history of the University of Michigan-Flint*, Flint, Mich.

Silver, H.: *A higher education: the Council for National Academic Awards and British higher education*, New York.

Thomas, J. B. ed.: *British universities and teacher education: a century of change*, New York.

The U.S.S.R.

Additions to Earlier Lists

For 1979

Aristov, V. V., Shofman, A. S. and Mikhailova, S. M.: *Kazansky universitet 1804–1979: Ocherki istorii* (K. Univ. 1804–1979. Hist. sketches), Kazan.

Bagir-zade, F. M. and Kaziyev, M. A.: *Azerbaijansky gosudarstvenny universitet im. S. M. Kirova: 60 (let)* (The S.M.K. state univ. in A. 60 yrs), Baku. (Summary in Eng., Arabic, Germ., Persian, French.)

Bidrute, Z., Babarskaite, R. and Gaigaliene, L.: *Vilnussky universitet 1579–1832* (V. Univ 1579–1832), Vilnius. (Cat. of exhib. In Lithuanian and Russian.)

Mavrodin, V. V. and Tishkin, G. A.: Leningradsky universitet i zhenskoye obrasovaniye v Rossii (L. Univ. and women's educ. in R.), *Vestnik LGU*, 2(1): 5–9.

Sladkevich, I. G. and Tishkin, G. A. eds: *Peterburgsky universitet i revolutsionnoye dvizheniye v Rossii* (P. Univ. and the revol. movt in R.), Leningrad.

Publications 1980

Belyavsky, T. M.: *Ikh imena uvekovecheny v Moskve: Ucheniye i pitomtsy Mosk. un-ta* (Their names are immortalised in M.: learning and the alumni of M. Univ.), Moscow.

Fedosova, E. P.: *Bestuzhevskiye kursy: pervy zhensky universitet v Rossii 1878–1918* (B. courses. The 1st women's univ. in R.), Moscow.

Gentshke, L. V., Dmitriyev, G. P., Orazimbetov, S. O. and Rachimov, M. G.: *Ocherki istorii Tashkentskogo gosudarstvennogo universiteta im. V.I.Lenina* (Hist. sketches of the V.I.L. Univ. of T.), Tashkent.

Glavatsky, M. Y., Chufarov, V. G. and Adamov, V. V.: *Uralsky gosudarstvenny universitet* (The state univ. of the Urals), Sverdlovsk.

Rybalka, I. K., Chernyakov, M. V. and Kucher A. Y.: *Kharkovsky gosudarstvenny universitet 1805–1980: Istor. ocherk* (K. state univ. 1805–1980. Hist. sketch), Kharkov.

Sinyayev, V. S., Kirsanova, Y. S. and Plotnikova, M. Y.: *Tomsky universitet 1880–1980: Ocherk istorii i deyatelnosti* (T. Univ. 1880–1980. An outline of its hist. and activities), Tomsk.

Publications 1981

Garibyan, G., Sagatelyan, V. and Tonoyan, R.: *Yerevansky gosudarstvenny universitet: Istor. ocherk* (Y. state univ. Hist. outline), Yerevan. (In Armenian.)

Sobolyev, V. V.: Sto let astronomicheskoy observatorii LGU (100 years of the L. Univ. astron. observatory), *Vestnik Leningrad. un-ta. 7. Matematika, Mekhanika, Astronomiya*, 2: 5–9.

Publications 1982

Arsharuni, A. M.: *Moskovsky universitet i armyanskaya peredovaya intelligentsia* (M. Univ. and the progressive Armenian intelligencia), Ayastan. (Enlarged 2nd ed. In Armenian.)

Bukeliene, E., Gadeikis, L. and Pakeriene, V.: *Vilnussky universitet na styke vecov* (V. Univ. at the turn of the cents), Vilnius.

Drevo nadezhdy (The tree of hope), Tbilisi. (Materials relating to 400th anniv. of Vilnius Univ. In Georgian and Armenian.)

Istoriya Kharkovskogo universiteta: sist. ukaz lit. 1. 1917–80 (Hist. of K. Univ. A systematic lit. index. 1. 1917–80), Kharkov.

Istoriya Tartusskogo universiteta 1632–1982 (Hist. of Tartu Univ. 1632–1982). 3 vols, Tallinn. (In Estonian.)

Koop, A. V.: *350 let Tartuskomu universitetu 1632–1982* (350th anniv. of Tartu Univ. 1632–1982), Tallinn.

Mavrodina, V. V. and Yezhova, V. A. gen. eds: *Leningradsky universitet v vospominaniyakh sovremennikov. 2. Peterburgsky-Petrogradsky universitet 1895–1917* (L. Univ. through the recollections of contemporaries. 2. P.-P. Univ. 1895–1917), Leningrad.

Piirinäe, H., Siilivask, K. and Ruutsoo, R.: *Istoriya Tartuskogo universiteta 1632–1982* (Hist. of T. Univ.), Tallinn.

Tankler, H.: *Vospitanniki Tartusskogo universiteta-chleny Akademii nauk SSSR* (Alumni of T. Univ. Members of the Soviet Acad. of Sciences), Tallinn. (In Estonian.)

Tishkina, G. A. ed.: *Ocherki po istorii Leningradskogo universiteta. 4* (Essays on the hist. of L. Univ. 4), Leningrad.

Publications 1983

Abramyan, A. G.: *Gladzorsky universitet: Kratky ocherk* (G. Univ. A short essay), Yerevan. (In Armenian and Russian.)

Aizenshtadt, L. M., Kuibysheva, K. S. and Senderovich, E. A.: *Moskovsky universitet za 225 let: Ukaz. lit.* (225 yrs of M. Univ. Lit. index), Moscow.

Arevshatyan, S. S. and Matevosyan, A. S.: *Gladzorsky universitet—tsentr prosvecheniya srednevekovoy Armenii* (G. Univ. A centre of enlightenment of medieval A.), Yerevan.

Margolis, Y. D.: *T. G. Shevchenko i Peterburgsky universitet* (T.G.S. and P. Univ.), Leningrad.

Revishvili, S. I.: *Letopis druzhby dvukh universitetov: Yena–Tbilisi 1966–83 gg.* (Annals of friendship between 2 univs. J.-T. 1966–83), Tbilisi. (Summary in German.)

Saarmaa, E.: *Literatura o Tartuskom universitete: bibliogr. ukazat. za 1940–80 gg.* (Lit. about T. Univ. Bibliog. for 1940–80), Tartu. (Partly in Estonian.)

Yesakov, V. A.: *Geografiya v Moskovskom universitete: Ocherki org., prepodavaniya, razvitiya geogr. mysli (do 1917 g.)* (Geog. in M. Univ.

Outlines of the organis. of teaching and of the devel. of geog. thought to 1917), Moscow.

Publications 1984

Kievsky universitet 1834–1984 (K. Univ. 1834–1984), Kiev.

Kupaygorodskaya, A. P.: *Vysshaya shkola Leningrada v pervyje gody Sovetskoy vlasti 1917–25 gg.* (The Higher Schl. at L. in the 1st yrs of Soviet power), Leningrad.

Latviyskomu gosudarstvennomu universitetu im. Petra Stuchki 60 let (For the 60th anniv. of the P.S. Latvian state univ.), Riga. (Collection of materials and docs. In Lettish. Summaries in Russian, Germ., Eng. and French.)

Marakhov, G. I.: *Kievsky universitet v revolutsionno-demokraticheskom dvizhenii* (K. Univ. in the revol. democratic movt), Kiev.

Margolis, Y. and Tishkin, G.: Skolko let Peterburgskomu universitetu (How old in P. Univ.?). *Neva*, 11: 118–95.

Remezovsky, I. D.: *Kievsky universitet: stranitsy revolutsionnoy borby 1834–1984* (K. Univ.: leaves in the revol. struggle 1834–1984), Kiev.

Sergiyenko, G. Y. and Sergeyenko, Y. S.: *Kievsky universitet i T.G. Shevchenko* (K. Univ. and T.G.S.), Kiev. (In Ukrainian.)

Tishkina, G. A. ed.: *Ocherki po istorii Leningradskogo universiteta. 5* (Essays on the hist. of L. Univ. 5), Leningrad.

Publications 1985

Chernyayev, S. V., Romanyuk, V. Y. and Vdovin, A. I.: *Moskovsky universitet v Velikoy Otechestvennoy voyne* (M. Univ. in the Great Patriotic War), Moscow. (Revised edition.)

Dmitriyev, P. A. and Safronov, G. I.: K 150-letiyu kafedr slavyanskoy filologii v otechestvennukh universitetakh (For the 150th anniv. of the Slavonic lang. depts in our native univs), *Vestnik Leningr. un-ta. Istoriya, Yazyk, Literature*, 23(4): 52–8. (Slavonic lang. depts established at univs. of Moscow, St Petersburg, Kharvov and Kazan in 1835.)

Eimontova, R. G.: *Russkiye universitety na grani dvukh epokh: Ot Rossii krepostnoy k Rossii kapitalisticheskoy* (R. univs on the boundary between epochs: from the R. of serfdom to the R. of capitalism), Moscow.

Elango, A. Y.: Tri sistemy universitetskoy podgotovki uchiteley (3 systems of univ. teacher training), in *Formirovaniye aktivnosti uchaschikhsya i studentov v kollektive*, Riga: 71–6. (From the 2nd half of the 17th cent. to the present day, in Russia, in the USSR and in other countries.)

Ionenko, I. M. and Popov, V. A.: *Kazansky universitet v gody Velikoy Otechestvennoy voyny* (K. Univ. during the yrs of the Great Patriotic War), Moscow.

Kalnin, V. V.: Iz istorii nauchnykh svyazey Tartuskogo i Moskovskogo universitetov v oblasti meditsiny (19 i nachalo 20 v.) (Aspects of the hist. of scientif. links between T. and M. Univs in med. in 19th and early 20th cents), *Tartu; ülikodi ajaloo küsimusi—Voprosy istorii Tart. un-ta*, 18: 72–8.

Piirimäe, H., Siilivask, K. and Ruutsoo, R.: *Istoriya Tartuskogo universiteta 1632–1982* (Hist. of T. Univ. 1632–1982), Tallinn. (In Estonian.)

Zhdanova, Y. A. ed.: *Rostovsky gosudarstvenny universitet 1915–85: Ocherki* (R. state univ. 1915–85. Essays), Rostov-na-Donu.

Publications 1986

Baik, L., Bobich, O. I. and Volyanyuk, N. M.: *Lvovsky universitet 1661–1986* (L. Univ. 1661–1986), Lvov.

Chugailov, V. P. etc. eds: *Lvivsky universitet 1661–1986* (L. Univ. 1661–1986), Lvov. (In Ukrainian.)

Garibdzhanyan, G. B.: *Ot Gladzora do Yerevanskogo universiteta* (From G. to Y. Univ.), Yerevan.

Isakov, S. ed.: *Vospominaniya o Tartuskom universitete (17–19 vv.): Sborn* (Recollections of T. Univ. (17th–19th cents). Collection), Tallinn. (In Estonian.)

Kodasma, S. etc. eds: *Spravochnik o sostave studenchestva Tartuskogo universiteta* (Ref. books on student composition in T. Univ.). *Album academicum universitatis Tartuensis 1889–1918*. 3, Tartu.

Mikhailova, S. M.: Rol Kazanskogo universiteta v prosveschenni narodov Sibiri (The role of K. Univ. in the educ. of Siberian peoples), *Sov. pedagogica*, 1: 114–20.

Viksia, A. A.: *Derptsky universitet* (D. Univ.), Riga. (In Lettish.)

Zhivopistsev, V. P.: *Den otkrytykh dverey: Perm. gos. un-tu-70 let, 1916–86* (The day of opened doors. For the 70th anniv. of P. state univ. 1916–86), Perm.

Publications 1987

Aristov, V. V.: *Stranitsy slavnoy istorii: Rasskazy o Kazan, un-te* (Pages of glorious hist. Stories of K. Univ.), Kazan.

Belyavsky, M. T.: Shkola i obrazovaniye (Schl and educ.), in *Ocherki russkoy kultury 18 veka*, Moscow: 258–93. (The formation of secular educ. in Russia; the fndation of the Acad. univ. in St Petersburg in 1725, the fndation of Moscow Univ., military schools.)

Kertman, L. Y., Vasilyeva, N. Y. and Shustov, S. G.: *Pervy na Urale: (Perm. gos. un-t im. A.M. Gorkogo 1916–86)* (First in the Urals. A.M.G.P. state univ. 1916–86), Perm.

Matulaitite, S.: Biblioteka staroy observatorii Vilnius-skogo universiteta v 18 veke (The library of V. Univ's old observatory in the 18th cent.), *Lietuv. TSR aukstuju mokyklu mokalo = Nauch. trudy vusov Lit. SSR. Knigovedeniye*, 13: 68–85. (In Lithuanian. Summaries in Russian and English.)

Safrazyan, N. L.: *Stanovleniye marksistsko-leninskogo gumanitarnogo obrazovaniya v Moskovskom universitete (oktyabr 1917–25 gg)* (The formation of M.-L. humanitarian educ. at M. Univ. (Oct. 1917–25)), Moscow.

Vain, A.: 125 let biomekhanicheskikh issledovaniy v Tartuskom universitete (125 yrs of biomechanical research at T. Univ.), *Tartu Ülikodi ajlookküsimusi= Voprosy istorii Tartuskogo un-ta*: 227–32. (In Estonian.)

Publications 1988

Aleksandrov, Y. V.: Astronomiya v Kharkovskom universitete (Astron. at K. Univ.), *Ocherki yestestvoznaniya i tekhniki*, 34: 57–65.

Bagbaya, I. D. and Todia M. V.: Problemy podgotovki uchiteley fiziki v Rossii (do 1917 g.) (Problems in training Physics teachers in R. before 1917), *A. M. Gorky ikhz zkhyu Apenyt i akh yntkarrat universitetic shromeberi= Tr. Abkhaz. gos. un-ta im. A. M. Gorkogo*, 6: 224–50.

Gurgenidze, I.: Gruzinskomu nauchnomu khramu 70 let (The Georgian temple of sciences is 70 yrs old), *Ekonomisti*, 10: 23–7. (In Georgian. The 70th anniv. of Tbilisi State University.)

Gurgenidze, I. K.: Rektory Tbilisskogo universiteta (The rects of T. Univ.), Tbilisi.

Khizzhnyak, Z. I.: *Kievo-Mogylyanskaya akademiya* (The K.-M. acad.), Kiev.

Kroychik, L. Y. eds: *Rozhdenny revolyutsiyey: Voronezhsky gos, un-t im. Leninskogo komsomola: Dokumenty, vospominaniya* (Born of the Revoln. The L.K. state univ. of V. Docs; recollections), Voronezh.

Kruzhalova, N. Y. and Knyazev, Y. A.: Universitet Shanyavskogo—volnaya vyschaya shkola (S.'s univ. A free higher schl), *Vestnik vysch. shk.*, 4: 79–85. (Hist. of the peoples univ. in Moscow.)

Margolis, Y. D. and Tishkin, G. A.: *Otechestvu na polzu, a rossiyanam vo slavu: Iz istorii universitet. obrazovaniya v Peterburge v 18–nachale 19 v* (For the good of the fatherland: to the glory of the Russians. Aspects of the hist. of univ. educ. in St Petersburg in the 18th and early 19th cents), Leningrad.

Ozhigova, Y. P.: V. A. Steklov i voprosy vyschego obrazovaniya (V.A.S. and questions of higher educ.), *Ocherki istorii yestestvoznaniya i tekhniki*, 35: 28–34. (V.A.S.'s activities as organiser of univ. educ. in R. end of 19th cent. and in 1920s.)

Pilinchuk, O. Y. and Chernenko, K. A.: Kievskoye obschestvo yestestvoispytateley i yego rol v izuchenii fauny Ukrainy (The K. Soc. of Naturalists and its role in the study of fauna of the U.), in *Istoricheskiye traditsii i opyt razvitiya otechestvennoy nauki i tekhniki*, Kiev (henceforth noted as *Istoricheskiye traditsii*): 65–7. (The activities of K. Naturalist Soc. at K. Univ. 1869–1917.)

Raudsepp, M. P. and Tamul, S. Y.: Traditsii issledovaniya tochnykh nauk v muzeye istorii Tartuskogo gosudarstvennogo universiteta (The research tradits of the exact sciences in T. state univ's Museum of Hist.) in *Istoricheskiye traditsii*: 62–5.

Teliya, A.: Tak stroilsya universitet (In this way a univ. was built), *Ekonomisty*, 10: 11–22. (In Georgian. The 70th anniv. of Tbilisi State University.)

Vaskovsky, O. A.: 50-letiye istfaka Uralskogo universiteta (The 50th anniv. of the hist. fac. of the univ. of the Urals), *Vopr. istorii*, 10: 176–78.

Vozniknoveniye universitetskogo slavyanovedeniya. Osnovnyye resultaty slavisticheskikh issledovaniy v Rossii 30–50-kh godov 19 v (The emergence of Slavonic studies in univs. Basic results of Slav research in R. from 1830s–1850s), in *Slavyanovedeniye v dorevolyutsionnoy Rossii*, Moscow: 66–75.

Vusalinova, G. A.: M. V. Lomonosov i osnovaniye Moskovskogo universiteta v osveschenii otechestvennykh istorikov (M.V.L and the fndation of M. Univ. as interpreted by native historians), in *Opyt raboty nauchnoy biblioteki MGU*, Moscow: 57–67.

Publications 1989

Goldfarb, S. I. ed.: *Irkutsky gosudarstvenny universitet: 70 let: Khronika sobytiy* (1. state univ. 70 yrs. A chronicle of events), Irkutsk.

Korobeinik, Y. F., Yerusalimsky, Y. M., Nalbandyan, M. B. and Rozhanskaya, N. N.: *Mekhaniko-matematichesky fakultet Rostovskogo gosudarstvennogo universiteta: Kratky ist. ocherk* (R. univ's fac. of mechanics and maths: a short hist. outline), Rostov-na-Donu.

Moskovsky universitet v vospominaniyakh sovremennikov 1755–1917 (Univ. of M. through the recollections of contemps), Moscow.

Shidlauskas, A. I.: *Istoriya v Vilniusskom universitete v kontse 16–nachale 19 veka* (Hist. in V. Univ. from the late 16th to early 19th cents), Vilnius. (In Lithuanian.)

Tering, A. ed.: *Akademicheskiye svyazi mezhdu Gettingenskim universitetom i Pribaltikoy v 18–nachale 19 veka* (Acad. links between G. Univ. and the Baltic States in 18th and early 19th cents), Tartu. (Cat. of an exhibition.)

Tishkin, G. A. ed.: *Ocherki po istirii Leningradskogo universiteta. 6* (Essays on the hist. of L. Univ. 6), Leningrad.

Zhuravsky, Y. I., Zaitsev, B. P. and Migal, B. K.: *Kharkovsky universitet v gody Velicoy Otechestvennoy voyny* (K. Univ. during the yrs of the Great Patriotic War), Kharkov.

Index of Continents, Towns and Institutions